Fast Track Financial Analysis and Forecasting

Jae K. Shim, Ph.D.
Joel G. Siegel, Ph. D., CPA

PRENTICE HALL

Library of Congress Cataloging-in-Publication Data

Shim, Jae K.
  Fast track financial analysis and forecasting (with CD ROM) / Jae K. Shim, Joel G. Siegel.
      p. cm.
  Includes index.
  ISBN 0-13-060191-8 (cloth
     1. Business enterprises—Finance. 2. Business forecasting. I. Siegel, Joel G. II. Title.

HG4026.S454 2001
658.15—dc21

2001045111

Acquisitions Editor: John Hiatt
Production Editor: Mariann Hutlak
Interior Design/Composition: DM Cradle Associates

© 2001 by Prentice Hall

All rights reserved. No part of this book may be reproduced, in any form or by any means, without permission in writing from the publisher.

This publication is designed to provide accurate and authoritative information in regard to the subject matter covered. It is sold with the understanding that the publisher is not engaged in rendering legal, accounting, or other professional service. If legal advice or other expert assistance is required, the services of a competent professional person should be sought.

  ...From the Declaration of Principles jointly adopted by a Committee of the American Bar Association and a Committee of Publishers and Associations.

Printed in the United States of America   *Printed in the United States of America*
10 9 8 7 6 5 4 3 2 1   *10 9 8 7 6 5 4 3 2 1*

ISBN 0-13-060191-8 (CD)   ISBN 0-13-043303-9 (URL)

ATTENTION: CORPORATIONS AND SCHOOLS

Prentice Hall books are available at quantity discounts with bulk purchase for educational, business, or sales promotional use. For information, please write to: Prentice Hall Direct Special Sales, 240 Frisch Court, Paramus, NJ 07652. Please supply: title of book, ISBN, quantity, how the book will be used, date needed.

PRENTICE HALL
Paramus, NJ 07652

http://www.phdirect.com

To

Chung Shim
Dedicated Wife

and
Roberta M. Siegel
Loving Wife and Expert Typist

and
Jack Siegel
I miss him so much

About the Authors

Jae K. Shim, Ph.D., is Professor of Finance and Accountancy at California State University, Long Beach. Dr. Shim, a financial and operations research consultant, received his M.B.A. and Ph.D. degrees from the University of California at Berkeley (Haas School of Business).

Dr. Shim has published numerous refereed articles in such journals as *Financial Management, Econometrica, Decision Sciences, Management Science, Long Range Planning, Journal of Business Forecasting, Advances in Accounting, Corporate Controller, The CPA Journal, CMA Magazine, Management Accounting, OMEGA, Journal of Operational Research Society*, and *Journal of Systems Management*.

Professor Shim is a coauthor of *Strategic Business Forecasting, Encyclopedic Dictionary of Accounting and Finance, Financial Management, Barron's Accounting Handbook, Managerial Accounting, Complete Budgeting Workbook and Guide, The Vest-Pocket CPA, The Vest-Pocket CFO*, and the best-selling *Vest-Pocket MBA*. He is also a coeditor of *Readings in Cost and Managerial Accounting* and a coauthor of the *AICPA's Variance Analysis for Cost Control and Profit Maximization* and *Accounting for and Evaluation of Process Cost Systems*.

Dr. Shim has 45 other professional and college books to his credit and was a recipient of the 1982 Credit Research Foundation Outstanding Paper Award for his article on financial forecasting.

Joel G. Siegel, Ph.D., CPA, is Professor of Accounting and Information Systems at Queens College of the City University of New York and an accounting and financial consultant. He was previously associated with Coopers and Lybrand, CPAs, and Arthur Anderson, CPAs. Dr. Siegel has acted as a consultant to numerous companies, including International Telephone and Telegraph, Citicorp, Carrier Corporation, and Person-Wolinsky Associates. He is the author of 63 books and about 200 articles, which have appeared in numerous financial and information systems journals, including *The Financial Analysis Journal, The Financial Executive, Managerial Planning, Long Range Planning, Decision Sciences, Credit and Financial Management*, and *International Journal of Systems Science*. He has served on the book review editorial board of *The CPA Journal* and acted as a technical reviewer for Dryden Press, Harper and Row, Prentice Hall, Barron's, and the American

Institute of CPAs. In 1972, he was the recipient of the Outstanding Educator of America Award. Dr. Siegel is listed in *Who's Where Among Writers* and in *Who's Who in the World*.

Credit lines *for* Computer Software Products

Crosstalk is a registered trademark of Microstuf Corporation. EXPRESS is a trademark of Management Decision Systems. Huttonline is a trademark of E.F. Hutton. Interactive Financial Planning System (IFPS) is a trademark of Comshare. Lotus 1-2-3 is a trademark of Lotus Development Corporation. Excel is a trademark of Microsoft Corporation. Profit Impact of Market Strategy is a trademark of Strategic Planning Institute. SAS is a trademark of SAS Institute. Simplan is a trademark of Social Systems. Venture is a trademark of Team Tech Systems. Encore Plus is a trademark of Ferox Microsystems. Micro FCS is a trademark of Pilot Executive Software. Quattro Pro is a trademark of Corel. Spss is a trademark of Spss Inc.

Acknowledgments

We wish to express our deep gratitude to the late Bette Schwartzberg, Ellen Schneid Coleman, and Luis Gonzalez for their outstanding editoral assistance during the first and second editions. The input and efforts are much recognized and appreciated. Many thanks also go to Cathy Johnson and Mariann Hutlak for her excellent editorial contributions in the production stage.

Special thanks to: Dr. Marc Levine, CPA, Professor of Accounting and Information Systems at Queens College, for contributing his expertise in Chapter 5; Professor Leonard Ledereich, JD, MBA, CPA, Area Coordinator of Business and Accounting at Hostos Community College, for his contribution to Chapter 8; Dr. Peter Chiu of the Department of Accounting and Information Systems at Queens College, an investment and real estate advisor, for his invaluable help with Chapter 10.

Contents

What This Book Will Do for You   xvii

A Word from the Authors   xx

PART I: Financial Analysis 1

1: How to Use Break-even, Operating Leverage, and Contribution Margin 3

    Break-even Analysis   3
    Measuring and Examining the Effects
       of Operating Leverage   11
    Contribution Margin Analysis   14
    Conclusion   22

2. Applying Discounting and Compounding Analysis Techniques 23

    Future Value of $1   25
    Future Value of an Annuity of $1   28
    Future Value of an Annuity Due of $1   31
    Present Value of $1   32
    Present Value of an Annuity of $1   32
    Present Value of an Annuity Due of $1   37
    Perpetuities   38
    Conclusion   38

3. How Evaluating Capital Investment Proposals Leads to Sound Decision Making 41

    Accounting (Simple) Rate of Return   43
    Payback Period   44
    Discounted Payback Period   46
    Net Present Value   46
    Profitability Index   51
    Contingent Proposals   53

x   Contents

    Internal Rate of Return (Time-Adjusted
      Rate of Return)   53
    Nondiscretionary Projects   56
    Comparison of Methods   57
    Capital Budgeting Process   58
    Risk and Uncertainty   60
    Conclusion   66

4. **How to Analyze Financial Position** 67
    Analyzing Asset Quality   67
    Liabilities   75
    Liquidity Analysis   77
    Appraisal of Solvency   81
    Analyzing the Statement of Cash Flows   82
    Potential for Business Failure   89
    Conclusion   93

5. **Techniques for Analyzing Operating
   Performance** 95
    Quality of Earnings   95
    Analysis of Discretionary Costs   97
    Cash Flow from Operations   99
    The Role of Taxable Income   100
    Residual Income   101
    Accounting Estimates   101
    Internal Control and Management Honesty   103
    Auditor Relations and Reports   103
    Conclusion   103

6. **How to Analyze the Financial Structure
   of the Firm** 105
    How to Measure the Stability of Earnings   105
    Stability Elements   108
    Product Line Characteristics   109
    Measuring a Company's Success   113
    Risk   114
    Industry Characteristics   115
    Economic Factors   116

Political Factors   119
Conclusion   120

7. Using Variance Analysis as a Financial Tool 121

Usefulness of Variance Analysis   122
Standard Setting   122
Sales Variances   123
Cost Variances   124
Variances to Evaluate Marketing Effort   129
Conclusion   132

PART II: Evaluating Assets, Liabilities, and Potential Acquisitions 133

8. How to Evaluate Business Segments 135

Appraising Manager Performance   135
Cost Center   136
Profit Center   138
Investment Center   144
Conclusion   151

9. Tools and Techniques for Analyzing Cash, Accounts Receivable, and Inventory 153

Evaluating Working Capital   153
Cash Management   154
Management of Accounts Receivable   159
Inventory Planning and Control   166
Conclusion   172

10. Portfolio Investment Analysis Information You Need 173

Accounting Aspects   173
Analytical Implications   174
Obtaining Information   175
Risk Versus Return   178
Financial Assets   180
Real Assets   188

xii Contents

    Portfolio Analysis   190
    Mutual Funds   190
    Fundamental Analysis   192
    Technical Analysis   192
    Conclusion   203

11. How to Finance the Business 205

    Financial Planning   205
    Short- and Intermediate-Term Financing Sources   206
    Comparing Short- to Long-Term Financing   210
    Long-Term Financing   211
    Cost of Capital   213
    Conclusion   217

12. Techniques for Analyzing Mergers
    and Acquisitions 219

    Mergers   220
    Deciding on Acquisition Terms   222
    Acquisition of Another Business   225
    Impact of Merger on Earnings per Share
        and Market Price per Share   227
    Risk   230
    Holding Company   231
    Methods of Accounting for a Business
        Combination   232
    Conclusion   235

PART III: Financial Forecasting 237

13. Forecasting and Financial Planning
    as Management Tools 239

    Who Uses Forecasts?   239
    Forecasting Methods   241
    Selection of Forecasting Method   242
    The Qualitative Approach   244
    Common Features and Assumptions
        Inherent in Forecasting   246

Contents xiii

Steps in the Forecasting Process 247
Conclusion 247

14. Forecasting Methods for Financial Planning 249

Naive Models 249
Smoothing Techniques 249
The Computer and Exponential Smoothing 254
Forecasting Using Decomposition
   of Time Series 255
Conclusion 264

15. How to Forecast with Regression
and Markov Methods .265

Regression Analysis Sales and Earnings
   Projection 265
Regression Statistics 271
Statistics to Look for in Multiple Regressions 276
Evaluation of Forecasts 279
Checklists—How to Choose the Best
   Forecasting Equation 287
Use of a Computer Statistical Package
   for Multiple Regression 288
Models Based on Learned Behavior—Markov Model 291
Conclusion 301

16. Financial Forecasting, Planning,
and Budgeting Techniques 303

Financial Forecasting 303
Budgeting and Financial Planning 306
How the Budgets Work: An Example 307
A Shortcut Approach to Formulating
the Budget 323
Computer-Based Models and Spreadsheet
   Program Models for Budgeting 324
Zero-Base Budgeting 324
The CPA's Involvement and Responsibility
   with Prospective Financial Statements 325
Conclusion 329

xiv   Contents

17. How to Forecast Cash Inflows for Budgeting ...331

    Probability Matrix Approach   332
    Regression Approach   335
    Is Cash Flow Software Available?   342
    Conclusion   343

PART IV: FINANCIAL MODELING 345

18. Using Corporate Planning Models 347

    Types of Analysis   348
    Typical Questions About Corporate Modeling   348
    Types of Models   350
    History of Models   350
    Current Trends in Modeling   351
    Attitudes and Problems   353
    MIS, DSS, EIS, and Personal Computers   359
    The Future of Corporate Planning Models   360
    Conclusion   361
    Bibliography and Additional Readings   361

19. Financial Modeling—Simulation 363

    Financial Model   363
    Applications and Uses of Financial Models   364
    Putting Financial Modeling into Practice   365
    Quantitative Techniques Used
       in Financial Models   366
    Developing Financial Models   367
    Model Specification   369
    Comprehensive Financial Model   375
    Conclusion   377

20. Techniques to Use to Develop
    Optimal Budgets 379

    Linear Programming   379
    Goal Programming   385
    Conclusion   387

Contents xv

21. How to Use Spreadsheet and Financial
    Modeling Languages 391

    Use of a Spreadsheet Program
      for Financial Modeling   392
    Forecasting Business Failures with Z Scores   395
    Financial Modeling Languages   400
    Interactive Financial Planning   System (IFPS)   400
    SIMPLAN: A Planning and Modeling System   409
    EXPRESS   412
    ENCORE! Plus   414
    Budget Maestro   415
    Conclusion   415

22. How to Use and Apply Management
    Games for Executive Training 421

    Executive Management Games   423
    Advantages and Disadvantages
      of Executive Games   426
    Validating the Game   430
    A New Role for Computerized Executive Games   431
    Conclusion   431
    Bibliography and Additional Readings   431

23. Corporate Valuations 435

    Steps in Valuation   437
    Business Valuation Methods   443
    Conclusion   453
    Additional Readings   454

24. Security Valuation 455

    How to Value a Security   455
    How to Value Bonds   456
    How to Value Common Stock   458
    How to Forecast Stock Price—
      A Pragmatic Approach   460
    What Are the Determinants of the Price–
      Earnings Ratio?   461

How to Read Beta   462
What Does It Mean When a Firm's Stock
   Sells on a High or Low P/E Ratio?   463
Conclusion   464

25. Forensic Accounting 465

What Is Forensic Accounting?   465
Why Is Forensic Accounting Necessary?   467
When Does One Employ a Forensic Accountant?   467
Where is a Forensic Accountant Used?   468
How Does a Forensic Accountant Work?   469
A Case in Forensic Accounting   470

Appendix 487

Budgeting, Financial Analysis,
   and Optimization Software   487

Forecasting and Statistical Software   492

Index   499

What This Book Will Do for You

This handbook is your practical reference of proven techniques, strategies, and approaches that are successfully used by professionals to diagnose the financial and operating health of businesses. You too can benefit from these tested techniques and use them to enhance your skills in analyzing and making decisions that affect your company's financial future.

You'll find many new, up-to-date methods and techniques, and you'll learn which ones to use when, what to look for, what to watch out for, and exactly what to do and how to do it. Equally important, this book will show you how to evaluate the results of your analyses so that you can quickly adopt tactics for increasing profits or reducing losses. You will be guided every step of the way by computational examples and illustrations, which you can quickly tailor to your own needs.

This handbook is a tool chest to help you with financial decision making. Checklists summarize each of the major areas covered; the ratios, formulas, models, and statistical techniques have all been proven successful. And, to help you evaluate your company's present and future financial health more accurately, there are specific guidelines and yardsticks to use to measure and predict analysis results. You'll get step-by-step procedures so that you can move quickly to take advantage of favorable or unfavorable situations.

Here is the guide that will help you make smart decisions in all areas of financial management and operations. It will be your daily problem-solver for financial situations professionals face—in all companies, large or small.

- Part I provides guidelines for evaluating your company's financial health. You'll get proven techniques for analyzing financial position, operating performance, and corporate structure. There are applications for handling marketing effectiveness, budgeting, and appraisal of divisional performance. Through variance analysis techniques you'll be able to evaluate proposals for profit potential and problem areas. You'll get all the tested tools and strategies that will help you improve the bottom line for your company.

- Part II supplies management and financing techniques so that you can derive the best financial position and rate of return, while trying to reduce the level of risk. You'll learn how to manage working capital, cash, and accounts receivable, as well as how to analyze investment portfolios.

xviii   *What This Book Will Do for You*

Finally, you'll be provided with the tested tools for business financing as well as the analysis techniques for evaluating a potential acquisition.

- Part III provides the strategies and techniques for short- and long-term forecasting and budgeting. This includes trend analysis, exponential smoothing, time series, regression, econometrics, Markov analysis, and sales forecasting. And, equally important, you'll learn how to evaluate the quality of your forecast results.
- Part IV gives you the techniques necessary for financial modeling, including risk-return analysis, optimization models, sensitivity analysis, simulation, linear programming, shadow pricing, and goal programming. You'll learn the effect of using management game techniques and applications, as well as future trends in financial modeling and their impact—including management information systems, modeling languages, and networking.

The practical benefits of this handbook are unlimited. This book:

- Presents the techniques necessary to measure and evaluate financial position and operating performance—all of which can be practically applied
- Shows you how to measure the degree of operational stability
- Explains how to measure and appraise the risk level, with specific recommendations for application
- Lists "red flags" to watch out for in operations
- Provides the signs of future business failure so you can avoid them
- Recommends proven ways to correct financial sickness and inefficiency
- Illustrates break-even and contribution analysis to evaluate business opportunities
- Provides applications of discounting and compounding techniques for specific business situations
- Shows how to evaluate business proposals using different methods of capital budgeting
- Presents measures that enable you to evaluate corporate liquidity, solvency, potential for failure, and profitability
- Offers tested techniques for analyzing the financial structure of your business

- Shows you how to measure the impact of inflationary and recessionary trends
- Provides techniques and guidelines for measuring marketing effectiveness
- Provides interpretation of variances indicating inefficiencies in the organization
- Highlights the various types of budgets and provides guidelines for use
- Gives you the tools for spotting financially strong or weak business segments
- Shows you how to manage assets and liabilities to achieve optimal overall performance
- Provides evaluative criteria and measures for mergers
- Gives you forecast preparation techniques and tools to assist management in decision making
- Shows you how to use and evaluate forecast quality
- Gives proven techniques and guidelines for using forecasting models, including time-series regression
- Provides computer-assisted applications in forecasting, including a guide to available software packages
- Gives you tested procedures for using financial modeling to solve business problems, and opportunities, including risk-return optimization, sensitivity, and simulation
- Illustrates quantitative decision-making techniques, such as linear programming, queuing, and learning curve, and shows how to apply them to daily business situations

This handbook provides you with a veritable tool chest of guidelines, illustrations, and how-to's for the business financial decision maker. Keep it handy as an easy-to-use, frequent reference.

A Word from the Authors

Financial analysis is necessary for evaluating internal operations and activities to optimize profit and efficiency, while at the same time reducing the risk. Problem areas must be identified so that corrective, timely action may be taken.

Break-even analysis determines what level of sales of a product line is necessary to cover costs. Contribution margin evaluation indicates what selling price to charge given a special order situation.

To determine where funds should be expended in the business, capital budgeting techniques include present value, internal rate of return, and payback. Applications of various types of investment opportunities are addressed.

Analyzing the balance sheet, income statement, and overall financial structure shows the company's financial strengths and deficiencies, and identifies problem areas for management attention. How the business is viewed financially by investors and creditors affects the firm's chances of financing, cost of capital, and the market price of its stock.

Knowing how to evaluate segmental performance is essential to recognizing the relative performance of divisions within the firm, with techniques for comparisons to similar divisions in competing companies. Measures of performance include return on investment and residual income.

The management of current assets and liabilities positively affects the bottom line and reduces risk. Some examples of this are accelerating cash inflow, delaying cash outflow, inventory planning, and investment portfolio management. By acquiring other companies, diversification and earning power may be enhanced. Selecting the right financing instrument to obtain funds is critical; it affects both cost of capital and restrictiveness of funds.

Financial planning models are used to generate proforma financial statements and financial ratios—the basic tools for budgeting and profit planning. There are user-oriented computer software systems specifically designed for corporate planners and executives. Technological advances in computers, such as networking and data base management systems, have made more companies use modeling for making day-to-day operational and strategic planning decisions. Financial planning models, which is one functional branch of a general corporate model, may be used for many purposes. Among these applications are

- Financial forecasting
- Budgeting
- Risk analysis
- Cash management

- Tax planning
- Profit planning
- Capital budgeting
- Merger and acquisition analysis
- New venture analysis

Supported by the expanded capabilities provided by models, many companies are increasingly successful in including long-term strategic considerations in their business plans, thus enabling them to investigate the possible impact of their current decisions on future profitability and cash flow. For example, companies are able to examine the effects of proposed mergers and acquisitions with much more certainty and to estimate with more confidence the potential profits from new markets. The applications of and benefits deriving from the use of well-designed and sophisticated planning models are unlimited. The model is, in short, a technique for "risk" analysis and "what-if" experiments. Modeling allows for strategic planning and for accomplishing operational and tactical decisions for immediate planning problems.

With the ever-increasing technology in the areas of spreadsheets, data base management systems, graphics, and the like, businesspeople will use financial models more effectively. With the applications found throughout this book, you will be able to use modeling for analytical decisions without having to know programming.

The book shows you:

- How to develop a new model
- How to select the best user-oriented planning package to meet the specific needs and resources available
- How to use your spreadsheet program on a personal computer for various modeling purposes
- How to tie the financial model to the overall management information system framework

This is your guidebook for more effective financial management. Use it often, to keep continuous tabs on your company's financial health.

Jae K. Shim
Joel G. Siegel

PART I:
Financial Analysis

1
How to Use Break-even, Operating Leverage, and Contribution Margin

The first step is to familiarize yourself with *break-even analysis* (cost–volume–profit analysis, or CVP), which refers to the sales necessary to cover costs so that there is zero profit or loss. *Operating leverage* is the degree to which fixed costs exist in a company's cost structure and measures operating risk arising from high fixed costs. *Contribution margin* analysis is useful in your decisions regarding pricing strategy and which product lines to emphasize.

BREAK-EVEN ANALYSIS

A fixed cost is one that remains constant regardless of activity (such as rent), while variable cost is one that varies with activity (such as materials).

Cost–Volume–Profit Analysis

Cost–volume–profit analysis relates to the way in which profit and costs change with a change in volume. It examines the impact on earnings of changes in such factors as variable cost, fixed cost, selling price, volume, and product mix, and therefore aids in the planning process. *Recommendation:* Do a break-even analysis to determine whether or not the break-even point can be achieved. Break-even analysis is useful when starting a new project, expanding a project, or subtracting from the project.

Your business objective is not just to break even but to earn a profit. You can extend break-even analysis to concentrate on a desired earnings figure.

3

How to Compute the Break-even Point

The break-even point can be computed using either the equation, contribution, or graphical approach.

In the graphical approach (Figure 1.1), revenue, total cost, and fixed cost are plotted on the vertical axis, and volume is plotted on the horizontal axis. The break-even point is where the revenue line intersects the total cost line. The chart shown in Figure 1.1 also depicts profit potentials over a wide range of activity.

The relevant range is the area within which the break-even chart maintains its validity. Beyond it, on the up side, total fixed cost increases; below it, on the down side, a point where the amount of loss exceeds management's tolerance limit is ultimately reached. Within the relevant range, variable cost per unit remains constant.

CVP analysis aids in determining:

- Sales volume necessary to break even
- Sales volume necessary to earn a desired profit
- The effect on earnings of changing selling price, variable cost, fixed cost, and output

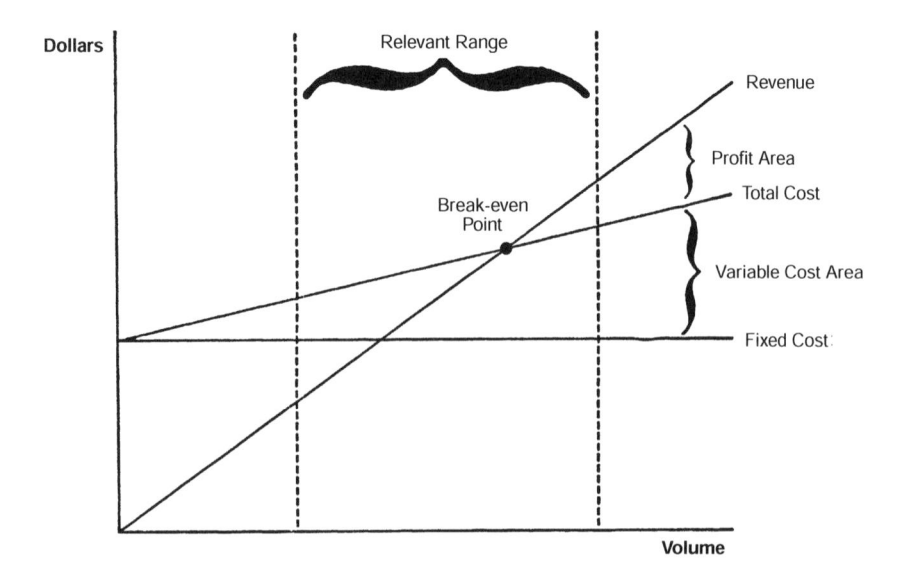

FIGURE 1.1 Break-even Chart

Chapter 1: Break-even, Operating Leverage, and Contribution Margin   5

- The impact of a change in product mix on the break-even point and target income

Benefits of Break-even Analysis

- Aids in profit planning
- Illustrates the effect of operating leverage on earnings
- Illustrates the impact of volume changes on profitability
- Assists in determining the optimal proportion of fixed cost to variable cost

Applications of Break-even Analysis

- Introducing a new product or service
- Modernizing facilities
- Starting a new business
- Evaluating production and administrative activities

Assumptions of Break-even Analysis

- Selling price is constant, which in turn requires the following assumptions:
  —Demand elasticity is very high for the selling price to remain the same when sales volume increases.
  —Selling price is stable over the income period.
  —*Tip:* In practice, neither assumption is likely to hold, making it difficult to forecast selling price.
- There is only one product or a constant sales mix.
- Manufacturing efficiency is constant.
- Inventories do not materially change from period to period.
- Variable cost per unit is constant.
- Total fixed cost is constant.
- Fixed cost and variable cost are properly separated, identified, and quantified.
- The only factor affecting variable cost is volume.

Note: There is a relevant range of activity over which assumptions are valid.

Guidelines for Breaking Even

- An increase in selling price lowers break-even sales.
- An increase in variable cost increases break-even sales.
- An increase in fixed cost increases break-even sales.

The margin of safety is the amount by which sales may decrease before losses begin. It is a risk indicator.

$$\text{Margin of safety} = \frac{\text{Budget sales} - \text{Break-even sales}}{\text{Budget sales}}$$

The lower the ratio, the more risk there is of reaching the break-even point.

EXAMPLE 1.1

Expected sales are $40,000 and break-even sales are $34,000.

$$\text{Margin of safety} = \frac{\$40,000 - \$34,000}{\$40,000} = \underline{15\%}$$

EXAMPLE 1.2

Assume fixed cost is $270,000 and variable cost is 70% of sales. The break-even sales are:

$$S = FC + VC$$
$$1S = \$270,000 + 0.7S$$
$$0.3S = \$270,000$$
$$S = \$900,000$$

where

S = sales
FC = fixed cost
VC = variable cost

If the selling price per unit is $100, break-even units are 9,000 ($900,000/$100). If the desired profit is $40,000, the sales necessary to obtain that profit (P) are:

$$S = FC + VC + P$$
$$1S = \$270{,}000 + 0.7S + \$40{,}000$$
$$0.3S = \$310{,}000$$
$$S = \$1{,}033{,}333$$

EXAMPLE 1.3

Selling price per unit $30
Variable cost per unit $20
Fixed cost $400,000

Break-even units (U) are:

$$S = FC + VC$$
$$\$30U = \$400{,}000 + \$20U$$
$$\$10U = \$400{,}000$$
$$U = \underline{\$40{,}000}$$

Break-even dollars are:
40,000 units × $30 = $\underline{\$1{,}200{,}000}$

EXAMPLE 1.4

You sell 800,000 units of an item. The variable cost is $2.50 per unit. Fixed cost totals $750,000. The selling price per unit should be $3.44 to break even.

$$S = FC + VC$$
$$\$800{,}000\ SP = \$750{,}000 + \$2.50\ (800{,}000)$$
$$\$800{,}000\ SP = \$2{,}750{,}000$$
$$SP = \underline{\$3.44}\ \text{(rounded)}$$

EXAMPLE 1.5

Assume the following:

Sales volume	20,000 units
Selling price	$40
Variable cost	$15
Fixed cost	$120,000
After-tax profit	$60,000
Tax rate	40%

Based on the above information, you want to know how much you have available to spend on research (R).

$$S = VC + FC + P + R$$
$$(\$40 \times 20{,}000) = (\$15 \times 20{,}000) + \$120{,}000 + \$100{,}000^a + R$$
$$\$280{,}000 = R$$

EXAMPLE 1.6

Assume the following:

Selling price	$40
Variable cost	$24
Fixed cost	$150,000
After-tax profit	$240,000
Tax rate	40%

You want to determine how many units you must sell to make the after-tax profit.

$$S = FC + VC + P$$
$$\$40U = \$150{,}000 + \$24U + \$400{,}000^b$$
$$\$16U = \$550{,}000$$
$$U = \underline{34{,}375} \text{ units}$$

EXAMPLE 1.7

Assume the following:

Selling price	$50
Variable cost	$30
Sales volume	60,000 units
Fixed cost	$150,000
Tax rate	30%

You want to determine the after-tax profit.

---

[a]After-tax profit = $60,000 = 0.6 × Before-tax profit
$$\frac{\$60{,}000}{0.6} = \text{Before-tax profit}$$
$$\$100{,}000 = \text{Before-tax profit}$$

[b]0.6 × Before-tax profit = After-tax profit
0.6 Before-tax profit = $240,000
$$\text{Before-tax profit} = \frac{\$240{,}000}{0.6} = \$400{,}000$$

$$S = FC + VC + P$$
$$(\$50 \times 60{,}000) = \$150{,}000 + (\$30 \times 60{,}000) + P$$
$$\underline{\$1{,}050{,}000} = P$$
After-tax profit = $\$1{,}050{,}000 \times 0.70 = \underline{\$735{,}000}$

EXAMPLE 1.8

You are considering making a product that is currently purchased outside for $0.12 per unit. The fixed cost is $10,000 and the variable cost per unit is $0.08. The number of units you must sell so the annual cost of your machine equals the outside purchase cost is:

$$\$0.12U = \$10{,}000 + \$0.08U$$
$$\$0.04U = \$10{,}000$$
$$U = \underline{250{,}000}$$

Sales Mix

Break-even analysis requires additional computations when more than one product is produced and sold. Different selling prices and different variable costs can result in different contribution margins. As a consequence, break-even points change depending on the proportions of the products sold, which is referred to as sales mix. *Tip*: You have to predetermine the sales mix and then compute a weighted-average contribution margin. An assumption must be made that sales mix does not change for a specified period.

EXAMPLE 1.9

You manufacture products X and Y, which have the following data:

		X	Y
Selling price		$30	$20
Variable cost		14	10
Contribution margin		$16	$10
Sales mix		60%	40%
Fixed cost	$80,000		

The weighted-average contribution margin per unit equals:

$$(\$16 \times 0.6) + (\$10 \times 0.4) = \underline{\$13.6}$$

Part I: Financial Analysis

Break-even units equal:

$$\frac{\text{Fixed cost}}{\text{Contribution margin}} = \frac{\$80,000}{\$13.60} = \underline{5,882} \text{ units (rounded)}$$

The 5,882 units are allocated as follows:

Product X: 5,882 × 0.6 = 3,529
Product Y: 5,882 × 0.4 = 2,353
Total: = 5,882

An assumption in break-even analysis for a multiproduct business is that the sales mix will not change during the planning period. If the sales mix does change, the break-even point will also change.

EXAMPLE 1.10

You manufacture and sell products X, Y, and Z.

	X	Y	Z	Total
Sales	$40,000	$70,000	$30,000	$140,000
Sales mix	28.6%	50%	21.4%	100%
Less variable cost	$16,000	$35,000	$ 8,000	$ 59,000
Contribution margin	$24,000	$35,000	$22,000	$ 81,000
Contribution margin ratio	60%	50%	73.3%	57.9%

Total fixed cost = $30,000

$$\text{Break-even dollars} = \frac{\text{Fixed cost}}{\text{Contribution margin ratio}} = \frac{\$30,000}{0.579}$$

$$= \underline{\$51,813.47}$$

The break-even dollars will be divided by the sales percentage of each product, as follows:

X: $51,813.47 × 0.286 = $14,818.65
Y: 51,813.47 × 0.50 = 25,906.74
Z: 51,813.47 × 0.214 = 11,088.08
                        $51,813.47

Cash Break-even Point

If you have a minimum of available cash or if the opportunity cost of holding excess cash is high, you may want to determine the sales volume needed to cover all cash expenses during a period. Not all fixed costs require cash payment (for example, depreciation expense). *What to Do:* In coming up with the cash break-even point, reduce fixed cost by the noncash charges. Hence, the cash break-even point will be less than the usual break-even point.

EXAMPLE 1.11

Selling price is $40, variable cost per unit is $10, and fixed cost is $64,000 (including depreciation of $4,000).

Break-even units are calculated as follows:

$$S = FC + VC$$
$$\$40U = \$60,000 + \$10U$$
$$\$30U = \$60,000$$
$$U = \underline{2,000}$$

An alternative break-even formula is:

$$\text{Break-even units} = \frac{\text{Fixed cost}}{\text{Contribution margin}^a}$$

$$\text{Break-even dollars} = \frac{\text{Fixed cost}}{\text{Contribution margin ratio}^b}$$

MEASURING AND EXAMINING THE EFFECTS OF OPERATING LEVERAGE

Leverage applies to the fixed cost of the entity constituting risk to the business. Operating leverage measures operating risk. High operating leverage magnifies changes in profit caused by small changes in sales. When high degrees of operating leverage are combined with highly elastic product demand, earnings fluctuation will be high.

The impact of operating leverage decreases as revenue increases above the break-even point because the bases to which increases in earnings are compared get progressively larger. *What to Do:* Analyze the rela-

---

[a] Contribution margin = Selling price – Variable cost

[b] Contribution margin ratio = $\dfrac{\text{Contribution margin}}{\text{Sales}}$

12   Part I: Financial Analysis

tionship between sales and the break-even point when appraising your entity's earnings stability. *Caution:* If your break-even point is high, you are vulnerable to economic declines.

Your company's cost structure affects earnings as volume changes. If you have high operating leverage there is high risk because fixed cost cannot be decreased when revenue declines.

What to Look for: A high ratio of variable cost to total cost points to stability. It is easier to adjust variable cost than fixed cost when product demand declines.

Some ratios that should be calculated in measuring operating leverage are

- Fixed cost/total cost
- Percent change in operating income/percent change in sales
- Net income/fixed cost

When there is an increase in the first two or a decrease in the third, higher fixed costs are indicated. These may result in earnings variability. Other useful comparisons are

- Fixed cost/variable cost
- Break-even point to sales

EXAMPLE 1.12

Assume the following:

Selling price	$30
Variable cost	$18
Fixed cost	$40,000
Volume	8,000 units

You want to determine the degree of operating leverage. Degree of operating leverage equals:

$$\frac{(\text{Selling price} - \text{Variable cost}) (\text{Units})}{(\text{Selling price} - \text{Variable cost}) (\text{Units}) - \text{Fixed cost}}$$

$$\frac{(\$30 - \$18)(8,000)}{(\$30 - \$18)(8,000) - 40,000} = \frac{\$96,000}{\$56,000} = \underline{\$1.71} \text{ (rounded)}$$

Chapter 1: Break-even, Operating Leverage, and Contribution Margin   13

Interpretation: If sales increase by 10%, net income will increase by 1.71 times that amount, or 17.10%.

EXAMPLE 1.13

Your comparative income statement follows:

	20X0	20X1
Net income	$100,000	$102,000
Fixed costs	40,000	55,000
Variable costs	25,000	27,000

The operating leverage in 20X1 relative to 20X0 was higher, as evidenced by the increase in the ratio of fixed costs to total costs and the decrease in the ratio of net income to fixed costs. Thus, there is greater earnings instability.

	20X0	20X1
Fixed costs to total costs	61.5%	67.1%
Net income to fixed costs	2.5	1.86

EXAMPLE 1.14

You want to appraise your operating leverage. Assume the following:

Selling price	$2
Fixed cost	$50,000
Variable cost per unit	$1.10

Sales Volume	Dollar Sales	−	Fixed Cost	−	Variable Cost	=	Profit
100,000	$200,000	−	$50,000	−	$110,000	=	$40,000
130,000	260,000	−	50,000	−	143,000	=	67,000

The ratio of the percentage change in operating income to the percentage change in sales volume is

$$\frac{\text{Change in profit}}{\text{Profit}} \Big/ \frac{\text{Change in quantity}}{\text{Quantity}} = \frac{\$67,000 - \$40,000}{\$40,000} \Big/ \frac{130,000 - 100,000}{100,000} = \frac{\$27,000}{\$40,000} \Big/ \frac{\$40,000}{30,000} \Big/ \frac{100,000}{100,000} = \frac{67.5\%}{30.0} = 2.25$$

14 Part I: Financial Analysis

CONTRIBUTION MARGIN ANALYSIS

Contribution margin analysis is used to evaluate the performance of the manager and activity. Contribution margin equals sales less variable cost. The contribution margin income statement looks at cost behavior. It shows the relationship between variable cost and fixed cost, irrespective of the functions associated with a given cost item.

Illustrative Contribution Margin Income Statement

- Sales
- Less variable cost of sales
- Manufacturing contribution margin
- Less variable selling and administrative expenses
- Contribution margin
- Less fixed cost
- Net income

Advantages of Contribution Margin Income Statement

- Aids in decision making, such as whether to drop or push a product line
- Aids in deciding whether to ask a selling price below the normal price

Tip: When idle capacity exists, an order should be accepted at below the normal selling price as long as contribution margin is earned, because fixed cost will not change.

Disadvantages of Contribution Margin Income Statement

- Not accepted for financial reporting or tax purposes
- Ignores fixed overhead as a product cost
- Difficult to segregate fixed cost and variable cost

EXAMPLE 1.15

Assume the following information:

Selling price	$15
Variable manufacturing cost per unit	$7

Chapter 1: Break-even, Operating Leverage, and Contribution Margin

Variable selling cost per unit	$2
Fixed manufacturing overhead	$150,000
Fixed selling and administrative expenses	$60,000
Sales volume	600,000
Beginning inventory	50,000 units
Ending inventory	70,000 units

Production is:

Sales	600,000
Add ending inventory	70,000
Need	670,000
Less beginning inventory	50,000
Production	620,000

Contribution margin income statement follows.

Sales (600,000 × $15)		$9,000,000
Less variable cost of sales		
Beginning inventory		
(50,000 × $7)	$ 350,000	
Variable cost of goods manufactured		
(620,000 × $7)	4,340,000	
Variable cost of goods available	$4,690,000	
Less ending inventory		
(70,000 × $7)	490,000	
Total variable cost of sales		4,200,000
Manufacturing contribution margin		$4,800,000
Less variable selling and administrative expenses (600,000 × $2)		1,200,000
Contribution margin		$3,600,000
Less fixed costs		
Fixed overhead	$ 150,000	
Fixed selling and administrative	60,000	
Total fixed costs		210,000
Net income		$3,390,000

You are sometimes faced with a decision whether to process an item further.

EXAMPLE 1.16

Product X may be sold at split-off or processed further. Relevant data follow:

	Sales Value	Additional Cost and Sales Value for Further Processing	
Production	at Split-Off	Sales	Cost
5,000	$95,000	$120,000	$18,000

Incremental revenue ($120,000 – $95,000)	$25,000
Incremental cost	18,000
Incremental gain	$ 7,000

You should process this product further because it results in incremental earnings.

Contribution margin analysis can be used to ascertain the best way of utilizing capacity.

EXAMPLE 1.17

You can make a raw metal that can either be sold at this stage or processed further and sold as an alloy. Relevant data follow.

	Raw Metal	Alloy
Selling price	$200	$315
Variable cost	90	120

Total fixed cost is $400,000, and 100,000 hours of capacity are interchangeable between the products. There is unlimited demand for both products. Three hours are needed to make the raw metal, and five hours are required to manufacture the alloy. Contribution margin per hour follows.

	Raw Metal	Alloy
Selling price	$200	$315
Less variable cost	90	120

	Raw Metal	Alloy
Contribution margin	$110	$195
Hours per ton	3	5
Contribution margin per hour	$ 36.67	$ 39

Chapter 1: Break-even, Operating Leverage, and Contribution Margin   17

You should sell only the alloy because it results in the highest contribution margin per hour. Fixed costs are not considered because they are constant and are incurred regardless of which product is manufactured.

You should accept an order at less than the normal selling price when there is idle capacity because fixed costs are constant as long as you earn a contribution margin on the order.

EXAMPLE 1.18

You currently sell 8,000 units at $30 per unit. Variable cost per unit is $15. Fixed costs are $60,000 (fixed cost per unit is thus $7.50: $60,000/8,000). Idle capacity exists. A potential customer is willing to purchase 500 units at $21 per unit.

You should accept this order because it increases your profitability.

Sales (500 × $21)	$10,500
Less variable costs (500 × $15)	7,500
Contribution margin	$ 3,000
Less fixed costs	0
Net income	$ 3,000

Note: When idle capacity exists, the acceptance of an additional order does not increase fixed cost. If fixed cost were to go up, say by $1,000 to purchase a special tool just for this job, it still is financially feasible to accept this order because a positive profit of $2,000 ($3,000 − $1,000) would result.

EXAMPLE 1.19

You manufacture a product. You can produce 200,000 units per year at a total variable cost of $800,000 and a total fixed cost of $500,000. You estimate that you can sell 150,000 units at a normal selling price of $4 each. Further, a special order has been placed by a customer for 50,000 units at a 25% discount.

Your profit will rise by $50,000 due to this special order.

$$\text{Variable cost per unit} = \frac{\$800{,}000}{200{,}000} = \$4$$

Special order price 0.75 × $4	3
Incremental profit per unit	$ 1
Incremental earnings $1 × 50,000 units =	$50,000

EXAMPLE 1.20

Financial information follows:

Selling price	$15
Direct material	$2
Direct labor	$1.90
Variable overhead	$0.50
Fixed overhead ($100,00/20,000 units) = $5	

Selling and administrative expenses are fixed except for sales commissions, which are 14% of the selling price. Idle capacity exists.

You receive an additional order for 1,000 units from a potential customer at a selling price of $9.

Even though the offered selling price of $9 is significantly less than the current selling price of $15, the order should be accepted.

Sales (1,000 × $9)	$9,000
Less variable manufacturing costs (1,000 × $4.40)*	4,400
Manufacturing contribution margin	$4,600
Less variable selling and administrative expenses (14% × $9,000)	1,260
Contribution margin	$3,340
Less fixed cost	0
Net income	$3,340

EXAMPLE 1.21

You want a markup of 40% over cost on a product. Relevant information about the product follows.

Direct material	$ 5,000
Direct labor	12,000
Overhead	4,000
Total cost	$21,000
Markup on cost (40%)	8,400
Selling price	$29,400

---

*Variable manufacturing cost = $2 + $1.90 + $0.50 = $4.40.

Chapter 1: Break-even, Operating Leverage, and Contribution Margin   19

Total direct labor for the year is $1,800,000. Total overhead for the year equals 30% of direct labor. The overhead is broken down into 25% fixed and 75% variable. A customer offers to buy the item for $23,000. Idle capacity exists. You should accept the incremental order because additional profitability is earned.

Selling price		$23,000
Less variable costs		
Direct material	$ 5,000	
Direct labor	12,000	
Variable overhead ($12,000 × 22.5%)*	2,700	19,700
Contribution margin		$ 3,300
Less fixed cost		0
Net income		$ 3,300

Variable overhead = 22.5% of direct labor, calculated as follows:

$$\frac{\text{Variable overhead}}{\text{Direct labor}} = \frac{0.75 \times \$540,000}{\$1,800,000} = \frac{\$405,000}{\$1,800,000} = \underline{22.5\%}$$

Contribution margin analysis assists in formulating a bid price on a contract to produce an item or render a service.

EXAMPLE 1.22

You receive an order for 10,000 units. You want to know the minimum bid price that will result in a $20,000 increase in earnings. The current income statement follows.

Sales (50,000 units × $25)		$1,250,000
Less cost of sales		
Direct material	$120,000	
Direct labor	200,000	
Variable overhead ($200,000 × 0.30)	60,000	
Fixed overhead	100,000	480,000
Gross margin		$ 770,000
Less selling and administrative expenses		
Variable (includes freight costs of $0.40 per unit)	$ 60,000	
Fixed	30,000	90,000
Net income		$ 680,000

*Total overhead 0.30 × $1,800,000 = $540,000.

Part I: Financial Analysis

If the contract is awarded, cost patterns for the incremental order are the same except that:

- Freight costs will be absorbed by the customer.
- Special tools of $8,000 will be needed only for this order and are not going to be used again.
- Direct labor time for each unit under the order will be 20 percent longer.

Preliminary calculations:

	Per Unit Cost
Direct material ($120,000/50,000)	$2.40
Direct labor ($200,000/50,000)	4.00
Variable selling and administrative expense ($60,000/50,000)	1.20

A forecasted income statement follows.

	Current	Forecasted	Explanation
Units	50,000	60,000	
Sales	$1,250,000	$1,372,400	Computed last[a]
Cost of Sales			
Direct material	$ 120,000	$ 144,000	($2.40 × 60,000)
Direct labor	200,000	248,000	($200,000 + [10,000 × $4.80[b]])
Variable overhead	60,000	74,400	($248,000 × .30)
Fixed overhead	100,000	108,000	
Total	$ 480,000	$ 574,400	
Selling and Administrative Expenses			
Variable	$ 60,000	$ 68,000	($60,000 + [10,000 × .$80[c]])
Fixed	$ 30,000	$ 30,000	
Total	$ 90,000	$ 98,000	
Net income	$ 680,000	$ 700,000[d]	

[a] Net income + Selling and administrative expenses + Cost of sales = Sales
$700,000 + $98,000 + $574,400 = $1,372,400
[b] 4 × 1.2 = $4.80
[c] $1.20 − $.40 = $.80
[d] $680,000 + $20,000 = $700,000

Chapter 1: Break-even, Operating Leverage, and Contribution Margin

The contract price for the 10,000 units should be $122,400 ($1,372,400 − $1,250,000), or $12.24 per unit ($122,400/10,000).

The contract price per unit of $12.24 is less than the $25 current selling price per unit. Keep in mind that total fixed cost is the same except for the $8,000 expenditure on the special tool.

Contribution margin analysis assists in determining how to derive the same profit as last year even though there is a drop in sales volume.

EXAMPLE 1.23

In 20X1, sales volume was 200,000 units, selling price was $25, variable cost per unit was $15, and fixed cost was $500,000.

In 20X2, sales volume is expected to total 150,000 units. As a result, fixed costs have been slashed by $80,000. On 4/1/20X2, 40,000 units have already been sold. You want to determine the contribution margin that has to be earned on the remaining units for 20X2.

Net income computation for 20X1:

$$S = FC + VC + P$$
$$\$25 \times 200{,}000 = \$500{,}000 + (\$15 \times 200{,}000) + P$$
$$\$1{,}500{,}000 = P$$

Contribution margin to be earned in 20X2:

Total fixed cost ($500,000 − $80,000)	$ 420,000
Net income	1,500,000
Contribution margin needed for year	$1,920,000
Contribution margin already earned:	
(Selling price − variable cost) × units	
($25 − $15) = $10 × 40,000 units	400,000
Contribution margin remaining	$1,520,000

$$\text{Contribution margin per unit needed} = \frac{\text{Contribution margin remaining}}{\text{Units remaining}}$$

$$= \frac{\$1{,}520{,}000}{110{,}000 \text{ units}} = \underline{\$13.82}$$

CONCLUSION

Break-even analysis assists you in making management decisions concerning the feasibility of introducing products or services. The impact of fixed costs in the cost structure must be considered in evaluating corporate operational risk. Contribution margin analysis reveals whether to accept a below-normal selling price, which products to emphasize, how to optimize utilization of capacity, and how to formulate a bid price on a contract.

2
Applying Discounting and Compounding Analysis Techniques

You cannot treat today's and tomorrow's dollars the same. This chapter looks at the relationship between *present* (discounted) and *future* (compound, amount of) values of money. Applications of present values and future values include loans, leases, bonds, sinking fund, growth rates, capital budgeting investment selection, and effect of inflation on the organization. You can solve for many different types of unknowns, such as interest rate, annual payment, number of periods, present amount, and future amount. Present value and future value calculations have many applications in accounting, financial, and investment decisions.

Assumptions of Present Value and Future Value Techniques

- Present value and future value variables (e.g., interest rate, number of periods, annual cash flows) are known with certainty.
- The interest rate is constant.
- All amounts in a series are equal.

We will be using the following tables throughout this chapter:

Future Value of $1	Table 2.1
Future Value of an Annuity of $1	Table 2.2
Present Value of $1	Table 2.3
Present Value of an Annuity of $1	Table 2.4

Future value is sometimes called amount of, sum of, or compound value. Present value is sometimes called discounted value, year zero value, or current value.

Some rules for using the present and future value tables throughout this chapter follow.

Present Value Table

- A present value table is used if you want to determine the current amount of receiving future cash flows.
- The Present Value of $1 table is used if you have unequal cash flows each period or a lump-sum cash flow.
- The Present Value of an Annuity of $1 table is used if the cash flows each period are equal and occur at the end of the period.
- The Present Value of an Annuity Due (which requires modification of the Present Value of an Annuity table) is used if the cash flows each period are equal and occur at the beginning of the period.

Future Value Table

- A future value table is used if you want to determine the future (later) amount of giving cash flows.
- The Future Value of $1 table is used if you have unequal cash flows each period or a lump-sum cash flow.
- The Future Value of an Annuity of $1 table is used if the cash flows each period are equal and occur at the end of the period.
- The Future Value of an Annuity Due (which requires modification of the Future Value of an Annuity table) is used if the cash flows each period are equal and occur at the beginning of each period.

Both Present Value and Future Value Tables

- If you want to determine a total dollar amount either in the present or future, you have a multiplication problem.
- If you want to calculate an annual payment, interest rate, or number of periods, you have a division problem. In such a case, what you put in the numerator of a fraction determines which table to use. For example, if you put in the numerator a future value that involves equal year-end payments, you have to use the Future Value of an Annuity table.

- If you are given a present value amount, it goes in the numerator of the fraction. On the other hand, if you are given a future value amount, that value goes in the numerator.
- If you are solving for an annual payment, you divide the numerator by the factor corresponding to the interest rate (i) and the number of periods (n).
- If you are solving for an interest rate, divide the numerator by the annual payment to get a factor. Then, to find the interest rate, find that factor on the table opposite the number of years. The interest rate will be indicated at the top of the column where the factor is located.
- If you are solving for the number of years, you divide the numerator by the annual payment to get the factor. Then find the factor in the appropriate interest rate column. The number of years will be indicated in the far left-hand column.

Now let us look at examples using the different tables.

FUTURE VALUE OF $1 (TABLE 2.1)

EXAMPLE 2.1

You put $400 in a savings account earning 10% interest compounded annually for 6 years. You will have accumulated

$$\$400 \times 1.7716 = \underline{\$708.64}$$

EXAMPLE 2.2

You deposit $10,000 in an account offering an annual interest rate of 20%. You will keep the money on deposit for 5 years. The interest rate is compounded quarterly. The accumulated amount at the end of the fifth year is

$$n = 5 \times 4 = 20$$
$$i = 20\%/4 = 5\%$$
$$\$10,000 \times 2.6533 = \underline{\$26,533}$$

EXAMPLE 2.3

On 1/1/00 you deposit $10,000 to earn 10% compounded semiannually. Effective 1/1/04 the interest rate is increased to 12%, and at that time you

TABLE 2.1 Future Value of $1

Interest Rate

Number of Years	1%	2%	3%	4%	5%	6%	7%	8%	9%	10%	12%	14%	15%	16%	18%	20%	24%	28%	32%	36%
1	1.0100	1.0200	1.0300	1.0400	1.0500	1.0600	1.0700	1.0800	1.0900	1.1000	1.1200	1.1400	1.1500	1.1600	1.1800	1.2000	1.2400	1.2800	1.3200	1.3600
2	1.0201	1.0404	1.0609	1.0816	1.1025	1.1236	1.1449	1.1664	1.1881	1.2100	1.2544	1.2996	1.3225	1.3456	1.3924	1.4400	1.5376	1.6384	1.7424	1.8496
3	1.0303	1.0612	1.0927	1.1249	1.1576	1.1910	1.2250	1.2597	1.2950	1.3310	1.4049	1.4815	1.5209	1.5609	1.6430	1.7280	1.9066	2.0972	2.3000	2.5155
4	1.0406	1.0824	1.1255	1.1699	1.2155	1.2625	1.3108	1.3605	1.4116	1.4641	1.5735	1.6890	1.7490	1.8106	1.9388	2.0736	2.3642	2.6844	3.0360	3.4210
5	1.0510	1.1041	1.1593	1.2167	1.2763	1.3382	1.4026	1.4693	1.5386	1.6105	1.7623	1.9254	2.0114	2.1003	2.2878	2.4883	2.9316	3.4360	4.0075	4.6526
6	1.0615	1.1262	1.1941	1.2653	1.3401	1.4185	1.5007	1.5869	1.6771	1.7716	1.9738	2.1950	2.3131	2.4364	2.6996	2.9860	3.6352	4.3980	5.2899	6.3275
7	1.0721	1.1487	1.2299	1.3159	1.4071	1.5036	1.6058	1.7138	1.8280	1.9487	2.2107	2.5023	2.6600	2.8262	3.1855	3.5832	4.5077	5.6295	6.9826	8.6054
8	1.0829	1.1717	1.2668	1.3686	1.4775	1.5938	1.7182	1.8509	1.9926	2.1436	2.4760	2.8526	3.0590	3.2784	3.7589	4.2998	5.5895	7.2058	9.2170	11.703
9	1.0937	1.1951	1.3048	1.4233	1.5513	1.6895	1.8385	1.9990	2.1719	2.3579	2.7731	3.2519	3.5179	3.8030	4.4355	5.1598	6.9310	9.2234	12.166	15.916
10	1.1046	1.2190	1.3439	1.4802	1.6289	1.7908	1.9672	2.1589	2.3674	2.5937	3.1058	3.7072	4.0456	4.4114	5.2338	6.1917	8.5944	11.805	16.059	21.646
11	1.1157	1.2434	1.3842	1.5395	1.7103	1.8983	2.1049	2.3316	2.5804	2.8531	3.4785	4.2262	4.6524	5.1173	6.1759	7.4301	10.657	15.111	21.198	29.439
12	1.1268	1.2682	1.4258	1.6010	1.7959	2.0122	2.2522	2.5182	2.8127	3.1384	3.8960	4.8179	5.3502	5.9360	7.2876	8.9161	13.214	19.342	27.982	40.037
13	1.1381	1.2936	1.4685	1.6651	1.8856	2.1329	2.4098	2.7196	3.0658	3.4523	4.3635	5.4924	6.1528	6.8858	8.5994	10.699	16.386	24.748	36.937	54.451
14	1.1495	1.3195	1.5126	1.7317	1.9799	2.2609	2.5785	2.9372	3.3417	3.7975	4.8871	6.2613	7.0757	7.9875	10.147	12.839	20.319	31.691	48.756	74.053
15	1.1610	1.3459	1.5580	1.8009	2.0789	2.3966	2.7590	3.1722	3.6425	4.1772	5.4736	7.1379	8.1371	9.2655	11.973	15.407	25.195	40.564	53.358	100.71
16	1.1726	1.3728	1.6047	1.8730	2.1829	2.5404	2.9522	3.4259	3.9703	4.5950	6.1304	8.1372	9.3576	10.748	14.129	18.488	31.242	51.923	84.953	136.96
17	1.1834	1.4002	1.6528	1.9479	2.2920	2.6928	3.1588	3.7000	4.3276	5.0545	6.8660	9.2765	10.761	12.467	16.672	22.186	38.740	66.461	112.13	186.27
18	1.1961	1.4282	1.7024	2.0258	2.4066	2.8543	3.3799	3.9960	4.7171	5.5599	7.6900	10.575	12.375	14.462	19.673	26.623	48.038	85.070	148.02	253.33
19	1.2081	1.4568	1.7535	2.1068	2.5270	3.0256	3.6165	4.3157	5.1417	6.1159	8.6129	12.055	14.231	16.776	23.214	31.948	59.567	108.89	195.39	344.53
20	1.2202	1.4859	1.8061	2.1911	2.6533	3.2071	3.8697	4.6610	5.6044	6.7275	9.6463	13.743	16.366	19.460	27.393	38.337	73.864	139.37	257.91	468.57
21	1.2324	1.5157	1.8603	2.2788	2.7860	3.3996	4.1406	5.0338	6.1088	7.4002	10.803	15.667	18.821	22.574	32.323	46.005	91.591	178.40	340.44	637.26
22	1.2447	1.5460	1.9161	2.3699	2.9253	3.6035	4.4304	5.4365	6.6586	8.1403	12.100	17.861	21.644	26.186	38.142	55.206	113.57	228.35	449.39	866.67
23	1.2572	1.5769	1.9736	2.4647	3.0715	3.8197	4.7405	5.8715	7.2579	8.9543	13.552	20.361	24.891	30.376	45.007	66.247	140.83	292.30	593.19	1178.6
24	1.2697	1.6084	2.0328	2.5633	3.2251	4.0489	5.0724	6.3412	7.9111	9.8497	15.178	23.212	28.625	35.236	53.108	79.496	174.63	374.14	783.02	1602.9
25	1.2824	1.6406	2.0938	2.6658	3.3864	4.2919	5.2474	6.8485	8.6231	10.834	17.000	26.461	32.918	40.874	62.668	95.396	216.54	478.90	1033.5	2180.0
26	1.2953	1.6734	2.1566	2.7725	3.5557	4.5497	5.8074	7.3964	9.3992	11.918	19.040	30.166	37.856	47.414	73.948	114.47	268.51	612.99	1364.3	2964.9
27	1.3082	1.7069	2.2213	2.8834	3.7335	4.8223	5.8074	7.9881	10.245	13.110	21.324	34.389	43.535	55.000	87.259	137.37	332.95	784.63	1800.9	4032.2
28	1.3213	1.7410	2.2879	2.9987	3.9201	5.1117	6.6488	8.6271	11.167	14.421	23.883	39.204	50.065	63.800	102.96	164.84	412.86	1004.3	2377.2	5483.8
29	1.3345	1.7758	2.3566	3.1187	4.1161	5.4184	7.1143	9.3173	12.172	15.863	26.749	44.693	57.575	74.008	121.50	197.81	511.95	128.5	3137.9	7458.0
30	1.3478	1.8114	2.4273	3.2434	4.3219	5.7435	7.6123	10.062	13.267	17.449	29.959	50.950	66.211	85.849	143.37	237.37	634.81	1645.5	4142.0	10143.

Chapter 2: Discounting and Compounding Analysis Techniques   27

decide to double your balance. You want to determine how much will be accumulated in your account on 1/1/10.

$$1/1/00-1/1/04: \quad n = 4 \times 2 = 8$$

$$i = \frac{10\%}{2} = 5\%$$

$$\$10,000 \times 1.4475 = \$14,775$$

1/1/04: Double balance   14,775

1/1/04: Total balance $29,550

$$1/1/04-1/1/10: \quad n = 6 \times 2 = 12$$

$$i = \frac{12\%}{2} = 6\%$$

$$\$29,550 \times 2.0122 = \$59,460.51$$

EXAMPLE 2.4

You want to have $1,000,000 at the end of 15 years. The interest rate is 8%. You have to deposit today the following sum to accomplish your objective:

$$\frac{\$1,000,000}{3.1722} = \frac{\$315,238.63}{}$$

EXAMPLE 2.5

At an interest rate of 12%, you want to know how long it will take for your money to double.

$$\frac{\$2}{\$1} = 2$$

$$n = 6 \text{ years}$$

EXAMPLE 2.6

You want to have $250,000. Your initial deposit is $30,000. The interest rate is 12%. The number of years it will take to reach your goal is:

$$\frac{\$250,000}{\$\ 30,000} = 8.333$$

$n = 18.5$ years (approximately)
(Factor falls about midway between 18 and 19 years.)

EXAMPLE 2.7

You agree to pay back $3,000 in 6 years on a $2,000 loan made today. You are being charged an interest rate of:

$$\frac{\$3,000}{\$2,000} = 1.5$$

$$i = 7\%$$

EXAMPLE 2.8

Your earnings per share was $1.20 in 20X1, and eight years later it was $3.67. The compound annual growth rate is:

$$\frac{\$3.67}{\$1.20} = 3.059$$

$$\text{Growth rate} = 15\%$$

FUTURE VALUE OF AN ANNUITY OF $1 (TABLE 2.2)

EXAMPLE 2.9

You plan to pay into a sinking fund $20,000 year-end payments for the next 15 years. The fund earns an interest of 8% compounded once a year. The accumulated balance at the end of the fifteenth year is:

$$\$20,000 \times 27.152 = \underline{\$543,040}$$

EXAMPLE 2.10

You deposit $30,000 semiannually into a fund for 10 years. The annual interest rate is 8%. The amount accumulated at the end of the tenth year is calculated as follows:

$$n = 10 \times 2 = 20$$

$$i = \frac{8\%}{2} = 4\%$$

$$\$30,000 \times 29.778 = \underline{\$893,340}$$

EXAMPLE 2.11

You borrow $300,000 for 20 years at 10%. At the end of the 20-year period, you will have to pay:

$$\$300,000 \times 6.7275 = \underline{\$2,018,250}$$

TABLE 2.2 Future Value of an Annuity of $1

Interest Rate

Number of Years	1%	2%	3%	4%	5%	6%	7%	8%	9%	10%	12%	14%	15%	16%	18%	20%	24%	28%	32%	36%
1	1.0000	1.0000	1.0000	1.0000	1.0000	1.0000	1.0000	1.0000	1.0000	1.0000	1.0000	1.0000	1.0000	1.0000	1.0000	1.0000	1.0000	1.0000	1.0000	1.0000
2	2.0100	2.0200	2.0300	2.0400	2.0500	2.0600	2.0700	2.0800	2.0900	2.1000	2.1200	2.1400	2.1500	2.1600	2.1800	2.2000	2.2400	2.2800	2.3200	2.3600
3	3.0301	3.0604	3.0909	3.1216	3.1525	3.1836	3.2149	3.2464	3.2781	3.3100	3.3744	3.4396	3.4725	3.5056	3.5724	3.6400	3.7776	3.9184	4.0624	4.2096
4	4.0604	4.1216	4.1836	4.2465	4.3101	4.3746	4.4399	4.5061	4.5731	4.6410	4.7793	4.9211	4.9934	5.0665	5.2154	5.3680	5.6842	6.0156	6.3624	6.7251
5	5.1010	5.2040	5.3091	5.4163	5.5256	5.6371	5.7507	5.8666	5.9847	6.1051	6.3528	6.6101	6.7424	6.8771	7.1542	7.4416	8.0484	8.6999	9.3983	10.146
6	6.1520	6.3081	6.4684	6.6330	6.8019	6.9753	7.1533	7.3359	7.5233	7.7156	8.1152	8.5355	8.7537	8.9775	9.4420	9.9299	10.980	12.135	13.405	14.798
7	7.2135	7.4343	7.6625	7.8983	8.1420	8.3938	8.6540	8.9228	9.2004	9.4872	10.089	10.730	11.066	11.413	12.141	12.915	14.615	16.533	18.695	21.126
8	8.2857	8.5830	8.8923	9.2142	9.5491	9.8975	10.259	10.636	11.028	11.435	12.299	13.232	13.726	14.240	15.327	16.499	19.122	22.163	25.678	29.731
9	9.3685	9.7546	10.159	10.582	11.026	11.491	11.978	12.487	13.021	13.579	14.775	16.085	16.785	17.518	19.085	20.798	24.712	29.369	34.895	41.435
10	10.462	10.949	11.463	12.006	12.577	13.180	13.816	14.486	15.192	15.937	17.548	19.337	20.303	21.321	23.521	25.958	31.643	38.592	47.061	57.351
11	11.566	12.168	12.807	13.486	14.206	14.971	15.783	16.645	17.560	18.531	20.654	23.044	24.349	25.732	28.755	32.150	40.237	50.398	63.121	78.998
12	12.682	13.412	14.192	15.025	15.917	16.869	17.888	18.977	20.140	21.384	24.133	27.270	29.001	30.850	34.931	39.580	50.894	65.510	84.320	108.43
13	13.809	14.680	15.617	16.626	17.713	18.882	20.140	21.495	22.953	24.522	28.029	32.088	34.351	36.786	42.218	48.496	64.109	84.852	112.30	148.47
14	14.947	15.973	17.086	18.291	19.598	21.015	22.550	24.214	26.019	27.975	32.392	37.581	40.504	43.672	50.818	59.195	80.496	109.61	149.23	202.92
15	16.096	17.293	18.598	20.023	21.578	23.276	25.129	27.152	29.360	31.772	37.279	43.842	47.580	51.659	60.965	72.035	100.81	141.30	197.99	276.97
16	17.257	18.639	20.156	21.824	23.657	25.672	27.888	30.324	33.003	35.949	42.753	50.980	55.717	60.925	72.939	87.442	126.01	181.86	262.35	377.69
17	18.430	20.012	21.761	23.697	25.840	28.212	30.840	33.750	36.973	40.544	48.883	59.117	65.075	71.673	87.068	105.93	157.25	233.79	347.30	514.66
18	19.614	21.412	23.414	25.645	28.132	30.905	33.99	37.450	41.301	45.599	55.749	68.394	75.836	84.140	103.74	128.11	195.99	300.25	459.44	700.93
19	20.810	22.840	25.116	27.671	30.539	33.760	37.379	41.446	46.018	51.159	63.439	78.969	88.211	98.603	123.41	154.74	244.03	385.32	607.47	954.27
20	22.019	24.297	26.870	29.778	33.066	36.785	40.995	45.762	51.160	57.275	72.052	91.024	102.44	115.37	146.62	186.68	303.60	494.21	802.86	1298.8
21	23.239	25.783	28.676	31.969	35.719	39.992	44.865	50.442	56.764	64.002	81.698	104.76	118.81	134.84	174.02	225.02	377.46	633.59	1060.7	1767.3
22	24.471	27.299	30.536	34.243	38.505	43.392	49.005	55.456	62.873	71.402	92.502	120.43	137.63	157.41	206.34	271.03	469.05	811.99	1401.2	2404.6
23	25.716	28.845	32.452	36.617	41.430	46.995	53.436	60.893	69.531	79.543	104.60	138.29	159.27	183.60	244.48	326.23	582.62	1040.3	1850.6	3271.3
24	26.973	30.421	34.426	39.082	44.502	50.815	58.176	66.764	76.789	88.497	118.15	158.65	184.16	213.97	289.49	392.48	723.46	1332.6	2443.8	4449.9
25	28.243	32.030	36.459	41.645	47.727	54.864	63.249	73.105	84.700	98.347	133.33	181.87	212.79	249.21	342.60	471.98	898.09	1706.8	3226.8	6052.9
26	29.525	33.670	38.553	44.311	51.113	59.156	68.676	79.954	93.323	109.18	150.33	208.33	245.71	290.08	405.27	567.37	1114.6	2185.7	4260.4	8233.0
27	30.820	35.344	40.709	47.084	54.669	63.705	74.483	87.350	102.72	121.09	169.37	238.49	283.56	337.50	479.22	681.85	1383.1	2798.7	5624.7	11197.9
28	32.129	37.051	42.930	49.967	58.402	68.528	80.697	95.338	112.96	134.20	190.69	272.88	327.10	392.50	566.48	819.22	1716.0	3583.3	7425.6	15230.2
29	32.450	38.792	45.218	52.966	62.322	73.689	87.346	103.96	124.13	148.63	214.58	312.09	377.16	456.30	669.44	984.06	2128.9	4587.6	9802.9	20714.1
30	34.784	40.568	47.576	56.084	66.438	79.058	94.460	113.28	136.30	164.49	241.33	356.78	434.74	530.31	790.94	1181.8	2640.9	5873.2	12940	28172.2

The interest amount equals:

$2,018,250   Maturity value
  300,000   Principal
$1,718,250   Interest

EXAMPLE 2.12

You want to determine the annual year-end deposit needed to accumulate $100,000 at the end of 15 years. The interest rate is 12%. The annual deposit is:

$$\frac{\$100,000}{37.279} = \underline{\$2,682.48}$$

EXAMPLE 2.13

You need a sinking fund for the retirement of a bond 30 years from now. The interest rate is 10%. The annual year-end contribution needed to accumulate $1,000,000 is:

$$\frac{\$1,000,000}{164.49} = \underline{\$6,079.40}$$

EXAMPLE 2.14

You want to have $600,000 accumulated in your fund. You make four deposits of $100,000 per year. The interest rate you must earn is:

$$\frac{\$600,000}{\$100,000} = 6$$

$$i = \underline{28\%} \text{ (approximately)}$$

EXAMPLE 2.15

You want to have $500,000 accumulated in a pension plan after 9 years. You deposit $30,000 per year. The interest rate you must earn is:

$$\frac{\$500,000}{\$\ 30,000} = 16.667$$

$$i = \underline{15\%} \text{ (approximately)}$$

EXAMPLE 2.16

You want $500,000 in the future. The interest rate is 10%. The annual payment is $80,000. The number of years it will take to accomplish this objective is:

$$\frac{\$500,000}{\$80,000} = 6.25$$

$$n = 5 \text{ years (approximately)}$$

FUTURE VALUE OF AN ANNUITY DUE OF $1 (TABLE 2.2. ADJUSTED)

Calculation of the future value of an annuity due of $1 requires a minor adjustment to the Future Value of an Ordinary Annuity of $1 table. To get the future value of an annuity due, add 1 to the number of years and then obtain the factor. Then subtract 1 from this factor.

EXAMPLE 2.17

You make $25,000 payments at the beginning of the year into a sinking fund for 20 years. The interest rate is 12%. The accumulated value of the fund at the end of the twentieth year is:

$n = 20 + 1 = 21$ Factor 81.698
                                  −1,000
                       Adjusted   80.698

$25,000 × 80.698 = $2,017,450

EXAMPLE 2.18

You want to accumulate $600,000 in an account. You are going to make eight yearly deposits. The interest rate is 12%. The annual deposit is:

$$n = 8 + 1 = 9$$

$$\frac{\$600,000}{14.775 - 1} = \frac{\$600,000}{13.775} = \$43,557.17$$

PRESENT VALUE OF $1 (TABLE 2.3)

EXAMPLE 2.19

You have an opportunity to receive $30,000 four years from now. You earn 12% on your investment. The most you should pay for this investment is:

$$\$30,000 \times 0.6355 = \underline{\$19,065}$$

EXAMPLE 2.20

You are thinking of starting a new product line that initially costs $30,000. The interest rate is 10%. Your annual net cash inflows are:

Year 1 $ 8,000
Year 2   15,000
Year 3   18,000

The net present value is positive, as indicated in the following calculations.

Year	Calculation	Net Present Value
0	−$30,000 × 1	−$30,000.00
1	8,000 × 0.9091	7,272.80
2	15,000 × 0.8264	12,396.00
3	18,000 × 0.7513	13,523.40
Net present value		$ 3,192.20

You should undertake the new product line.

PRESENT VALUE OF AN ANNUITY OF $1 (TABLE 2.4)

Annuities are often received from pension plans and insurance policies. The Present Value of $1 table (Table 2.3) can be used to solve an annuity of equal payments by making separate calculations for each year's cash flow (multiplying the cash flow for the year by the present value of $1 factor) and adding them all up over the length of the proposal's life. This calculation can be done much faster using a Present Value of an Annuity of $1 table (Table 2.4). All that is required is to multiply the annual cash payment by the factor in the table.

TABLE 2.3 Present Value of $1

Interest Rate

Number of Years	1%	2%	3%	4%	5%	6%	7%	8%	9%	10%	12%	14%	15%	16%	18%	20%	24%	28%	32%	36%
1	0.9901	0.9804	0.9709	0.9615	0.9524	0.9434	0.9346	0.9259	0.9174	0.9091	0.8929	0.8772	0.8696	0.8621	0.8475	0.8333	0.8065	0.7813	0.7576	0.7353
2	0.9803	0.9612	0.9426	0.9246	0.9070	0.8900	0.8734	0.8573	0.8417	0.8264	0.7972	0.7695	0.7561	0.7432	0.7182	0.6944	0.6504	0.6104	0.5739	0.5407
3	0.9706	0.9423	0.9151	0.8890	0.8638	0.8396	0.8163	0.7938	0.7722	0.7513	0.7118	0.6750	0.6575	0.6407	0.6086	0.5787	0.5245	0.4768	0.4348	0.3975
4	0.9610	0.9238	0.8885	0.8548	0.8227	0.7921	0.7629	0.7350	0.7084	0.6830	0.6355	0.5921	0.5718	0.5523	0.5158	0.4823	0.4230	0.3725	0.3294	0.2923
5	0.9515	0.9057	0.8626	0.8219	0.7835	0.7473	0.7130	0.6806	0.6499	0.6209	0.5674	0.5194	0.4972	0.4761	0.4371	0.4019	0.3411	0.2910	0.2495	0.2149
6	0.9420	0.8880	0.8375	0.7903	0.7462	0.7050	0.6663	0.6302	0.5963	0.5645	0.5066	0.4556	0.4323	0.4104	0.3704	0.3349	0.2751	0.2274	0.1890	0.1580
7	0.9327	0.8706	0.8131	0.7599	0.7107	0.6651	0.6227	0.5835	0.5470	0.5132	0.4523	0.3996	0.3759	0.3538	0.3139	0.2791	0.2218	0.1776	0.1432	0.1162
8	0.9235	0.8535	0.7894	0.7307	0.6768	0.6274	0.5820	0.5403	0.5019	0.4665	0.4039	0.3506	0.3269	0.3050	0.2660	0.2326	0.1789	0.1388	0.1085	0.0854
9	0.9143	0.8368	0.7664	0.7026	0.6446	0.5919	0.5439	0.5002	0.4604	0.4241	0.3606	0.3075	0.2843	0.2630	0.2255	0.1938	0.1443	0.1084	0.0822	0.0628
10	0.9053	0.8203	0.7441	0.6756	0.6139	0.5584	0.5083	0.4632	0.4224	0.3855	0.3220	0.2697	0.2472	0.2267	0.1911	0.1615	0.1164	0.0847	0.0623	0.0462
11	0.8963	0.8043	0.7224	0.6496	0.5847	0.5268	0.4751	0.4289	0.3875	0.3505	0.2875	0.2366	0.2149	0.1954	0.1619	0.1346	0.0938	0.0662	0.0472	0.0340
12	0.8874	0.7885	0.7014	0.6246	0.5568	0.4970	0.4440	0.3971	0.3555	0.3186	0.2567	0.2076	0.1869	0.1685	0.1372	0.1122	0.0757	0.0517	0.0357	0.0250
13	0.8787	0.7730	0.6810	0.6006	0.5303	0.4688	0.4150	0.3677	0.3262	0.2897	0.2292	0.1821	0.1625	0.1452	0.1163	0.0935	0.0610	0.0404	0.0271	0.0184
14	0.8700	0.7579	0.6611	0.5775	0.5051	0.4423	0.3878	0.3405	0.2992	0.2633	0.2046	0.1597	0.1413	0.1252	0.0985	0.0779	0.0492	0.0316	0.0205	0.0135
15	0.8613	0.7430	0.6419	0.5553	0.4810	0.4173	0.3624	0.3152	0.2745	0.2394	0.1827	0.1401	0.1229	0.1079	0.0835	0.0649	0.0397	0.0247	0.0155	0.0099
16	0.8528	0.7284	0.6232	0.5339	0.4581	0.3936	0.3387	0.2919	0.2519	0.2176	0.1631	0.1229	0.1069	0.0930	0.0708	0.0541	0.0320	0.0193	0.0118	0.0073
17	0.8444	0.7142	0.6050	0.5134	0.4363	0.3714	0.3166	0.2703	0.2311	0.1978	0.1456	0.1078	0.0929	0.0802	0.0600	0.0451	0.0258	0.0150	0.0089	0.0054
18	0.8360	0.7002	0.5874	0.4936	0.4155	0.3503	0.2959	0.2502	0.2120	0.1799	0.1300	0.0946	0.0808	0.0691	0.0508	0.0376	0.0208	0.0118	0.0068	0.0038
19	0.8277	0.6864	0.5703	0.4746	0.3957	0.3305	0.2765	0.2317	0.1945	0.1635	0.1161	0.0829	0.0703	0.0596	0.0431	0.0313	0.0168	0.0092	0.0051	0.0029
20	0.8195	0.6730	0.5537	0.4564	0.3769	0.3118	0.2584	0.2145	0.1784	0.1486	0.1037	0.0728	0.0611	0.0514	0.0365	0.0261	0.0135	0.0072	0.0039	0.0021
25	0.7798	0.6095	0.4776	0.3751	0.2953	0.2330	0.1842	0.1460	0.1160	0.0923	0.0588	0.0378	0.0304	0.0245	0.0160	0.0105	0.0046	0.0021	0.0010	0.0005
30	0.7419	0.5521	0.4120	0.3083	0.2314	0.1741	0.1314	0.0994	0.0754	0.0573	0.0334	0.0196	0.0151	0.0116	0.0070	0.0042	0.0016	0.0006	0.0002	0.0001

TABLE 2.4 Present Value of an Annuity of $1

Interest Rate

Number of Years	1%	2%	3%	4%	5%	6%	7%	8%	9%	10%	12%	14%	15%	16%	18%	20%	24%	28%	32%
1	0.9901	0.9804	0.9709	0.9615	0.9524	0.9434	0.9346	0.9259	0.9174	0.9091	0.8929	0.8772	0.8696	0.8621	0.8475	0.8333	0.8065	0.7813	0.7576
2	1.9704	1.9415	1.9135	1.8861	1.8594	1.8334	1.8080	1.7833	1.7591	1.7355	1.6901	1.6467	1.6257	1.6052	1.5656	1.5278	1.4568	1.3916	1.3315
3	2.9410	2.8839	2.8286	2.7751	2.7232	2.6730	2.6243	2.5771	2.5313	2.4869	2.4018	2.3216	2.2832	2.2459	2.1743	2.1065	1.9813	1.8684	1.7663
4	3.9020	3.8077	3.7171	3.6299	3.5460	3.4651	3.3872	3.3121	3.2397	3.1699	3.0373	2.9137	2.8550	2.7982	2.6901	2.5887	2.4043	2.2410	2.0957
5	4.8534	4.7135	4.5797	4.4518	4.3295	4.2124	4.1002	3.9927	3.8897	3.7908	3.6048	3.4331	3.3522	3.2743	3.1272	2.9906	2.7454	2.5320	2.3452
6	5.7955	5.6014	5.4172	5.2421	5.0757	4.9173	4.7665	4.6229	4.4859	4.3553	4.1114	3.8887	3.7845	3.6847	3.4976	3.3255	3.0205	2.7594	2.5342
7	6.7282	6.4720	6.2303	6.0021	5.7864	5.5824	5.3893	5.2064	5.0330	4.8684	4.5638	4.2883	4.1604	4.0386	3.8115	3.6046	3.2423	2.9370	2.6775
8	7.6517	7.3255	7.0197	6.7327	6.4632	6.2098	5.9713	5.7466	5.5348	5.3349	4.9676	4.6389	4.4873	4.3436	4.0776	3.8372	3.4212	3.0758	2.7860
9	8.5660	8.1622	7.7861	7.4353	7.1078	6.8017	6.5152	6.2469	5.9952	5.7590	5.3282	4.9464	4.6389	4.6065	4.3030	4.0310	3.5655	3.1842	2.8681
10	9.4713	8.9826	8.5302	8.1109	7.7217	7.3601	7.0236	6.7101	6.4177	6.1446	5.6502	5.2161	4.9464	4.8332	4.4941	4.1925	3.6819	3.2689	2.9304
11	10.3676	9.7868	9.2526	8.7605	8.3064	7.8869	7.4987	7.1390	6.8052	6.4951	5.9377	5.4527	5.2337	5.0286	4.6560	4.3271	3.7757	3.3351	2.9776
12	11.2551	10.5753	9.9540	9.3851	8.8633	8.3838	7.9427	7.5361	7.1607	6.8137	6.1944	5.6603	5.4206	5.1971	4.7932	4.4392	3.8514	3.3868	3.0133
13	12.1337	11.3484	10.6350	9.9856	9.3936	8.8527	8.3577	7.9038	7.4889	7.1034	6.4235	5.8424	5.5831	5.3423	4.9095	4.5327	3.9124	3.4272	3.0404
14	13.0037	12.1062	11.2961	10.5631	9.8986	9.2950	8.7455	8.2442	7.7862	7.3667	6.6282	6.0021	5.7245	5.4675	5.0081	4.6106	3.9616	3.4834	3.0609
15	13.8651	12.8493	11.9379	11.1184	10.3797	9.7122	9.1079	8.5595	8.0607	7.6061	6.8109	6.1422	5.8474	5.5755	5.0916	4.6755	4.0013	3.4834	3.0764
16	14.7179	13.5777	12.5611	11.6523	10.8378	10.1059	9.4466	8.8514	8.3126	7.8237	6.9740	6.2651	5.9542	5.6685	5.1724	4.7296	4.0333	3.5026	3.0882
17	15.5623	14.2919	13.1661	12.1657	11.2741	10.4773	9.7632	9.1216	8.5436	8.0216	7.1196	6.3729	6.0472	5.7487	5.2223	4.7746	4.0591	3.5177	3.0971
18	16.3983	14.9920	13.7535	12.6593	11.6896	10.8276	10.0591	9.3719	8.7556	8.2014	7.2497	6.4674	6.1280	5.8178	5.2732	4.8122	4.0799	3.5294	3.1039
19	17.2260	15.6785	14.3238	13.1339	12.0853	11.1581	10.3356	9.6036	8.9501	8.3649	7.3658	6.5504	6.1982	5.8775	5.3162	4.8435	4.0967	3.5386	3.1090
20	18.0456	16.3514	14.8775	13.5903	12.4622	11.4699	10.5940	9.8181	9.1285	8.5436	7.4694	6.6231	6.2593	5.9288	5.3527	4.8696	4.1103	3.5458	3.1129
25	22.0232	19.5235	17.4131	15.6221	14.0939	12.7834	11.6536	10.6748	9.8226	9.0770	7.8431	6.8729	6.4641	6.0971	5.4669	4.9476	4.1474	3.5640	3.1220
30	25.8077	22.3965	19.6004	17.2920	15.3725	13.7648	12.4090	11.2578	10.2737	9.4269	8.0552	7.0072	6.5660	6.1772	5.5168	4.9789	4.1601	3.5693	3.1242

EXAMPLE 2.21

You are trying to determine the price you are willing to pay for a $1,000, 5-year U.S. bond paying $50 interest semiannually, which is sold to yield 8%.

$$i = \frac{8\%}{2} = 4\%$$

$$n = 5 \times 2 = 10$$

Present Value of $1 (Table 2.3) for $n = 10$, $i = 4\%$:

| $1,000 \times 0.6756$ | $675.60 |

Present Value of an Annuity of $1 (Table 2.4) for $n = 10$, $i = 4\%$:

| $ 50 \times 8.1109 | 405.55 |
| Present value | $1,081.15 |

EXAMPLE 2.22

You incur the following expenditures to lease an item:

Year 0	$3,000
Year 1	4,000
Year 2	5,000
Years 3–10	12,000*

The interest rate is 10%.

For years 1 and 2, use the Present Value of $1 table (Table 2.3).

The net present value is:

Year	Calculation	Present Value
0	− $3,000 × 1	−$3,000.00
1	− 4,000 × 0.9091	− 3,636.40
2	− 5,000 × 0.8264	− 4,132.00
3–10	− 12,000 × (6.1446 − 1.7355)[a]	−52,909.20
Net present value		−$63,677.60

[a]Year 10 factor − year 2 factor.

---

* You are paying $12,000 each from year 3 to year 10. While you can calculate it using the Present Value of $1 table, it is significantly faster and more accurate to use the Present Value of an Annuity of $1 table (Table 2.4).

Each loan payment comprises principal and interest. The breakdown is usually shown in a loan amortization table. The interest is higher in the early years than the later years because it is multiplied by a higher loan balance.

EXAMPLE 2.23

You borrow $200,000 for 5 years at an interest rate of 14%. The annual year-end payment on the loan is:

$$\frac{\$200,000}{3.4331} = \underline{\$58,256.39}$$

EXAMPLE 2.24

You take out a $30,000 loan payable monthly over 5 years. The annual interest rate is 24%.

$$n = 5 \times 12 = 60$$

$$i = \frac{24\%}{2} = 2\%$$

$$\frac{\$30,000}{34.7609} = \underline{\$863.04}$$

EXAMPLE 2.25

You borrow $300,000 payable $70,000 a year. The interest rate is 14%. The number of years you have to pay off the loan is:

$$\frac{\$300,000}{\$\ 70,000} = 4.2857$$

$$n = 7 \text{ years (approximately)}$$

EXAMPLE 2.26

You borrow $20,000 to be repaid in 12 monthly payments of $1,891.20. The monthly interest rate is

$$\frac{\$20,000.00}{\$\ 1,891.20} = 10.5753$$

$$i = 2\%$$

Chapter 2: Discounting and Compounding Analysis Techniques

EXAMPLE 2.27

You borrow $1,000,000 and agree to make payments of $100,000 per year for 18 years. The interest rate you are paying is:

$$\frac{\$1,000,000}{\$\ 100,000} = 10$$

$$i = 7\% \text{ (approximately)}$$

EXAMPLE 2.28

You buy a note for $14,000. You will receive annual payments of $2,000 on it for 10 years. Your annual yield is:

$$\frac{\$14,000}{\$\ 2,000} = 7$$

$$i = 7\%$$

EXAMPLE 2.29

When you retire you want to receive an annuity of $80,000 at the end of each year for 10 years. The interest rate is 8%. The amount that must be in your retirement account at the date of retirement is calculated as follows.

Using the Present Value of an Annuity of $1 table (Table 2.4):

$$\$80,000 \times 6.7101 = \underline{\$536,808}$$

You also want to know how much you have to deposit into your pension plan at the end of each year to have $536,808 if you are going to make 20 annual contributions. The interest rate is 6%.

Using the Future Value of an Annuity of $1 table (Table 2.2):

$$\frac{\$536,808}{36.785} = \underline{\$14,593.12}$$

PRESENT VALUE OF AN ANNUITY DUE OF $1 (TABLE 2.4 ADJUSTED)

To get the present value of an annuity due, which refers to equal beginning-of-year payments, find the present value of an ordinary annuity of $1 for one period less than the life of the annuity. Then add 1 to this number.

EXAMPLE 2.30

You will receive 10 payments of $5,000 at the beginning of each year. The interest rate is 14%. The present value of the cash receipts is:

$n = 10 - 1 = 9$	Factor	4.9464
	Add	1.0000
	Adjusted factor	5.9464

$5,000 \times 5.9464 = \underline{\$29,732}$

EXAMPLE 2.31

You owe $800,000 and will make 15 beginning-of-year payments to pay it off. The interest rate is 18%. The annual payment is:

$n = 15 - 1 = 14$	Factor	5.0081
	Add	1.0000
	Adjusted factor	6.0081

$$\frac{\$800,000}{6.0081} = \underline{\$133,153.57}$$

PERPETUITIES

Annuities that go on indefinitely are referred to as perpetuities. An example is preferred stock having an indefinite constant dollar dividend.

$$\text{Present value of a perpetuity} = \frac{\text{Receipt}}{\text{Discount rate}}$$

EXAMPLE 2.32

A perpetual bond has a $50 per year interest payment, and the discount rate is 8%. The present value of this perpetuity equals:

$$\frac{\$50}{0.08} = \underline{\$625}$$

CONCLUSION

The Present Value of $1 table is used when you want to determine the current value of receiving unequal cash receipts. If the cash flows each year are equal, you use the Present Value of an Annuity of $1 table. The Future Value of $1 table is employed to find the compounded amount of making unequal deposits. If the cash deposits are equal each period, you use the Future Value of an Annuity of $1 table. The present value and future value tables are used to solve for unknowns such as annual payment, interest rate, and the number of years. They can be used to solve many business-related problems.

3
How Evaluating Capital Investment Proposals Leads to Sound Decision Making

Capital budgeting relates to planning for the best selection and financing of long-term investment proposals. The two basic types of investment decisions are selecting between proposed projects and replacement decisions, which requires judgments concerning future events over which you have no direct knowledge. You have to consider timing and risk, and minimize your chances of being wrong. To help you deal with uncertainty, you may use the risk–return trade-off method. Discounted cash flow methods are more realistic than methods that do not take into account the time value of money in appraising investments, which becomes more essential in inflationary periods. Capital budgeting can be used in profit and nonprofit industries.

Planning for capital expenditures requires you to determine the "optimal" proposal, the number of dollars to be spent, and the amount of time required for completion. Requirements are evaluating current programs, looking at new proposals, and coordinating interrelated proposals within the firm. In planning a project, consideration should be given to time, cost, and quality, which all interreact. For control, a comparison should be made between budgeted cost and time versus actual cost and time.

Capital budgeting decisions must conform to your cash position, financing strategy, and growth rate. Will the project earn a return exceeding the long-range expected return of the business? Projects must be tied into the firm's long-range planning, with consideration of corporate strengths and weaknesses. The goals of the business and the extent to which they depend on economic variables (e.g., inflation, interest rate), production (e.g., technological changes), and market factors must be established. Also, the capital budget may have to be modified after considering financial, economic, and political conditions. But consideration should be given to "sunk" and "fixed" costs that are difficult to revise once the initial decision is made.

Recommendation: Use cost–benefit analysis. Is there excessive effort for the proposal? Can it be performed internally or must it be done externally (e.g., make or buy)? Is there a more efficient means and less costly way of accomplishing the end result? Further, problem areas must be identified. An example is when long-term borrowed funds are used to finance a project where sufficient cash inflows will not meet debt at maturity.

Suggestion: Measure cash flows of a project using different possible assumed variations (e.g., change in selling price of a new product). By modifying the assumptions and appraising the results, you can see the sensitivity of cash flows to applicable variables. An advantage is the appraisal of risk in proposals based on varying assumptions. An increase in risk should result in a higher return rate.

Taxes have to be considered in making capital budgeting decisions because a project that looks good on a before-tax basis may not be acceptable on an after-tax basis. Taxes have an effect on the amount and timing of cash flows.

Factors to Consider in Determining Capital Expenditures

- Rate of return
- Budget ceiling
- Probability of success
- Competition
- Tax rate
- Dollar amounts
- Time value of money
- Risk
- Liquidity
- Long-term business strategy
- Forecasting errors

Types of Capital Budgeting Decisions to Be Made

- Cost-reduction program
- Undertaking an advertising campaign

- Replacement of assets
- Merger analysis
- Refinancing an outstanding debt issue
- New and existing product evaluation

This chapter discusses the various capital budgeting methods, including accounting rate of return, payback, discounted payback, net present value, profitability index, and internal rate of return. Consideration is also given to contingent proposals, capital rationing, and nondiscretionary projects. The incorporation of risk into the analysis is also dealt with.

ACCOUNTING (SIMPLE) RATE OF RETURN

Accounting rate of return (ARR) measures profitability by comparing the required investment (sometimes average investment) to future annual earnings. *Rule of Thumb:* Select the proposal with the highest ARR.

EXAMPLE 3.1

Initial investment	$8,000
Life	15 years
Cash inflows per year	$1,300

$$\text{Depreciation} = \frac{\text{Cost} - \text{Salvage value}}{\text{Life}} = \frac{\$8,000 - 0}{15} = \$533$$

$$\text{ARR} = \frac{\text{Cash inflows per year} - \text{Depreciation}}{\text{Initial investment}}$$

$$\frac{\$1,300 - \$533}{\$8,000} = \frac{\$767}{\$8,000} = \underline{9.6\%}$$

If you use average investment, ARR is

$$\text{ARR} = \frac{\$767}{\$8,000 / 2} = \frac{\$767}{\$4,000} = \underline{19.2\%}$$

Note: When average investment is used rather than the initial investment, ARR is doubled.

Advantages of ARR

- Easy to comprehend and calculate
- Considers profitability
- Numbers relate to financial statement presentation
- Considers full useful life

Disadvantages of ARR

- Ignores time value of money
- Uses income data rather than cash flow data

PAYBACK PERIOD

Payback is the number of years it takes to recover your initial investment. Payback assists in evaluating a project's risk and liquidity. A shorter payback period is desirable because it indicates less risk, improved liquidity, and faster rate of return. A benefit of payback is that it permits companies with a cash problem to evaluate the turnover of scarce resources in order to recover invested funds earlier.

Supporters of the payback period point to its use where preliminary screening is more essential than precise figures and in situations where a poor credit position is a major factor. Some believe that payback should be used in unstable, uncertain industries subject to rapid technological change because the future is so unpredictable that there is no point in guessing what cash flows will be more than two years from now.

Advantages of Payback

- Easy to use and understand
- Effectively handles investment risk
- Can be used as a supplement to other more sophisticated techniques because it does indicate risk

Deficiencies of Payback

- Ignores the time value of money
- Does not consider cash flows received after the payback period
- Does not measure profitability

Warning: Do not select a proposal simply because the payback method indicates acceptance. You still have to use the discounting methods such as present value and internal rate of return.

EXAMPLE 3.2

You are considering a new product. It will initially cost $250,000. Expected cash inflows are $80,000 for the next 5 years. You want your money back in 4 years.

$$\text{Payback period} = \frac{\text{Initial investment}}{\text{Annual cash inflow}} = \frac{\$250,000}{\$80,000} = \underline{3.125}$$

Because the payback period (3.125) is less than the cutoff payback period (4), you should accept the proposal.

EXAMPLE 3.3

You invest $40,000 and receive the following cash inflows:

Year 1	$15,000
Year 2	$20,000
Year 3	$28,000

$$\$35,000 + \frac{\$\ 5,000}{\$28,000}$$

$$2 \text{ years} + .18 = 2.18 \text{ years}$$

$$\text{Payback period} = \underline{2.18 \text{ years}}$$

If there are unequal cash inflows each year, to determine the payback period just add up the annual cash inflows to come up with the amount of the cash outlay. The answer is how long it takes to recover your investment.

DISCOUNTED PAYBACK PERIOD

You can take into account the time value of money by using the discounted payback method. The payback period will be longer using the discounted method because money is worth less over time. *How to Do It:* Discounted payback is computed by adding the present value of each year's cash inflows until they equal the investment.

EXAMPLE 3.4

Assume the same facts as in Example 3.3 and a cost of capital of 10%.

$$\text{Discounted payback} = \frac{\text{Initial cash outlay}}{\text{Discounted annual cash inflows}}$$

Year 1		Year 2		Year 3
$15,000	+	$20,000	+	$28,000
× 0.9091		× 0.8264		× 0.7513
$13,637	+	$16,528	+	$21,036
		$30,165	+	$9,835
				$21,036
		2 years	+	0.47 years = 2.47 years

NET PRESENT VALUE

The present value method compares the present value of future cash flows expected from an investment project to the initial cash outlay for the investment. Net cash flows are the difference between forecasted cash inflow received because of the investment to the expected cash outflow of the investment. You should use as a discount rate the minimum rate of return earned on your money. A company uses its cost of capital. *Rule of Thumb:* If a proposal is supposed to provide you with a return, invest in it only if it provides a positive net present value. If two proposals are mutually exclusive (acceptance of one precludes the acceptance of another), accept the proposal with the highest present value. An advantage of net present value is that it considers the time value of money. A disadvantage is the subjectivity in determining expected annual cash inflows and expected period of benefit.

Chapter 3: Evaluating Capital Investment Proposals   47

The net present value method typically provides more reliable signals than other methods. By employing net present value and using best estimates of reinvestment rates, you can select the most advantageous project.

EXAMPLE 3.5

You are considering replacing Executive 1 with Executive 2. Executive 2 requires a payment upon contract signing of $200,000. He will receive an annual salary of $300,000. Executive 1's current annual salary is $140,000. Because Executive 2 is superior in talent, you expect there will be an increase in annual cash flows from operations (ignoring salary) of $350,000 for each of the next 10 years. The cost of capital is 12%.

As indicated in the following calculations, as there is a positive net present value, Executive 1 should be replaced with Executive 2.

Year	Explanation	Amount	× Factor	= Present Value
0	Contract signing bonus	−$200,000 × 1		−$200,000
1–10	Increased salary ($300,000 − $140,000)	−$160,000 ×	5.6502[a]	−$904,032
1–10	Increase in annual cash flow from operations			
	Net present value	+$350,000 ×	5.6502[a]	$1,977,570
				$ 873,538

[a]Factor is obtained from Table 2.4 representing the intersection of 12% and 10 years.

EXAMPLE 3.6

You own a business for which you have received a $1,000,000 offer. If you do not sell, you will remain in business for 8 years and will invest another $50,000 in your firm. If you stay, you will sell your business in the eighth year for $60,000.

You expect yearly sales to increase by 50% from its present level of $500,000. Direct material is proportional to sales. Direct labor is proportional to sales, but will increase by 30% for all labor. Variable overhead varies with sales, and annual fixed overhead will total $70,000, including depreciation. Straight-line depreciation will increase from $7,000 to $10,000. At the end of 8 years, all fixed assets will be fully depreciated. Selling and administrative expenses are assumed to remain constant. The cost of capital is 14%.

Your current year's income statement is:

Sales		$500,000
Less cost of sales		
Direct material	$100,000	
Direct labor	120,000	
Variable overhead	50,000	
Fixed overhead	65,000	335,000
Gross margin		$165,000
Less selling and administrative expenses*		40,000
Net income		$125,000

Your forecasted income statement for each of the next 8 years follows.

Sales ($500,000 × 1.5)		$750,000
Less cost of sales		
Direct material ($100,000 × 1.5)	$150,000	
Direct labor ($120,000 × 1.5 × 1.3)	234,000	
Variable overhead ($50,000 × 1.5)	75,000	
Fixed overhead	70,000	529,000
Gross margin		$221,000
Less selling and administrative expenses		40,000
Net income		$181,000

Your annual cash flow from operations is:

Net income	$181,000
Add:	
Depreciation	10,000
Salary	20,000
Annual cash flow from operations	$211,000

A comparison of your alternatives follows.

Sell business: +$1,000,000

Stay in business:

Year	Explanation	Amount	×	Factor	=	Present Value
0	Investment in assets	−$50,000	×	1		−$ 50,000
1–8	Annual cash inflow	+$211,000	×	4.6389		+$978,808
8	Sales price of business	+$ 60,000	×	0.3506		+$ 21,036
	Net present value					+$949,844

Since the net present value is higher to sell the business ($1,000,000) than staying in business ($949,844), you should sell now.

---

*Includes your salary of $20,000.

EXAMPLE 3.7

You are considering replacing an old machine with a new one. The old machine has a book value of $800,000 and a remaining life of 10 years. The expected salvage value of the old machine is $50,000, but if you sold it now you would obtain $700,000. The new machine costs $2,000,000 and has a salvage value of $250,000. The new machine will result in an annual savings of $400,000. The tax rate is 50%, and the cost of capital is 14%. Use straight-line depreciation to determine whether to replace the machine.

The net increase in annual cash flow is:

	Net Income	Cash Flow	
Annual savings		$400,000	$400,000
Less incremental depreciation			
New machine = $\frac{\$2,000,000 - \$250,000}{10}$			
= $175,000			
Old machine = $\frac{\$800,000 - \$50,000}{10}$			
= $75,000			
Incremental depreciation		100,000	
Income before tax		$300,000	
Tax (50%)		150,000	150,000
Income after tax		$150,000	
Net cash inflow			$250,000

The net present value follows.

Year	Explanation	Amount	Factor	Present Value
0	Cost of new machine	−$2,000,000 × 1.000		−$2,000,000
0	Sale of old machine	700,000 × 1.000		700,000
1	Tax benefit from loss on sale of old machine	50,000 × 0.877		43,850
1–10	Yearly increase in cash flows	250,000 × 5.216		1,304,000
10	Incremental salvage value	200,000 × 0.270		54,000
				$101,850

The replacement of the old machine with a new machine should be made because of the resulting positive net present value.

Part I: Financial Analysis

Deciding whether to lease or purchase involves comparing the leasing and purchasing alternatives.

EXAMPLE 3.8

You have decided to acquire an asset costing $100,000 with a life of 5 years and no salvage value. The asset can be purchased with a loan or it can be leased. If leased, the lessor wants a 12% return. Lease payments are made in advance at the end of the year prior to each of the 10 years. The tax rate is 50%, and the cost of capital is 8%.

$$\text{Annual lease payment} = \frac{\$100{,}000}{1 + 3.3073} = \frac{\$100{,}000}{4.3073} = \underline{\$23{,}216} \text{ rounded}$$

Year	Lease Payment	Tax Savings	After-Tax Cash Outflow	Factor	Present Value
0	$23,216		$23,216	1.0000	$23,216
1–4	23,216	$11,608[a]	11,608	3.3121	38,447
5		11,608	(11,608)	0.6806	(7,900)
					$53,763

[a]23,216 x 50% = 11,608

If you buy the asset, you will take out a 10% loan. Straight-line depreciation is used with no salvage value.

$$\text{Depreciation} = \frac{\$100{,}000}{5} = \$20{,}000$$

$$\text{Annual loan payment} = \frac{\$100{,}000}{3.7906} = \underline{\$26{,}381}$$

The loan amortization schedule follows.

Year	Loan Payment	Beginning-of-Year Principal	Interest[a]	Principal[b]	End-of-Year Principal
1	26,231	100,000	10,000	16,381	83,619
2	26,231	83,619	8,362	18,019	65,600
3	26,231	65,600	6,560	19,821	45,779
4	26,231	45,779	4,578	21,803	23,976
5	26,231	23,976[c]	2,398	23,983[c]	

[a]10% × Beginning-of-year principal
[b]Loan payment – Interest
[c]Slight difference due to rounding

The computation of the present value of borrowing follows:

Year	(1) Loan Payment	(2) Interest	(3) Depreciation	(4) Total Deduction[a]
1	26,381	10,000	20,000	30,000
2	26,381	8,362	20,000	28,362
3	26,381	6,560	20,000	26,560
4	26,381	4,578	20,000	24,578
5	26,381	2,398	20,000	22,398

(5) Tax Savings[b]	(6) Cash Outflow[c]	(7) Present Value Factor (8%)	(8) Present Value of Cash Outflow[d]
15,000	11,381	0.9259	10,538
14,181	12,200	0.8573	10,459
13,280	13,101	0.7938	10,400
12,289	14,092	0.7350	10,358
11,199	15,182	0.6806	10,333
			52,088

[a] (4) = (2) + (3)
[b] (5) = (4) × 50%
[c] (6) = (1) − (5)
[d] (8) = (6) × (7)

The present value of borrowing ($52,088) is less than the present value of leasing ($53,763). Thus, the asset should be bought.

PROFITABILITY INDEX

The profitability (ranking) index is a net instead of an aggregate index and is employed to differentiate the initial cash investment from later cash inflows. If you have budget constraints, proposals of different dollar magnitude can be ranked on a comparative basis.

$$\text{Profitability index} = \frac{\text{Present value of cash inflows}}{\text{Present value of cash outflows}}$$

Rule of Thumb: Accept a proposal with a profitability index equal to or greater than 1.

Warning: A higher profitability index does not always coincide with the project with the highest net present value.

Capital rationing takes place when a business is not able to invest in projects having a net present value greater than or equal to zero. Typically, the firm establishes an upper limit to its capital budget based on budgetary constraints. *Special Note:* With capital rationing, the project with the highest ranking index rather than the net present value should be selected for investment.

EXAMPLE 3.9

You have the following information regarding two proposals:

	Proposal A	Proposal B
Initial investment	$100,000	$10,000
Present value of cash inflows	$500,000	$90,000

The net present value of Proposal A is $400,000 and that of Proposal B is $80,000. Based on net present value, Proposal A is better. However, this is very misleading when a budget constraint exists. In this case, Proposal B's profitability index of 9 far surpasses Proposal A's index of 5. Thus, profitability index should be used in evaluating proposals when budget constraints exist. The net result is that Proposal B should be selected over Proposal A.

EXAMPLE 3.10

Projects	Investment	Present Value	Profitability	Index Ranking
A	$ 70,000	$112,000	1.6	1
B	100,000	145,000	1.45	2
C	110,000	126,500	1.15	5
D	60,000	79,000	1.32	3
E	40,000	38,000	0.95	6
F	80,000	95,000	1.19	4

The budget constraint is $250,000. You should select projects A, B, and D, as indicated by the following calculations:

Project	Investment	Present Value
A	$ 70,000	$112,000
B	100,000	145,000
D	60,000	79,000
	$230,000	$336,000

where net present value = $336,000 − $230,000 = $106,000.

CONTINGENT PROPOSALS

A contingent proposal is one that requires acceptance of another related one. Hence, the proposals must be looked at together. You compute a profitability index for the group.

EXAMPLE 3.11

Proposal	Present Value of Cash Outflow	Present Value of Cash Inflow
A	$160,000	$210,000
B	60,000	40,000
Total	$220,000	$250,000

$$\frac{\$250,000}{\$220.000} = 1.14$$

INTERNAL RATE OF RETURN (TIME-ADJUSTED RATE OF RETURN)

The internal rate of return is the return earned on a given proposal. It is the discount rate equating the net present value of cash inflows to the net present value of cash outflows to zero. The internal rate of return assumes cash inflows are reinvested at the internal rate.

This method involves trial and error computations. However, the use of a computer or programmable calculator simplifies the process.

The internal rate of return can be compared with the required rate of return (cutoff or hurdle rate). *Rule of Thumb:* If the internal rate of return equals or exceeds the required rate, the project is accepted. The required rate of return is typically a company's cost of capital, sometimes adjusted for risk.

An advantage of internal rate of return is that it considers the time value of money. Disadvantages are that with internal rate of return it is difficult and time-consuming to compute, particularly when there are uneven cash flows. Also, it does not consider the varying size of investment in competing projects and their respective dollar profitabilities.

To solve for internal rate of return where unequal cash inflows exist, you can use the trial and error method while working through the present value tables. Guidelines in using trial and error follow:

- Compute net present value at the cost of capital, denoted here as r_1.
- See if net present value is positive or negative.
- If net present value is positive, use a higher rate (r_2) than r_1. If net present value is negative, use a a lower rate (r_2) than r_1. The exact internal rate of return at which net present value equals zero is somewhere between the two rates.
- Compute net present value using r_2.
- Perform interpolation for exact rate.

EXAMPLE 3.12

A project costing $100,000 is expected to produce the following cash inflows:

Year	
1	$50,000
2	30,000
3	20,000
4	40,000

Using trial and error, you can calculate the internal rate as follows:

Year	10%	Present Value	16%	Present Value	18%	Present Value
1	0.909	$ 45,450	0.862	$ 43,100	0.847	$ 42,350
2	0.826	24,780	0.743	22,290	0.718	21,540
3	0.751	15,020	0.641	12,820	0.609	12,180
4	0.683	27,320	0.552	22,080	0.516	20,640
		+$112,570		+$100,290		+$ 96,710
Investment		− 100,000		− 100,000		− 100,000
Net present value		+$ 12,570		+ $ 290		−$ 3,290

The internal rate of return on the project is a little more than 16% because at that rate the net present value of the investment is approximately zero.

If the return on the investment is expected to be in one lump sum after a period of years, you can use the Present Value of $1 table (Table 2.3) to find the internal rate.

EXAMPLE 3.13

You are considering two mutually exclusive investment proposals. The cost of capital is 10%. Expected cash flows are as follows:

Project	Investment	Year 1	Year 6
A	$10,000	$12,000	
B	$10,000		$20,000

Internal rates of return are:

$$\text{Project A } \frac{\$10,000}{\$12,000} = 0.8333$$

Looking across 1 year on the table, 0.8333 corresponds to an internal rate of 20%.

$$\text{Project B } \frac{\$10,000}{\$20,000} = 0.5000$$

Looking across 6 years on the table, an internal rate of 12% corresponds most closely with 0.5000.

Project A should be selected because it has a higher internal rate of return than Project B.

If the cash inflows each year are equal, the internal rate of return is computed first by determining a factor (which happens to be the same as the payback period) and then looking up the rate of return on the Present Value of an Annuity of $1 table (Table 2.4).

EXAMPLE 3.14

You invest $100,000 in a proposal that will produce annual cash inflows of $15,000 a year for the next 20 years.

$$\text{Internal rate of return} = \frac{\$100,000}{\$ 15,000} = 6.6667$$

Now we go to the Present Value of an Annuity of $1 table (Table 2.4). Looking across 20 years, we find that the factor closest to 6.6667 is 6.6231, in the 14% column. Hence, the internal rate is about 14%.

EXAMPLE 3.15

Initial investment	$12,950
Estimated life	10 years
Annual cash inflows	$ 3,000
Cost of capital	12%

The internal rate of return (IRR) calculation follows, including interpolation to get the exact rate.

$$\text{Present value of annuity factor} = \frac{\$12,950}{3,000} = \underline{4.317}$$

The value 4.317 is somewhere between 18 and 20% in the 10-year line of Table 2.4. Using interpolation you get

	Present Value of Annuity Factor	
18%	4.494	4.494
IRR		4.317
20%	4.192	
Difference	0.302	0.177

Therefore, $\text{IRR} = 18\% + \frac{0.177}{0.302}(20\% - 18\%)$

$= 18\% + 0.586\,(2\%) = 18\% + 1.17\% = \underline{19.17\%}$

Because the internal rate of return (19.17%) exceeds the cost of capital (12%), the project should be accepted.

NONDISCRETIONARY PROJECTS

Some investments are made out of necessity rather than profitability (e.g., pollution control equipment, safety equipment). Here you will have solely a negative cash flow. Hence, your discretionary projects must earn a return rate in excess of the cost of capital to make up for the losses on nondiscretionary projects.

EXAMPLE 3.16

A company's cost of capital is 14% and it has $30 million of capital projects, 25% of which are nondiscretionary projects. It thus has to earn $4.2

million per year (14% × $30 million). The $22.5 million of discretionary projects ($30 million less 25%) must earn 18.7% ($4.2 million/$22.5 million) rather than 14% to achieve the overall corporate earnings goal of $4.2 million.

COMPARISON OF METHODS

In general, the discounting cash flow methods (net present value, internal rate of return, and profitability index) come to the same conclusions for competing proposals. But these methods can give different rankings to mutually exclusive proposals in certain cases. Any one of the following conditions can cause contradictory rankings:

- Project lives differ.
- There is a higher cost for one project relative to another.
- The trend in cash flow of one project is the reverse of that of another.

One of the following characteristics of the company may also produce conflicting rankings:

- Future investment opportunities are expected to be different from the present, and the investor knows whether they will be better or worse.
- There is capital rationing, a maximum level of funding for capital investments.

The major cause for different rankings of alternative projects under present value and internal rate of return methods relates to the varying assumptions regarding the reinvestment rate employed for discounting cash flows. The net present value method assumes cash flows are reinvested at the cost of capital rate. The internal rate of return method assumes cash flows are reinvested at the internal rate. *Tip:* The net present value method typically provides a correct ranking because the cost of capital is a more realistic reinvestment rate. *Note:* Determining which method is best for a business really depends on which reinvestment rate is nearest the rate the business can earn on future cash flows from a project.

The minimum rate of return required for a proposal may be waived in a situation where the proposal has significant future benefit (e.g., research and development), applies to a necessity program (e.g., safety requirement), and has qualitative benefit (e.g., product quality).

CAPITAL BUDGETING PROCESS

Questions to Be Asked in the Capital Budgeting Process

- How is risk incorporated into the analysis?
- Is risk versus return considered in choosing projects?
- Prior to making a final decision, are all the results of the capital budgeting techniques considered and integrated?
- In looking at a proposal, are both dollars and time considered?
- Is the proposal consistent with long-term goals?
- Does each project have a cost–benefit analysis?
- Do you know which are your most profitable proposals and products? How much business is in each?
- Are there projects of an unusual nature?
- Do you periodically track the performance of current programs in terms of original expectations?
- In the capital budgeting process, are qualitative factors also considered, such as marketing, production, and economic and political variables?
- Has the proposal been considered incorporating the company's financial health?
- What is the quality of the project?
- Given the current environment, are your capital investments adequate?
- Are you risk prone or risk averse?
- Is the discounted payback method being used?
- How are probable cash flows computed?
- How do you come up with the expected life?

To look at the entire picture of the capital budgeting process, a comprehensive example is provided.

EXAMPLE 3.17

You are deciding whether to buy a business. The initial cash outlay is $35,000. You will receive annual net cash inflows (excluding depreciation) of $5,000 per year for 10 years. The cost of capital is 10%. The tax rate is 50%. You want to evaluate whether you should buy this business.

The annual cash inflow for years 1 to 10 follows:

	Net Income	Cash Flow
Annual cash savings	$5,000	+$5,000
Depreciation ($35,000/10)	3,500	
Income before tax	$1,500	
Tax (50%)	750	− 750
Net income	$ 750	
Net cash inflow		+$4,250

Average rate of return on investment:

$$\frac{\text{Net income}}{\text{Average investment}} = \frac{\$750}{\$35,000/2} = \frac{\$750}{\$17,500} = \underline{4\%}$$

Payback period:

$$\frac{\text{Initial investment}}{\text{Annual net cash inflow}} = \frac{\$35,000}{\$4,250} = \underline{8.2 \text{ years}}$$

Net present value:

Year	Explanation	Amount × Factor	= Present Value
0	Initial investment	−$35,000 × 1	−$35,000
1–10	Annual net cash inflow	+ 4,250 × 6.1446	26,095
	Net present value		−$ 8,905

Profitability index:

$$\frac{\text{Present value of cash inflow}}{\text{Present value of cash outflow}} = \frac{\$26,095}{\$35,000} = \underline{0.74}$$

Internal rate of return:

$$\text{Factor} = \frac{\text{Initial outlay}}{\text{Annual cash inflow}} = \frac{\$35,000}{\$4,250} = \underline{8.2}$$

Going to Table 2.4, we look for the intersection of 10 years and a factor of 8.2. Looking up the column we find 4%, which is the internal rate.

Conclusion: The business should not be bought for the following reasons:

- An average rate of return of 4% is low.
- The payback period is long.
- The net present value is negative.
- The internal rate of return of 4% is less than the cost of capital of 10%.

RISK AND UNCERTAINTY

You must consider the interrelation of risk among all investments. By properly diversifying, you can obtain the best combination of expected net present value and risk. *Tip:* Do not automatically reject a high-risk project. For example, a new product with much risk may be accepted if there is a chance of a major breakthrough in the market. The business may be able to afford a few unsuccessful new products if one is developed for extraordinary return.

Probabilities can be assigned to expected cash flows based on risk. The probabilities are multiplied by the monetary values to derive the expected monetary value of the investment. A probability distribution function can be generated by computer. *Special Note:* The tighter the probability distribution of expected future returns, the lower the risk associated with a project.

Several methods to incorporate risk into capital budgeting are risk-adjusted discount rate, standard deviation and coefficient of variation, certainty equivalent, semivariance, simulation, sensitivity analysis, and decision (probability) trees.

Risk-Adjusted Discount Rate

Risk can be included in capital budgeting by computing probable cash flows on the basis of probabilities and assigning a discount rate based on the riskiness of alternative proposals.

Using this approach, an investment's value is determined by discounting the expected cash flow at a rate allowing for the time value of money and for the risk associated with the cash flow. The cost of capital (discount rate) is adjusted for a project's risk. A profitable investment is indicated by a positive net present value. Using the method, you judge the risk class of the proposed capital investment and the risk-adjusted discount rate appropriate for that class.

Tip: If doubtful of your results, check them by estimating the cost of capital of other companies specializing in the type of investment under consideration.

EXAMPLE 3.18

You are evaluating whether to accept Proposal A or B. Each proposal mandates an initial cash outlay of $12,000 and has a 3-year life. Annual net cash flows along with expected probabilities are as follows.

Proposal A

Expected Annual Cash Inflow	Probability
$5,800	.4
6,400	.5
7,000	.1

Proposal B

Expected Annual Cash Inflow	Probability
$ 3,400	.3
8,400	.5
11,000	.2

The inflation rate and interest rate are estimated at 10%. Proposal A has a lower risk because its cash flows show greater stability than those of Proposal B. Since Proposal A has less risk, it is assigned a discount rate of 8%, while Proposal B is assigned a 10% discount rate because of the greater risk.

Proposal A

Cash Flow	Probability	Probable Cash Flow
$5,800	.4	$2,320
6,400	.5	3,200
7,000	.1	700
Expected annual cash inflow		$6,220

Proposal B

Cash Flow	Probability	Probable Cash Flow
$ 3,400	.3	$1,020
8,000	.5	4,000
11,000	.2	2,200
Expected annual cash inflow		$7,220

Part I: Financial Analysis

Proposal A

Year	Explanation	Amount	× Factor	= Present Value
0	Initial investment	−$12,000 × 1	=	−$12,000
1–3	Annual cash flow	+ 6,220 × 2.5771[a]	=	+ 16,030
	Net present value			+$ 4,030

[a] Using an 8% discount rate.

Proposal B

Year	Explanation	Amount	× Factor	= Present Value
0	Initial investment	−$12,000 × 1	=	−$12,000
1–3	Annual cash flow	+ 7,220 × 2.4869[a]	=	+ 17,955
	Net present value			+$ 5,955

[a] Using a 10% discount rate.

Even though Project B has more risk, it has a higher risk-adjusted net present value. Project B should thus be selected.

Standard Deviation and Coefficient of Variation

Risk is a measure of dispersion around a probability distribution. It is the variability of cash flow around the expected value. Risk can be measured in either absolute or relative terms. First, the expected value, $\overline{A}$, is

$$\overline{A} = \sum_{i=1}^{n} A_i p_i$$

where

A_i = the value of ith possible outcome
p_i = the probability that the ith outcome will take place
n = the number of possible outcomes

Then, the absolute risk is determined by the standard deviation σ:

$$\sigma = \sqrt{\sum_{i=1}^{n}(A_i - \overline{A})^2 p_i}$$

The relative risk is expressed by the coefficient of variation

$$\frac{\sigma}{\overline{A}}$$

EXAMPLE 3.19

You are considering investing in one of two projects. Depending on the state of the economy, the projects would provide the following cash inflows in each of the next 5 years:

Economic Condition	Probability	Proposal A	Proposal B
Recession	.3	$1,000	$ 500
Normal	.4	2,000	2,000
Boom	.3	3,000	5,000

We now compute the expected value ($\overline{A}$), the standard deviation (σ), and the coefficient of variation ($\sigma/\overline{A}$).

Proposal A

A_i	p_i	$A_i p_i$	$(A_i - \overline{A})$	$(A_i - \overline{A})^2$
$1,000	.3	$ 300	−$1,000	$1,000,000
2,000	.4	800	0	0
3,000	.3	900	1,000	1,000,000
		$\overline{A}$ = $2,000	σ^2 =	$2,000,000

Because $\sigma^2 = \$2{,}000{,}000$, $\sigma = \$1{,}414$. Thus

$$\frac{\sigma}{\overline{A}} = \frac{\$1{,}414}{\$2{,}000} = \underline{0.71}$$

Proposal B

A_i	p_i	$A_i p_i$	$(A_i - \overline{A})$	$(A_i - \overline{A})^2$
$ 500	.3	$ 150	−$1,950	$ 3,802,500
2,000	.4	800	− 450	202,500
5,000	.3	1,500	2,550	6,502,500
		$\overline{A}$ = $2,450	σ^2 =	$10,507,500

Since $\sigma^2 = \$10{,}507{,}500$, $\sigma = \$3{,}242$. Thus

$$\frac{\sigma}{\overline{A}} = \frac{\$3{,}242}{\$2{,}450} = \underline{1.32}$$

Therefore, Proposal A is relatively less risky than Proposal B, as measured by the coefficient of variation.

Certainty Equivalent

The certainty equivalent approach relates to utility theory. You specify at what point the company is indifferent to the choice between a certain sum of dollars and the expected value of a risky sum. The certainty equivalent is multiplied by the original cash flow to obtain the equivalent certain cash flow. You then use normal capital budgeting. The risk-free rate of return is employed as the discount rate under the net present value method and as the cutoff rate under the internal rate of return method.

EXAMPLE 3.20

A company's cost of capital is 14% after taxes. Under consideration is a 4-year project that will require an initial investment of $50,000. Assume the following data:

Year	After-Tax Cash Flow	Certainty Equivalent Coefficient
1	$10,000	.95
2	15,000	.80
3	20,000	.70
4	25,000	.60

The risk-free rate of return is 5%.

Equivalent certain cash inflows are:

Year	After-Tax Cash Inflow	Certainty Equivalent Coefficient	Equivalent Certain Cash Inflow	× Present Value Factor at 5%	= Present Value
1	$10,000	.95	$ 9,500	0.9524	$ 9,048
2	15,000	.80	12,000	0.9070	10,884
3	20,000	.70	14,000	0.8638	12,093
4	25,000	.60	15,000	0.8227	12,341
					$44,366

Net present value:
Initial investment   −$50,000
Present value of cash inflows   + 44,366
Net present value   −$ 5,634

Using trial and error, an internal rate of 4% is determined.

The proposal should be rejected because of the negative net present value and an internal rate (4%) less than the risk-free rate (5%).

Semivariance

Semivariance is the expected value of the squared negative deviations of the possible outcomes from an arbitrarily chosen point of reference. Semivariance appraises risks applicable to different distributions by referring to a fixed point designated by you. In computing semivariance, positive and negative deviations contribute differently to risk, whereas in computing variance, a positive and negative deviation of the same magnitude contribute equally to risk. In effect, since there is an opportunity cost of tying up capital, the risk of an investment is measured principally by the prospect of failure to earn the return.

Simulation

You obtain probability distributions for a number of variables (e.g., investment outlays, unit sales) when doing a simulation. Selecting these variables from the distributions at random results in an estimated net present value.

Sensitivity Analysis

Forecasts of many calculated net present values under various alternatives are compared to identify how sensitive the net present value is to changing conditions. You see if one or more variable significantly affects net present value once that variable is changed.

Decision Trees

A decision (probability) tree graphically shows the sequence of possible outcomes. The capital budgeting tree shows cash flows and net present value of the project under different possible circumstances. Advantages of this approach are that it shows possible outcomes of the contemplated project, makes you more cognizant of adverse possibilities, and depicts the conditional nature of later years' cash flows. The disadvantage is that many problems are too complex to allow for a year-by-year depiction. For example, a 3-year project with three possible outcomes following each year has 27 paths.

EXAMPLE 3.21

You want to introduce one of two products. The probabilities and present values of expected cash inflows are

Product	Investment	Present Value of Cash Inflows	Probability
A	$225,000		
		$450,000	.4
		200,000	.5
		−100,000	.1
B	80,000		
		320,000	.2
		100,000	.6
		−150,000	.2

	(1) Initial Investment	(2) Probability	(3) Present Value of Cash Inflows	(4) Present Value of Cash Inflows*
Product A	$225,000	.40	$450,000	$180,000
		.50	$200,000	100,000
		.10	−100,000	− 10,000
				$270,000
or				
Product B	$80,000	.20	$320,000	$64,000
		.60	100,000	60,000
		.20	−150,000	− 30,000
				$94,000

*(2) × (3) = (4).

Net present value:
Product A $270,000 − $225,000 = $45,000
Product B $ 94,000 = $ 80,000 = $14,000

Product A should be selected.

CONCLUSION

Net present value, internal rate of return, and profitability index are equally effective in selecting economically sound, independent investment proposals. But the payback method is inadequate since it does not consider the time value of money. For mutually exclusive projects, net present value, internal rate of return, and profitability index methods are not always able to rank projects in the same order; it is possible to come up with different rankings under each method. Risk should be taken into account in the capital budgeting process by using probabilities, simulation, and decision trees.

4 How to Analyze Financial Position

Your analysis of the balance sheet assists in appraising earnings quality. For example, if there is an overstatement in assets, net income will be overstated as well because reported results do not include charges necessary to reduce assets to their proper valuations.

When computing ratios for *analytical* purposes, you should use the realistic values for balance sheet accounts rather than reported amounts. For example, marketable securities are shown at the lower of cost or market applied on a total portfolio basis. Thus, if cost is $100,000 and market is $180,000, the portfolio would be shown at $100,000. But realistically the securities are worth $180,000 in today's market.

This chapter explores the analysis of asset and liability accounts, evaluates corporate liquidity, analyzes business solvency, covers the analytical implications of the sources and uses of funds, and looks to signs of possible business failure. Besides analyzing an entity's financial health, recommendations for improvement to financial officers are also offered.

ANALYZING ASSET QUALITY

Asset quality applies to the certainty associated with the amount and timing of the realization of the assets in cash. *Tip:* Determine the dollar frequency of a company's assets in the high-risk category. *What to Do:* Calculate the ratios for: (1) high-risk assets to total assets and (2) high-risk assets to sales. If high risk exists in assets, earnings quality is poor because of the potential of later charge-offs. For instance, the realization of goodwill is more doubtful than that of equipment. Also evaluate the risk of each major asset category. For example, receivables from an economically unstable government (e.g., Mexico) has greater risk than a receivable from ITT. *Special Note:* Single-purpose assets have greater risk than multipurpose ones. *What to Watch Out for:* Assets with no separable value that cannot be sold easily, such as intangibles and work in process. On the contrary, marketable securities are readily salable.

Cash

How much of the cash balance is unavailable for use or restricted? Examples are a compensating balance and cash held in a foreign country where remission restrictions exist.

You should determine the ratio of sales to cash. A high turnover rate may indicate a deficient cash position.

EXAMPLE 4.1

A company reports the following data:

	20X1	20X2
Cash	$500,000	$400,000
Sales	8,000,000	9,000,000
Industry norm for cash turnover rate	15.8 times	16.2 times

The turnover of cash is 16 ($8,000,000/$500,000) in 20X1 and 22.5 ($9,000,000/$400,000) in 20X2. It is clear that the company has a cash deficiency in 20X2, which implies a possible liquidity problem.

You should distinguish between two types of cash: that needed for operating purposes and that required for capital expenditures. While the former must be paid, the latter is postponable.

Accounts Receivable

In appraising the realization risk of receivables, look at the nature of the receivable balance. *What to Do:* Search out high-risk receivables, such as a customer with severe financial problems. Are the receivables diversified or are they concentrated in just a few customers? *Note:* Receivables from consumers have higher risk than those from industry.

$$\text{Accounts receivable turnover} = \frac{\text{Credit sales}}{\text{Average accounts receivable}}$$

Caution: If sales vary greatly during the year, proper averaging is necessary to avoid a distorted ratio. Here, quarterly sales figures may be used.

$$\text{Collection period} = \frac{365 \text{ days}}{\text{Turnover}}$$

Also look for a buildup over time in the ratio of accounts receivable to total assets as indicative of a receivable collection problem. Receivables outstanding in excess of the expected payment date and relative to industry norm implies a higher probability of uncollectibility.

You should evaluate the trends in the ratios of (1) bad debts to accounts receivable and (2) bad debts to net sales. Unwarranted reductions in bad debts mean overstated earnings. On the other hand, a company may overstate the bad debt provision to provide for an accounting cushion, thus understating profits.

EXAMPLE 4.2

A company reports the following information:

	20X1	20X2
Sales	$100,000	$130,000
Accounts receivable	30,000	40,000
Bad debts	2,000	2,200

You conclude that the company is selling to more risky customers in 20X2 relative to 20X1.

Relevant ratios follow.

	20X1	20X2
Bad debts to sales	2.0%	1.7%
Bad debts to accounts receivable	6.7%	5.5%

Because the company is selling to more marginal customers, its bad debt provision should increase in 20X2. However, the ratios of bad debts to sales and bad debts to accounts receivable actually decreased. The impact of understating bad debts is to overstate net income and accounts receivable. Thus, net income should be lowered for the incremental profit arising from the unwarranted lowering of bad debts. If you decide that a realistic bad debt percentage to accounts receivable is 6.5%, then the bad debt expense should be $2,600 ($40,000 × 6.5%). Net income should thus be reduced by $400 ($2,600 less $2,200).

If there is an upward trend in the ratios of sales returns to sales and sales returns to accounts receivable, this indicates poor-quality merchandise.

Inventory

An inventory buildup may mean realization problems. The buildup may be at the plant, wholesaler, or retailer. A sign of a buildup is when inventory increases at a much faster rate than the increase in sales. *What to Watch Out for:* A decline in raw materials coupled with a rise in work in process and finished goods pointing to a future production slowdown.

Calculate the turnover rate for each major inventory category as well as by department. Possible reasons for a low turnover rate are overstocking, obsolescence, and product line deficiencies. *Note:* The turnover rate may be unrepresentatively high when the business uses a "natural year-end" because at that time the inventory balance will be exceptionally low. *What to Do:* Compute the number of days inventory is held and compare it to the industry norm and previous years.

$$\text{Inventory turnover} = \frac{\text{Cost of goods sold}}{\text{Average inventory}}$$

$$\text{Age of inventory} = \frac{365 \text{ days}}{\text{Turnover}}$$

Also look at the trend in inventory to sales.

What to Watch Out for: Merchandise that is susceptible to price variability, "fad," specialized, perishable, and luxurious goods. On the contrary, low realization risk is with standardized, staple, and necessity items.

Note: Raw material inventory is safer than finished goods or work in process since raw material has more universal and varied uses.

Questions to be asked:

- Is inventory collateralized against a loan?
- Is there adequate insurance in case of loss?
- Is it subject to political risk (e.g., big cars and an oil crisis)?
- Is a change in depreciation method appropriate or is it designed to create illusory earnings growth?
- Is there an unusual change related to inventory in the fourth quarter?

Warning: The more technical a product and the more dependent the valuation on internally developed cost records, the more susceptible are cost estimates to misstatement. Also, sudden inventory write-offs should make you suspicious of a company's deferral policy.

EXAMPLE 4.3

A company presents the following makeup of inventory:

	20X1	20X2
Raw materials	$89,000	$78,000
Work in process	67,000	120,000
Finished goods	16,000	31,000

Your analysis of the inventory shows there was a material divergence in the inventory components between 20X1 and 20X2. There was a reduction in raw material by 12.4% ($11,000/$89,000), while work in process rose by 79.1% ($53,000/$67,000) and finished goods rose by 93.8% ($15,000/$16,000). The lack of consistency in the trend between raw materials relative to work in process and finished goods may imply a forthcoming cutback in production. An obsolescence problem may also exist applicable to work in process and finished goods due to the sizable buildup.

Fixed Assets

Is there sufficient maintenance of productive assets to ensure current and future earning power? Lessened operational efficiency occurs when obsolete assets have not been replaced and/or required repairs made. *What to Do*: Determine the age and condition of each major asset category, as well as the cost to replace old assets. Determine output levels, downtime, and temporary discontinuances. Is the rate of return on assets satisfactory? Are the fixed assets specialized or risky, making them susceptible to obsolescence?

Ratio trends to be calculated are:

- Fixed asset acquisitions to total assets
- Repairs and maintenance to fixed assets
- Repairs and maintenance to sales
- Sales to fixed assets
- Net income to fixed assets

Recommendation: Use a depreciation method that best approximates the decline in usefulness of the fixed asset. Compare the depreciation rate to the industry norm. *What to Do*: Calculate the trend in depreciation expense to fixed assets and depreciation expense to sales. If there are decreasing trends, inadequate depreciation charges may exist. Compare the book depreciation rate to the tax depreciation rate.

What to Watch Out for: A material decline in sales coupled with a significant increase in capital expenditures may be inconsistent. It could point to overexpansion and later write-offs.

Has there been a decline in depreciation expense caused by unwarranted changes in lives or salvage values of fixed assets? If so, downwardly adjust net income for the impact of the change.

Intangible Assets

Realization risk is indicated when there is a high ratio of intangible assets to total assets. The amounts recorded for intangibles may be overstated relative to their market value or to their future income-generating capacity. Intangibles should be treated with suspicion. For instance, in a recessionary environment, goodwill on the books may be worthless. Since APB Opinion 17 provides for a 40-year amortization period for intangibles, some companies tend to ignore economic reality by making only minimum amortization provisions. Further, intangibles acquired before the effective date of the opinion are not even subject to such minimum amortization.

What to Do: Calculate trends in the following ratios:

- Intangible assets to total assets
- Intangible assets to stockholders' equity
- Intangible assets to sales
- Intangible assets to net income
- Specific, questionable intangible assets (e.g., goodwill) to total assets
- Change in intangible assets to change in net income

EXAMPLE 4.4

A company shows the following data:

	20X1	20X2
Intangible assets	$ 58,000	$187,000
Total assets	512,000	530,000
Sales	640,000	655,000
Net income	120,000	140,000

Relevant ratios can now be computed as follows:

	20X1	20X2
Intangible assets to total assets	11.3%	35.3%
Intangible assets to sales	9.1%	28.5%

Higher realization risk in intangibles is indicated by the higher ratios of intangible assets to total assets and intangible assets to sales. Also, the 222.4% increase in intangibles along with the 16.7% increase in net income imply that earnings have been overstated as a result of the failure to incorporate items that have been expensed rather than capitalized.

What to Watch Out for: Unwarranted extension in the amortization period for intangibles, which overstates profits.

Note: In some instances, intangible assets may be undervalued, such as a highly successful patented product. However, can the patent product be infringed upon by minor alteration? What are the expiration dates of patents, and are new ones coming on stream?

In evaluating goodwill, you should determine whether in fact the business enjoys superior earnings potential relative to competition. If not, goodwill should be written down. However, there may exist internally developed goodwill not recorded in the accounts (e.g., the good name of IBM).

Deferred Charges

Deferred charges depend on estimates of future probabilities and developments to a greater extent than do other assets. These estimates are often overly optimistic. Is the business deferring an item that has no future economic benefit only to defer costs so as not to burden reported results? Further, deferred charges do not constitute cash-realizable assets, and thus cannot meet creditor claims. Examples of questionable deferred costs are start-up costs, rearrangement costs, and promotional costs.

What to Do: Calculate trends in the ratios of (1) deferred charges to sales, (2) deferred charges to net income, and (3) deferred charges (e.g., advertising) to total expenditures (e.g., total advertising). Watch out for increasing trends.

Red Flag: A high ratio of intangibles and deferred charges to total assets points to realization risk.

EXAMPLE 4.5

A company presents the following information:

	20X1	20X2
Deferred charges	$ 47,000	$121,000
Total assets	580,000	650,000
Sales	680,000	720,000
Net income	190,000	205,000

Relevant ratios are now calculated as follows:

	20X1	20X2
Deferred charges to total assets	8.1%	18.6%
Deferred charges to sales	6.9%	16.8%
Deferred charges to net income	24.7%	59.0%

Greater realization risk is indicated from the higher ratios. The net income for 20X2 is most likely overstated, because items that should have been expensed are probably included in the deferred charge balance.

Asset Profile

Assets that are interdependent create a financial disadvantage for the company. For example, the sale of equipment on the assembly line may adversely affect the remaining equipment. On the other hand, you can sell one marketable security without affecting another.

Sharp vacillation in the price of assets is a negative sign, because the company may be forced to sell an asset at a time of financial need at great loss (i.e., market value is significantly less than book value).

Greater liquidity risk exists with noncurrent assets than with current assets because of the greater disposition difficulty.

You must also determine whether off-balance-sheet assets (unrecorded resources) exist. Examples are a tax loss carry-forward benefit, expected rebates, and a purchase commitment to acquire an item at a price lower than the prevailing price. You should also review for assets that are reflected on the balance sheet at an amount substantially less than their real value. Examples are patents recorded at cost, even though the present value of future benefits substantially exceeds it, and land that does not reflect its appreciated value.

LIABILITIES

The provision for estimated liabilities for future costs and losses (e.g., lawsuits, warranties) may impair the significance of net income and should be viewed with skepticism. *Advice*: In evaluating the adequacy of estimated liability accounts, you should carefully examine footnote disclosures and familiarize yourself with the financial and accounting characteristics of the industry. *What to Do*: Eliminate arbitrary adjustments of estimated liabilities in arriving at corporate earning power. If you find that reserves are used to manage earnings, add back the amounts charged to earnings, and subtract amounts credited to earnings.

What to Watch Out for: An unrealistically low provision for future costs. For example, it is inconsistent for a firm to decrease its warranty provision when previous experience indicates a poor-quality product.

Be on guard against an overprovision of estimated liabilities, such as when earnings are too high and management wants to decrease them. Note when more operating expenses and losses are being charged to reserve accounts compared to prior years, since this represents a lower earnings quality source.

EXAMPLE 4.6

A company reports the following data:

	20X1	20X2	20X3
Estimated liability for warranties	$ 30,000	$ 33,000	$ 40,000
Sales	100,000	130,000	190,000

From 20X1 to 20X3, the company reports that there has been a higher rate of defective merchandise that has to be repaired.

Relevant ratios follow.

	20X1–20X2	20X2–20X3
Percentage increase in the estimated liability account	10.0%	21.2%
Percentage increase in sales	30.0%	46.2%

The percentage increase in the estimated liability account is materially less than the percentage increase in sales. Since the firm is experiencing quality problems, it is clear that the estimated liability account is understated. Hence, net income is overstated because a sufficient provision for warranty expense has not been established.

Calculate the trends in the ratios of:

- Current liabilities to total liabilities
- Current liabilities to stockholders' equity
- Current liabilities to sales

Increasing trends point to liquidity difficulty. *Caution*: Stretching short-term payables is not a good sign.

Determine the trend in "patient" (e.g., supplier) to "pressing" (e.g., bank) liabilities. When liquidity problems exist, you are better off with patient creditors who will work with you. Thus, a high ratio of pressing liabilities to total liabilities is disadvantageous.

EXAMPLE 4.7

A company presents the following information:

Current Liabilities	20X1	20X2
Trade payables	$ 33,000	$ 28,000
Bank loans	51,000	78,000
Commercial paper	35,000	62,000
Taxes payable	8,000	12,000
Total current liabilities	$127,000	$180,000
Total noncurrent liabilities	$310,000	$315,000
Total liabilities	$437,000	$495,000
Total revenue	$1,100,000	$1,150,000

Relevant ratios are:

Current liabilities to total revenue	11.5%	15.7%
Current liabilities to total liabilities	29.1%	36.4%
Pressing current liabilities to patient current liabilities	2.85	5.43

There is more liquidity risk in 20X2, as reflected by the higher ratios. In fact, pressing liabilities has significantly risen in terms of percentage.

Avenues of Financing

The company's ability to obtain financing at reasonable rates is affected by external considerations (e.g., Federal Reserve policy) and internal considerations (e.g., degree of existing debt).

The extent of loan restrictions on the company should be examined. How close is the company to violating a given restriction, which may in turn call the loan? Can the company issue commercial paper and short-term bank debt? If there is a loan, has the collateral value of the loan diminished relative to the balance of the loan? If so, additional security may be required. Also examine the trend in the effective interest rate and compensating balance requirement relative to competition. Does the client's weighted-average debt significantly exceed the year-end debt balance?

Overstated Liabilities

Certain liabilities shown in the balance sheet should not be considered obligations for analytical purposes because they may not require future payment. Examples are:

- The deferred tax credit account if it applies to a temporary difference that will keep recurring (e.g., depreciation as long as capital expansion occurs)
- Unearned revenue related to passive income sources, such as rents
- Convertible bonds with an attractive conversion feature

Undervalued or Unrecorded Liabilities

Corporate obligations that are not recorded in the balance sheet must be considered when evaluating the entity's going-concern potential. Examples are lawsuits, dispute under a government contract, operating leases, and commitments for future loans to a troubled company.

An equity account may be in essence a liability, such as preferred stock with a maturity date.

LIQUIDITY ANALYSIS

Liquidity is your ability to convert noncash assets into cash or to obtain cash to meet impending obligations. You have to look at the stock and flow of liquid resources and the timing of the cash inflows and outflows.

Liquidity is affected by your ability to obtain financing (e.g., lines of credit) and to postpone cash payments. Also considered is the mixture of current assets and current liabilities and how "close to cash" are the assets and liabilities.

What to Watch Out for: When evaluating a seasonal business, year-end financial data are not representative. Instead, use averages based on quarterly or monthly information to level out seasonal effects.

Can you adjust to unexpected difficulties by changing the amount and timing of future cash flows? Consideration should be given to the closeness to cash of assets, ability to obtain further financing, degree of nonoperating assets that can be sold, ability to change operating and investing activities, and short payback periods on projects.

Funds Flow Ratios

- Current ratio = $\dfrac{\text{Current Assets}}{\text{Current liabilities}}$

- Quick ratio = $\dfrac{\text{Cash + Marketable securities + Accounts receivable}}{\text{Current liabilities}}$

This is a more stringent test of liquidity than the current ratio because it excludes inventories and prepaid expenses.

- Working capital = Current assets − Current liabilities

This is a liquid reserve available to meet uncertainties. A high working capital position is required if the business is not able to borrow on short notice. Working capital can also be related to sales and total assets. Working capital to sales indicates whether the business is optimally employing its liquid balance.

- $\dfrac{\text{A specific current asset}}{\text{Total current assets}}$

For example, a shift of cash to inventory indicates less liquidity.

- $\dfrac{\text{Sales}}{\text{Current assets}}$

A high ratio infers deficient working capital.

- $\dfrac{\text{Working capital provided from operations}}{\text{Net income}}$

A high ratio is desirable because it indicates the profits are backed up by liquid funds.

- $\dfrac{\text{Working capital provided from operations}}{\text{Total liabilities}}$

This shows the extent to which internally generated working capital can meet obligations.

- $\dfrac{\text{Cash + Marketable securities}}{\text{Current liabilities}}$

This reflects the cash available to meet short-term debt.

- $\dfrac{\text{Quick assets}}{\text{Year's cash expenses}}$

This tells how many days of expenses the highly liquid assets could meet.

- $\dfrac{\text{Sales}}{\text{Short-term trade liabilities}}$

This indicates whether the business could partly finance its operations with cost-free funds. If the firm can readily get trade credit, this is a positive sign.

- $\dfrac{\text{Net income}}{\text{Sales}}$

A decline in the ratio points to difficulty in loan repayment due to a lack of earnings.

- $\dfrac{\text{Fixed Assets}}{\text{Short-term debt}}$

If you finance long-term assets with current debt, there may be a problem in meeting the debt when due because the return and proceeds from the fixed asset will not be realized before the maturity dates of the current debt.

- $\dfrac{\text{Short-term debt}}{\text{Long-term debt}}$

A high ratio indicates greater liquidity risk. The entity has vulnerability in a money-market squeeze.

- $\dfrac{\text{Accounts payable}}{\text{Average daily purchases}}$

This indicates the number of days required for the firm to pay creditors.

- Liquidity index.

This applies to the number of days current assets are removed from cash. A shorter period is preferred.

EXAMPLE 4.8

The following information is presented for a company:

	Amount	×	Days Removed from Cash	=	Total
Cash	$ 10,000	×	—		—
Marketable securities	40,000	×	20		$ 800,000
Accounts receivable	50,000	×	35		1,750,000
Inventory	65,000	×	48		3,120,000
	$165,000				$5,670,000

$$\text{Index} = \frac{\$5,670,000}{\$165,000} = 34.4 \text{ days}$$

EXAMPLE 4.9

The following data are presented:

Current assets	$ 390,000
Noncurrent assets	780,000
Current liabilities	460,000
Noncurrent liabilities	510,000
Revenue	5,200,000
Working capital provided from operations	125,000

Industry averages are:

Noncurrent assets to current liabilities	3.8 times
Current liabilities to noncurrent liabilities	47%
Revenue to current assets	9.0 times
Working capital provided from operations to total liabilities	33%

Applicable ratios are now calculated:

Noncurrent assets to current liabilities	1.7 times
Current liabilities to noncurrent liabilities	90.2%
Revenue to current assets	13.3 times
Working capital provided from operations to total liabilities	12.9%

All of the liquidity ratios are poor relative to the industry benchmark. Current liabilities are high and current assets are low compared to the industry norms. Working capital provided from operations to meet total debt is also weak.

You should analyze the debt footnote. Is the business cleaning up its debt position at year-end in order to improve the debt-equity ratio? Such maneuvers are revealed if the weighted-average debt for the year significantly exceeds the year-end balance.

APPRAISAL OF SOLVENCY

Solvency depends upon corporate earning power because a business will not be able to meet its obligations unless it is profitable. Also, there should be a high ratio of long-term assets to long-term liabilities. *Recommendation*: Use the market value of assets rather than the book value of assets in ratio computations since market value is more reflective of reality.

Stability in earnings and cash flow from operations enhances confidence in the client's ability to meet debt. Long-term debt-related ratios to be examined include:

- *Long-term debt to net worth*. High financial leverage indicates risk in meeting the principal and interest on debt. High interest charges also result in earnings instability.
- *Cash flow from operations to long-term debt*. This ratio shows whether internally generated cash funds are adequate to meet noncurrent liabilities.
- *Interest coverage (Net income + Interest + Taxes/Interest)*. This reveals the adequacy of earnings to meet interest charges. A high ratio is desired.
- *Cash flow from operations plus interest to interest*. This indicates the number of times interest is covered via internal cash earnings.
- *Cash flow from operations plus fixed costs to fixed costs*. This ratio points to the adequacy of cash earnings to meet fixed charges, which becomes particularly essential in an economic downturn.
- *Fixed assets to noncurrent liabilities*. Long-term debt will be met from the return on and proceeds from noncurrent assets.
- *Retained earnings to total assets*. This reflects the long-term earning ability of the business.

The liquidation value of a company may be estimated by using J. Wilcox's gambler's ruin prediction formula:

Cash + (marketable securities at market value) + (70% of inventory, accounts receivable, and prepaid expenses) + (50% of other assets) − (current liabilities + long-term liabilities).

EXAMPLE 4.10

Selected financial data for Murray Company follow:

Noncurrent assets	$680,000
Noncurrent liabilities	470,000
Net worth	290,000
Income before tax	75,000
Cash flow from operations	98,000
Interest	18,000

Ratios of a competitor, Bette Corporation, are:

Noncurrent assets to noncurrent liabilities	1.90
Noncurrent liabilities to net worth	.70
Cash flow from operations to noncurrent liabilities	.28
Income before tax plus interest to interest	7.50

Murray's ratios are:

Noncurrent assets to noncurrent liabilities	1.40
Noncurrent liabilities to net worth	1.62
Cash flow from operations to noncurrent liabilities	.21
Income before tax plus interest to interest	5.17

Murray's solvency is worse than Bette's due to the larger degree of long-term debt in the financing structure and the lower times-interest-earned ratio.

ANALYZING THE STATEMENT OF CASH FLOWS*

An analysis of the Statement of Cash Flows will provide vital information regarding the company's cash reciepts and cash payments for a period as they relate to operating, investing, and financing activities. The Statement assists in the evaluation of the impact on the firm's financial position of cash and noncash investing and financing transactions.**

Comparative Statements of Cash Flows must be thoroughly appraised because they hold clues to a company's earnings quality, risk, and liquidity. They show the degree of repeatability of the company's sources of funds, their costs, and whether such sources may be relied upon

---

* This section was taken from J. Siegel, *How to Analyze Businesses, Financial Statements and the Quality of Earnings* (2nd edition), 1991.
** J. Siegel, "A Financial Analysis and Evaluation of the Statement of Cash Flows," *Practical Accountant* (June 1989), pp. 71–73.

in the future. Uses of funds for growth as well as for maintaining competitive share are revealed. An analysis of Comparative Statements of Cash Flows holds the key to a complete and reliable analysis of corporate financial health in the present and future. It aids in planning future ventures and financing needs. Comparative data help financial analysts identify abnormal or cyclical factors as well as changes in the relationship among each flow component.

The Statement serves as a basis to forecast earnings based on plant, property, and equipment posture. It assists in evaluating growth potential and incorporates cash flow requirements, highlighting specific fund sources and future means of payment. Will the company be able to meet its obligations and pay cash dividends?

The Statement reveals the type and degree of financing required to expand long-term assets and to bolster operations.

For analytical purposes, cash flow per share equal to net cash flow divided by number of shares should be calculated. A high ratio is desirable because it indicates the company is in a very liquid position.

We now discuss the analysis of the operating, investing, and financing sections of the Statement of Cash Flows.

Operating Section

An analysis of the operating section of the Statement of Cash Flows helps determine the adequacy of cash flow from operating activities to satisfy company requirements. Can the firm obtain positive future net cash flows? The reconciliation tracing net income to net cash flow from operating activities should be examined to see the effect of noncash revenue and noncash expense items.

An award under a lawsuit is a cash inflow from operating activities that results in a nonrecurring source of revenue.

An operating cash outlay for refunds given to customers for deficient goods indicates a quality problem with the firm's merchandise.

Payments of penalties, fines, and lawsuit damages are operating cash outflows, which show poor management because a problem arose that required a nonbeneficial expenditure to the organization.

Investing Section

An analysis of the Investing Section of the Statement of Cash Flows enables identification of an investment in another company that may point to an attempt at eventual control for diversification purposes. It may also indicate a change in future direction or change in business philosophy.

An increase in fixed assets indicates capital expansion and future growth. An analysis should be made as to which assets have been purchased. Are they assets for risky (specialized) ventures or are they stable (multipurpose) ones? An indication exists as to risk potential and expected returns. The nature of the assets provides signs as to future direction and earning potential with regard to the introduction or reinforcement of product lines, business segments, etc. Are these directions sound and viable?

Is there a contradiction in the business arising from the sale of fixed assets without adequate replacement? Is the problem corporate (e.g., product line is weakening) or industry-wide (e.g., industry is on the downturn)? If corporate, management is not optimistic regarding the future. Nonrecurring gains may occur because of the sale of low-cost basis fixed assets (e.g., land). Such gains cause temporary increases in profits above normal levels and represent low quality of earnings sources, and should be discounted.

Financing Section

An evaluation of the Financing Section will provide an opinion regarding the company's capability to meet its obligations. The financial mixture comprising bonds, long-term loans from banks, and equity instruments affect the cost of financing. One major advantage of debt is the tax deductibility of interest while dividends are not deductible. Further, during inflation, paying back debt will result in purchasing power gains since the payback is made in cheaper dollars. However, there is greater risk associated with debt financing because the company must have adequate funds to pay interest and retire the obligation at maturity. If funds are insufficient, higher interest sources may have to be used (e.g., factors). The stability of the fund source must be appraised to determine if it may be relied upon continuously, even during tight money markets. Otherwise, potential difficulties in maintaining corporate operations during recessionary periods exist. The question is: Where can the company go for funds during times of cash squeezes?

By evaluating the financing sources, the financing preferences of management are revealed. Is there an inclination toward risk or safety? Creditors would prefer to see equity issuances as protection of their loans. Excessive debt may be a problem during economic downturn.

The ability of a company to finance with the issuance of common stock on attractive terms (high stock price) indicates that the investing public is optimistic about the financial well-being of the entity.

The issuance of preferred stock may be a negative sign since it may mean the company has difficulty issuing common stock.

An appraisal should be made of the company's ability to satisfy debt. If debt is excessive, it points to greater corporate risk. The problem is acute if earnings are unstable or declining. On the other hand, the reduction in long-term debt is favorable because it points to less risk associated with the firm.

A financing cash outflow for the early extinguishing of debt will result in an extraordinary gain or loss resulting in a one-time effect upon earnings.

The firm's dividend paying ability should be analyzed. Stockholders favor a company that has a high dividend payout.

Is there a purchase of treasury stock resulting in an artificial increase in earnings per share?

Schedule of Noncash Financing and Investing Activities

A bond conversion is a positive sign about the entity's financial health because it indicates that bondholders are optimistic about the company's financial health or that the market price of the common stock has risen. A conversion of preferred stock is also favorable because it shows that preferred stockholders feel positive about the company's future and are willing to have a lower priority in the event of corporate liquidation.

Note that bond and preferred stock conversions affect the existing position of long-term creditors and stockholders. For example, a reduction in debt by conversion to stock protects to a greater degree the loans of the remaining bondholders and banks.

Conclusion

Current profitability is only one important factor for corporate success. Also essential are the current and future cash flows. In fact, a profitable company may have a cash crisis.

Management is responsible for planning how and when cash will be used and obtained. When planned expenditures necessitate more cash than planned activities are likely to produce, managers must decide what to do.

They may decide to obtain debt or equity financing or to dispose of some fixed assets or a whole business segment. Alternatively, they may decide to cut back on planned activities by modifying operational plans, such as ending a special advertising campaign or delaying new acquisitions. Or, they may decide to revise planned payments to financing sources, such as delaying bond repayment or reducing dividends. Whatever is decided, the manager's goal is to balance, over both the short and the long term, the cash available and the needs for cash.

Managerial planning is aided when evaluating the Statement of Cash Flows in terms of coordinating dividend policy with other corporate activities, financial planning for new products and types of assets needed, strengthening weak cash posture and credit availability, and ascertaining the feasibility and implementation of existing top management plans.

The analysis and evaluation of the Statement of Cash Flows is essential if an entity's cash flows from operating, investing, and financing activities are to be properly appraised. The company's liquidity and solvency positions as well as future directions are revealed. Inadequacy in cash flow has possible serious implications—it may lead to declining profitability, greater financial risk, and even bankruptcy.

EXAMPLE 4.11

X Company provides the following financial statements:

X Company
Comparative Balance Sheets
December 31
(In Millions)

	20X0	20X1
Assets		
Cash	$ 47	$ 40
Accounts receivable	35	30
Prepaid expenses	2	4
Land	35	50
Building	80	100
Accumulated depreciation	(6)	(9)
Equipment	42	50
Accumulated depreciation	(7)	(11)
Total assets	$228	$254

Liabilities and Stockholders' Equity		
Accounts payable	$ 16	$ 20
Long-term notes payable	20	30
Common stock	100	100
Retained earnings	92	104
Total liabilities and stockholders' equity	$228	$254

X Company
Income Statement
For the Year Ended December 31, 20X0
(In Millions)

Revenue		$300
Operating expenses (excluding depreciation)	$200	
Depreciation	7	207
Income from operations		$ 93
Income tax expense		32
Net income		$ 61

Additional information:
1. Cash dividends paid: $49.
2. The company issued long-term notes payable for cash.
3. Land, building, and equipment were acquired for cash.

We can now prepare the Statement of Cash Flows under the *indirect method* as follows:

X Company
Statement of Cash Flows
For the Year Ended December 31, 20X0
(In Millions)

Cash flow from operating activities		
Net income		$ 61
Add (deduct) items not effecting cash		
Depreciation expense	$ 7	
Decrease in accounts receivable	5	
Increase in prepaid expenses	(2)	
Increase in accounts payable	4	14
Net cash flow from operating activities		$ 75
Cash flow from investing activities		
Purchase of land	($ 15)	
Purchase of building	(20)	
Purchase of equipment	(8)	(43)

88   Part I: Financial Analysis

Cash flow from financing activities		
Issuance of long-term notes payable	$ 10	
Payment of cash dividends	(49)	(39)
Net decrease in cash		$ 7

A financial analysis of the Statement of Cash Flows reveals that the profitability and operating cash flow of X Company improved. This indicates good earnings performance as well as the fact that earnings are backed up by cash. The decrease in accounts receivable may reveal better collection efforts. The increase in accounts payable is a sign that suppliers are confident in the company and willing to give interest-free financing. The acquisition of land, building, and equipment points to a growing business undertaking capital expansion. The issuance of long-term notes payable indicates that part of the financing of assets is through debt. Stockholders will be happy with the significant dividend payout of 80.3% (dividends divided by net income, or $49/$61, in millions). Overall, there was a decrease in cash of $7 million but this should *not* cause alarm because of the company's profitability and the fact that cash was used for capital expansion and dividend payments. We recommend that the dividend payout be reduced from its high level and the funds be reinvested in the profitable business. Also, the curtailment of dividends by more than $7 million would result in a positive net cash flow for the year. Cash flow is needed for immediate liquidity needs.

EXAMPLE 4.12

Y Company presents the following statement of cash flows.

Y Company
Statement of Cash Flows
For the Year Ended December 31, 20X1

Cash flows from operating activities		
Net income		$134,000
Add (deduct) items not effecting cash		
Depreciation expense	$21,000	
Decrease in accounts	10,000	
Increase in prepaid expenses	(6,000)	
Increase in accounts payable	35,000	60,000
Net cash flow from operating activities		$194,000

Chapter 4: How to Analyze Financial Position   89

Cash flows from investing activities		
Purchase of land	($70,000)	
Purchase of building	(200,000)	
Purchase of equipment	(68,000)	
Cash used by investing activities		(338,000)
Cash flows from financing activities		
Issuance of bonds	150,000	
Payment of cash dividends	(18,000)	
Cash provided by financing activities		132,000
Net decrease in cash		$ 12,000

An analysis of the Statement of Cash Flows reveals that the company is profitable. Also, cash flow from operating activities exceeds net income, which indicates good internal cash generation. The ratio of cash flow from operating activities to net income is a solid 1.45 ($194,000/$134,000). A high ratio is desirable because it shows that earnings are backed up by cash. The decline in accounts receivable could indicate better collection efforts. The increase in accounts payable shows the company can obtain interest-free financing. The company is definitely in the process of expanding for future growth as evidenced by the purchase of land, building, and equipment. The debt position of the company has increased indicating greater risk. The dividend payout was 13.4% ($18,000/$134,000). Stockholders look positively on a firm that pays dividends. The decrease in cash flow for the year of $12,000 is a negative sign.

POTENTIAL FOR BUSINESS FAILURE

Bankruptcy occurs when the company is unable to meet maturing financial obligations. We are thus particularly interested in predicted cash flow. Financial difficulties affect the price–earnings ratio, bond ratings, and the effective interest rate.

A comprehensive quantitative indicator used to predict failure is Altman's "Z-score," which equals

$$\frac{\text{Working capital}}{\text{Total assets}} \times 1.2 + \frac{\text{Retained earnings}}{\text{Total assets}} \times 1.4$$

$$\frac{\text{Operating income}}{\text{Total assets}} \times 3.3 + \frac{\text{Market value of common and preferred}}{\text{Total liabilities}} \times 0.6$$

$$+ \frac{\text{Sales}}{\text{Total assets}} \times 0.999$$

The scores and the probability of short-term illiquidity follow.

Score	Probability of Illiquidity or Failure
1.80 or less	Very high
1.81–2.99	Not sure
3.0 or greater	Unlikely

EXAMPLE 4.13

A company presents the following information:

Working capital	$280,000
Total assets	875,000
Total liabilities	320,000
Retained earnings	215,000
Sales	950,000
Operating income	130,000
Common stock	
Book value	220,000
Market value	310,000
Preferred stock	
Book value	115,000
Market value	170,000

The Z-score equals:

$$\frac{\$280,000}{\$875,000} \times 1.2 + \frac{\$215,000}{\$875,000} \times 1.4 + \frac{\$130,000}{\$875,000} \times 3.3 + \frac{\$480,000}{\$320,000}$$

$$\times .6 + \frac{\$950,000}{\$875,000} \times 0.999 = 0.384 + 0.344 + 0.490 + 0.9$$

$$+ 1.0846 = 3.2026$$

The probability of failure is not likely.

Quantitative Factors in Predicting Corporate Failure

- Low cash flow to total liabilities.
- High debt-to-equity ratio and high debt to total assets.
- Low return on investment.
- Low profit margin.
- Low retained earnings to total assets.

- Low working capital to total assets and low working capital to sales.
- Low fixed assets to noncurrent liabilities.
- Inadequate interest-coverage ratio.
- Instability in earnings.
- Small-size company measured in sales and/or total assets.
- Sharp decline in price of stock, bond price, and earnings.
- A significant increase in beta. (Beta is the variability in the price of the company's stock relative to a market index. This is discussed in more detail in Chapter 6.)
- Market price per share is significantly less than book value per share.
- A significant rise in the company's weighted-average cost of capital.
- High fixed cost to total cost structure (high operating leverage).
- Failure to maintain capital assets. An example is a decline in the ratio of repairs to fixed assets.

Qualitative Factors in Predicting Failure

- New company.
- Declining industry.
- Inability to obtain adequate financing, and when obtained there are significant loan restrictions.
- A lack in management quality.
- Moving into new areas in which management lacks expertise.
- Failure of the company to keep up to date, especially in a technologically oriented business.
- High business risk (e.g., positive correlation in the product line; susceptibility to strikes).
- Inadequate insurance coverage.
- Fraudulent actions (e.g., misstating inventories to stave off impending bankruptcy).
- Cyclicality in business operations.
- Inability to adjust production to meet consumption needs.
- Susceptibility of the business to stringent governmental regulation (e.g., companies in the real estate industry).

- Susceptibility to energy shortages.
- Susceptibility to unreliable suppliers.
- Renegotiation of debt and/or lease agreements.
- Deficient accounting and financial reporting systems.

If a client has a going-concern problem, appropriate reference should be made in the audit opinion. Footnote disclosure may also be advisable.

Quantitative Financial Factors That Minimize Potential for Failure

- Have open lines of bank credit.
- Dispose of losing divisions.
- Manage assets for maximum return and minimum risk.
- Stagger and extend the maturity dates of debt.
- Use quantitative techniques such as multiple regression analysis to compute the correlation between given variables and the likelihood of business failure.
- Have a negative correlation in product line and in investments held.
- Lower dividend payouts.

Nonfinancial Factors That Minimize the Potential for Failure

- Vertically and horizontally diversify the product line and operations.
- Diversify geographically.
- Enhance the marketing effort (e.g., advertise in the right place).
- Engage in cost-reduction programs.
- Improve productivity (e.g., use timely and detailed variance analysis).
- Implement computer technology (e.g., microcomputers).
- Minimize the adverse effect of inflation and recession on the entity (e.g., price on a next-in, first-out basis).
- Invest in multipurpose, rather than single-purpose, assets, because of lower risks.
- Reconsider entering new industries that have a predicted high rate of past failure.

- Have many projects, rather than only a few, that significantly affect operations.
- Consider introducing product lines that are unaffected by the business cycle and that possess stable demand.
- Avoid going from a labor-intensive to a capital-intensive business, because the latter has a high degree of operating leverage.
- Avoid fixed-fee contracts to customers. Rather, incorporate inflation adjustment and energy-cost indexes in contracts.
- Avoid entering markets that are on the downturn or that are already highly competitive.

CONCLUSION

An analysis of a company's financial position and funds flow is essential in ascertaining its ability to continue and prosper. Areas of deficiency and potential ramifications can be highlighted so that corrective action may be taken. Investors are interested in making optimal portfolio decisions, while creditors are concerned with repayment of loans. Managers closely scrutinize segmental operations to identify areas of risk and poor profit potential.

5 Techniques for Analyzing Operating Performance

You should be familiar with the accounting factors involved in analyzing the income statement, including the nature of the accounting policies used, the degree of certainty in accounting estimates, discretionary costs, tax reporting, and verifiability of earnings. It is your task to adjust net income to derive an earnings figure that is most relevant to your needs.

QUALITY OF EARNINGS

Quality of earnings is relative, not absolute. It is a comparison of the favorable and unfavorable characteristics of the net incomes of competing companies. It involves looking at quantitative (e.g., ratio analysis) and qualitative factors (e.g., pending litigation). Reported earnings are adjusted to make them relevant to the user for analytical purposes. Data in the footnotes will assist in the restatement process.

Earnings quality indicates the degree by which net income is overstated or understated, as well as the stability of income statement elements. Earnings quality affects the price–earnings ratio, bond rating, effective interest rate, compensating balance requirement, availability of financing, and desirability of the firm as either an acquirer or acquiree. Earnings quality attributes exist in different proportions and intensities in the earnings profiles of companies.

You must be very careful of the quality of earnings of high-accounting-risk companies, including a company in a high-risk environment or one that shows "glamour," such as one with consistently strong growth.

Unwarranted accounting changes (principles and estimates) lower earnings quality and distort the earnings trend. Justification for an accounting change is present in a new FASB statement, AICPA Industry Audit Guide, and IRS regulations.

EXAMPLE 5.1

An asset was acquired for $12,000 on 1/1/20X1. The life is 8 years, and has a salvage value of $2,000. On 1/8/20X4, the company unrealistically changed the original life to 10 years, with a salvage value of $3,000.

The adjustment required to 20X4's net income is as follows:

Depreciation expense after change in estimate		$750
Original cost	$12,000	
Less accumulated depreciation ($1,250 × 3)	3,750	
Book value (12/31/20X3)	$ 8,250	
New salvage value	3,000	
Amount to be depreciated	$ 5,250	
New remaining life (10 – 3) 7 years		
Recorded depreciation expense ($5,250/7) = $750		
Depreciation expense should be		1,250
Downward adjustment to 20X4 net income		$ 500

Income smoothing lowers the quality of earnings. Examples are:

- Future revenue is reported in the current period.
- Income is transferred from good years to bad years.
- Expenses are shifted among the years.

A weak relationship between revenue and reported earnings may point to the existence of earnings management.

EXAMPLE 5.2

The ratio of net income to revenue for the period 20X1 to 20X4 was

20X1	20X2	20X3	20X4
14%	2%	22%	(4)%

The weak association implies the existence of income management.

The immediate recognition of revenue without the rendering of substantial services imparts lower earnings quality. An example is a health spa, which reflects income, as membership fees are collected at the beginning of the earnings cycle. On the other hand, the belated recognition of revenue results in understated earnings. Also watch out for the reversal of previously recorded items, such as profits or a prior write-off of an asset.

The underaccrual or overaccrual of expenses or losses results in poor earnings quality. For example, by underaccruing for warranty expense, net income is overstated. *What to Watch Out for:* The reduction of expenses for exaggerated expected recoveries of excess costs under contracts causing an overstatement in earnings. Also, is there a higher expense provision in the current year because of an inadequate provision in a previous year? This distorts the earnings trend. *Be on Guard Against:* A company taking a "financial bath" by writing down overstated assets all of a sudden and providing for expense and loss provisions that realistically apply to the future. This sometimes occurs when new management takes over and wants to reduce earnings, blaming old management for a bad year, or when the current management feels that since operations are so bad anyway, a further decrease in earnings will not have a material negative effect on the market price.

What to Watch Out for: Deferring items to an asset that should preferably be expensed. An example is advertising.

ANALYSIS OF DISCRETIONARY COSTS

Discretionary costs can be changed at management's will. *What to Do:* Examine the current level of discretionary costs relative to previous years and to future requirements. An index number may be used to compare the current-year discretionary cost to the base amount. A reduction in discretionary costs lowers earnings quality if their absence will have a detrimental effect on the future (e.g., advertising, research, repairs). *Recommendation:* Analyze the trend in the following ratios: (1) discretionary costs to sales and (2) discretionary costs to assets. If, in connection with a cost-reduction program, material cuts are made in discretionary costs, earnings quality has declined. However, cost control is warranted when (1) discretionary expenditures were excessive in prior years and (2) competition has decreased. A material increase in discretionary costs in a given year may have a significant positive impact on corporate earning power and future growth. Income smoothing is indicated when discretionary costs as a percentage of revenue fluctuate each year.

EXAMPLE 5.3

The following data are supplied:

	20X1	20X2	20X3
Sales	$95,000	$125,000	$84,000
Research	9,000	14,000	3,000

The most representative year (base year) is 20X1. After 20X4, you believe that research is essential for the company's success because of technological factors in the industry.

	20X1	20X2	20X3
Research to sales	9.5%	11.2%	3.6%

Looking in base dollars, 20X1 represents 100. 20X2 is 156 ($14,000/$9,000). 20X3 has an index of 33 ($3,000/$9,000).

A red flag is posted for 20X3. Research is lower than in previous periods. There should have been a boost in research in light of the technological updating needed for 20X4.

EXAMPLE 5.4

The following information applies for a company with respect to its plant assets:

	20X1	20X2
Equipment	$ 4,500	$ 4,800
Less accumulated depreciation	3,000	3,200
Book value	$ 1,500	$ 1,600
Repairs	400	320
Replacement cost of equipment	6,800	7,700
CPI value of equipment	7,400	8,500
Revenue	48,000	53,000
Working capital	2,900	2,600
Cash	1,100	970
Debt-to-equity ratio	42%	71%
Downtime of equipment	2%	5%

Finance company loans have increased relative to bank loans over the year.

You want to analyze equipment and repairs.

Repairs to gross equipment decreased from 8.9% in 20X1 ($400/$4,500) to 6.7% in 20X2 ($320/$4,800). In a similar vein, repairs to revenue went from 0.83% in 20X1 ($400/$48,000) to 0.6% in 20X2 ($320/$53,000).

Over the year there was a greater variation between replacement cost and book value and CPI value and book value, indicating equipment is aging.

As indicated by the greater amount of downtime, more equipment malfunction is taking place.

Equipment purchased over the year was minimal, 6.7% ($300/$4,500).

The company's capital maintenance is deficient. Repairs to fixed assets and repairs to revenue are down, and insufficient replacements are being made. Perhaps these are the causes for the greater downtime.

It may be a problem for the company to purchase fixed assets when required because of the deterioration in its liquidity position. Financial leverage has significantly increased over the year. It is more difficult for the company to obtain adequate financing at reasonable interest rates, as evidenced by the need to borrow to a greater extent from finance companies than from banks.

CASH FLOW FROM OPERATIONS

You should evaluate the trend in the ratio of cash flow from operations to net income. High earnings quality is present when revenue and expenses are recorded close to cash recognition, since the transaction is more objective.

EXAMPLE 5.5

The following condensed income statement appears for a company.

Sales		$1,300,000
Less cost of sales		400,000
Gross margin		$ 900,000
Less operating expenses		
Wages	$150,000	
Rent	80,000	
Electricity	50,000	
Depreciation expense	90,000	
Amortization expense	70,000	
Total operating expenses		440,000
Income before other items		$460,000

Other revenue and expenses
Interest $60,000
Amortization of deferred revenue 20,000
Total other items 40,000
Net income $420,000

The ratio of cash flow from operations to net income is:

Net income $420,000
Plus noncash expenses
  Depreciation expense $90,000
  Amortization expense 70,000 160,000
Less noncash revenue
  Amortization of deferred revenue (20,000)
Cash flow from operations $560,000

$$\frac{\text{Cash flow from operations}}{\text{Net income}} = \frac{\$560,000}{\$420,000} = 1.33$$

THE ROLE OF TAXABLE INCOME

A material overstatement of net income compared to taxable income may reflect lower earnings quality, since liberal accounting policies may have been used for book reporting while conservative ones were used for tax reporting. The difference between the two may be reflected in a widening increase in the deferred tax credit account and/or in the tax return.

Also determine the effective tax rate, which equals tax expense divided by income before tax. A low effective tax rate for the current year due to a one-time source results in lower earnings quality.

Higher earnings quality occurs if the company's earnings and growth do not rely on a lowered tax rate that is vulnerable to a future change in the tax law or that places material restrictions on the firm.

EXAMPLE 5.6

The following information is presented for a company:

	20X1	20X2	20X3
Deferred income tax credit	$102	$118	$298
Revenue	9,600	10,800	11,400
Net income	3,900	4,000	3,600

Chapter 5: Techniques for Analyzing Operating Performance   101

Relative to base dollars, the deferred income tax credit account was 115.7 in 20X2 ($118/$102) and 292.2 in 20X3 ($298/$102).

	20X1	20X2	20X3
Deferred income tax credit to revenue	1.1%	1.1%	2.6%
Deferred income tax credit to net income	2.6%	3.0%	8.3%

The deferred tax credit account significantly rose in 20X3, pointing to a widening difference between net income and taxable income.

RESIDUAL INCOME

The higher the ratio of residual income to net income, the higher the quality of earnings. Residual income represents an economic income, taking into account the opportunity cost of tying up money in the business.

Residual income = Net income − Minimum return (cost of capital) × Total assets

(Residual income is fully discussed in Chapter 8.)

EXAMPLE 5.7

A company's net income is $800,000, total assets are $4,600,000, and cost of capital is 13.40%.

Residual income equals:
Net income $800,000
Less minimum return × total assets
  13.40% × $4,600,000   616,400
Residual income $183,600

The ratio of residual income to net income is 23% ($183,600/$800,000).

ACCOUNTING ESTIMATES

The greater the degree of subjective accounting estimates in the income measurement process, the lower the quality of earnings. *What to Do:* Examine the difference between actual experience and the estimates employed.

The wider the difference, the lower the quality of earnings. Look at the variation over time between a loss provision and the actual loss. A continually understated loss provision means inaccurate estimates and/or an intent to overstate earnings. Sizable gains and losses on the sale of assets may infer inaccurate depreciation estimates.

Examine the trend in the following ratios:

- High estimation assets (e.g., fixed assets) to total assets
- Cash expenses to revenue
- Estimated expenses to revenue
- Cash revenue to revenue
- Estimated revenue to revenue
- Estimated expenses to net income
- Estimated revenue to net income

Higher estimation is indicated by long-term construction work using the percentage-of-completion contract method, and a material amount of estimated liability provisions.

EXAMPLE 5.8

The following information applies to a company:

	20X1	20X2
Cash and near-cash revenue	$ 98,000	$107,000
Noncash revenue items	143,000	195,000
Total revenue	$241,000	$302,000
Cash and near-cash expenses	$ 37,000	$ 58,000
Noncash expenses	67,000	112,000
Total expenses	$104,000	$170,000
Net income	$137,000	$132,000

Estimation-related ratios can now be calculated.

	20X1	20X2
Estimated revenue to total revenue	59%	65%
Estimated revenue to net income	104%	148%
Estimated expenses to total expenses	64%	66%
Estimated expenses to total revenue	28%	37%
Estimated expenses to net income	49%	85%

In every case, there was greater estimation involved in the income measurement process in 20X2 relative to 20X1. The higher degree of estimation resulted in lower earnings quality.

INTERNAL CONTROL AND MANAGEMENT HONESTY

Deficient internal control casts doubt upon the integrity of the earnings stream. Look at the trend in audit fees and in audit time over the years. Increasing trends may point to internal control and audit problems. Examine disclosure of errors that cast doubt upon the integrity of financial reporting. Are there any indicators of a dishonest management, such as corporate bribes, payoffs, or hiding of defective merchandise?

AUDITOR RELATIONS AND REPORTS

You should examine the turnover rate in auditors. High turnover rates as a result of accounting disagreements reflect negatively on earnings quality. When a conflict of opinion regarding an accounting change results in a change in auditors, determine the effect on net income if the new auditor agrees to the policy change; compare the net income computed under the new policy with that computed under the old policy.

Examine the type of audit opinion rendered (unqualified, qualified, disclaimer, or adverse), and consider why that format was selected. Questions to be asked are:

- What is the subject of a qualified opinion?
- Why was a disclaimer opinion called for?
- What uncertainties are present?
- Is there adequate footnote disclosure?
- Is there a significant subsequent event?
- Are there related party transactions?

CONCLUSION

Quality of earnings involves those factors that would influence investors or creditors considering investing or giving credit to firms exhibiting the same reported earnings. Specifically, two firms in a given industry may report identical earnings, but may be quite different in terms of operational performance. This is because identical earnings may possess different degrees of quality. The key in evaluating a company's earnings quality is to compare its earnings profile (the mixture and degree of favorable and unfavorable characteristics associated with reported results) with the earnings profile of other companies in the same industry. Analysts attempt to assess earnings quality in order to render the earnings comparable, and to determine what valuation should be placed upon them.

You must address the problem of evaluating earnings of competitive companies that report substantially different net incomes. The earnings quality of the firm reporting higher net income may in fact be inferior if the firm is burdened with more undesirable characteristics in earnings than its low-income competitor.

When two competitive companies use alternative accounting policies, you should adjust their net incomes to a common basis in order to reduce the diversity in accounting that exists. The best basis for adjusting earnings for comparative purposes is to derive net income figures, assuming that realistic accounting policies were used.

Quality of earnings can be looked at only in terms of accounting and financial characteristics that have an effect on the earning power of a firm, as shown in its net income figure. These characteristics are complex and inter-related, and are subject to wide varieties of interpretation depending upon your own analytical objective. Further, measurements of some of the characteristics may be very difficult. Nevertheless, you cannot avoid sorting through the characteristics to determine which of them are favorable in terms of earnings quality and which are unfavorable, and to determine the degree to which they exist. You are then in a position to rank the relative quality of earnings of companies in an industry as well as to restate companies' net incomes.

6 How to Analyze the Financial Structure of the Firm

A lack of stability indicates riskiness associated with the business. A company's stability and financial structure can be measured in numerous ways. Corporate and industry characteristics that have bearing upon stability must be considered. A key area is the company's marketing efforts. Finally, external factors, such as economic and political variables, can have a significant affect upon the firm's basic business operations.

HOW TO MEASURE THE STABILITY OF EARNINGS

Various quantitative measurements can be used to analyze a firm's stability over time. Comparisons can then be made to prior years of the firm, competing companies, and industry norms.

Types of Stability Measurements

Trend in Average Reported Earnings
Average earnings over a relatively long period (such as 5 years) will level out abnormal and erratic income statement components as well as cyclical effects upon the business.

Average Pessimistic Earnings
Average earnings in the worst possible case (minimum earnings) are useful in analyzing a high-risk business where creditors and potential investors wish to appraise such risk.

One-time Gains or Losses to Net Income and/or Sales

A high percentage of nonrecurring items to reported earnings indicates instability in income statement components, pointing to uncertainty and unrepresentativeness of what is typical. An example is the gain on the sale of low-cost basis land.

Standard Deviation

$$SD = \sqrt{\frac{\Sigma(y - \bar{y})^2}{n}}$$

where

y = net income for period t
$\bar{y}$ = average net income
n = number of periods

The higher the standard deviation, the greater the instability.

Coefficient of Variation

$$CV = \frac{SD}{\bar{y}}$$

The coefficient of variation is a relative measure of instability to facilitate a comparison between competing companies. The higher the coefficient, the greater the risk.

Instability Index of Earnings

$$I = \sqrt{\frac{\Sigma(y - y^T)^2}{n}}$$

where

y^T = trend earnings for period t, and is determined as follows:
$y^T = a + bt$

where

a = dollar intercept
b = slope of trend line
t = time period

Chapter 6: How to Analyze the Financial Structure of the Firm

Trend income is computed using a simple trend equation solved by computer. The index reflects the deviation between actual income and trend income. A higher index is reflective of greater instability.

Beta

Beta is calculated by a computer run based on the following equation:

$$r_{jt} = a_j + \beta_j\, r_{Mt} + E_{jt}$$

where

r_{jt} = return of security j for period t
a_j = constant
β_j = beta for security j
r_{Mt} = return on a market index such as the New York Stock Exchange index
E_{jt} = error term

Beta measures the systematic risk of a stock. A beta greater than one indicates the company's market price of stock vacillates more than the change in the market index, pointing to a risky security. Fluctuation in stock price implies greater business risk and instability with the firm. For example, a beta of 1.3 means the company's stock price rises or falls 30% faster than the market. A beta of one means the company's stock price moves the same as the market index. A beta of less than one indicates the company's stock price vacillates less than the stock market index, pointing to lower corporate risk. Of course, a company's beta may change over time. Betas for individual companies may be taken from various sources, such as Standard & Poor's.

EXAMPLE 6.1

A company shows the following trend in reported earnings:

20X0	$100,000
20X1	110,000
20X2	80,000
20X3	120,000
20X4	140,000

$$SD = \sqrt{\frac{\Sigma(y - \bar{y})^2}{n}}$$

$$\bar{y} = \frac{\Sigma y}{n} = \frac{100{,}000 + 110{,}000 + 80{,}000 + 120{,}000 + 140{,}000}{5}$$

$$= \frac{550{,}000}{5} = 100{,}000$$

Year	$(y - \bar{y})$	$(y - \bar{y})^2$
20X0	− 10,000	100,000,000
20X1	0	0
20X2	− 30,000	900,000,000
20X3	+ 10,000	100,000,000
20X4	+ 30,000	900,000,000
		2,000,000,000

$$SD = \sqrt{\frac{2{,}000{,}000{,}000}{5}} = \sqrt{4{,}000{,}000{,}000} = \underline{20{,}000}$$

$$CV = \frac{SD}{\bar{y}}$$

$$= \frac{20{,}000}{110{,}000} = \frac{18.2\%}{}$$

STABILITY ELEMENTS

When looking at earnings stability, it should be noted that the trend in income is more important than its absolute size.

Stable Revenue Sources

Stable revenue sources include the following:

- Nonoperating income that is recurring and serves as a cushion to total income. Examples are royalty income under long-term contracts with financially secure parties and rental income under long-term leases. Increased trends in the percentage of stable revenue sources to gross income and to net income are positive indicators.
- Obtaining further revenue from original sales. An example is maintenance services and replacement parts derived from selling an item. You should calculate the trend in replacement and maintenance revenue as a percentage of (1) new sales, (2) total revenue, and (3) net income.
- Sales to diversified industries (industries affected in different ways by cyclical factors).

- Good employee relations. Labor tranquility can be appraised by determining the number and duration of previous strikes, degree of union militancy, and employee turnover.

Abnormal and erratic income statement items (e.g., gain on the sale of land) distort the current year's net income as a predictor of future earnings. *Warning:* Watch out for a company that starts selling off part of its fixed assets, because it may be in a state of contraction.

Unstable Revenue Sources

Examples of unstable revenue sources are listed below.

- Export sales to a major foreign market that will disappear as that country develops a domestic capacity to manufacture the item.
- An opportunist market (e.g., electronic calculators) is a nonrepetitive source of earnings, since the saturation of a company's market will reduce its potential to derive continued earnings.
- Short-term schemes (e.g., a single government contract) increase earnings temporarily. You should determine the percentage of short-lived income to total revenue and to net income.
- The loss of a unique advantage in the near future that will hurt future years' revenues, such as the exhaustion of mineral rights.

PRODUCT LINE CHARACTERISTICS

A company's product line deeply affects its overall business stability and profitability. Where possible, product risk should be minimized, such as by moving toward negative correlation among products.

Product Line Measures

The degree of correlation between products is evident from a correlation matrix determined by a computer run.

Product demand elasticity is determined as follows:

$$\frac{\text{Percentage change in quantity}}{\text{Percentage change in price}}$$

110   Part I: Financial Analysis

If > 1   Elastic demand
If = 1   Unitary demand
If < 1   Inelastic demand

Red Flag: Products that are positively correlated and have elastic demands are of high risk. On the other hand, companies with product lines having negative correlations and inelastic demand (e.g., health-care products) are stable. Further, products with different seasonal peaks should be added to stabilize production and marketing operations.

EXAMPLE 6.2

The correlation matrix of a product line follows.

Product	A	B	C	D	E	F
A	1.0	.13	−.02	−.01	−.07	.22
B	.13	1.0	−.02	−.07	.00	.00
C	−.02	−.02	1.0	.01	.48	.13
D	−.01	−.07	.01	1.0	.01	−.02
E	−.07	.00	.48	.01	1.0	.45
F	.22	.00	.13	−.02	.45	1.0

Obviously, perfect correlation exists with the same product. For instance, the correlation between product F and product F is 1.0.

High positive correlation exists between products E and C (.48) and products E and F (.45). Because these products are tightly interwoven, risk exists.

Low negative correlation exists between products A and D (−.01) and products A and C (−.02).

No correlation is present between products B and E (.00) and products B and F (.00).

It would be better if some products had significant negative correlations (e.g., −.7) but such is not the case.

EXAMPLE 6.3

Data for products X and Y follow.

	X	Y
Selling price	$10	$8
Unit sales	10,000	13,000

Chapter 6: How to Analyze the Financial Structure of the Firm   111

If the selling price of product X is increased to $11, it is predicted that sales volume will decrease by 500 units. If the selling price of product Y is raised to $9.50, sales volume is anticipated to fall by 4,000 units.

Product demand elasticity equals:

$$\frac{\text{Percentage change in quantity}}{\text{Percentage change in price}}$$

Inelastic demand exists with product X:

$$\frac{\frac{500}{10,000}}{\frac{\$1}{\$10}} = \frac{.05}{.10} = .5$$

Elastic demand occurs with product Y:

$$\frac{\frac{4,000}{13,000}}{\frac{\$1.50}{\$8.00}} = \frac{.307}{.188} = 1.63$$

Variances in the product line may exist for volume, price, and cost. The greater the fluctuation in each, the wider the variability in earnings. You should examine variability for each major product by:

- Charting via graphs to uncover trends
- Determining the standard deviation
- Computing variances (discussed in Chapter 7)

Product Lines Promoting Stability

- Necessity items.
- Retail trade (mostly low-priced items appealing to a wide market).
- Growth and mature products.
- Low unit-cost items. These have a greater chance of succeeding in periods of economic health and also have greater resistance to declining demand in recessionary periods. If a firm with low-priced goods also provides a substitute for more expensive items (e.g., cereal for meat), it has a built-in hedge in inflationary and recessionary periods.

- "Piggy-back" product base where similar products are associated with the company's basic business.
- Ability to introduce new products. What is the number of patented products that come on stream annually?

Product Lines Causing Instability

- Novelty and nonessential goods.
- High-priced items (e.g., expensive jewelry) that add to variable demand during recessionary times. An exception is high-priced quality goods serving a select market, such as Mercedes-Benz, because the wealthy are not materially impacted by a temporary decline in economic conditions.
- Heavy goods and raw materials, because reduction in buying is magnified as it goes from the consumer to the source of production. For raw materials, there is price fluctuation in commodity markets as well as instability in demand for end products. With capital good sales, industry can postpone purchases of durable equipment.
- A single-product company since it has less stability and more obsolescence risk than a multiproduct one. *Recommendation:* Have a diversified product line to guard against adverse effects resulting from differing economic conditions. It is best to have negatively correlated items (e.g., winter clothing and summer clothing) to promote stability, as revenue obtained from one product increases while revenue obtained from the other decreases. At a minimum, there should be no correlation (e.g., food and office furniture). *Danger:* If a positive correlation exists between products (e.g., autos and steel), there is significant risk, since product demand moves in the same direction for both.
- Those that are susceptible to rapid changes in consumer tastes, such as novelty goods that depend on fads.
- Those closely tied to changes in real gross national product. You should try to move toward stable demand items.
- Those for which demand is obtained from a very few large industrial users. The loss of one customer can have a significant negative effect.
- Those with unusual demand coupled with skyrocketing prices (e.g., copper).
- High percentage of developmental products.
- Low profit margin products.

Ways to Measure Marketing Effectiveness

- Evaluate product warranty complaints and their dispositions.
- Calculate revenue, cost, and profit by product line, customer, industry segment, geographic area, distribution channel, type of marketing effort, and average order size.
- Evaluate new products in terms of risk and profitability.
- Appraise strengths and weaknesses of competition as well as their reactions to your promotion efforts.
- Determine revenue, marketing costs, and profits prior to, during, and subsequent to promotion programs.
- Appraise sales generated by different types of selling efforts (e.g., direct mail, television, newspaper).
- Analyze sales force effectiveness by determining the profit generated by salespeople, call frequency, sales incentives, sales personnel costs (e.g., auto), and dollar value of orders obtained per hour spent.
- Determine revenue and/or net income per employee.
- Examine the trend in the ratio of marketing costs to sales.
- Determine marketing share.
- Evaluate the trend in inventory at wholesalers and retailers, including order processing, packaging, warehousing, carrier, and customer services.

MEASURING A COMPANY'S SUCCESS

Compare Growth Rate to Competitors

A company's growth rate should be compared to that of competitors and industry norms.

Measures of Growth Rate

- $\dfrac{\text{Change in retained earnings}}{\text{Stockholders' equity at beginning of year}}$

- $\dfrac{\text{EPS (end of year)} - \text{EPS (beginning of year)}}{\text{EPS (beginning of year)}}$

The growth rate in sales, dividends, total assets, and the like may be computed in a similar fashion.

Look at Gross Profit

A high ratio of gross profit to sales is a good indicator, since it may mean the business is able to control its manufacturing costs.

Consider Raw Materials

In analyzing raw materials, we should determine variability in cost. *Recommendation:* Review trade publications for price instability. A problem exists if there is a lack of alternative raw material sources, especially if the current source of supply is unreliable. *Special Note:* Vertical integration reduces price and supply risk.

Management Quality

The success of a business depends greatly on the quality of executive decisions. Deficient competence in management holds in question the viability of the enterprise.

Signs of Poor Management Quality

- Instability and lack of experience of leadership
- Previous incidents of mismanagement
- Past occurrence of corporate bankruptcy
- Prior inaccurate management projections (e.g., overexaggerated predictions in the president's letter in the annual report)
- Inability to adjust to changing times (e.g., nature of the business)

RISK

In evaluating risk, you should compare the company's risk exposure to the competition and to past trends of the firm. Uncertainty about the business makes it difficult to reliably predict future performance.

Types of Risk

The following list covers some of the main risks you should consider:

- Corporate risk, such as overdependence on a few key executives or the underinsurance of assets (e.g., declining trend in insurance expense to fixed assets, unusual casualty losses). One means of minimizing corporate risk is to diversify operations.
- Social risk, such as a company experiencing customer boycotts or bias suits. One way of reducing social risk is to have some degree of community involvement by the firm.
- Environmental risk, such as a product line or service susceptible to changes in the weather. A way to lower this risk is to have counter-seasonal products.
- Industry risk, such as an industry under public and governmental scrutiny (e.g., real estate tax shelters). An approach to diminish industry risk is to move toward a variable-cost-oriented business.
- Economic risk, such as the effect of a depression on product demand. Curtail this risk by having a low-priced product substitute for a high-priced item (i.e., cereal for meat).
- Political risk, such as the need for lobbying efforts. Avoid operations in strictly regulated areas.

INDUSTRY CHARACTERISTICS

Corporate earnings are worth more if earned in a healthy, expanding industry than in an unhealthy, declining one. For example, an expanding and mature industry in which a restricted number of companies control a high percentage of the market and whose selling prices can be upwardly adjusted for rising costs, is in a strong position.

Labor-intensive businesses typically have greater stability than capital-intensive ones, since the former have a higher percentage of variable costs whereas the latter has a higher percentage of fixed costs. Capital-intensive industries have a higher susceptibility to cyclical performance. Companies in a staple industry have greater stability because of inelastic product demand.

A company may have variability because of an industry cycle. An example is the steel industry, which has a 5-to-10-year cycle because of the refurbishing of steel furnaces.

Industry Characteristics Indicative of Greater Risk

- High degree of competition. What is the ease of entry, price wars, and cheaper imports?

- Highly technological (e.g., computers), causing obsolescence risk and difficulty in keeping up to date.
- Overly dependent on energy, making it prone to energy shortages and price rises.
- Subject to tight governmental regulation, such as by a utility regulatory commission.
- Susceptibility to cyclical effects.
- High-risk product line without sufficient insurance coverage. If you have difficulty obtaining insurance in your industry, try to pool risks by setting up mutual insurance companies.

ECONOMIC FACTORS

If a company is insulated from the effect of changing economic conditions, it will have greater stability. *Recommendation:* To lessen the exposure to economic cycle effects, you should enter noncyclical or countercyclical lines of business. Further, geographic diversification reduces susceptibility to regional economic declines.

To the extent net income includes inflationary profits, it is overstated in an economic sense, because such profits arise from changes in the consumer price index (CPI) and/or replacement cost instead of from operational performance. You should thus compare CPI adjusted net income and current cost net income with the reported earnings. If the amount of reported earnings is significantly greater than the other net income measures, reported net income is overstated. Compare the following ratios: (1) constant dollar earnings to net income and (2) current cost earnings to net income. The lower the ratios, the lower the quality of earnings.

EXAMPLE 6.4

A company's net income for 20X1 is $4,000,000. CPI net income is $3,500,000, and current cost net income is $3,200,000. Its competitor reports net income for 20X1 of $2,000,000. It has CPI net income of $1,900,000 and current cost net income of $1,800,000.

Ratios showing inflationary effects for the companies follow.

	Company	*Competitor*
CPI net income to net income	87.5%	95.0%
Current cost net income to net income	80.0%	90.0%

The company's quality of earnings is lower than its competitor's, as evidenced by its lower ratios of CPI net income to net income and current cost net income to net income. The company's historically determined net income relative to inflation-adjusted profits is proportionately overstated compared with that of the competitor. The more that a company's net income exceeds the inflationary adjusted net income, the lower is its quality of earnings.

The absolute amount of reported net income is irrelevant.

Means to Counteract Inflation by Financial Management

Selling Price Strategy

- Upwardly adjust selling prices at short intervals (e.g., monthly).
- Have the ability to quickly modify price catalogues and sales literature. Different selling prices by distribution channel can be color coded—retail, distributor, stocking, repacker, etc.
- Keep price quotations only for short periods of time (e.g., 2 months).
- Base selling prices on a next-in, first-out basis to take into account replacement cost so that pricing is done ahead of inflation.
- Have cost-plus provisions in long-term contracts, perhaps tied to the CPI.

Cost Control

- Avoid product components that often experience excessive price increases.
- Substitute cheaper raw materials in products while maintaining control of quality and product warranty claims.
- Enter into futures contracts to lock yourself in to raw materials at currently lower prices.
- Contract for long-term purchase agreements and encourage suppliers to quote firm prices. Change a supplier if better terms are forthcoming.
- Periodically change insurance carriers when cost beneficial.
- Redesign truck logistics to reduce transportation costs.
- Segregate projects into self-contained economic units so success does not depend on the completion of the whole project to control rising costs.
- Hire temporary employees to handle peak work periods.

- To reduce high electric bills due to peak time usage, consider operating more shifts to level out the usage. Also, avoid a peak load period, such as by shutting off an air conditioner briefly when a furnace is turned on via a minicomputer-controlled energy system.
- Have a preventive maintenance program.

Marketing Strategy

- De-emphasize products significantly affected by inflation (e.g., production, promotion). Emphasize inflation-resistant product substitutes.
- Avoid marketing proposals mandating significant investments and long payback periods.
- Do not introduce unprofitable products unless technological change or design improvement can make them profitable in the future.

Labor Aspects

- Move toward automation to decrease the labor force.
- Tie salary increases to productivity improvements.

Financial Considerations

- Try to retain leased property at the end of the lease rather than encourage lessee purchase, because the lessor will be able to sell the property at a higher price (due to inflation) than the originally expected salvage value.
- Invest in real estate as an inflation hedge.
- Borrow from insurance companies against the cash surrender value of life insurance, because the rates are usually lower than the going interest rate.
- Do not pay out dividends in excess of inflation-adjusted earnings.
- Debt is advantageous: It results in a purchasing power gain because you are paying creditors back in cheaper dollars. On the other hand, holding monetary assets (e.g., cash, receivables) results in a purchasing power loss. Determine the ratio of monetary assets to monetary liabilities.

Obtaining Tax Benefits

- Companies depending on investments in fixed assets are in a poorer tax position than those relying on research and development (R&D). With

fixed assets, depreciation is charged over the asset's life so the tax reduction comes gradually. The present value of future tax savings should be ascertained here. Companies with R&D receive an immediate benefit; the full deductibility of such costs results in immediate cash flow.
- Adoption of the last-in, first-out inventory method results in lower taxable income since current costs are being matched against current revenue.

POLITICAL FACTORS

Political risk refers to foreign operations and governmental regulation. Multinational companies with significant foreign activities have uncertainties with respect to repatriation of funds, currency fluctuations, and local customs and regulations. Operations in politically and economically unstable foreign regions means instability.

Ratios to Be Examined
- Questionable foreign revenue to total revenue
- Questionable foreign earnings to net income
- Total export revenue to total revenue
- Total export earnings to net income
- Total assets in "questionable" foreign countries to total assets
- Total assets in foreign countries to total assets

Considerations in Foreign Operations

Foreign Exchange Rates
Red Flag: Vacillating foreign exchange rates, which can be measured by the percentage change over time and/or its standard deviation. When foreign assets are appropriately balanced against foreign liabilities, you are better insulated from changes in exchange rates, thus stabilizing earnings. Evaluate your exposed position for each foreign country in which there is a major operation. When the dollar is devalued, net foreign assets and income in countries with strong currencies are worth more dollars. Forward exchange contracts should be viewed positively, since the company is trying to minimize its foreign currency exposure by hedging against exchange risks emanating from foreign currency transactions.

You should also consider the foreign country's tax rate and duties.

Government Contracts and Subsidies

Companies dependent on government contracts and subsidies have more instability, since government spending is vulnerable to changing political whims of legislators and war-threatening situations. *Suggestion:* Determine the percentage of earnings obtained from government contract work and subsidies, and the extent to which such work and subsidies are recurring.

Look at the degree of government regulation over the company because it affects the bottom line (e.g., utility rate increases are less than that which has been asked for). *Recommendation:* Examine present and prospective effects of governmental interference on the company by reviewing current and proposed laws and regulations of governmental bodies. Possible sources of such information are legislative hearings, trade journals, and newspapers. Stringent environmental and safety regulations may eat into profits.

Analyze the effect on the company of present and proposed tax legislation. What are the areas of IRS scrutiny?

CONCLUSION

Analysis and evaluation of the company's financial structure and stability are needed to ascertain profit potential, degree of risk, and viability. Areas of analysis include sources of earnings, economic and inflationary effects, political aspects, industry characteristics, and marketing effectiveness. Quantitative measurements can be looked at over time to gauge performance.

7 Using Variance Analysis as a Financial Tool

A standard cost is a predetermined cost of manufacturing, servicing, or marketing an item during a given future period. It is based on current and projected future conditions. The norm is also dependent upon quantitative and qualitative measurements. Standards are set at the beginning of the period. Examples are sales quotas, standard costs (e.g., material price, wage rate), and standard volume.

Variance analysis compares standard to actual performance. Variances may be as detailed as necessary, considering the cost–benefit relationship. Evaluation of variances may be done yearly, quarterly, monthly, daily, or hourly, depending on the importance of identifying a problem quickly. Because you do not know actual figures (e.g., hours spent) until the end of the period, variances can only be arrived at then. A material variance requires highlighting who is responsible and taking corrective action. Insignificant variances need not be looked into further unless they recur repeatedly and/or reflect potential difficulty.

One measure of materiality is to divide the variance by the standard cost. A variance of less than 5% may be deemed immaterial. In some cases, materiality is looked at in terms of dollar amount or volume level. For example, you may set a policy looking into any variance that exceeds $10,000 or 20,000 units, whichever is less. Guidelines for materiality also depend upon the nature of the particular element as it affects corporate performance and decision making. For example, where the item is critical to the future functioning of the business (e.g., critical part, promotion, repairs), limits for materiality should be such that reporting is encouraged. Further, statistical techniques can be used to ascertain the significance of cost and revenue variances.

Often the reason for the variance is out-of-date standards or a poor budgetary process. Thus, it may not be due to actual performance.

USEFULNESS OF VARIANCE ANALYSIS

Standards and variance analyses resulting therefrom are essential in financial analysis and decision making.

Advantages of Standards and Variances

- Assist in decision making.
- Sell price formulation.
- Set and evaluate corporate objectives.
- Cost control.
- Highlight problem areas through the "management by exception" principle.
- Pinpoint responsibility for undesirable performance so that corrective action may be taken. Variances in product activity (cost, quantity, quality) are typically the foreman's responsibility; variances in sales are often the responsibility of the marketing manager; variances in profit usually relate to overall operations. It should be noted that if variances indicate strengths, further advantage of them should be taken.
- Facilitate communication within the organization.
- Assist in planning by forecasting needs (e.g., cash requirements).
- Establish bid prices on contracts.

STANDARD SETTING

Standards are based on the particular situation being appraised. Some examples follow:

Situation	Standard
Cost reduction	Tight
Pricing policy	Realistic
High-quality goods	Perfection

Types of Standards

- *Basic.* These are not changed from period to period. They form the basis to which later period performance is compared. What is unrealistic about it is that no consideration is given to a change in the environment.
- *Maximum efficiency.* These are perfect standards assuming ideal, optimal conditions. Realistically, certain inefficiencies will occur.
- *Currently attainable.* These are based on efficient activity. They are possible but difficult to achieve. Considered are normal occurrences, such as anticipated machinery failure.
- *Expected.* These are expected figures, which come very close to actual figures.

SALES VARIANCES

Sales variances are computed to gauge the performance of the marketing function.

EXAMPLE 7.1

Western Corporation's budgeted sales for 20X1 were:

Product A: 10,000 units at $6.00 per unit	$ 60,000
Product B: 30,000 units at $8.00 per unit	240,000
Expected sales revenue	$300,000

Actual sales for the year were:

Product A: 8,000 units at $6.20 per unit	$ 49,600
Product B: 33,000 units at $7.70 per unit	254,100
Actual sales revenue	$303,700

There is a favorable sales variance of $3,700, consisting of the sales price variance and the sales volume variance.

The sales price variance equals:

Actual selling price vs. Budgeting selling price × Actual units sold

Product A ($6.20 vs. $6.00 × 8,000)	$1,600	Favorable
Product B ($7.70 vs. $8.00 × 33,000)	9,900	Unfavorable
Sales price variance	$8,300	Unfavorable

The sales volume variance equals:

Actual quantity vs. Budgeted quantity × Budgeted selling price
Product A (8,000 vs. 10,000 × $6.00) $12,000 Unfavorable
Product B (33,000 vs. 30,000 × $8.00)   24,000 Favorable
Sales volume variance $12,000 Favorable

Proof:

Sales price variance $ 8,300 Unfavorable
Sales volume variance   12,000 Favorable
Sales variance $ 3,700 Favorable

COST VARIANCES

When a product is made or a service is performed, you have to compute these three measures:

- Actual cost equals actual price times actual quantity, where actual quantity equals actual quantity per unit of work times actual units of work produced.
- Standard cost equals standard price times standard quantity, where standard quantity equals standard quantity per unit of work times actual units of work produced.
- Control variance equals actual cost less standard cost.

Control variance has the following elements:

- Price (rate, cost) variance (standard price versus actual price times actual quantity).
- Quantity (usage, efficiency) variance (standard quantity versus actual quantity times standard price).

These are computed for both material and labor. A variance is unfavorable when actual cost is higher than standard cost.

Material Variances

You can use the material price variance to evaluate the activity of the purchasing department and to see the impact of changes in raw material cost on profitability. The material quantity variance is the responsibility of the production supervisor.

EXAMPLE 7.2

The standard cost of one unit of output (product or service) was $15: three pieces at $5 per piece. During the period, 8,000 units were made. Actual cost was $14 per unit: two pieces at $7 per piece.

Material Control Variance:

Standard quantity × Standard price (24,000 × $5)	$120,000
Actual quantity × Actual price (16,000 × $7)	112,000
	$ 8,000 F

Material Price Variance:

Standard price versus Actual price × Actual quantity ($5 vs. $7 × 16,000)	$ 32,000 U

Material Quantity Variance:

Standard quantity versus Actual quantity × Standard price (24,000 vs. 16,000 × $5)	$ 40,000 F

You cannot control material price variances when higher prices are due to inflation or shortage situations.

The reason and responsible party for an unfavorable material variance follows:

Reason	Responsible Party
Overstated price paid	Purchasing
Failure to detect defective goods	Receiving
Inefficient labor or poor supervision	Foreman
Poor mix in material	Production manager
Rush delivery of materials	Traffic
Unfavorable quantity variance	Foreman
Unexpected change in production volume	Sales manager

To correct for an unfavorable material price variance, you can increase selling price, substitute cheaper materials, change a production method or specification, or engage in a cost-reduction program.

Labor Variances

The standard labor rate should be based on the contracted hourly wage rate. Where salary rates are set by union contract, the labor rate variance will usually be minimal. Labor efficiency standards are typically estimated by engineers on the basis of an analysis of the production operation.

Labor variances are determined in a manner similar to that in which material variances are determined.

EXAMPLE 7.3

The standard cost of labor is four hours times $9 per hour, or $36 per unit. During the period, 7,000 units were produced. The actual cost is six hours times $8 per hour, or $48 per unit.

Labor Control Variance:

Standard quantity × Standard price (28,000 × $9)	$252,000
Actual quantity × actual price (42,000 × $8)	336,000
	$ 84,000 U

Labor Price Variance:

Standard price versus Actual price × Actual quantity ($9 vs. $8 × 42,000)	$ 42,000 F

Labor Quantity Variance

Standard quantity versus Actual quantity × Standard price (28,000 vs. 42,000 × $9)	$126,000 U

Possible reasons for a labor price variance and the one responsible follow.

Reason	Responsible Party
Use of overpaid or excessive number of workers	Production manager or union contract
Poor job descriptions	Personnel
Overtime	Production planning

In the case of a shortage of skilled workers, it may be impossible to avoid an unfavorable labor price variance.

The cause and responsibility entity for an unfavorable labor efficiency variance follows:

Cause	Responsible Entity
Inadequate supervision	Foreman
Improper functioning of equipment	Maintenance
Insufficient material supply or poor quality	Purchasing

Overhead Variances

The overhead variance comprises the controllable and volume variances. Relevant computations follow:

- Overhead control variance equals actual overhead versus standard overhead (standard hours times standard overhead rate).
- Controllable variance equals actual overhead versus budget adjusted to standard hours. *Note:* Budget adjusted to standard hours equals fixed overhead plus variable overhead (standard hours times standard variable overhead rate).
- Volume variance equals standard overhead versus budget adjusted to standard hours.

EXAMPLE 7.4

The following data are provided:

Budgeted overhead (includes fixed overhead of $7,500 and variable overhead of $10,000)	$17,500
Budgeted hours	10,000
Actual overhead	$ 8,000
Actual units produced	800
Standard hours per unit of production	5

Preliminary calculations:

Budgeted fixed overhead ($7,500/10,000 hr)	$0.75
Budgeted variable overhead ($10,000/10,000 hr)	1.00
Total budgeted overhead ($17,500/10,000 hr)	$1.75
Standard hours (800 units × 5 hr per unit)	4,000

Overhead Control Variance:

Actual overhead		$8,000
Standard overhead		
Standard hours	4,000 hr	
Standard overhead rate	× $1.75	7,000
		$1,000 U

Controllable Variance:

Actual overhead		$8,000
Budget adjusted to standard hours		
Fixed overhead	$7,500	
Variable overhead (Standard hours		
× Standard variable overhead rate)		
(4,000 × $1)	4,000	11,500
		$ 3,500 F

Volume Variance:

Standard overhead	$ 7,000
Budget adjusted to standard hours	11,500
	$ 4,500 U

The controllable variance is the responsibility of the foreman, since he influences actual overhead incurred. The volume variance is the responsibility of management executives and production managers, since they are involved with plant utilization.

Variable overhead variance information is helpful in arriving at the output level and output mix decisions. It also assists in appraising decisions regarding variable inputs. Fixed overhead variance data provide information regarding decision-making astuteness when buying some combination of fixed plant size and variable production inputs.

Possible Reasons for a Recurring Unfavorable Overhead Volume Variance

- Buying the wrong size plant
- Improper scheduling
- Insufficient orders
- Shortages in material
- Machinery failure

- Long operating time
- Inadequately trained workers

When idle capacity exists, this may indicate long-term operating planning problems.

VARIANCES TO EVALUATE MARKETING EFFORT

Prior to setting a marketing standard in a given trade territory, you should examine prior, current, and forecasted conditions for the company itself and that given geographical area. Standards will vary depending upon geographical location. In formulating standard costs for the transportation function, minimum cost traffic routes should be selected on the basis of the given distribution pattern.

Standards for advertising cost in particular territories will vary depending upon the types of advertising media needed, which are in turn based on the type of customers the advertising is intended to reach as well as the nature of the competition.

Some direct selling costs can be standardized, such as product presentations for which a standard time per sales call can be established. Direct selling expenses should be related to distance traveled, frequency of calls made, etc. If sales commissions are based on sales generated, standards can be based on a percentage of net sales.

Time and motion studies are usually a better way of establishing standards than prior performance, since the past may include inefficiencies.

Cost variances for the selling function may pertain to the territory, product, or personnel.

Salesperson Variances

You should appraise your sales force within a territory, including time spent and expenses incurred.

EXAMPLE 7.5

Sales data for your company follow.

Standard cost	$240,000
Standard salesperson days	2,000
Standard rate per salesperson day	$ 120

130   Part I: Financial Analysis

Actual cost $238,000
Actual salesperson days 1,700
Actual rate per salesperson day $ 140

Total Cost Variance:

Actual cost $238,000
Standard cost 240,000
$ 2,000 F

The control variance is broken down into salesperson days and salesperson costs.

Variance in Salesperson Days:

Actual days versus Standard days × Standard rate per day
(1,700 vs. 2,000 × $120) $ 36,000 F

The variance is favorable because the territory was handled in fewer days than expected.

Variance in Salesperson Costs:

Actual rate versus Standard rate × Actual days
($140 vs. $120 × 1,700) $ 34,000 U

An unfavorable variance results because the actual rate per day is greater than the expected rate per day.

EXAMPLE 7.6

A salesperson called on 55 customers and sold each an average of $2,800 worth of merchandise. The standard number of calls is 50, and the standard sale is $2,400. Variance analysis looking at calls and sales follows.

Total Variance:

The elements of the $34,000 variance are

Actual calls × Actual sale   55 × $2,800 $154,000
Standard calls × Standard sale 50 × $2,400   120,000
$ 34,000

Variance in Calls:

Actual calls versus Standard calls × Standard sale
(55 vs. 50 × $2,400) $12,000

Variance in Sales:

Actual sale versus Standard sale × Standard calls
($2,800 vs. $2,400 × 50) $20,000

Joint Variance:

(Actual calls versus Standard calls) × (Actual sale versus Standard sale)
(55 vs. 50) × ($2,800 vs. $2,400) $ 2,000

Variances in Warehousing Costs

Variances in warehousing costs can be calculated by looking at the cost per unit to store the merchandise and the number of orders anticipated.

EXAMPLE 7.7

The following information applies to a product:

Standard cost	$12,100
Standard orders	5,500
Standard unit cost	$2.20
Actual cost	$14,030
Actual orders	6,100
Actual unit cost	$2.30

Total Warehousing Cost Variance:

Actual cost	$14,030
Standard cost	12,100
	$ 1,930 U

The total variance is segregated into the variance in orders and variance in cost.

Variance in Orders:

Actual orders versus Standard orders × Standard unit cost
6,100 vs. 5,500 × $2.20 $1,320 U

Variance in Cost:

Actual cost per unit versus Standard cost per unit × Actual orders
$2.30 vs. $2.20 × 6,100 $610 U

CONCLUSION

Variance analysis is essential in the organization for the appraisal of all aspects of the business, including manufacturing, marketing, and service. Significant unfavorable variances must be examined to ascertain whether they are controllable by management or uncontrollable because they solely relate to external factors. When controllable, immediate corrective action must be undertaken to handle the problem. If a variance is favorable, an examination should be made of the reasons for it so that corporate policy may include the positive aspects found. Further, the responsible entity for a favorable variance should be recognized and rewarded.

PART II:

Evaluating Assets, Liabilities, and Potential Acquisitions

8 How to Evaluate Business Segments

Analysis of segmental performance assists in determining the success or failure of the divisional manager as well as the division itself. Divisional performance measures are concerned with the contribution of the division to profit and quality and whether the division meets the overall goals of the company.

APPRAISING MANAGER PERFORMANCE

In appraising manager performance, you must determine which factors were under the manager's control (e.g., advertising budget) and which factors were not (e.g., economic conditions). Comparison should be made of one division in the company to other divisions, as well as to a similar division in a competing company. Appraisal should also be made of the risk and earning potential of a division.

Importance of Measuring Performance of Divisional Manager

- Assists in formulating management incentives and controlling operations to meet corporate goals
- Directs upper management attention where it would be most productive
- Determines whom to reward for good performance
- Determines who is not doing well so corrective action may be taken
- Provides job satisfaction since the manager receives feedback

In decentralization, profit responsibility is assigned among subunits of the company. Decentralization is most effective in organizations where cost and profit measurements are necessary and in organizations where subunits are totally independent and autonomous.

Advantages of Decentralization

- Top management has more time for strategic planning.
- Decisions are made by managers with the most knowledge of local conditions.
- There is greater managerial input in decision making.
- Managers have more control over results resulting in greater motivation.

Disadvantages of Decentralization

- Managers become "narrow-sighted" and look solely at the division rather than the company as a whole.
- Duplication of services can result.
- There is an increased cost in obtaining additional information.

For comparison purposes, replacement cost instead of historical cost should be employed. It furnishes a relative basis of comparison because it represents the comparable necessary investment at the end of a reporting period. Evaluating replacement cost assists in comparing asset valuation to current productivity. If replacement cost cannot be determined, valuation can be based on the present value of future net cash flows.

The major means of analyzing divisional performance are cost center, profit center, and investment center.

COST CENTER

A cost center is typically the smallest segment of activity or responsibility area for which costs are accumulated. This approach is usually employed by departments rather than divisions. Departmental profit is difficult to derive because of problems in allocating revenue and costs.

In the cost center approach, you compare budgeted cost to actual cost. Variances are investigated to determine the reasons for them, necessary corrective action is taken to correct problems, and efficiencies are accorded recognition. The cost center approach is useful when a manager possesses control over costs at a specified operating level. *Recommendation:* Use this approach when problems arise in relating financial measures to output. *Suggestion:* Cost center evaluation is most suitable for the following functions: accounting and financial reporting, legal, computer services, marketing, personnel, and public relations and similar areas where there is a problem in quantifying the output in financial terms.

Note: You will find the cost center approach appropriate for nonprofit and governmental units where budgetary appropriations are assigned. Actual expenditures are compared to budgetary amounts. A manager's performance depends on his or her ability to achieve output levels given budgetary constraints.

When looking at a manager's performance, say at bonus time, the relevant costs are those incremental costs he or she has control over. Incremental costs are those expenditures that would not exist if the center were abandoned. Hence, allocated common costs (e.g., general administration) should not be included in appraising manager performance. Such costs should, however, be allocated in determining the profit figure for the entire division. Cost allocation must conform to goal congruence and autonomy, and should be applied consistently among divisions.

Cost center evaluation will not be worthwhile unless reliable budget figures exist. If a division's situation significantly changes, an adjustment to the initial budget is necessary. In such a case, actual cost should be compared with the initial budget figure (original goal) and the revised budget. Flexible budgets should be prepared to enable you to look at costs incurred at different levels of capacity. For example, if figures are budgeted for expected capacity, optimistic capacity, and pessimistic capacity, better comparisons of budget to actual can thus be made given changing circumstances.

When a transfer occurs between cost centers, the transfer price should be based upon actual cost, standard cost, or controllable cost. Transfer price is the price charged between divisions for a product or service. *Warning:* Using actual cost has the problem of passing cost inefficiencies onto the next division. There is no incentive for the transfer to control costs. *Solution:* Using standard cost corrects the problem of transferring cost inefficiencies to the next division, but it should be noted that standard cost includes allocated fixed cost, which might be subjective.

A good transfer price is a controllable cost. *What to Do:* Charge the cost center with actual controllable cost, and credit it with standard controllable cost for the assembled product or service to other divisions. *Rectifying the Problem:* By including just controllable cost, the subjectivity of the allocation of fixed noncontrollable cost does not exist.

In evaluating administrative functions, prepare performance reports examining dollar indicators such as executive salaries and service department costs as well as nondollar measures such as number of files handled, phone calls taken, and invoices processed.

PROFIT CENTER

A profit center has revenue and expenses associated with it. *Benefits:* The profit center approach enhances decentralization and provides units for decision-making purposes. *When to Use:* Use it when there is a self-contained division (with its own manufacturing and distribution facilities) and when there are a limited number of interdivision transfers. The reason for this is that the profit reported by the division is basically independent of other divisions' operating activities. Each division's profit should be independent of performance efficiency and managerial decisions elsewhere in the company. Further, divisional earnings should not be increased by any action reducing overall corporate profitability. Also use profit center when divisional managers have decision-making authority in terms of the quantity and mix of goods or services manufactured. With a profit center you determine net income as if the division were a separate economic entity; therefore, the manager is more cognizant of outside market considerations. There are different ways of expressing profit, such as net income, contribution margin, gross profit, controllable profit, and incremental profit.

It is not essential that fixed costs be allocated. Hence, contribution margin may be a good indicator of divisional performance. If each division meets its target contribution margin, excess contribution margin will be adequate to cover general corporate expenses. A contribution margin income statement can be prepared to evaluate divisional and managerial performance. It also aids in computing selling price, the price to accept an order given an idle capacity situation, output levels, maximization of resource uses, and break-even analysis. The contribution margin income statement is illustrated in Figure 8.1. *Note:* Controllable costs are under the division manager's control. They are the incremental costs of operating a division. In effect, they are costs that could have been avoided by the company if the division was shut down. Noncontrollable costs are common to a group of divisions that are rationally allocated to them.

FIGURE 8.1 Contribution Margin Income Statement for Divisional Performance Evaluation

- Sales
- Less variable production cost of sales
- Manufacturing contribution margin
- Less variable selling and administrative expenses
- Contribution margin
- Less controllable fixed costs (i.e., salesperson salaries)
- Controllable contribution margin by manager (measures performance of the segment manager)
- Less uncontrollable fixed costs (i.e., depreciation, property taxes, insurance)
- Segment contribution margin (measures performance of the division)
- Less unallocated costs to divisions (excessively difficult to allocate objectively or illogical to allocate, such as the president's salary, corporate research)
- Income before taxes (measures performance of the company in its entirety)

A difficulty with the profit center idea is that profit is calculated after subtracting noncontrollable costs or costs not directly related to divisional activity that have been arbitrarily allocated. The ensuing profit figure may hence be erroneous. However, cost allocation is required, because divisions must incorporate nondivisional costs that must be met before the company will show a profit. *Special Note:* Policies optimizing divisional earnings will likewise optimize corporate earnings even before the allocation of nondivisional expenses.

Advantages of the profit center approach are that it creates competition in a decentralized company, provides goal congruence between a division and the company, and aids performance evaluation. A drawback is that profits can be "messaged," since expenses may be shifted among periods. Examples of discretionary costs where management has wide latitude are research and repairs. Also, not considered is the total assets employed in the division to obtain the profit.

EXAMPLE 8.1

You can sell a product at its intermediate point in Division A for $170 or its final point in Division B at $260. The outlay cost in Division A is $120, while the outlay cost in Division B is $110. Unlimited product demand exists for both the intermediate product and the final product. Capacity is interchangeable. Divisional performance follows.

	Division A	Division B
Selling price	$170	$260
Outlay cost—A	(120)	(120)
Outlay cost—B	—	(110)
Profit	$ 50	$ 30

Sell at the intermediate point because of the higher profit.

Other measures in appraising divisional performance that are not of a profit nature that must be considered are

- Productivity measures, including input–output relationships. An example is labor hours in a production run. We have to consider the input in terms of time and money, and the resulting output in terms of quantity and quality. Does the maintenance of equipment ensure future growth?
- Personnel development (e.g., number of promotions)
- Market measures (e.g., market share, product leadership)
- Product leadership indicators (e.g., patented products, innovative technology)
- Human resource relationships (e.g., employee turnover rate, customer relations, including on-time deliveries)
- Social responsibility measures (e.g., consumer medals)

Transfer Pricing

A transfer price has to be formulated so that a realistic and meaningful profit figure can be determined for each division. It should be established only after proper planning. The transfer price is the one credited to the selling division and charged to the buying division for an internal transfer of an assembled product or service. It is the same for each as if an "arm's length" transaction had taken place.

Recommendation: The best transfer price is the negotiated market value of the assembled product or service, since it is a fair price and treats each profit center as a separate economic entity. It equals the outside service fee or selling price for the item, less internal cost savings that result from dealing internally within the organization (e.g., advertising, sales commission, delivery charges). The market value of services performed is based on the going rate for a specific job (e.g., equipment tuneup) and/or the standard hourly rate (e.g., the hourly rate for a plumber). If two divisions cannot agree on the transfer price, it will be settled by arbitration at a higher level. A temporarily low transfer price (due to oversupply of the item, for example) or high transfer price (due to a strike situation causing a supply shortage, for example), should not be employed.

Solution: Use the average long-term market price. If the outside market price is not ascertainable (e.g., new product, absence of replacement market), you should use budgeted cost plus profit markup, because this transfer price approximates market value and will spot divisional inefficiencies. Profit markup should take into account the particular characteristics of the division rather than the overall corporate profit margin. There is an incentive to the selling division to control its costs because it will not be credited for an amount in excess of budgeted cost plus a markup. Thus, if the selling division's inefficiencies resulted in actual costs being excessive, it would have to absorb the decline in profit to the extent that actual cost exceeded budgeted cost. Profit markup should be as realistic as possible given the nature of the division and its product.

Note: Even though actual cost plus profit markup is used by some, it has the drawback of passing on cost inefficiencies. In fact, the selling division is encouraged to be cost-inefficient, since the higher its actual cost, the higher will be its selling price (since it shows a greater profit). Some use actual cost as the transfer price, but the problem there is that no profit is shown by the selling division, and cost inefficiencies are passed on.

Incremental cost is another transfer pricing possibility. Incremental costs are the variable costs of making and shipping goods and any costs directly and exclusively traceable to the product. This cost is quite good for use for the company as a whole, but does little for measuring divisional performance. The incremental cost approach assumes the selling division has sufficient capacity to satisfy internal company demands as well as demands of outside customers.

Another way of setting the transfer price is dual pricing. It occurs when the buying division is charged with variable cost ($1) and the selling division is credited with absorption cost and markup ($1.50 plus 60%). Under dual pricing, there is a motivational effect, since each division's performance is enhanced by the transfer. However, profit for the company as a whole will be less than the sum of the division's profits.

A last possibility is allocating profit among divisions, say, based on input by departments (e.g., time spent, costs incurred).

Factors to Consider in Selecting a Transfer Price

- *Goal congruence.* Does the transfer price promote organizational goals to divisions?
- *Performance evaluation.* Does the transfer price come up with the best reflection of value of the transferred product or service that is fair to the selling division and buying division?
- *Autonomy.* Does the transfer price preserve autonomy among divisions?
- *Conformity with requirements.* Does the transfer price meet tax requirements, legal restrictions, and tariff considerations?

EXAMPLE 8.2

Division A manufactures an assembled product that can be sold to outsiders or transferred to Division B. Relevant information for the period follows.

Division A	Units
Production	1,500
Transferred to Division B	1,200
Sold outside	300
Selling price $25	
Unit cost $ 5	

The units transferred to Division B were processed further at a cost of $7. They were sold outside at $45. Transfers are at market value.

Division profit is:

	Division A	Division B	Company
Sales	$ 7,500	$54,000	$61,500
Transfer price	30,000		
	$37,500	$54,000	$61,500
Product cost	$ 7,500	$ 8,400	$15,900
Transfer price		30,000	
	$ 7,500	$38,400	$15,900
Profit	$30,000	$15,600	$45,600

EXAMPLE 8.3

Zeno Corporation manufactures radios. It has two production divisions (assembly and finishing) and one service division (maintenance). The assembly division both sells assembled radios to other companies and transfers them for further processing to the finishing division. The transfer price used is market value. Relevant data follow.

Assembly Division:
Outside sales: 1,000 assembled radios at $30 (included in the price is selling commission fees of $1 per unit and freight costs of $2 per unit).
Transferred to finishing division: 10,000 assembled radios.
Direct costs $80,000
Indirect costs $45,000

Finishing Division:
Outside sales: 10,000 finished radios at $55
Direct costs $90,000
Indirect costs $30,000

Maintenance Division:
Direct costs (direct labor, parts) $80,000
Indirect costs $25,000
9,000 hours rendered for servicing to Assembly Division
12,000 hours rendered for servicing to Finishing Division
Standard hourly rate: $8

A schedule of the gross profit of the separate divisions and the gross profit of Zeno Corporation is shown in Table 8.1.

EXAMPLE 8.4

An assembly division wants to charge a finishing division $80 per unit for an internal transfer of 800 units. The variable cost per unit is $50. Total fixed cost in the assembly division is $200,000. Current production is 10,000 units. Idle capacity exists. The finishing division can purchase the item outside for $73 per unit.

The maximum transfer price should be $73, which is the cost to buy it from outside. The finishing division should not have to pay a price greater than the outside market price.

Whether the buying division should be permitted to buy the item outside or be forced to buy inside depends on what is better for overall corporate profitability. Typically, the buying division is required to purchase inside at the maximum transfer price ($73), since the selling division still has to meet its fixed cost when idle capacity exists. The impact on corporate profitability of having the buying division go outside is determined as follows:

TABLE 8.1 Gross Profit, Zeno Corporation

	Assembly	Finishing	Maintenance	Transfers	Zeno
Revenue					
Sales	$ 30,000	$550,000			$580,000
Transfers	270,000			$270,000	
			$ 72,000	72,000	
			96,000	96,000	
Total	$300,000	$550,000	$168,000	$438,000	$580,000
Costs					
Direct	$ 80,000	$ 90,000	$ 80,000		$250,000
Indirect	45,000	30,000	25,000		100,000
Transfers:					
—Maintenance	72,000	96,000		$168,000	
—Assembly		270,000		270,000	
Total Costs	$197,000	$486,000	$105,000	$438,000	$350,000
Gross Profit	$103,000	$ 64,000	$ 63,000	—	$230,000
Assembly revenue					
Sales $30 × 1000					
Transfer price $27 × 10,000					

Savings to assembly division (units × variable cost per unit): 800 × $50 $40,000

Cost to finishing division (units × outside selling price): 800 × $73   58,400

Stay inside $18,400

The buying division will be asked to purchase inside the company, because if it went outside, corporate profitability would decline by $18,400.

INVESTMENT CENTER

A divisional investment is the amount placed in that division and placed under division management control. Two major divisional performance indicators are return on investment (ROI) and residual income. We should use available total assets in these measures to take into account all assets in the division, whether used or not. By including nonproductive assets in the base, the manager is motivated either to retain or sell them. Assets assigned to a division include direct assets in the division and allocated corporate assets. Assets are reflected at book value. *Suggestion*: Include facilities being constructed in the investment base if the division is committing the funds for the new asset.

You should distinguish between controllable and noncontrollable investment. While the former is helpful in appraising a manager's performance, the latter is used to evaluate the entire division. Controllable investment depends on the degree of a division's autonomy.

In obtaining divisional investment, there has to be an allocation of general corporate assets to that division. These allocated assets are not considered part of controllable investment. Assets should be allocated to divisions on the basis of usage measures (e.g., area occupied). *What to Do:* The allocated investment should be part of the division's investment base, but not as an element of controllable investment. Do not allocate general corporate assets attributable to the company as a whole (e.g., security investments). *Advice:* Do not allocate an asset if it requires excessive subjectivity.

The optimal way to assign cash to a division is to agree upon a cash level that meets the minimum needs of the division. If cash is held in excess of this level, there should be an interest income credit using current interest rates. Because the division typically earns a higher return rate on investment than the prevailing interest rate, it will voluntarily return excess cash to the company. This policy maximizes the overall corporate return. Accounts receivable should be assigned to divisions based on sales. Finished goods should be included in the asset base. The division manager has control over it because he or she determines the production level on the basis of expected sales. Excessive finished goods inventory is partly due to a division's inadequate planning. *Recommendation:* Use the opportunity cost of funds tied up in inventory that could be invested elsewhere for a return in determining divisional profit. Plant and equipment should be allocated on the basis of square footage.

The valuation of assets can be based on book value, gross cost, consumer price index (CPI) adjusted cost, replacement cost, or sales value. Typically, historical cost measures are employed in practice because of availability and consistency with balance sheet valuation. *Warning:* Using book value for asset valuation will artificially increase divisional return on investment as assets become older, since the denominator using book value becomes lower over time. Gross cost corrects for this decline in value, but it still does not consider inflationary cost increases. However, an advantage of using gross book value to value assets is that it is not affected by changes in expansion rates. *Note:* CPI adjusted value takes into account changing price levels. *Recommendation:* Replacement cost is ideal because it truly reflects the current prices of assets. Alternative ways exist to determine replacement cost (e.g., present value of future cash flows, specific price index of item, and current market value). *Tip:* Inventory accounted for using LIFO should be adjusted to the FIFO basis or the replacement value, so that inventory is stated at current prices.

Current liabilities should be subtracted in determining the asset base because divisional financing policy depends on the decision of upper management.

Return on Investment

Net income determination for return on investment (ROI) purposes requires that divisional earnings measurements comply with the following guidelines:

- Divisional earnings should not be tied to operational efficiency and quality of managerial decisions of other segments.
- Divisional earnings should include all items the divisional manager has control over.
- Divisional earnings should not be increased because of any action that negatively affects current or future profits.

ROI is a superior indicator when the investment employed is outside of the manager's determination. *Caution:* If a manager can significantly determine the capital employed, the return rate is a weakened tool.

$$\text{ROI} = \frac{\text{Net income}}{\text{Available total assets}}$$

Alternative measures are:

$$\frac{\text{Operating profit}}{\text{Available total assets}}$$

$$\frac{\text{Controllable operating profit}}{\text{Controllable net investment} \left(\text{Controllable assets} - \text{Controllable liabilities} \right)}$$

Note: With respect to the last measure, depreciation is a controllable cost since changes in the asset base are controllable by the division manager. *Interesting Point:* Excluded from controllable investment is equipment the manager wants to sell but is unable to because the company is trying to get an alternative use by another division or central headquarters. *Recommendation:* Transfer this asset from the division's controllable investment base. Also, controllable fixed assets allocated to divisions (e.g., research facilities, general administrative offices) should be excluded from controllable investment.

Advantages of ROI

- Highlights unprofitable divisions. Perhaps some should be disposed of?
- Can be used as a base against which to evaluate divisions within the company and to compare the division to a comparable division in a competing company.
- Assigns profit responsibility.
- Aids in appraising divisional manager performance.
- When a division maximizes its ROI, the company similarly maximizes its ROI.
- Places emphasis on high-return items.

Disadvantages of ROI

- Alternative profitability measures could be used in the numerator besides net income (e.g., gross profit, contribution margin, segment margin).
- Different assets in the division must earn the same return rate regardless of the assets' riskiness.
- To boost profits, needed expenditures may not be incurred (e.g., repairs, research). Here, look at the ratio over time of discretionary costs to sales.
- A division may not want to acquire fixed assets because it will lower its ROI.
- A labor-intensive division generally has a higher ROI than a capital-intensive one.
- ROI is a static indicator; it does not show future flows.
- A lack of goal congruence may exist between the company and a division. For instance, if a company's ROI is 12%, a division's ROI is 18%, and a project's ROI is 16%, the division manager will not accept the project because it will lower the ROI, even though the project is best for the entire company.
- It ignores risk.

EXAMPLE 8.5

You are concerned about your company's current return on investment. Your company's income statement for year 20X1 follows.

Sales (100,000 units @ $10)	$1,000,000
Cost of sales	300,000
Gross margin	$ 700,000
Selling and general expenses	200,000
Income before taxes	$ 500,000
Taxes (40%)	200,000
Net income	$ 300,000

On December 31, total assets available consist of current assets of $300,000 and fixed assets of $500,000.

You forecast that sales for 20X2 will be 120,000 units at $11 per unit. The cost per unit is estimated at $5. Fixed selling and general expenses are forecasted at $60,000, and variable selling and general expenses are anticipated to be $1.50 per unit. Depreciation for the year is expected to be $30,000.

Forecasted earnings for 20X2 are calculated as follows:

Sales (120,000 @ $11)		$1,320,000
Cost of sales (120,000 @ $5)		600,000
Gross margin		$ 720,000
Selling and general expenses		
Fixed	$ 60,000	
Variable (120,000 @ $1.50)	180,000	
Total		240,000
Income before tax		$ 480,000
Tax (40%)		192,000
Net income		$ 288,000

The investment expected at December 31, 20X2 is:

Ratio of current assets to sales in 20X1:		
$300,000/$1,000,000		30%
Expected current assets at December 31, 20X2:		
30% × $1,320,000		$396,000
Expected fixed assets at December 31, 20X2:		
Book value on January 1	$500,000	
Less depreciation for 20X2	30,000	470,000
Total investment		$866,000

$$\text{ROI} = \frac{\$288,000}{\$866,000} = \underline{33.3\%}$$

Residual Income

The optimal measure of divisional performance is residual income, which equals divisional net income less minimum return times average available total assets.

EXAMPLE 8.6

Divisional earnings are $250,000, average available total assets are $2,000,000, and the cost of capital is 9%.

Residual income equals:

Divisional net income	$250,000
Less minimum return × Average available total assets	
9% × $2,000,000	180,000
Residual income	$ 70,000

The minimum rate of return is based upon the company's overall cost of capital adjusted for divisional risk. The cost of capital should be periodically calculated and used because of shifts in the money rate over time.

A target residual income may be formulated to act as the division manager's objective. The trend in residual income to total available assets should be examined in appraising divisional performance (see Figure 8.2).

A division manager's performance should be appraised on the basis of controllable residual income. A manager should not be penalized for uncontrollable matters. To evaluate a division, we use net residual income after taxes. This is a key figure, because it aids in the decision to make new investments or withdrawals of funds in that division.

Advantages of Residual Income

- The same asset may be required to earn the same return rate throughout the company irrespective of the division the asset is in.
- Different return rates may be employed for different types of assets, depending on riskiness.

FIGURE 8.2 Residual Income Statement for Divisional Evaluation Purposes

Sales	$1,200,000	
Transfers at market value to other divisions	400,000	
Total		$1,600,000
Less		
Variable cost of goods sold and transferred	$ 800,000	
Variable divisional expenses	200,000	
Total		1,000,000
Variable income		$ 600,000
Less		
Controllable divisional overhead	$ 200,000	
Depreciation on controllable plant and equipment	110,000	
Property taxes and insurance on controllable fixed assets	40,000	
Total		$ 350,000
Controllable operating income		$ 250,000
Add		
Nonoperating gains	$ 300,000	
Nonoperating losses	20,000	
Net nonoperating gains		280,000
Total		$ 530,000
Less interest on controllable investment		30,000
Controllable residual income		$ 500,000
Less		
Uncontrollable divisional overhead (e.g., central advertising)	$ 40,000	
Incremental central expenses chargeable to the division	10,000	
Interest on noncontrollable investment	50,000	
Total		100,000
Residual income before taxes		$ 400,000
Less income taxes (40%)		160,000
Net residual income after taxes		$ 240,000

- Different return rates may be assigned to different divisions, depending on the risk associated with those divisions.
- Provides an economic income, taking into account the opportunity cost of tying up assets in the division.
- Identifies operating problem areas.
- Precludes the difficulty that a division with a high ROI would not engage in a project with a lower ROI even though it exceeds the overall corporate ROI rate. This is because residual income maximizes dollars instead of a percentage. It motivates divisional managers to take into account all profitable investments. Unprofitable investments are not included.

Disadvantages of Residual Income

- Assignment of a minimum return involves estimating a risk level that is subjective.
- It may be difficult to determine the valuation basis and means of allocating assets to divisions.
- If book value is used in valuing assets, residual income will artificially increase over time, since the minimum return times total assets becomes lower as the assets become older.

CONCLUSION

It is essential to evaluate a segment's performance to identify problem areas. Factors that are controllable or not controllable by the division manager must be considered. The various means of evaluating performance include cost center, profit center, and investment center. The calculations for each method along with proper analysis are vital in appraising operating efficiency. You should understand the advantages and disadvantages of each method as well as when each is most appropriate.

9

Tools and Techniques for Analyzing Cash, Accounts Receivable, and Inventory

The proper management of working capital, cash, accounts receivable, and inventory will result in maximizing return and minimizing liquidity and business risk. There are many ways of managing assets, including using quantitative techniques to find optimal asset levels. Also, you want to achieve the best mixture of assets in the total asset structure.

The amount invested in any current asset may change daily and requires close appraisal. Improper asset management occurs when funds tied up in the asset can be used more productively elsewhere. A buildup in an asset account also implies risk (e.g., obsolete inventory). However, an excessively low asset base may also result in less profit (e.g., inadequate stocking of inventory resulting in lost sales).

EVALUATING WORKING CAPITAL

Working capital equals current assets less current liabilities. Management of working capital involves regulating the various types of current assets and current liabilities. Involved are decisions on how assets should be financed (e.g., short-term debt, long-term debt, or equity). Managing working capital involves a trade-off between return and risk. If funds go from fixed assets to current assets, there is a reduction in liquidity risk, greater ability to obtain short-term financing, and enhanced flexibility, because the entity can more readily adjust current assets to changes in sales volume. But less of a return is earned because the yield on fixed assets is more than that of current assets. Financing with noncurrent debt has less liquidity risk than financing with current debt. However, long-term debt often has a higher cost than short-term debt because of the greater uncertainty, which detracts from your overall return.

What to Do: Use the hedging approach of financing where assets are financed by liabilities of similar maturity. In this way, there are sufficient funds to satisfy debt when due. For example, permanent assets should be financed with long-term debt rather than short-term debt.

Rule of Thumb: The longer the time period involved to buy or produce goods, the more working capital is required. Working capital also applies to the volume of purchases and the cost per unit. For example, if you can receive a raw material in two weeks, you need less of an inventory level than if two months lead time is involved. *Tip:* Purchase material early if significantly lower prices are available and if the material's cost savings exceed inventory carrying costs.

CASH MANAGEMENT

The purpose of cash management is to invest excess cash for a return and at the same time have adequate liquidity to meet future needs. The proper cash balance should exist, neither excessive nor deficient. Do you know how much cash you need, how much you have, and where the cash is? Proper cash forecasting is needed to determine (1) the optimal time to incur and pay back debt and (2) the amount to transfer daily between accounts. *Recommendation:* Analyze each bank account as to type, balance, and cost. Do not have an excessive cash balance because no return is earned. When quick liquidity is needed, invest in marketable securities.

Factors in Determining the Amount of Cash to Be Held

- Your utility preferences regarding liquidity risk.
- Proper use of cash management.
- Expected future cash flows, considering the probabilities of different cash flows under alternative circumstances.
- Maturity period of debt.
- Your ability to borrow on short notice and on favorable terms.
- Probability of different cash flows under varying circumstances.

What to Watch Out for: Having an "excessive" line of credit with the bank, which involves a commitment fee. Watch the amount of the compensating balance, since the portion of a loan that serves as collateral is restricted and unavailable for your use. Is cash unnecessarily tied up in other accounts (e.g., loans to employees, insurance deposits)? *Warning:* Liquid asset holdings are required during a downturn in a company's cycle, when funds from operations decline.

Recommendation: Do not seek to fund peak seasonal cash requirements internally. Rather, borrow on a short-term basis to enable internal funds to be used more profitably throughout the year, such as by investing in plant and equipment.

Acceleration of Cash Inflow

You should evaluate the causes and take corrective action for delays in having cash receipts deposited. *What to Do:* Ascertain how and where cash receipts come, how cash is transferred from outlying accounts to the main corporate account, and banking policy regarding availability of funds.

Types of Delays in Processing Checks

- Mail float: Time required for a check to move from debtor to creditor.
- Processing float: Time needed for the creditor to enter the payment.
- Deposit collection float: Time for a check to clear.

Means of Accelerating Cash Receipts

- Lockbox arrangement where the collection point is placed near customers. Customer payments are sent to strategic post office boxes geographically situated to expedite mailing and depositing time. Banks collect from these boxes several times a day and make deposits to the corporate account. *Recommendation:* Undertake a cost–benefit analysis to ensure that instituting a lockbox arrangement will result in net savings. Determine the average face value of checks received, cost of operations eliminated, reducible overhead, reduction in "mail float" days, and per-item processing cost. *Tip:* Compare the return earned on freed cash to the cost of the lockbox arrangement.
- Concentration banking, where funds are collected in local banks and transferred to a main concentration account.
- Transfer funds between banks by wire.
- Accelerate billing.
- Send customers preaddressed, stamped envelopes.

- Require deposits on large or custom orders or progress billings as the work progresses.
- Charge interest on accounts receivable after a certain amount of time.
- Use personal collection efforts.
- Offer discounts for early payment.
- Have postdated checks from customers.
- Have cash-on-delivery terms.
- Deposit checks immediately.

EXAMPLE 9.1

You are determining whether to start a lockbox arrangement that will cost $150,000 annually. Its daily average collections are $700,000. The system will reduce mailing and processing time by 2 days. Your rate of return is 14%.

Return on freed cash (14% × 2 × $700,000)	$196,000
Annual cost	150,000
Net advantage of lockbox system	$ 46,000

EXAMPLE 9.2

You presently have a lockbox arrangement with Bank A in which it handles $5 million a day in return for an $800,000 compensating balance. You are thinking of canceling this arrangement and further dividing your western region by entering into contracts with two other banks. Bank B will handle $3 million a day in collections with a compensating balance of $700,000, and Bank C will handle $2 million a day with a compensating balance of $600,000. Collections will be half a day quicker than the current situation. Your return rate is 12%.

Accelerated cash receipts	
($5 million per day × 0.5 day)	$2,500,000
Increased compensating balance	500,000
Improved cash flow	$2,000,000
Rate of return	× 0.12
Net annual savings	$ 240,000

Delay of Cash Outlay

You should delay cash payments to earn a greater return on your money. Evaluate who your payees are and to what extent you can reasonably stretch time limits.

Ways of Delaying Cash Payments

- Centralize the payables operation so that debt may be paid at the most profitable time and so that the amount of disbursement float in the system may be ascertained.
- Make partial payments.
- Use payment drafts, where payment is *not* made on demand. Instead, the draft is presented for collection to the bank, which in turn goes to the issuer for acceptance. When approved, the company deposits the funds. *Net Result:* Less of a required checking balance.
- Draw checks on remote banks (e.g., a New York company using a Texas bank).
- Mail from post offices with limited service or where mail has to go through numerous handling points. *Tip:* If you utilize float properly you can maintain higher bank balances than the actual lower book balances. For instance, if you write checks averaging $200,000 per day and three days are necessary for them to clear, you will have a $600,000 checking balance less than the bank's records.
- Use probability analysis to determine the expected date for checks to clear. *Suggestion:* Have separate checking accounts (e.g., payroll, dividends) and monitor check clearing dates. For example, payroll checks are not all cashed on the payroll date, so funds can be deposited later to earn a return.
- Use a computer terminal to transfer funds between various bank accounts at opportune times.
- Use a charge account to lengthen the time between buying goods and paying for them.
- Stretch payments as long as possible as long as there is no associated finance charge or impairment in credit rating.

- Do not pay bills before due dates.
- Utilize noncash compensation and remuneration methods (e.g., stock).
- Delay the frequency of your company payrolls.
- Disburse commissions on sales when the receivables are collected rather than when they are made.

You can use a stochastic model for cash management where major uncertainty exists regarding cash payments. The Miller–Orr model places an upper and lower limit for cash balances. When the upper limit is reached, a transfer of cash to marketable securities is made. When the lower limit is reached, a transfer from securities to cash takes place. A transaction will not occur as long as the cash balance falls within the limits.

Factors taken into account in the Miller–Orr model are the fixed costs of a securities transaction (F), assumed to be the same for buying as well as selling, the daily interest rate on marketable securities (i), and the deviation in daily net cash flows (σ^2). The objective is to meet cash requirements at the lowest possible cost. A major assumption is the randomness of cash flows. The two control limits in the Miller–Orr model may be specified as "d" dollars as an upper limit and zero dollars at the lower limit. When the cash balance reaches the upper level d, less z dollars of securities are bought and the new balance becomes z dollars. When the cash balance equals zero, z dollars of securities are sold and the new balance again reaches z. Of course, practically speaking you should note that the minimum cash balance is established at an amount greater than zero due to delays in transfer as well as to having a safety buffer.

The optimal cash balance z is computed as follows:

$$z = \sqrt[3]{\frac{3F\sigma^2}{4i}}$$

The optimal value for d is computed as $3z$.

The average cash balance will approximate $\dfrac{(z + d)}{3}$.

EXAMPLE 9.3

You wish to use the Miller–Orr model. The following information is supplied.

Fixed cost of a securities transaction	$10
Deviation in daily net cash flows	$50
Daily interest rate on securities (10%/360)	0.0003

The optimal cash balance, the upper limit of cash needed, and the average cash balance follow:

$$z = \sqrt[3]{\frac{3(10)(50)}{4(0.0003)}} = \sqrt[3]{\frac{3(10)(50)}{.0012}} = \sqrt[3]{\frac{1{,}500}{0.0012}}$$

$$= \sqrt[3]{1{,}250{,}000}$$

$$= \underline{\$102}$$

The optimal cash balance is $102.

The upper limit is $306 (3 × $102).

The average cash balance is $136 $\frac{(\$102 + \$306)}{3}$.

A brief elaboration on these findings is needed for clarification. When the upper limit of $306 is reached, $204 of securities ($306 − $102) will be purchased to bring you to the optimal cash balance of $102. When the lower limit of $0 dollars is reached, $102 of securities will be sold to again bring you to the optimal cash balance of $102.

MANAGEMENT OF ACCOUNTS RECEIVABLE

In accounts receivable management, you should consider that there is an opportunity cost associated with holding receivable balances. A key concern is the amount and credit terms given to customers. Receivable management bears on your bottom line.

Means of Managing Accounts Receivable

- "Cycle bill" to produce greater uniformity in the billing process.
- Mail customer statements within 24 hours of the close of the accounting period.

- Send an invoice to customers when you process the order at the warehouse instead of when merchandise is shipped.
- Bill for your services periodically when work is performed or charge a retainer. *Tip:* Bill large sales immediately.
- Use seasonal datings. *Recommendation:* When business is slow, sell to customers with delayed payment terms to stimulate demand for customers who are unable to pay until later in the season. *What to Do:* Compare profitability on incremental sales plus the reduction in inventory carrying costs, which have to exceed the opportunity cost on the additional investment in average accounts receivable.
- Carefully analyze customer financial statements before giving credit. Also, obtain ratings from financial advisory sources such as Dun and Bradstreet.
- Avoid typically high-risk receivables (e.g., customers in a financially troubled industry).
- Modify credit limits based on changes in customers' financial health.
- Ask for collateral in support of questionable accounts. *Tip:* The collateral value should equal or exceed the account balance.
- Factor accounts receivable when net savings ensue.
- Use outside collection agencies where warranted.
- Consider marketing factors, since a stringent credit policy might result in a loss of business.
- Consumer receivables have greater risk of default than corporate receivables.
- Age accounts receivable to spot delinquent customers. Aged receivables can be compared to prior years, industry norms, and competitive norms. *Note:* Bad debt losses are typically higher for smaller companies than for larger ones.
- Accelerate collections from customers currently having financial problems.
- Have credit insurance to guard against unusual bad debt losses.

What to Consider: In deciding whether to get this insurance, take into account expected average bad debt losses, financial capability of the firm to withstand the losses, and the cost of insurance.

Attributes of a Good Credit System

- Clear, quick, and uniform in application.
- Does not intrude on customer's privacy.

- Inexpensive (e.g., centralization of credit decisions by experienced staff).
- Based upon past experience, considering characteristics of good, questionable, and bad accounts. *Tip:* Determine the correlation between customer characteristics and future uncollectibility.

You often have to determine your dollar investment tied up in accounts receivable.

EXAMPLE 9.4

You sell on terms of net/30. Your accounts are on average 20 days past due. Annual credit sales are $600,000. Your investment in accounts receivable is

$$\frac{50}{360} \times \$600,000 = \underline{\$83,333.28}$$

EXAMPLE 9.5

The cost of a product is 30% of selling price, and the cost of capital is 10% of selling price. On average, accounts are paid 4 months after sale. Average sales are $70,000 per month.

The investment in accounts receivable from this product is:

Accounts receivable (4 months × $70,000)	$280,000
Investment in accounts receivable [$280,000 × (0.30 + 0.10)]	$112,000

Should you offer customers a discount for the early payment of account balances? You have to compare the return on freed cash resulting from customers' paying sooner to the cost of the discount.

EXAMPLE 9.6

The following data are provided:

Current annual credit sales	$14,000,000
Collection period	3 months
Terms	net/30
Minimum rate of return	15%

You are considering offering a 3/10, net/30 discount. You expect 25% of the customers to take advantage of it. The collection period will decline to 2 months.

Part II: Evaluating Assets, Liabilities, and Potential Acquisitions

The discount should be offered, as indicated in the following calculations.

Advantage:
Increased profitability:
Average accounts receivable balance before a change in policy

$$\frac{\text{Credit sales}}{\text{Accounts receivable turnover}} = \frac{\$14,000,000}{4} \quad \$3,500,000$$

Average accounts receivable balance after a change in policy

$$\frac{\text{Credit sales}}{\text{Accounts receivable turnover}} = \frac{\$14,000,000}{6}$$

	2,333,333
Reduction in average accounts receivable balance	$1,166,667
Rate of return	× 0.15
Return	$ 175,000

Disadvantage:

Cost of the discount (0.03 × 0.25 × $14,000,000)	$ 105,000
Net advantage of discount	$ 70,000

Should you give credit to marginal customers? You have to compare the earnings on sales obtained to the added cost of the receivables. *Note:* If you have idle capacity, the additional earnings is the contribution margin on the incremental sales because fixed costs are constant. The additional cost on the additional receivables results from the greater number of bad debts and the opportunity cost of tying up funds in receivables for a longer time period.

EXAMPLE 9.7

Sales price per unit	$120
Variable cost per unit	80
Fixed cost per unit	15
Annual credit sales	$600,000
Collection period	1 month
Minimum return	16%

If you liberalize the credit policy, you project that:

- Sales will increase by 40%.
- The collection period on total accounts will be 2 months.
- Bad debts on the increased sales will be 5%.

Preliminary calculations:

Current units ($600,000/$120)	5,000
Additional units (5,000 × 0.4)	2,000

Chapter 9: Analyzing Cash, Accounts Receivable, and Inventory   163

The new average unit cost is now calculated:

	Units × Unit Cost	= Total Cost
Current units	5,000 × $95	$475,000
Additional units	2,000 × $80	160,000
Total	7,000	$635,000

$$\text{New average unit cost} = \frac{\text{Total cost}}{\text{Units}} = \frac{\$635,000}{7,000} = \underline{\$90.71} \text{ (rounded)}$$

Note that at idle capacity, fixed cost remains constant. Thus, the incremental cost is only the variable cost of $80 per unit. This will cause the new average unit cost to drop.

Advantage:
Additional profitability:
Incremental sales volume × Contribution margin per unit   2,000 units
(Selling price – variable cost) $120 – $80   × $40
Incremental profitability $80,000

Disadvantage:
Incremental bad debts:
Incremental units × Selling price
2,000 × $120 $240,000
Bad debt percentage   × 0.05
Additional bad debts $ 12,000

Opportunity cost of funds tied up in accounts receivable: Average investment in accounts receivable after change in policy:

$$\frac{\text{Credit sales}}{\text{Accounts receivable turnover}} \times \frac{\text{Unit cost}}{\text{Selling price}} \qquad \$105,828$$

$$\frac{\$840,000^a}{6} \times \frac{\$90.71}{\$120}$$

Current average investment in accounts receivable:

$$\frac{\$600,000}{12} \times \frac{\$95}{\$120} \qquad\qquad\qquad\qquad 39,583$$

Additional investment in accounts receivable $ 66,245
Minimum return   × 0.16
Opportunity cost of funds tied up $ 10,599

---
[a]7,000 units × $120 = $840,000.

Net advantage of relaxation in credit standards:
Additional earnings $80,000
Less
   Additional bad debt losses $12,000
   Opportunity cost 10,599   22,599
Net savings $57,401

You may have to decide whether to extend full credit to presently limited credit customers or no-credit customers. Full credit should be given only if net profitability occurs.

EXAMPLE 9.8

Category	Bad Debt Percentage	Collection Period	Credit Policy	Increase in Annual Sales if Credit Restrictions Are Relaxed
X	2%	30 days	Unlimited	$80,000
Y	5%	40 days	Restricted	600,000
Z	30%	80 days	No credit	850,000

Gross profit is 25% of sales. The minimum return on investment is 12%.

	Category Y	Category Z
Gross profit		
$600,000 × .25	$150,000	
$850,000 × .25		$212,500
Less bad debts		
$600,000 × .05	−30,000	
$850,000 × .30		−255,000
Incremental average investment in accounts receivable		
$\dfrac{40}{360} \times (0.75 \times \$600,000)$	$50,000	
$\dfrac{80}{360} \times (0.75 \times \$850,000)$		$141,667

Chapter 9: Analyzing Cash, Accounts Receivable, and Inventory 165

Opportunity cost of incremental investment in accounts receivable	×0.12 − 6,000	×0.12 −17,000
Net earnings	$114,000	$(59,500)

Credit should be extended to category Y.

EXAMPLE 9.9

You are planning a sales campaign in which you will offer credit terms of 3/10, net/45. You expect the collection period to increase from 60 days to 80 days. Relevant data for the contemplated campaign follow.

	Percent of Sales Before Campaign	Percent of Sales During Campaign
Cash sales	40%	30%
Payment from		
1–10	25	55
11–100	35	15

The proposed sales strategy will probably increase sales from $8 million to $10 million. There is a gross margin rate of 30%. The rate of return is 14%. Sales discounts are given on cash sales.

	Without Sales Campaign	With Sales Campaign
Gross margin (0.3 × $8,000,000)	$2,400,000	(0.3 × $10,000,000) $3,000,000
Sales subject to discount		
0.65 × $8,000,000	$5,200,000	
0.85 × $10,000,000		$8,500,000
Sales discount	× 0.03 − 156,000	× 0.03 − 255,000

Investment in average
accounts receivable

$$\frac{60}{360} \times \$8{,}000{,}000 \times 0.7 \quad \$933{,}333$$

$$\frac{80}{360} \times \$10{,}000{,}000 \times 0.7 \qquad \$1{,}555{,}555$$

Return rate	× 0.14 − 130,667	× 0.14 − 217,778
Net profit	$2,113,333	$2,527,222

You should undertake the sales campaign, because earnings will increase by $413,889 ($2,527,222 − $2,113,333).

INVENTORY PLANNING AND CONTROL

In inflationary and tight money periods, you have to be flexible in your inventory management. For example, the quantity to be ordered may have to be adjusted to reflect increased costs. Inventory risk must be appraised. High realization risk items include those that are technological, perishable, fashionable, inflammable, and specialized.

Ways of Managing Inventory

- Do not carry excessive inventory balances, because of the opportunity cost and carrying cost.
- Evaluate the efficiency related to buying and controlling inventory. If there is a lack of control, restrict inventory balances.
- Have a safety stock balance to guard against material shortages that could cause shutdowns and lost sales.
- Search out slow-moving items to be discarded to aid cash flow and lower carrying costs.
- Ensure that inventory is received when needed so that production runs smoothly. *What to Do:* Compare vendor and production receipts to promised delivery due dates.
- Determine the degree of spoilage.
- Utilize computer techniques and operations research to properly control inventory.
- Evaluate future trends in material prices. If you expect price increases, buy more goods now.
- Appraise the cash flow position and the cost and availability of financing inventory acquisition. If problems exist, less inventory should be bought.

- Consider the number of back orders. A greater number of back orders will require a lower inventory balance because production planning and procurement have been facilitated. *What to Do:* Calculate the ratio of the value of backlog orders to average value of sales per day.
- Analyze the quality of received goods. *What to Do:* Calculate the ratio of purchase returns to purchases. An increasing trend in the ratio points to deteriorating quality, and thus new suppliers should be found.
- Implement approaches to reduce the lead time in buying, producing, packing, and shipping goods. *What to Do:* Calculate the ratio of the value of outstanding orders to average daily purchases to indicate the lead time for receiving orders from suppliers. The ratio indicates whether you should increase the inventory level or change your buying pattern.
- Enhance the supervision of warehouse and material handling personnel to improve efficiency and lessen the likelihood of theft.
- Appraise the level of raw materials, which depends on equipment quality, expected production, supplier reliability, and cyclicality in operations. *Recommendation:* Have sound material management guidelines to specify what and how much should be stored. Manufacturing requires an appropriate balance of parts to produce an end item. *What to Watch Out for:* A situation in which you have four of five needed components, because this results in having four excess inventories when a stock-out of the fifth occurs.
- In monitoring work in process, analyze the production time period from the inputting of raw material to the completion of the item. Quantitative engineering techniques should be used to expedite production.
- Examine the trend in the unit cost of manufactured items. *What to Watch Out for:* Higher unit cost due to management inefficiencies. However, rising costs beyond management control are understandable (e.g., strike at a supplier).
- Have controlled audit groups of work in process moving through the manufacturing process to see the accuracy with which work in process is documented.
- Employ the ABC approach. *What to Do:* Put more emphasis on higher cost, higher use, and critical parts. "A" items deserve more attention than "C" items. *Tip:* In looking at "A" items, carefully examine records, bills of material, customer orders, open purchase orders, and open manufacturing orders.

- Accuracy is needed for the bills of materials to indicate the parts and quantities received to produce an end product. *What to Do:* Conduct audits on the production floor when the parts are assembled.
- Have accurate inventory records and assign inventory responsibilities to managers. For instance, assign to the engineering manager responsibility for the bills of material. Do you have the necessary inventory measurement tools (e.g., scales)?
- Have "cycle counting" for inventory so a limited number of full-time experienced counters are used throughout the period, making it easier to spot errors. A benefit is that the plant does not have to be shut down at year-end. *Recommendation:* To lessen the time needed for counting, use standardized labeling procedures and quantity markings as well as orderly warehouse stocking. *Tip:* Take the count during nonworking hours to guard against duplicate counting. Alternatively, warehouse pickers could carefully enter daily movement when the cycle count takes place.

Inventory costs include ordering costs and carrying costs. Ordering costs include the cost of placing the order and receiving goods. Examples are freight charges and clerical costs. *Note:* Cost of scheduling is included for produced items. Order cost is assumed to be constant for each order, irrespective of the number of units in that order.

$$\text{Total number of orders} = \frac{S}{EOQ}$$

where

S = total usage

EOQ = economic order quantity: the optimum amount to order each time to minimize total inventory costs (ordering and carrying)

$$\text{Total order cost} = \frac{S}{EOQ} \times O$$

where

O = cost per order

Carrying costs include the storage, handling, property tax, and insurance costs, as well as the required return rate on the inventory investment. It is assumed constant per unit of inventory.

Chapter 9: Analyzing Cash, Accounts Receivable, and Inventory

$$\text{Total carrying cost} = \frac{EOQ}{2} \times C$$

where

$$C = \text{carrying cost per unit}$$

$$\frac{EOQ}{2} = \text{average inventory quantity for the period}$$

$$\text{Total inventory cost:} = \left(\frac{S}{EOQ} \times O\right) + \left(\frac{EOQ}{2} \times C\right)$$

A trade-off exists between order size and the carrying cost. The higher the order quantity (EOQ), the higher the carrying cost but the lower the ordering cost.

$$EOQ = \sqrt{\frac{2SO}{C}}$$

EXAMPLE 9.10

Usage = 500 units per month

O = $20 per order

C = $10 per unit

$$EOQ = \sqrt{\frac{(2)(500)(20)}{10}} = \sqrt{2,000} = \underline{45} \text{ units (rounded)}$$

Number of times per month to place an order $\frac{S}{EOQ} = \frac{500}{45} = \underline{11}$ (rounded)

An order should be placed about every 3 days (30/11).

EXAMPLE 9.11

You are determining the frequency of orders for an item from a supplier. Each item costs $20. Carrying cost is estimated at $500 per year. You anticipate selling 200 units per month. Average desired inventory is 110. Order cost is $8. You want to know the optimum quantity and order frequency.

$$EOQ = \sqrt{\frac{2SO}{C}} = \sqrt{\frac{(2)\,(2,400)^a\,(8)}{4.5^b}} = \sqrt{8458.15} = \underline{92} \text{ units (rounded)}$$

[a]$S = 12 \times 200 = 2,400$
[b]Calculation of C follows:

$$C = \frac{\text{Carrying cost}}{\text{Average inventory}}$$
(which equals unit cost × average quantity)

$$\frac{\$500}{\$20 \times \$110} = \frac{\$500}{\$2,200} = \underline{22.7\%}$$

C = Purchase price × Percentage of carrying cost to average investment

$C = \$20 \times 0.227 = \underline{\$4.54}$

$$\text{Number of orders per year} = \frac{S}{\text{EOQ}} = \frac{2,400}{92} = \underline{26} \text{ (rounded)}$$

An order should be placed about every 14 days (360/26).

Assumptions of the EOQ calculation are that demand is known with certainty and remains constant within the period, ordering and carrying costs are constant, and lead time is determinable (thus there are no shortage costs). Also, EOQ does not consider quantity discounts, which is often unrealistic to ignore.

Recommendation: Use EOQ model for a pure inventory system, specifically one for single-item, single-stage inventory decisions for which you can ignore joint costs and constraints.

Caution: When demand is not precisely known and/or other complications exist, you should not use the EOQ model, but rather a probabilistic one.

The economic order point (EOP) is the inventory level requiring an order at the EOQ amount. Included in the calculation is a safety stock level, which represents the minimum inventory amount needed acting as a safety buffer (guarding against unusual product demand or unanticipated delivery problems). A safety stock is required to protect against possible stock-outs when lead time and demand are uncertain.

The optimal safety stock level is the one in which increased carrying cost equals the opportunity cost applicable to a possible stock-out. The increased carrying cost equals the carrying cost per unit times the safety stock.

Stock-out cost = Number of orders (S/EOQ) × Stock-out units
× Unit stock-out cost × Probability of a stock-out

EXAMPLE 9.12

You use 250,000 units per year. Each order is for 25,000 units. Stock-out is 4,000 units. The tolerable stock-out probability is 25%. The per-unit stock-out cost is $4. The carrying cost per unit is $8.

Chapter 9: Analyzing Cash, Accounts Receivable, and Inventory

$$\text{Stock-out cost} = \frac{250{,}000}{25{,}000} \times 4{,}000 \times \$4 \times 0.25 = \underline{\$40{,}000}$$

$$\frac{\text{Amount of safety}}{\text{stock-needed}} = \frac{\text{Stock-out cost}}{\text{Carrying cost per unit}}$$

$$= \frac{\$40{,}000}{\$8} = \underline{5{,}000} \text{ units}$$

$$EOP = SL + F\sqrt{S(EOQ)(L)}$$

where

L = Lead time

F = Stock-out acceptance factor

EXAMPLE 9.13

You have the following information:

Usage = 2,000 units per month

EOQ = 400 units

Lead time = 0.5 month

F = 1.29, representing an acceptable stock-out percentage of 10% (the safety stock factor is gotten from a statistical table)

$$EOP = SL + F\sqrt{S(EOQ)(L)}$$

$$= 2{,}000 \,(0.5) + 1.29 \,\sqrt{2{,}000(400)(0.5)}$$

$$1{,}000 + 1.29 \,\sqrt{400{,}000}$$

$$1{,}000 + 1.29 \,(632.46) = \underline{1{,}816} \text{ (rounded)}$$

An optimal inventory level can be based on consideration of the incremental profitability resulting from having more merchandise to the opportunity cost of carrying the higher inventory balances.

EXAMPLE 9.14

The current inventory turnover is 12 times. Variable costs are 60% of sales. An increase in inventory balances is expected to prevent stock-outs, thus increasing sales. Minimum rate of return is 18%. Relevant data follow.

Sales	Turnover
$800,000	12
890,000	10
940,000	8
980,000	7

(1) Sales	(2) Turnover	(3) [(1)/(2)] Average Inventory Balance
$800,000	12	$ 66,667
890,000	10	89,000
940,000	8	117,500
980,000	7	140,000

(4) Opportunity Cost of Carrying Incremental Inventory[a]	(5) Increased Profitability[b]	(6) [(5)−(4)] Net Savings
—	—	—
$4,020	$36,000	$31,980
5,130	20,000	14,870
4,050	16,000	11,950

[a] Increased inventory × 0.18.
[b] Increased sales × 0.40.

The optimal inventory level is $89,000, because it results in the highest net savings.

CONCLUSION

By properly managing working capital, cash, accounts receivable, and inventory you can achieve maximum return at an acceptable level of risk. Emphasis should be placed on having the right mixture of working capital items. Quantitative models can be used to find optimal asset levels. The funds invested in a given asset category may change daily, and mandate close scrutiny.

10 Portfolio Investment Analysis Information You Need

Investment analysis evaluates the quality of an existing portfolio as well as determines what and when to buy or sell financial and real assets. Appropriate sources of investment information must be researched and evaluated for optimal decision making. A risk–return analysis is required to achieve a proper mix of securities in the portfolio. The types of financial assets and real assets to invest in must be known, along with their respective advantages and disadvantages. Diversification by investing in mutual funds is also addressed. Fundamental and technical analyses are discussed to assist you in selecting the right securities at the right time. Personal computers greatly aid in the investment analysis process.

ACCOUNTING ASPECTS

As per FASB No. 115, an investment portfolio of stocks is recorded at aggregate cost or market value. For trading securities, the unrealized loss or gain is shown in the income statement. For available-for-sale securities, the cumulative unrealized loss or gain is shown as a separate item in the stockholders' equity section.

EXAMPLE 10.1

A company reports a cumulative unrealized loss of $200,000 on available-for-sale securities in the stockholders' equity section of the balance sheet. For analytical purposes, the company's investment selections have done poorly.

ANALYTICAL IMPLICATIONS

Held-to-maturity debt securities must be retained at amortized cost, even though their market value is less or more. For analytical purposes, value held-to-maturity investments at market.

Be on Guard: Watch for declines in portfolio market values not fully reflected in the accounts. An indication of fair value is the revenue (interest income, dividend income) generated by the portfolio. A declining trend in the percentage of earnings on investments to carrying value may point to higher asset realization risk. If there has been a subsequent event disclosure in the annual report applicable to unrealized losses that have occurred on the securities' portfolio, downwardly adjust the investment to account for the decline.

EXAMPLE 10.2

A company reports the following information.

	20X1	20X2
Investments	$30,000	$33,000
Income from investments (dividends and interest)	4,000	3,200

The 20X2 annual report has a footnote titled "Subsequent Events," which indicates that there was a $5,000 decline in the investment portfolio as of March 3, 20X3.

The ratio of investment income to total investments went down from 13.3% ($4,000/$30,000) in 20X1 to 9.7% ($3,200/$33,000) in 20X2, pointing to higher realization risk in the portfolio. Further, the post–balance-sheet disclosure of a reduction in value of $5,000 in the portfolio should make you downwardly adjust the realizability of the year-end portfolio.

Indicators of Riskiness in a Portfolio

- *Volatile securities.* Diversify the portfolio by industry and economic sector. However, volatile securities can be more profitable in a bull market.
- *Positively correlated securities.* Try to have securities that are negatively correlated to each other in order to add price stability to the portfolio. With negatively correlated securities, some securities will go up in value while others go down in value.
- *Variability in rate of return.* Determine the standard deviation of the rate of return on the investment portfolio.

Considerations in Selecting an Investment

- Liquidity needs.
- Desired rate of return.
- Risk. *Rule:* The higher the risk, the higher the rate of return must be.
- Tax rate. If one is in a high tax bracket, tax-free securities may be preferred (e.g., municipal bonds).
- Rate of change in price.
- Annual income.
- Future prospects.
- Maturity period. A longer maturity period means a greater chance of price fluctuation.
- Amount of available funds.

OBTAINING INFORMATION

Prior to making an investment decision, you should be familiar with economic conditions, political environment, market status, industry surroundings, and corporate performance. Investment information is either descriptive or analytical. *Descriptive* information reveals prior performance of the economy, politics, market, and specific investment. *Analytical* information consists of current data, including forecasts and recommendations as to specific securities. Both types of investment information assist you in assessing the risk and return of a particular choice and enable you to see whether the investment satisfies your objectives.

"Almost free" information is contained in newspapers and magazines. You will have to pay for additional information from a financial advisory service publication like *Value Line*. Other sources of investment data include market information and indexes, economic and current events, and industry and company data.

Market Information and Indexes

Market price information provides past, present, and prospective prices of securities. Data on current and recent price behavior of stocks are contained in price quotations.

The Dow Jones Industrial Average is an average of the market prices of the 30 industrial stocks having wide ownership and volume activity as well as significant market value. Dow Jones calculates separate averages for public utilities, transportation, and the composite.

Standard & Poor's has five common stock indexes. The S&P Index compares the present price of a group of stocks to the base prices from 1941 to 1943. The S&P indexes are industrial (400 companies), financial (40 companies), transportation (20 companies), public utility (40 companies), and composite (500 companies). S&P also has indexes for consumer and capital goods companies as well as low-grade and high-grade common stocks.

The New York Stock Exchange Index includes all the stocks on the exchange. The American Stock Exchange Index reflects the price changes of its stocks. The National Association of Security Dealers Automated Quotation (NASDAQ) Index reflects activity in the over-the-counter market. Its composite index consists of about 2,300 companies traded on the NASDAQ system.

Barron's has a 50-stock average as well as the average price of the 20 most active and 20 lowest-priced stocks. Other averages and indexes are published by some financial advisory services. For example, *Value Line* has a composite of 1,700 companies as an indication of the overall behavior of the stock market.

There are also indicators of bond performance. Bond yields are typically quoted for a group of bonds of similar type and quality. Some sources of bond yield information are the Federal Reserve, Standard & Poor's, Moody's, and *Barron's*.

Economic and Political Events

The analysis of economic and political events provides information in forecasting national and international economic trends. *Recommendation:* Read the financial section of a good newspaper (e.g., *Barron's*) and business magazines (e.g., *Forbes*).

The *Federal Reserve Bulletin* provides data on the performance of the national economy. Included are a summary of business conditions; statistics on employment and retail prices; the Federal Reserve Board Index of industrial production; and information about gross national product, national income, interest rates, and yields.

The U.S. Department of Commerce issues monthly the *Survey of Current Business* and *Business Conditions Digest*. The *Survey* has a monthly update by industry of business information about exports, inventories, personal consumption, and labor market statistics. The *Digest* publishes cyclical indicators of economic activity, including leading, coincident, and lagging.

Subscription services publish data of economic and corporate developments. They also publish forecasts of business trends and detailed economic information and analysis. An example is the *Kiplinger Washington Letter*.

Industry and Company Analysis

You should select an industry that looks good before picking a particular company. You can obtain industry data by reading an industry trade publication such as the *Public Utilities Fortnightly*. Financial advisory reports on companies, such as Standard & Poor's and Moody's, may be helpful as well. Financial advisory reports typically present and analyze a company's financial history, current financial position, and future expectations. For example, Dun and Bradstreet issues *Key Business Ratios* and *Billion Dollar Directory*.

Brokerage research reports also provide useful analyses and recommendations on industries and companies.

Personal Computers and Electronic Data Bases

With the use of a PC, you have instant access to business data and immediate analytical ability (e.g., comparing data to predetermined criteria), and you can compute a rating of all your investments. Software exists for record keeping (shares, cost, selling price, revenue), graphics for plotting prices, timing buys and sells, and portfolio management. Some programs enable you to perform sophisticated fundamental and technical analysis and contain price and dividend history as well. Investment selection software aids in determining whether to buy or sell a stock. Investment monitoring software permits you to keep track of your portfolio by using investment information in data bases. You can add new prices to the files or modify old ones. Dividend information is also available. Tax investment software enables you to consider the tax aspects of certain securities. Investment programs can accommodate and track stocks, bonds, treasury securities, options, warrants, mutual funds, and commodities.

Dow Jones News/Retrieval contains many data bases, including current and historical Dow Jones Quotes, Corporate Earnings Estimator (earnings per share or EPS estimates), Disclosure II (corporate financial statements and footnote data), Media General Financial Services (stock performance related ratings; comparisons to market indicators; bond, mutual fund, and money market information), Merrill Lynch Research Service, Weekly Economic Survey and Update (economic data, trends, and analysis), and Wall Street Highlights. The Dow Jones Spreadsheet Link obtains financial information, such as stock prices from Dow Jones News/Retrieval, and puts them on a data disk. The data are then transferred to a spreadsheet for financial analysis calculations.

CompuServe's Executive Information Service provides financial data on companies, economic information and projections, money market trends, and earnings results and forecasts. Included are Value Line and Standard and Poor's information. CompuServe's MicroQuote gives a record of marketable securities, dividends, and interest paid on securities. CompuServe's mainframe will compute the worth of a portfolio for transfer to your terminal.

E.F. Hutton's Huttonline provides daily portfolio and account information, transaction activity, and investment research information.

Most investment programs communicate through computer terminals with other outside data bases and various brokerage firms (via stock bulletin board services). To access them you need a modem and telecommunications software (e.g., Crosstalk).

Standard & Poor's CompuStat tapes provides 20 years of annual financial data for more than 3,000 companies.

RISK VERSUS RETURN

Return from an investment comes from current income and appreciation in market value. The expected return rate on a security is the weighted average of possible returns, weights being probabilities. The holding period return is the total return you earn from holding an investment for a specified period of time, and equals

$$\text{Holding period return} = \frac{\text{Current income} + \text{Capital gain (or loss)}}{\text{Purchase price}}$$

EXAMPLE 10.3

You invest $100 in a security, sell it for $107, and earn a cash dividend of $13.

The holding period return is

$$\frac{\$13 + \$7}{\$100} = \frac{\$20}{\$100} = \underline{20\%}$$

Risk is the variability of possible returns applicable to an investment. Greater return is required to compensate for higher risk. Risk can be measured by the standard deviation (see Chapter 6), which is a measure of the dispersion of the probability distribution of possible returns. The higher the standard deviation, the wider the distribution, and thus the greater the investment risk. *Special Note:* Be careful using the standard deviation to compare risk, since it is only an absolute measure of dispersion (risk), and does not consider the dispersion of outcomes in relation to an expected return. *Recommendation:* In comparing securities with differing expected returns, you should use the coefficient of variation (see Chapter 6). The coefficient of variation equals the standard deviation for a security divided by its expected value. The higher the coefficient, the riskier the security.

EXAMPLE 10.4

Stock X has a standard deviation of 14.28% and an expected value of 19%. The coefficient of variation equals

$$\frac{14.28\%}{19\%} = \underline{0.75}$$

Types of Risk

- Business risk is due to earnings variability, which may be caused by variability in demand, selling price, and cost. It is the uncertainty surrounding the basic operations of the entity.
- Liquidity risk is the possibility that an asset may not be able to be sold for its market value on short notice.
- Default risk is the risk that the borrower will not be able to pay interest or principal on debt.
- Market risk applies to changes in stock price caused by changes in the stock market as a whole, regardless of the fundamental change in a company's earning power.
- Interest rate risk applies to fluctuation in the value of the asset as interest rate, money market, and capital market conditions change. Interest rate risk applies to all investment instruments, such as fixed income securities. For example, a decline in interest rates will result in an increase in bond and stock prices.
- Purchasing power risk applies to the possibility that you will receive less in purchasing power than originally invested. Bonds in particular are af-

fected by this risk, since the issuer will be paying back in cheaper dollars during an inflationary period. However, the return on common stock tends to move with the inflation rate.

- Systematic risk is nondiversifiable, resulting in situations beyond management's control, and is thus not unique to the particular security. Examples are interest rates, purchasing power, and market risks.
- Unsystematic risk is the portion of the security's risk that is controlled through diversification. It is the risk unique to a given security. Examples are liquidity, default, and business risks. Most of the unsystematic risk can be diversified away in an efficiently constructed portfolio.

FINANCIAL ASSETS

Investments may be in the form of financial assets or real assets. The former comprise all intangible investments representing equity ownership of a company, providing evidence that someone owes you debt, or your right to buy or sell an ownership interest at a later date. Financial assets include common stock, preferred stock, bonds, options and warrants, mutual funds, certificates of deposit, treasury bills, commercial paper, commodity and financial futures, savings accounts, and money market funds. Real assets are those that physically can be touched, including precious metals and real estate. Real assets are discussed in the next section.

Short-term securities (to be held one year or less) have minimal risk and provide liquidity. Long-term securities (to be held for more than one year) usually are invested in for capital appreciation and annual income.

Common Stock

Common stock is the equity investment representing ownership of a company. The margin requirement is 50% for common stock. Advantages of owning common stock are voting rights, appreciation in stock price, receipt of dividends, and a better hedge against inflation than fixed-income obligations. Disadvantages of common stock ownership are a decline in stock price in bearish markets, lack of sizable dividends, and higher risk than debt securities and preferred stock, since you are the last to be paid in corporate liquidation.

Types of Common Stock

- *Blue chip stock.* This is common stock of high-quality companies with a long record of earnings and dividends. They are typically held for a long term, have low risk, and generate modest but dependable return. An example is ITT.

- *Growth stocks.* These have a long record of higher-than-average earnings. Typically there is a low dividend payment, since funds are retained for expansion. They grow faster than the economy and industry. An example is high-tech firms.
- *Income stocks.* These stocks are suitable for those wishing higher current income instead of future capital gains with minimal risk. There are above-average returns and dividend payouts. Examples are utility stocks.
- *Cyclical stocks.* These are stocks that fluctuate in price depending on economic changes. An example is airlines.
- *Defensive stocks.* These are basically not affected by downswings in the business cycle, and are recession-resistant. An example is consumer products.
- *Speculative stocks.* These do not have a track record of high earnings and dividends. While profits are uncertain, they do have the potential for providing a substantial return. Speculative stocks are for you if you are willing to accept substantial risk in return for potentially high return. An example is cancer-related pharmaceuticals.
- *Penny stocks.* This refers to some over-the-counter stocks of high risk and low quality that nevertheless have potential for high return. Some are on the way toward failure, while others have just entered the market and are barely surviving.

Preferred Stock

Preferred stock is a hybrid of common stock and bonds. It is an equity investment (with no voting rights), but has many characteristics of a bond issue. The amount of dividend is typically fixed. There is an 80% dividend exclusion for dividends received on stock. Preferred stock is riskier than bonds, and as such has a higher return. Preferred stockholders take precedence over common stockholders in the receipt of dividends and in the event of liquidation. There is no maturity date, but preferred stock is often convertible into common stock. Preferred stock may be callable at the company's option, and it generally provides only dividend income rather than significant appreciation in price.

$$\text{Preferred dividend yield} = \frac{\text{Annual stated dividend income}}{\text{Preferred stock price}}$$

Bonds

A bond represents a long-term obligation to pay by a corporation or government. Bonds are typically in $1,000 denominations. You can buy or sell a bond before maturity at a price other than face value. Investment in bonds can provide you with both interest income and capital gains. Interest rates and bond prices move in opposite directions. A decrease in interest rate will result in an increase in bond price. Bonds are good for fixed income.

Corporate bonds have more risk than government bonds because companies can fail. A tax disadvantage to bonds is that interest income is fully taxed, while there is an 80% dividend exclusion. *Recommendation:* If you want stability in principal, buy variable rate bonds, because the interest rate is changed to keep the bonds at par.

Disadvantages of bond investment are constancy of interest income over the life of the bond, decrease in purchasing power during an inflationary period, sensitivity of prices to interest rate swings, and less marketability in the secondary market compared to stocks.

Convertible Securities

Convertible securities may be converted into common stock at a later date. Two examples of these securities are convertible bonds and convertible preferred stock. These securities provide fixed income in the form of interest (convertible bonds) or dividends (convertible preferred stock). You also benefit from the appreciation value of the common stock.

Warrants

A warrant permits you to purchase a given number of shares at a specified price during a given time period. Warrants are typically good for several years. They are often given as sweeteners for a bond issue. Warrants are not frequently issued, and are not available for all securities. There are no dividend payments or voting rights. A warrant permits you to take part indirectly in price appreciation of common stock and to derive a capital gain.

When the price per common share rises, you may either sell the warrant (because it also increases in value) or exercise it to obtain stock. Trading in warrants is speculative because of the possibility of variability in return, but the potential for high return exists.

EXAMPLE 10.5

A warrant in ABC Company stock permits you to buy one share at $10. If the stock rises in price prior to the expiration date, the warrant increases in value. If the stock drops below $10, the warrant loses value.

The warrant's exercise price is typically constant over its life. But the price of some warrants may increase as the expiration date becomes closer. Exercise price is adjusted for stock splits and stock dividends.

$$\text{Return on a warrant} = \frac{\dfrac{\text{Selling price} - \text{Purchase price}}{\text{Years}}}{\text{Average investment}}$$

EXAMPLE 10.6

You bought a warrant for $18 and sold it for $30 after 3 years. Your return rate is:

$$\frac{\dfrac{\$30 - \$18}{3}}{\dfrac{\$30 + \$18}{2}} = \frac{\$4}{\$24} = \underline{16.7\%}$$

Warrants are a speculative investment because their value depends on the price of common stock for which they may be exchanged. The value of a warrant varies as the related stock's price varies.

Value of a warrant = (Market price of common stock
 − Exercise price of warrant)
× Number of common shares bought for one warrant

EXAMPLE 10.7

The exercise price of a warrant is $40. Two warrants equal one share. The stock has a market price of $58.

Value of a warrant = ($58 − $40) × 0.5 = $\underline{\$9}$

Options

An option allows for the purchase of a security (or property) at a certain price during a specified time period. An option is neither debt nor equity. It is an opportunity to take advantage of an expected change in the price of a security. The option holder has no guaranteed return. The option may not be attractive to exercise, since the market price of the underlying common stock has not risen, for example, or the option time period may elapse. If this occurs, you will lose your investment. Thus, options involve considerable risk.

A *call* is an option to *buy*, whereas a *put* is an option to *sell*, a security at a specified price by a given date. Calls and puts can be bought in round lots, typically 100 shares. They are usually written for widely held and actively traded stock. Calls and puts are an alternative investment to common stock. They provide leverage opportunity and are speculative. You do not have to exercise a call or put to earn a return. You can trade them in the secondary market for their value at the time.

In purchasing a call you have the opportunity to make a substantial gain from a small investment, but you risk losing your entire investment if the stock price does not increase. Calls are in bearer form, with a life of one to nine months. Calls have no voting rights, ownership interest, or dividend income. However, option contracts are adjusted for stock splits and stock dividends. The value of a call rises as the underlying common stock increases in market price.

Value of call = (Market price of stock − Exercise price of call) × 100

EXAMPLE 10.8

The market price of a stock is $60, with an exercise price of $53.

Value of call = ($60 − $53) × 100 = $700

EXAMPLE 10.9

You have a 3-month call option permitting you to buy 700 shares of a company's stock at $15 per share. Within the time period, you exercise the option when the market price is $23. The gain is $5,600 ($8 × 700). If the price had declined or remained at $15 per share you would not have been able to exercise the call option, and would have lost the entire cost of the option.

In purchasing a call you buy common stock for a fraction of the cost of purchasing regular shares. Calls are bought at a much lower price than common stock. Leverage exists, since a little change in common stock price can result in a significant change in the call option's price. Part of the percentage gain in the call price is the speculative premium applicable to the remaining time period on the call. Calls let you control 100 shares of stock without making a significant dollar investment.

EXAMPLE 10.10

A stock has a price of $35. You can for $300 purchase a call that permits the acquisition of 100 shares at $35 each. The stock prices goes to $57, at which time you exercise the call. The profit is $22 on each of the 100 shares of stock in the call, or a total of $2,200, on an investment of only $300. The net return is 633% ($2,200 – $300/$300).

As previously mentioned, your return on a put comes when stock price declines.

Value of put = (Exercise price of put – Market price of stock) × 100

EXAMPLE 10.11

Stock price is $40. You acquire a put to sell 100 shares of stock at $40. The cost of the put is $250. When stock price goes to $27, you exercise the put. The profit is $1,300 ($13 × 100). Your net gain is $1,050 ($1,300 – $250). Your net return is 420% ($1,050/$250).

Investment strategies with calls and puts include hedging, straddles, and spreads.

If you own a call and put option you can *hedge* by holding on to two or more securities to lower risk and at the same time earn a profit. It may involve purchasing a stock and later buying an option on it. For instance, a stock may be acquired along with writing a call on it. Further, a holder of a security that has increased in price may acquire a put to bring about downside risk protection.

Straddling integrates a call and put on the identical security with the same exercise price and exercise date. It is employed by a speculator trading on both sides of the market. The speculator looks to a significant change in stock price in one direction in order to earn a gain exceeding the cost of both options. But if the large change in prices does not occur, there is a loss equal to the cost of the options. A straddle holder can increase risk and earning potential by closing one option prior to closing the other.

With a *spread*, you buy an option (long position) and write an option (short position) in the same security using call options. There is high risk and a potential for high return. With a spread, you buy one call and sell another. The net profit from a spread position depends on the change between two option prices as the stock price increases or decreases.

Straddles and spreads are not traded on listed exchanges, but rather must be bought through brokerage houses and members of the Put and Call Brokers and Dealers Association.

Futures Contracts

In the futures market you can trade in commodities and financial instruments. A future is a contract to buy or sell a specified amount of an item for a certain price by a given date. The seller of a futures contract agrees to deliver the item to the buyer of the contract, who agrees to buy the item. In the contract are specified the amount, valuation, method, quality, expiration date, manner of delivery, and exchange to be traded in.

Commodity contracts are assurances by a seller to deliver a commodity (e.g., wheat). Financial contracts are seller agreements to deliver a financial instrument (e.g., Treasury bill) or a given amount of foreign currency. Futures are high-risk investments partly because they depend on international economic conditions and the volatile nature of prices.

A "long position" is buying a contract in the hope that the price will increase. A "short position" is selling a contract with the expectation that the price will decline. The position may be terminated by reversing the transaction. For example, the long buyer may subsequently become a short seller of the same amount of the commodity or financial instrument. Practically all futures are offset prior to delivery.

A futures contract can be traded in the futures market. Trading is accomplished through specialized brokers, and some commodity firms deal only in futures. Fees depend on the contract amount and the price of the item.

Commodities Futures

Commodity contracts may last up to 1 year. There are standardized unit sizes of some commodity contracts (e.g., 50,000 pounds for cotton). You can invest in a commodity directly, indirectly through a mutual fund, or by a limited partnership involved in commodity investments. The latter is more conservative, because risk is spread among many owners and professional management runs the limited partnership. You may look to commodity trading for high rates of return and as an inflation hedge. *Recommendation:* To reduce your risk, diversify your portfolio.

Commodity and financial futures are traded in the Chicago Board of Trade, which is the largest exchange. There are other exchanges, some specializing in given commodities (e.g., New York Cotton Exchange).

The return on futures contracts is in the form of capital gain because no current income is earned. There is high return potential due to price volatility of the commodity and leverage effects from low margin requirements. But if things go the opposite way, the entire investment in the form of margin can be lost rapidly.

$$\text{Return on commodity contract} = \frac{\text{Selling price} - \text{Purchase price}}{\text{Margin deposit}}$$

EXAMPLE 10.12

You buy a commodity contract for $30,000 giving a margin deposit of $6,000. You sell the contract for $32,000.

$$\text{Return on commodity contract} = \frac{\$32,000 - \$30,000}{\$6,000} = \frac{\$2,000}{\$6,000} = 0.33$$

The margin on a commodity contract is low, typically from 5% to 10% of the contract's value.

Financial Futures

Financial futures may relate to interest rate futures, foreign currency futures, and stock–index futures. As a result of instability in interest and exchange rates, financial futures can be used to hedge. They can also be used to speculate, because of the possibility of major price changes. There is a lower margin requirement with financials than with commodities. For example, the margin on a U.S. Treasury bill is about 2%. For the most part, financial futures are for fixed-income debt securities to hedge or speculate on interest rate changes and foreign currency.

With an interest rate futures contract, you have the right to a certain amount of the applicable debt security at a subsequent date (typically no more than 3 years). Examples are Treasury bills and notes, certificates of deposit, and commercial paper.

The value of interest rate futures contracts is directly linked to interest rates. For instance, as interest rates decrease, the contract's value increases. As the price or quote of the contract increases, the buyer of the contract gains, while the seller loses.

If you are a speculator, financial futures are attractive because of the possibility of a significant return on a small investment. But there is much risk to interest futures because of their volatility, along with significant gain or loss potential.

With a currency futures contract you have the right to a certain amount of foreign currency at a later date. The contracts are standardized;

no secondary markets exist. Currency futures are expressed in dollars or cents per unit of the related foreign currency. The delivery period is usually no more than 1 year. There are standardized trading units for different currencies (e.g., the British pound has a 25,000 trading unit).

> **EXAMPLE 10.13**
>
> Assume a standardized contract of £100,000. In March you buy a currency futures contract for delivery in July. The contract price is $1, or £2. The total value of the contract is $50,000, and the margin requirement is $6,000. The pound strengthens until £1.8 equal $1. Thus, the value of your contract rises to $55,556, providing you with a return of 92.6%. However, if there was a weakening in the pound, you would have incurred a loss on the contract.

A stock-index futures contract is tied to a broad stock market index (e.g., S&P 500 Stock Index, New York Stock Exchange Composite Stock Index). They permit you to take part in the general change in the entire stock market. You are in effect purchasing and selling the market as a whole instead of a specific security. *When to Use:* If you believe there will be a bull market but are uncertain as to which individual stock will increase, buy (long position) a stock-index future. There is high risk involved, however.

REAL ASSETS

Real (tangible) assets are those that physically exist (e.g., can be touched). They include real estate, precious metals, gems, collectibles, common metals, and oil. We will discuss here only the first two, since they are relevant for corporate investors.

Real property can be used to diversify a portfolio, since it typically increases in value when financial assets are decreasing in value. Disadvantages of tangible assets are that there is less liquidity (a secondary market does not always exist), dealer commission rates are higher than with financial assets, there may be storage and insurance costs, a substantial capital investment is required, and no current income is provided (except for rental real estate).

Real Estate

Real estate ownership can take the form of residential property, commercial property, raw land, limited partnership in a real estate syndicate, and ownership of shares in a real estate investment trust (REIT).

Real estate generates capital appreciation potential. Some types of real estate investment property (residential and commercial) provide annual income. Advantages of investing in real estate are building equity, high yield, inflation hedge, and leverage opportunity. Leverage improves earnings when the return earned on borrowed funds is greater than the after-tax interest cost. Disadvantages of investing in real estate are possible governmental regulation (e.g., building codes), high property taxes, possible losses if property declines in value, and limited marketability.

Commercial and industrial properties have differing degrees of risk depending on the tenants. There are also significant operating expenses.

Raw land has the highest risk but possesses the greatest return potential. There is no annual income; return is from appreciation in value.

REITs issue shares to obtain investment, which along with borrowed funds is put into long-term mortgages and real estate projects. REITs are similar to mutual funds, and are traded on the exchanges or over the counter. Real estate investment trusts have liquidity because of the existence of a secondary market.

A limited partnership (real estate syndicate) is a tax-sheltered investment with capital gain potential. The general partner (decision maker) sells participation units to limited partners (whose obligations are typically limited to their investments). Besides making cash investments, the partnership often incurs debt in the acquisition of properties. The advantage of a limited partnership is the greater and more diversified holdings. Disadvantages of a limited partnership are that limited partners have minimal control over activities, high fees are charged by the general partner, foreclosure can occur if borrowed amounts are not paid, and there is no secondary market, which precludes their sale.

Considerations in a Real Estate Arrangement

- Possible lawsuits against the partnership
- Prior performance
- Previous delays in paying limited partners
- Where funds are invested (e.g., identifiable or nonidentifiable property)
- Whether the limited partnership investment is publicly or privately traded

Precious Metals

Precious metals (e.g., gold and silver) are volatile investments, but they do furnish a hedge against inflation. The price of precious metals typically increases during troubled times because of investor uncertainty and decreases during stable, predictable periods. When interest rates are high, it is expensive to invest in gold or silver. Precious metals are liquid (have international markets) and are not periodically taxed.

Gold

Gold acts as an inflation hedge and is a good investment when there is a depreciation in paper currency and when interest rates are low. Gold typically reacts opposite to the way in which common stock does. Gold may be acquired directly or indirectly (e.g., shares in a gold mine). Investment in shares of gold mines does provide portfolio diversification. Disadvantages of gold investment are high storage cost, high transaction costs, no dividend revenue, price volatility, and the fact that some types of gold are in bearer form. An advantage to owning gold is the possibility of large appreciation in price.

Silver

The return from silver comes from capital appreciation. While silver is much lower in price than gold, there is a relatively higher carrying cost. You may also buy stock in silver mining companies.

PORTFOLIO ANALYSIS

The investment portfolio should be diversified into many different types of securities in different industry groups as well as international markets. A balanced portfolio contains stocks, bonds, real estate, money market (e.g., commercial paper), precious metals, and options. There is a trade-off of return and risk. Portfolio risk can be minimized by diversifying. The degree of reduction in portfolio risk depends on the correlation between the assets being combined.

> **EXAMPLE 10.14**
>
> A portfolio has a risk-free rate of 10%, market portfolio return of 14%, and beta of 0.9. The expected rate of return is
>
> $$10\% + 0.9(14\% - 10\%) = \underline{13.6\%}$$

MUTUAL FUNDS

Mutual funds represent investment in a professionally managed portfolio of securities. You receive shares of stock in a mutual fund investment company. Advantages are diversification, excellent management, more informed decisions, size (e.g., bid buys may influence the price of a stock up), ownership in many securities with minimal capital investment, dividend reinvestment, check-writing options, and easy record keeping (it is done by the fund). Disadvantages are commission charges and professional management fees. Generally, mutual fund performance has not materially done better than the market as a whole. However, certain mutual funds are well known for excellent performance over the years, as rated by independent sources like *Forbes* and *Money* magazines. Examples are Fidelity and Twentieth Century.

Mutual funds may be classified by type depending on organization, fees charged, methods of trading funds, and investment purpose. With open-end funds, you can purchase from and sell shares back to the fund itself. On the other hand, closed-end funds have a fixed number of shares outstanding. These shares are traded similarly to common stock in secondary markets. All open- and closed-end funds charge management fees. Load funds charge sales commissions while no-load funds do not.

There are also specialized mutual funds (e.g., money market fund). Mutual funds may have different investment purposes: growth, safety and income, capital appreciation, and growth plus income, for instance. You may invest in index funds to control portfolio risk and assure market performance. An index fund follows the change in a selected broad market index (e.g., Standard & Poor's 500) by holding investment commitments in the same proportion as those that comprise the index itself.

Types of Mutual Funds

- *Growth*. The purpose is capital appreciation. The stocks invested in have growth potential, but greater risk.
- *Income*. The objective is to obtain current income (e.g., dividends, interest income). Typically, the portfolio comprises high-dividend common stock, preferred stock, and debt securities. Generally, high-quality securities are bought.
- *Balanced*. These funds provide capital gains and current income. A high percentage of the portfolio is in high-quality common stock to achieve capital appreciation with a lower percentage in fixed income securities. There is a safe return with minimal risk. It is a hybrid between growth and income funds.
- *Bonds*. An investment is made in different types and qualities of bonds. Interest income is the paramount concern. The funds provide liquidity,

safety, and diversification. Some bond funds invest only in municipal securities to obtain tax-free income.

- *Money market.* These funds invest in short-term money market securities such as commercial paper, so there is liquidity with low risk. Usually the return on the fund exceeds what can be earned on a bank account.

A fund may invest in only one industry (e.g., Fidelity Select) or a group of industries. They try to maximize the rate of return, but higher risk is usually involved.

The return from mutual funds comes in the form of dividends, capital gain, and change in capital or net asset value (NAV) of the fund.

$$\frac{\text{Holding}}{\text{period}} = \frac{\text{Dividends} + \text{Capital gain distribution} + \text{Change in net asset value}}{\text{Beginning net asset value}}$$

FUNDAMENTAL ANALYSIS

Fundamental analysis evaluates a stock by analyzing the company's financial statements. It considers overall financial health, economic and political conditions, industry factors, and future outlook of the company. It tries to determine whether stock is overpriced, underpriced, or correctly priced. Financial statement analysis provides you with much of the data you require to forecast earnings, dividends, and selling price.

You have to look at economic risk. What is the effect of business cycles on the firm? Business cycles arise from three conditions: (1) changes in demand; (2) diversification of customer base; and (3) product diversification. The greater the changes in product demand, the more the company is affected by the business cycle, and thus the greater the profit variability.

Fundamental analysis is discussed in detail in chapters 4, 5, and 6.

TECHNICAL ANALYSIS

According to technical analysis, the market can be predicted in terms of direction and magnitude. You can evaluate the stock market by employing numerous indicators, including studying economic factors within the marketplace. Stock prices tend to move with the market because they react to numerous demand and supply forces. You may attempt to forecast short-term price changes to properly time purchase and sale of securities. You try to recognize a recurring pattern in prices or a relationship between stock price changes and other market data. You can also employ charts and graphs of internal market data, such as price and volume.

The two major techniques of technical analysis are key indicators and charting.

Key Indicators

Key indicators of market and stock performance include trading volume, market breadth, Barron's Confidence Index, mutual fund cash position, short selling, odd-lot theory, and the Index of Bearish Sentiment.

Trading Volume

A reflection of the health of the stock market is the number of shares traded. Price follows volume. For instance, increased price usually occurs with increased volume. Trading volume is based on supply–demand relationships and indicates market strength or weakness. A strong market occurs when volume rises as prices increase. A weak market occurs when volume increases as prices decrease. If the demand of new stock offerings exceeds the supply, stock prices will increase. *Note:* Supply–demand evaluation is more concerned with the short term than the long term.

Volume is closely tied into stock price change. A bullish market occurs when there is a new high on heavy volume. But a new high with light trading volume is considered temporary. A new low with light volume is deemed significantly better than one with high volume, since fewer investors are involved. A bearish situation occurs when there is high volume with the new low price.

Watch out for a "selling climax," when prices decrease for a long period at an increased rate, coupled with increased volume. Subsequent to the climax, we expect prices to increase, and the low at the point of climax is not anticipated to be violated for a long time. A selling climax usually happens at the end of a bear market.

When prices have been going up for several months, a low price increase coupled with high volume is a bearish indicator.

An upside–downside index shows the difference between advances and decreases in stock volume typically based on a 10- or 30-day moving average. The index assists in predicting stock market turning points. A bull market continues only where buying pressures continue to be strong.

The final stage of a major increase in stock price is referred to as the "exhaustion move." It takes place when there is a rapid decline in volume and price. A trend reversal is indicated.

Market Breadth

Market breadth refers to the dispersion of a general price increase or decrease. You can use it as an advance reflection of major stock price declines or advances. It can be used to analyze the prime turning points of the market on the basis of stock market cycles. A bull market is a long time period in which securities approach their highs slowly, with the individual peaks increasing as market averages approach a turning point. In a bear market, many stock prices decrease materially in a short time period. Market weakness occurs when many stocks are decreasing in prices while the averages increase. In forecasting the end of a bear market, the degree of stock selling is considered.

A breadth measure looks at the activity of a broader range of securities than does a market average (e.g., Dow Jones Industrial). The Dow Jones stocks are not representative of the whole market, since the average is weighted toward large companies. Hence, all stocks on an exchange may be analyzed by considering advances and declines.

The Breadth Index computes on a daily basis the net advances or declining issues on the New York Stock Exchange. Net advances is a positive sign. The amount of strength depends on the spread between the number of advances and declines. *Recommendation:* Look at relevant figures in *The Wall Street Journal.*

$$\text{Breadth index} = \frac{\text{New advances or declines}}{\text{Number of securities traded}}$$

Advances less declines typically move in the same direction as a popular market average. However, they may go in the opposite direction at a market peak or bottom.

Breadth analysis concentrates on change instead of level. *Suggestion:* Chart the Breadth Index against a market average (e.g., Dow Jones Industrial). In most cases they move together. *Caution:* In a bull market, carefully watch an extended divergence between the Breadth Index, such as where it drops gradually, to new lows and the Dow Jones, such as where it goes to new highs. *Recommendation:* Compare the Breadth Index for the current period to a base year. When the Breadth Index and Dow Jones Industrial Average are both dropping, it points to market weakness.

EXAMPLE 10.15

Net declines are 24 on securities traded of 1,160. The Breadth Index is −2.1% (−24/1,160).

A possible sign to the end of a bull market is when the Dow Jones Industrial Average is rising but the number of daily declines exceeds the number of daily advances on a continual basis. This possibly reflects that conservative investors are purchasing blue chip stocks, but do not have confidence in the overall market. A market upturn is pointed to when the Dow Jones Industrial Average is dropping, but advances continually lead declines.

Market breadth can be applied to individual securities as well. Net volume (rises in price minus decreases in price) should be computed.

EXAMPLE 10.16

Sixty thousand shares are traded in Company X for 1 day: 45,000 are on the upside (rising in price), 10,000 are on the downside (decreasing in price), and 5,000 have no change. The net volume difference is 35,000, traded on upticks. You have to appraise any sign of divergence between the price trend and the net volume for the company. If there is a divergence, you may expect a reversal in the price trend. Accumulation occurs when price decreases and net volume increases.

Barron's Confidence Index

Barron's Confidence Index evaluates the trading pattern of bond investors. It helps in deciding when to buy and sell stocks. The assumption used is that bond traders have more knowledge than stock traders, and hence spot trends more quickly. If you know what bond traders are doing today, you can predict what stock traders will be doing next. Barron's Confidence Index is calculated as follows:

$$\frac{\text{Yield on Barron's 10 top-grade corporate bonds}}{\text{Yield on Dow Jones 40-bond average}}$$

EXAMPLE 10.17

The Dow Jones's yield is 15% and the Barron's yield is 14%.

Barron's Confidence Index = 93.3% (14%/15%)

The numerator has a lower yield relative to the denominator since it contains higher-quality bonds. Lower risk means lower return. Obviously, the index will always be less than 100%. In the case where bond investors are bullish, there will be a small yield difference between high-grade and low-grade bonds (probably around 95%). In bearish times, bond investors will look to high-quality issues. If investors continue to place money in lower-quality bonds, they will demand a higher yield to compensate for the increased risk. The Confidence Index will now be lower because of an increasing denominator. If confidence is high, investors will buy lower-grade bonds. Consequently, the yield on high-grade bonds will decrease while the yield on low-grade bonds will increase.

Mutual Fund Position

The buying pattern of mutual funds reflects the purchasing potential of large institutional investors. *Recommendation:* Look at the Investment Company Institute's monthly ratio of mutual fund cash and cash equivalents to total assets. A change in the ratio points to changes in institutional investor opinions. Typically, the ratio is between 5 and 25%. When a mutual fund's cash position is 15% of assets or higher, you can assume the fund represents significant purchasing power, which points to a possible market upturn. The higher the cash position of the fund, the more bullish the general market outlook. The investment of this cash will cause a rise in stock prices. On the other hand, a low ratio is a bearish indicator.

Short Selling

You can engage in short selling when you believe stock prices will go down. In effect, you sell high and buy low. In a short sale you make a profit if the market price of the security drops. To make a short sale, your broker borrows the security from someone else and then sells it for you to another. Subsequently, you buy the shares back. Of course, if market price goes up, you have a loss. You "sell short against the box" when you sell short shares you actually own.

EXAMPLE 10.18

You sell short 100 shares of Company Y stock, which has a market price of $60 per share. You later buy them back for $48 per share. Your profit is $1,200 ($12 per share × 100 shares).

Technical analysts evaluate the number of shares sold short. They also examine the ratio of latest reported short interest position for the month to the daily average volume for the month. Short interest refers to the number of shares sold short in the market at any given time. A high ratio is bullish and a low ratio is bearish. Typically, the ratio for all stockholders on the New York Stock Exchange has been between 1.0 and 1.75. A short interest ratio of 2.0 or greater indicates a market low.

The examination of short sales is an example of a "contrary opinion rule." Some analysts are of the opinion that a rise in the number of short sellers points to a bullish market. It is believed that short sellers overreact. Further, the short seller will subsequently buy the short-sold stock back, resulting in an increased market demand.

However, some analysts believe that increased short selling points to a downward and technically weak market, which results from investor pessimism.

The Wall Street Journal publishes the amount of short interest on the New York Stock Exchange and the American Stock Exchange. By monitoring short interests you can forecast future market demand and determine whether the current market is optimistic or pessimistic. *Advice:* A significant short interest in a stock should make you question the security's value.

Why not also look at odd-lot short sales? Many odd-lotters are uninformed. An odd-lotter ratio of 3.0 or more reflects pessimism.

Specialists make markets in various securities and are deemed "smart money" investors. *Recommendation:* Look at the ratio of specialists' short sales to the total number of short sales on an exchange.

Odd-Lot Theory

An odd lot is a transaction in which less than 100 shares of a security are involved. Odd-lot trading is indicative of popular opinion. It rests on the theory of contrary opinion. *Guideline:* Determine what losers are doing and then do the opposite. In essence, sophisticated investors should sell when small traders are buying and buy when they are selling. Refer to *The Wall Street Journal* for odd-lot trading information. Volume is typically expressed in shares instead of dollars. But some technical analysts employ the *SEC Statistical Bulletin*, where volume is expressed in dollars.

$$\text{Odd-lot index} = \frac{\text{Odd-lot purchases}}{\text{Odd-lot sales}}$$

The ratio typically is between 0.40 and 1.60.

You may also examine the ratio of odd-lot short sales to total odd-lot sales, and the ratio of total odd-lot volume (buys and sells) to round-lot volume on the New York Stock Exchange. These figures act to substantiate the conclusions reached by evaluating the ratio of odd-lot selling volume to odd-lot buying volume.

As per the odd-lot theory, the small trader is right most of the time but does not recognize key market turns. For instance, odd-lot traders correctly begin selling part of their portfolios in an upward market trend, but as the market continues to rise, small traders try to make substantial profits by becoming significant net buyers. However, this precedes a market fall.

Index of Bearish Sentiment

Investors Intelligence's Index of Bearish Sentiment is based on the opposite of the recommendations of investment advisory services. It is a contrary opinion rule. For example, if investment advisory services say buy, you should sell. According to Investors Intelligence, when 42% or more of the advisory services are bearish, the market will go up. On the other hand, when 17% or fewer of the services are bearish, the market will drop.

$$\text{Index of Bearish Sentiment} = \frac{\text{Bearish services}}{\text{Total number of services giving an option}}$$

When the ratio goes toward 10%, it means the Dow Jones Industrial Average is about to move from bullish to bearish. When the index approaches 60%, the Dow Jones Industrial Average is about to go from bearish to bullish. The reasoning of the theory is that advisory services are trend followers instead of anticipators.

Puts and Calls

You may look toward option trading activity to forecast market trends.

$$\text{Put-call ratio} = \frac{\text{Put volume}}{\text{Call volume}}$$

The index increases when there is more put activity because of pessimism around market bottom. The ratio goes down when there is more call activity because investors are optimistic around the market peak.

$$\text{Option buy call percentage} = \frac{\text{Open buy call transactions}}{\text{Total call volume}}$$

A high ratio points to investor optimism.

Charting

Charts are useful in analyzing market conditions and price behavior of individual securities. Reference can be made to Standard & Poor's *Trendline*, which provides charting data on companies. Chart interpretation requires the ability to evaluate formations and identify buy and sell indicators. The major types of charts are line (Figure 10.1), bar (Figure 10.2), and point-and-figure.

A chart provides information about resistance levels (points). A breakout from the resistance level notes market direction. The longer the sideways movement prior to a break, the more stock can increase in price.

Benefits of the chart are they help you to ascertain whether there is a major market upturn or downturn and whether the trend will reverse. You can further appraise what price may be achieved by a given stock or market average. Also, these charts help in forecasting the magnitude of a price swing.

Moving Average

Moving averages assist in analyzing intermediate and long-term stock movements. By evaluating the trend in current prices relative to the long-term moving average of prices, you can predict a reversal in a major uptrend in price of a company's stock or of the general market. The underlying direction and degree of change in volatile numbers are depicted in a moving average.

Moving average computation:

- *Step 1:* Average a portion of the series.
- *Step 2:* Add the following number to the numbers already averaged, omitting the first number.
- *Step 3:* Obtain a new average.

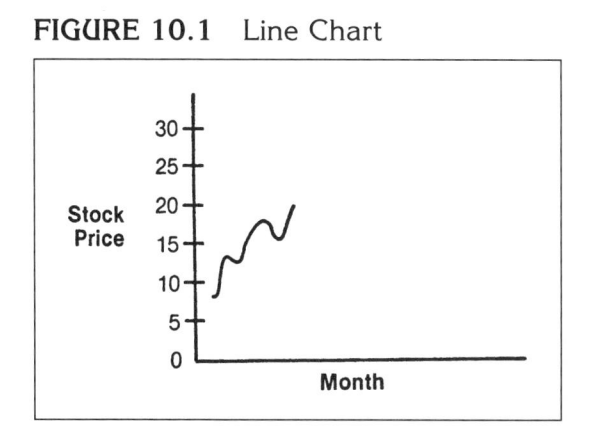

FIGURE 10.1 Line Chart

[Figure 10.2: Bar Chart showing Stock Price vs Month]

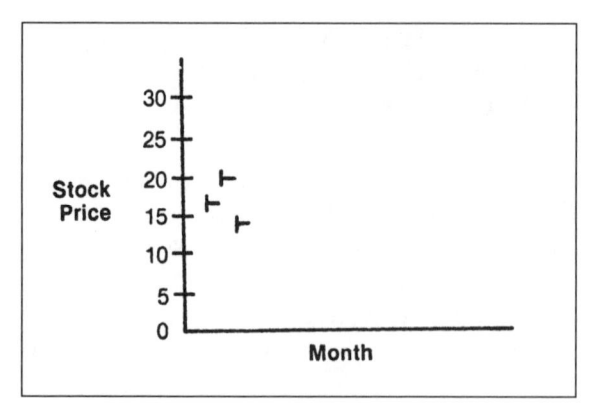

FIGURE 10.2 Bar Chart

Typically, a 200-day moving average of daily ending prices is used. The average is usually graphed to spot directions. *What to Do:* Buy when the 200-day average line becomes constant or increases after a decline and when the daily price of stock moves beyond the average line.

EXAMPLE 10.19

Day	Index	Three-Day Moving Total	Three-Day Moving Average
1	115		
2	126		
3	119	360 (days 1–3)	120 (360/3)
4	133	378 (days 2–4)	126 (378/3)

Suggestion: Buy when stock price surpasses the 200-day line, then goes down toward it but not through it, and then goes up again.

Relative Strength Analysis

Appraisal of relative strength assists in predicting individual stock prices.

$$\text{Relative strength (Method 1)} = \frac{\text{Monthly average stock price}}{\text{Monthly average market index (or industry group index)}}$$

$$\text{Relative strength (Method 2)} = \frac{\text{Specific industry group price index}}{\text{Total market index}}$$

What to Watch Out for: When a stock or industry group outperforms the market, that stock or industry is considered favorably because it should become even stronger. Some analysts distinguish between relative strength in a declining market and relative strength in an increasing market. When a stock does better than a major stock average in an advance, it may shortly turn around. However, when the stock is superior to the rest of the market in a decline, the stock will typically remain strong.

Support and Resistance Levels

A support level is the lower end of a trading range, while the resistance level is the upper end (Figure 10.3). Support may happen when a security goes to a lower trading level, since new investors may now desire to buy it. If such is the case, there will be new demand in the market. Resistance occurs when a stock goes to the high side of the normal trading range. If you purchase on an earlier high, you may see this as an opportunity to sell the security at a gain. When market price is higher than the resistance point or less than the support point, you may assume the stock is trading in a new range and that higher or lower trading values are imminent.

Dow Theory

Dow Theory applies to individual stocks and to the overall market. It is based on the movements of the Dow Jones Industrial Average and the Dow Jones Transportation Average. Stock market direction has to be confirmed by both averages. According to the theory, price trend in the overall mar-

FIGURE 10.3 Support and Resistance

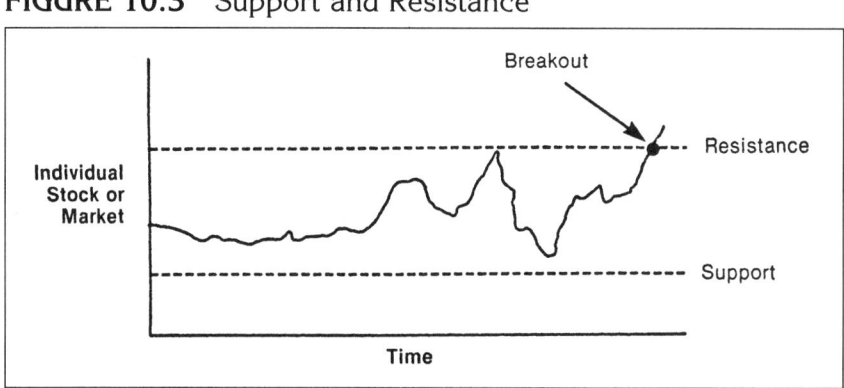

ket points to the termination of both bull and bear markets. It confirms when a reversal has taken place.

The following three movements in the market are assumed to occur simultaneously:

- *Primary*. A primary trend can be either bullish or bearish and typically lasts 28 to 33 months.
- *Secondary*. A secondary trend goes counter to the primary movement and typically lasts 3 weeks to 3 months.
- *Day-to-day*. This variability makes up the first two movements of the market.

Secondary movements and daily fluctuations reflect a long-term primary movement trend.

A major primary rise in market averages coexists with intermediate secondary downward reactions, eliminating a material amount of the previous increase. At the culmination of each reaction, a price recovery occurs that falls short of the previous rise. If, subsequent to an unsuccessful recovery, a downward reaction goes below the low point of the last prior reaction, it is inferred that the market is in a primary downturn (Figure 10.4.).

According to the Dow Theory, there is an upward market when the cyclical movements of the market averages increase over time and the suc-

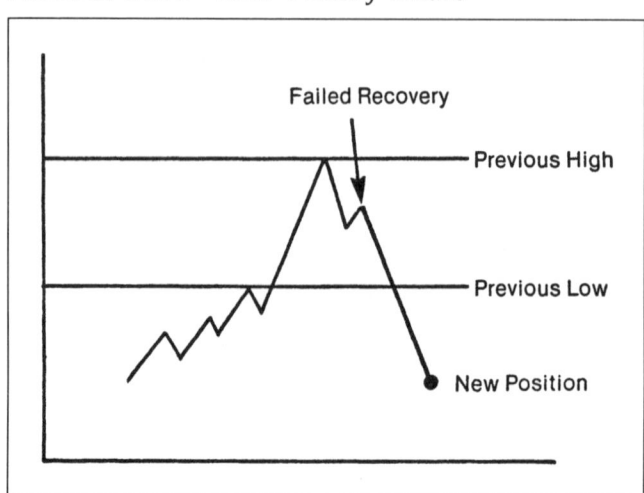

FIGURE 10.4 Dow Theory Chart

cessive market lows become higher. There is a downward market when the successive highs and successive lows in the market are lower than the previous highs and lows.

CONCLUSION

Portfolio investment analysis is needed to achieve maximum return on investments at minimal risk. A determination must be made of which investment vehicle is best under certain circumstances. Proper timing of buys and sells is also essential. Diversification is a must to guard against unusual price changes in one particular market.

11 How to Finance the Business

You can finance short-term (less than 1 year), intermediate-term (1 to 5 years), or long-term (in excess of 5 years). Each has its own merits and deficiencies. Under what circumstances is one better than the other? Are you able to adjust your financing strategy to meet changing times? Do you know the changing impact that economic, political, and industry conditions have on the entity's flow of funds? What is the degree of internally generated funds?

FINANCIAL PLANNING

After you have decided on the length of the financing, the proper type within the category must be chosen. In selecting a given financing instrument, you have to consider the following:

- Cost
- Risk
- Effect on financial ratios (e.g., solvency)
- Present debt in the capital structure
- Anticipated money market trends and availability of future financing
- Overall corporate objectives
- Tax effect
- Inflation rate
- Corporate profitability
- Cash flow and working capital levels

- Stability of operations
- Maturity of the firm

In looking at alternative financing sources, you have to consider not only satisfying current needs, but also undertaking business expansion. May the fund source be continually relied upon even in "tight money markets"? Otherwise there will be difficulties in maintaining corporate operations in recessionary times. If you think it is possible that you will be short of cash during certain times, you should arrange for financing in advance instead of waiting for an emergency. Is your financing policy inclined toward risk or safety? *Recommendation*: When debt levels are excessive, equity financing is preferred.

Small businesses can obtain equity financing economically by going to venture capital groups that take a position in a small business. A "finder" may act as an intermediary between the company and investing group. Alternatively, an ad may be placed in a newspaper. Another possibility is direct private placement to an institutional investor or a key customer or supplier. *Warning*: Avoid stringent restrictions that will curtail your freedom (e.g., minimum working capital requirement).

Suggestion: If you are materially affected by outside forces, you need more stability and reliability in your financing.

Advice: If you have financial problems, try to refinance short-term loans on a long-term basis, such as by lengthening the maturity date. Cash forecasting is essential to determine the amount of funds needed and for what length of time.

SHORT- AND INTERMEDIATE-TERM FINANCING SOURCES

Short- and intermediate-term financing sources include

- Trade credit
- Bank loan
- Finance company loan
- Commercial paper
- Receivable financing

- Inventory financing
- Leasing

Trade Credit

Trade credit is the amount owed to suppliers on account. Advantages are easy to obtain, no collateral is required, there is little or no interest, and trade creditors are more lenient than other creditors. However, the trade credit is limited to certain types of items. Further, the opportunity cost of not taking a discount on early payment should be determined, since it may be very costly.

> **EXAMPLE 11.1**
>
> A $10,000 purchase is made on terms of 2/20, net/60. The opportunity cost of not taking the discount is:
>
> $$\frac{\text{Discount foregone}}{\text{Proceeds from use of}} \times \frac{360}{\text{Days use of the money}}$$
>
> $$\frac{\$200}{\$9,800} \times \frac{360}{40} = 18.37\%$$
>
> You could most likely borrow at a lower rate than 18.37% in order to take advantage of the discount.

Bank Loan

Types of Bank Credit

- *Unsecured loan.* Recommended for financing projects that have immediate cash flow or for interim financing for a long-term project. *Suggestion*: Use for seasonal cash shortfalls, desired inventory buildups, or any situation in which you need immediate cash flow and can repay the loan quickly or shortly obtain longer-term financing. Disadvantages are its short term, higher interest rate, and the fact that it is repaid in a lump sum.
- *Line of credit.* A continuing agreement for loans up to a specified amount. *Recommendation*: Use if you work on large individual projects for a long time period and obtain minimal or no payments until the job is completed. Advantages are easy access to funds in tight money periods and abil-

ity to borrow only when needed, with quick repayment possibility. Disadvantages are that collateral is required and there are greater limitations (e.g., restrictions on capital expenditures). Determine whether your line of credit is adequate for your present and immediate future needs.

- *Revolving credit.* Notes are short term (typically 90 days). You may renew the loan or borrow additional funds up to a maximum amount. Advantages are readily available credit and fewer restrictions relative to the line-of-credit agreement. A disadvantage is the bank restrictions.
- *Installment loans.* These usually necessitate monthly payments. As the loan principal is lowered, refinancing may take place at lower interest rates. *Suggestion*: Tailor the loan to satisfy seasonal financing requirements.
- *Intermediate-term loans.* Recommended for financing fixed assets, acquiring another business, and to retire long-term debt. An advantage is that they may be adjusted more easily than a bond indenture or a preferred stock agreement. Disadvantages are possible collateral requirements, restrictive covenants (e.g., dividend restrictions), and periodic submission of financial reports.

Vital Question: If your bank chose to call your demand loans, could you obtain alternative financing without impairing your business?

Finance Company Loan

If you cannot obtain bank financing because of credit risks, you may be able to borrow from a finance company. Such borrowings are secured (collateral usually exceeds the loan balance) and they have higher interest rates than bank loans.

Commercial Paper

Commercial paper is unsecured and represents short-term notes issued by the highest-quality companies. Advantages are that the interest rate is lower than the bank borrowing rate, and no security is required.

EXAMPLE 11.2

You need $300,000 for the month of November. Your options are:

1. A 1-year line of credit for $300,000 with a bank. The commitment fee is 0.5%, and the interest charge on the used funds is 12%.

2. Issue 2-month commercial paper at 10% interest. Because the funds are only needed for one month, the excess funds ($300,000) can be invested in 8% marketable securities for December. The total transaction fee for the marketable securities is 0.3%.

The line of credit costs:

Commitment fee for unused period (0.005)(300,000)(11/12)	$1,375
Interest for one month (0.12)(300,000)(1/12)	3,000
Total cost	$4,375

The commercial paper costs:

Interest charge (0.10)(300,000)(2/12)	$5,000
Transaction fee (0.003)(300,000)	900
Less interest earned on marketable securities (0.08)(300,000)(1/12)	(2,000)
Total cost	$3,900

Note: The commercial paper arrangement is less costly.

Receivable Financing

Accounts receivable financing does not dilute ownership interest and allows you to avoid a long-term financing arrangement. *Factoring* is when accounts receivable are sold outright to a bank or finance company. Advantages to factoring are that you obtain cash immediately, you eliminate overhead expenses applicable to the accounts receivable function, you obtain management advice, you may receive cash advances on a seasonal basis, and you strengthen your balance sheet position. Disadvantages are the high cost and the potential of negative customer reaction. *Assignment* does not transfer ownership, but rather involves a cash advance based on a percent of the face value of the receivables. Disadvantages are the service charge, interest on the advance, retention of collection function, and absorbing bad debt losses. Advantages are immediate cash inflow, cash advances on a seasonal basis, and avoiding negative customer reaction.

Inventory Financing

Inventory financing typically takes place when you have already made full use of your ability to borrow on receivables. It requires that inventory be marketable, have a high turnover rate, not perishable, and not subject to rapid obsolescence. Raw materials and finished goods will usually be financed at about 75% of their value. The interest rate is usually several points above the prime interest rate.

EXAMPLE 11.3

You need $500,000 for a 3-month period. An insurance company has agreed to lend you the money at an 8% per annum interest rate using the inventory as collateral. A field warehouse agreement would be used, costing $1,300 per month.

For 3 months:

$$\text{Effective interest rate} = \frac{(3 \times 1{,}300) + (.08 \times 500{,}000 \times 3/12)}{500{,}000}$$

$$= \frac{13{,}900}{500{,}000} = 0.028$$

For 1 year:

$$0.028 \ (3 \text{ months}) \times 4 = \underline{0.112}$$

Leasing

Advantages of leasing are the absence of an immediate substantial cash outlay, the possibility of a bargain purchase option, the availability of the lessor's service technology, fewer restrictions, protection from technological obsolescence, and the fact that the obligation to pay does not necessarily have to be shown on the balance sheet. Disadvantages of leasing are higher cost than outright buying, the necessity of paying current prices at lease termination to enter into a new lease or acquire property, and having to use property no longer suitable or necessary.

COMPARING SHORT- TO LONG-TERM FINANCING

Short-term financing is easier to arrange, has lower cost, and is more flexible than long-term financing. However, short-term financing makes the borrower more subject to interest rate swings, requires refinancing more quickly, and is more difficult to repay. *Recommendation:* Use short-term financing as additional working capital, finance short-lived assets, or as interim financing on long-term projects. Long-term financing is more appropriate to finance long-term assets or construction projects.

LONG-TERM FINANCING

Types of long-term financing are:

- Mortgages
- Bonds
- Equity securities

Mortgages

Mortgages are notes payable to banks that are secured by real property, and are used to finance long-term needs (e.g., purchases of fixed assets, plant construction, and renovation). Advantages are favorable interest rates, fewer financing restrictions than other long-term sources, long payment schedules, and availability. A drawback is the collateral requirement.

Bonds

In a private placement, bonds are sold to a limited number of investors (usually institutional investors) without a public offering. Advantages are the elimination of underwriter fees and no need to register with the SEC.

Reasons to issue debt instead of equity securities are the tax deductibility of interest, and the fact that you will be paying back in cheaper dollars during inflation, there is no dilution of voting control, and flexibility in financing is possible by having a call provision in the bond indenture. Disadvantages are the need to make principal repayment and fixed interest charges and indenture restrictions.

Circumstances Favoring Long-Term Debt Issuance

- Stability in sales and earnings
- High net income
- High inflationary period
- Low debt–equity ratio
- Currently depressed market price of stock

Financial leverage should be used when a company's earnings are adequate to cover preferred stock dividends. But when a high degree of financial leverage exists, the company should try to reduce other risks (e.g., product risk). With a bond issue, a sinking fund is usually set up. *Recommendation:* If you expect interest rates to drop in the future, have a call provision in the bond indenture.

Convertible bonds have a number of positive attributes in terms of marketability, lower interest rates, and nonrepayment if converted to stock.

Warning: If the maturity structure of debt is such that large debt repayments will be due, stock issuance is recommended.

Equity Securities

Equity securities refer to common stock and preferred stock. Common stock is the real ownership interest in the company, because it carries voting rights. Advantages are that there are no fixed charge payments, no maturity date, no sinking fund requirements, you do not have to pay dividends in times of financial distress, and they improve the debt–equity ratio. Disadvantages are that you give up voting rights, ownership interest is diluted, there are higher flotation costs, investors receive dividends after preferred stockholders in case of liquidation, dividend payments are not tax deductible (unlike interest), and the cost is higher because greater risk exists with common stock than with preferred stocks and bonds.

Preferred stock comes after debt but before common stock in liquidation and in the distribution of earnings. With cumulative preferred stock, preferred dividends in arrears must be paid before any dividends can be paid to common stockholders. *Suggestion:* To avoid SEC disclosures and reduce issuance costs, private placement may be made.

The advantages of preferred stock relative to bonds are that you can omit a dividend but not interest, and there is no maturity date and no sinking fund requirement. Compared to common stock, there is no ownership dilution with preferred stock. Disadvantages of preferred stock relative to debt are that dividends are not tax deductible and there is a higher yield (because of the greater risk to the holder). *Recommendation:* Issue preferred stock where debt is already excessive and issuing common stock will result in control problems for the ownership group.

The cost of preferred stock usually follows changes in interest rates. Hence, the cost of preferred stock will most likely be low when interest rates are low. When the cost of common stock is high, preferred stock issuance may be achieved at a lower cost.

Suggestion: If you want to issue debt or preferred stock at a lower cost with fewer restrictions, warrants may be given as "sweeteners." Warrants are rights to buy common stock at a certain price at a later date.

COST OF CAPITAL

The cost of capital is the cost to the business of financing. An increase in the cost of capital rate of a company relative to the competition means it is viewed as being more risky in the eyes of the investment and credit community. As risk increases, interest rates and dividend yields increase. The cost of capital is also the discount rate that is used in present value analysis in capital budgeting. *Most Important*: A comparison should be made of the cost of capital rates determined under alternative financing strategies (e.g., mix of debt, preferred stock, and common stock within the capital structure). *Decision Rule*: Typically issue the financing instrument that results in the lowest overall cost of capital.

How is the cost of capital determined? It is a weighted average of the after-tax cost of debt and equity securities considering the percentage weights of each security type in the capital structure.

Cost of Short-Term Debt

The cost of a short-term obligation relates to the interest rate on bank or finance company loans.

$$\text{Cost of short-term debt} = \frac{\text{Interest}}{\text{Proceeds received}}$$

A bank typically discounts a loan, meaning that interest is deducted from the face of the loan to obtain the proceeds. A compensating balance also reduces the proceeds. As a result, the effective (real) interest rate on the loan exceeds the face interest, since the proceeds received are less than the face of the loan.

EXAMPLE 11.4

You take out a $320,000, 1-year, 11% loan with a compensating balance of 15%. The loan is made on a discount basis. The effective interest rate is:

$$\frac{11\% \times \$320{,}000}{\$236{,}800^a} = \frac{\$35{,}200}{\$236{,}800} = \underline{14.9\%}$$

Face of loan	$320,000
Less	
Interest	(35,200)
Compensating balance 15% × $320,000	(48,000)
Proceeds	$236,800

Note: The effective interest rate is materially greater than the stated interest rate.

---
[a] Proceeds received equals.

EXAMPLE 11.5

You need an additional $100,000. Your options are

1. A loan from a bank at 12% interest on a discount basis with a compensating balance of 10%.

or

2. A factoring arrangement where the factor is willing to purchase the accounts receivable and advance the invoice amount less a 4% factoring commission on the inventories bought. Sales are on 30-day terms. A 14% interest rate will be charged on the total invoice price and deducted in advance. With the factoring arrangement, the credit department will be eliminated, reducing monthly credit expenses by $1,500. Also, bad debt losses of 8% on the factored amount will be avoided.

To net you $100,000, the bank loan has to be:

$$\frac{\$100{,}000}{1 - (0.12 + .10)} = \frac{\$100{,}000}{0.78} = \underline{\$128{,}205}$$

To net you $100,000, the amount of accounts receivable to be factored is:

$$\frac{\$100{,}000}{1 - (0.04 + 0.14)} = \frac{\$100{,}000}{0.82} = \underline{\$121{,}951}$$

The effective interest rate on the bank loan is:

$$\frac{0.12}{0.78} = \underline{15.38\%}$$

The annual total dollar cost is:

Interest (0.12 × $128,205)	$15,385
Credit department ($1,500 × 12)	18,000
Bad debts (0.08 × $121,951)	9,756
Total cost	$43,141

The effective interest rate on the factoring arrangement is:

$$\frac{0.14}{0.82} = \underline{17.07\%}$$

The annual total dollar cost is:

Interest (0.14 × $121,951)	$17,073
Factoring (0.04 × $121,951)	4,878
Total cost	$21,951

Note: The bank loan is more costly in total dollar terms.

Cost of Long-Term Debt

The cost (yield) of a bond may be expressed as the simple (face) yield and the yield to maturity (effective interest rate). The latter is more difficult to calculate, but is considerably more accurate.

$$\text{Simple yield} = \frac{\text{Nominal (face) interest}}{\text{Present value of bond}}$$

$$\text{Yield to maturity} = \frac{\text{Nominal interest} + \left(\frac{\text{Discount}}{\text{years}} \text{ or } - \frac{\text{Premium}}{\text{years}}\right)}{\frac{\text{Present value} + \text{Maturity value}}{2}}$$

EXAMPLE 11.6

You issue a $500,000, 8%, 5-year bond for 98% of face value. Yield calculations follow.

Nominal interest payment (8% × $500,000)	$ 40,000
Proceeds of bond (98% × $500,000)	490,000
Bond discount (2% × $500,000)	10,000

$$\text{Simple yield} = \frac{\$40,000}{\$490,000} = \underline{8.2\%}$$

$$\text{Yield to maturity} = \frac{\$40,000 + \dfrac{\$10,000}{5}}{\dfrac{\$490,000 + \$500,000}{2}} = \frac{\$42,000}{\$495,000} = \underline{8.5\%}$$

Note: Since the bonds were issued at a discount, the yield is greater than the nominal interest rate.

Cost of Equity Securities

The cost of equity securities is the dividend.

$$\frac{\text{Common}}{\text{Stock}} = \frac{\text{Dividends per share}}{\text{Net proceeds per share}} + \text{Growth rate in individuals}$$

Explanatory Notes: The dividends per share are for the current year. The growth rate in dividends is constant.

The cost of preferred stock is the dividend rate. If the rate is not given, the cost of preferred stock is calculated in the same manner as that for common stock.

EXAMPLE 11.7

A company's net proceeds per share of common stock is $80. Long-term debt would be issued at 20%. Preferred stock could be issued with a 17% dividend rate. The tax rate is 40%. Dividends per share are $8. Growth rate in dividends is 6%.

The cost of common stock is 19.3% computed as follows:

$$\frac{\$8}{\$80} + 0.60 = \underline{16.0\%}$$

The cost of long-term debt after tax is 12% (20% × 60%). Preferred stock costs 17%.

In getting the overall cost of capital, consider the percentage of the total and after-tax cost of each financing instrument.

EXAMPLE 11.8

David Company presents the following from its financial statements:

Bonds payable (16%) $4 million
Preferred stock (13%)   1 million

		5 million
Common stock		
Total		$10 million

Dividends per share on common stock are $11; net proceeds per share are $80; growth rate in dividends is 4%, and tax rate is 40%.

The weighted average cost of capital is now determined.

	Percent	After-Tax Cost	Weighted-Average Cost
Bonds payable	0.40	0.096[a]	0.038
Preferred stock	0.10	0.130	0.013
Common stock	0.50	0.178[b]	0.089
	1.0		0.140

[a] Cost of bonds payable: $16\% \times 60\% = 0.096$.
[b] Cost of common stock = $\frac{\$11}{\$80} + 0.04 = 0.178$

CONCLUSION

In financing a business, you must select an appropriate category type as well as a maturity period. Many considerations are involved in deriving a financial strategy, including cost of capital, risk, liquidity, tax rate, and restrictions. A thorough analysis is required to determine which financing instrument is best suited in a particular situation.

12 Techniques for Analyzing Mergers and Acquisitions

External growth occurs when a business purchases the existing assets of another entity through a merger. You are often required to appraise the suitability of a potential merger as well as participate in merger negotiations. Besides the growth aspect, a merger may enable the reduction of corporate risk through diversification. The three common ways of joining two or more companies are a merger, consolidation, or a holding company.

In a *merger*, two or more companies are combined into one, where only the acquiring company retains its identity. Generally, the larger of the two companies is the acquiring company.

With a *consolidation*, two or more companies combine to create a new company. None of the consolidation firms legally survive. For example, companies A and B give all their assets, liabilities, and stock to the new company, C, in return for C's stock, bonds, or cash.

A *holding* company owns sufficient shares of common stock to possess voting control of one or more other companies. The holding company comprises a group of businesses, each operating as a separate entity. By possessing more than 50% of the voting rights through common stock, the holding company has effective control of another company with a smaller percent of ownership, such as 25%. The holding company is referred to as the *parent*, and each company controlled is termed a *subsidiary*.

Depending on the intent of the combination, there are three common ways in which businesses get together so as to obtain advantages in their market. They are:

- *Vertical merger*. This occurs when a company combines with a supplier or customer. An example is when a wholesaler combines with retailers.

- *Horizontal merger.* This occurs when two companies in a similar business combine. An example is the combining of two airlines.
- *Conglomerate merger.* This occurs when two companies in unrelated industries combine, such as where an electronics company joins with an insurance company.

MERGERS

A merger of two companies may be achieved in one of two ways. The acquirer may negotiate with the management of the prospective acquired company, which is the preferred approach. If negotiations are not successful, the acquirer may make a tender offer directly to the stockholders of the targeted company. A *tender offer* represents a cash offer for the common shares held by stockholders. The offer is made at a premium above the current market price of the stock. In some cases, the tender may be shares in the acquiring company rather than cash. Usually an expiration date exists for the tender. *Note*: A good takeover candidate includes a cash-rich business, a company with a low debt-to-equity ratio, and a company with significant growth potential.

In negotiating with management, the acquiring company usually makes a stock offer based on a specified exchange ratio. The merger may occur if the acquired company receives an offer at an acceptable premium over the current market price of stock. Sometimes contingent payments are also given, such as stock warrants.

There are various financing packages that buyers may use for mergers, such as common stock, preferred stock, convertible bonds, debt, cash, and warrants. A key consideration in choosing the final package is its effect on current earnings per share (EPS).

If common stock is exchanged, the seller's stock is given in exchange for the buyer's stock, resulting in a tax-free exchange. The drawback is that the stock issuance reduces earnings per share because the buyer's outstanding shares are increased. When an exchange of cash for common stock occurs, the selling company's stockholders receive cash, resulting in a taxable transaction. This type of exchange may increase earnings per share since the buying company is obtaining new earnings without increasing outstanding shares.

There are many reasons why a business might prefer external growth through mergers instead of internal growth.

Advantages of a Merger

- Aids in diversification, such as reducing cyclical and operational effects.
- Achieves a synergistic effect, which means that the results of a combination are greater than the sum of the parts. For example, greater profit may be derived from the combined entity than would occur from each individual company because of increased efficiency and cost savings. A greater probability of synergy exists with a horizontal merger because of the elimination of duplicate facilities.
- Provides a missed attribute; that is, a company gains something it lacked. For example, superior management quality or research capability may be obtained.
- Aids in the company's ability to raise funds when it combines with another possessing highly liquid assets and low debt.
- Enhances the market price of stock in certain cases, resulting in a higher P–E ratio for the stock. For instance, the stock of a larger company may be perceived to be more marketable, stable, and secure.
- Aids the company in financing an acquisition that would not otherwise be possible to obtain, such as where acquiring a company by exchanging stock is less costly than constructing new capital facilities, which would require a substantial outlay of cash. For example, a company may be unable to finance significant internal expansion but can accomplish it by buying a business already having such capital facilities.
- Generates a good return on investment when the market value of the acquired company is materially less than its replacement cost.
- Obtains a tax loss carry-forward benefit if the acquired company has been operating at a net loss. The acquirer may utilize the tax loss carry-forward benefit to offset its own profitability, thus lowering its taxes. The tax loss may be carried forward 20 years to reduce the acquiring company's future earnings. In essence, the government is financing part of the acquisition.

EXAMPLE 12.1

Harris Company is evaluating whether to buy Stone Company. Stone has a tax loss of $500,000. Harris Company expects pretax earnings of $400,000 and $300,000 for the next 2 years. The tax rate is 46%.

The taxes to be paid by Harris follow.

Year 1 $400,000 − $400,000 = 0

Year 2 $300,000 − $100,000 = $200,000 × 46% = $92,000

Disadvantages of a Merger

- Adverse financial effects because expected benefits were not forthcoming. For example, anticipated cost reductions did not occur.
- Problems are caused by dissenting minority stockholders.
- Government antitrust action delays or prevents the proposed merger.

Appraisal of a potential merger must consider its effect on the financial performance of the company, including:

- *Earnings per share.* The merger should result in higher earnings or improve its stability.
- *Dividends per share.* The dividends before and after the merger should be maintained to stabilize the market price of stock.
- *Market price per share.* The market price of the stock should be higher or at least the same after the merger.
- *Risk.* The merged business should have less financial and operating risk than before.

DECIDING ON ACQUISITION TERMS

When determining acquisition terms, you should consider the following:

- Earnings in terms of absolute dollars and percentage change
- Dividends
- Market price of stock
- Book value per share
- Net working capital per share

The weight of each of the aforementioned elements on a merger varies depending upon the circumstances involved.

Earnings

In determining the value of earnings in a merger, you should consider expected future earnings and projected P–E ratio. A rapidly growing company is anticipated to have a higher P–E multiple.

Dividends

Dividend receipts are desirable to stockholders. However, the more a company's growth rate and earnings, the less is the impact of dividends on market price of stock. On the other hand, if earnings are dropping, the greater is the effect of dividends on per share price.

Market Price of Stock

The price of a security considers projected earnings and dividends. The value assigned to the company in the acquisition will most likely be greater than the present market price in the following cases:

- The business is in a depressed industry.
- The acquired company is of greater value to the acquirer (e.g., has high-quality management, aids diversification) than to the stock market in general.
- A higher market price than the current one is offered to induce existing stockholders to give up their shares.

Book Value per Share

Since book value is based on historical cost rather than current value, it is not an important factor to consider. However, when book value is greater than market value, there may be an expectation that market price will go up after the merger because of improved circumstances (e.g., superior management).

Net Working Capital per Share

If the acquired business has a very low debt position or very liquid assets, the acquirer may borrow the funds for the acquisition by using the acquired company's strong liquidity position.

Factors to Consider in Determining the Price to Be Paid for a Business

- Financial analysis of the acquired company, such as the quality of earnings and growth rate.
- Future expected rate of return on assets and sales along with the probability of achieving those expected returns.

- Tax effects, such as unused tax credits.
- Management quality, such as experienced and dynamic management.
- Marketing position, such as favorable marketing image and market share.
- Degree of competition.
- Employee relations, such as the absence of unionization.
- Political environment, such as the absence of stringent governmental regulation and operations in politically unstable areas.
- Risk level, such as having sufficient insurance coverage for assets.
- Economic environment, including recession-resistant business.
- Corporate characteristics, including having negatively correlated product lines.
- Industry characteristics, such as being in a growing industry rather than a declining one. For example, in 1981, Sohio's acquisition of Kennecott Copper for $1.77 billion resulted in financial disaster because of downside trends in the industry.
- Structure of the arrangement, making it taxable or nontaxable.
- Effect of the acquisition on the acquiring company's financial strength and operating performance (e.g., liquidity, solvency). For example, Baldwin United's acquisition of Mortgage Guaranty Insurance eventually forced both companies into bankruptcy. There was a clear failure to properly evaluate the effect of the acquisition on financial posture.
- Enhancement of integration and/or diversification.
- Legal implications, such as the likelihood of stockholder liability suits.
- Possible attack for antitrust violation.

Be Careful: Detailed financial planning and analysis are required in the acquisition process. An example of an acquisition that did not work out well is the 1980 acquisition by Pan American of National Airlines for $400 million. A major purpose of the acquisition was to enable Pan Am to use National's routes to feed its overseas routes. But management did not make progress in rescheduling for almost 2 years.

Warning: If an acquiring company overpays for a target company, this negatively affects its financial stature. For instance, was it worth it to J. Ray McDermott to fight off United Technologies to obtain control of Babcock and Wilcox, even though it pushed the stock price up from approximately $35 to $65?

ACQUISITION OF ANOTHER BUSINESS

Should stock or assets be given in the acquisition?

Advantages of Giving Stock

- Quick.
- Simple in terms of document preparation. There is a transfer of stock certificates in exchange for immediate or deferred payment.
- Typically, stockholder votes authorizing the purchase or sale are not required.
- Minority stockholders may not have appraisal rights.

Disadvantages of Giving Stock

- The acquirer in buying stock of the target company assumes its liabilities, whether disclosed or not.
- If the target is liquidated after acquisition, much work is required in conveying the target company's assets as part of the liquidation.

Advantages of Giving Assets

- Acquirer has full control over the assets it buys and the liabilities it assumes.
- Typically, no acquiring company stockholder vote is needed.

Disadvantages of Giving Assets

- Difficult to determine the fair value of each asset.
- Target company's stockholders must approve.
- State transfer taxes must be paid.
- Creditor agreement may be required for certain transfers and assignments.
- Must conform to bulk sales laws.

In evaluating whether to buy another business, capital budgeting techniques may be used. Also, the effect of the new capital structure on the entity's overall cost of capital has to be projected.

EXAMPLE 12.2

Weiss Corporation is considering buying Poczter Corporation for $95,000. Weiss' current cost of capital is 12%. Poczter's estimated overall cost of capital after the acquisition is 10%. Projected cash inflows from years 1 through 8 are $13,000.

The net present value is:

Year	Present Value
0 (−$95,000 × 1)	−$95,000
1–8 (13,000 × 5.334926)	+ 69,354[a]
Net present value	−$25,646

[a]Using 10% as the discount rate.

The acquisition is not feasible because of the negative net present value.

EXAMPLE 12.3

Charles Company desires to purchase certain fixed assets of Blake Company. However, the latter wants to sell out its business. The balance sheet of Blake Company follows.

Assets:

Cash	$ 4,000
Accounts receivable	8,000
Inventory	10,000
Equipment 1	16,000
Equipment 2	28,000
Equipment 3	42,000
Building	110,000
Total assets	$218,000

Liabilities and Stockholders' Equity:

Total liabilities	$ 80,000
Total equity	138,000
Total liabilities and equity	$218,000

Charles wants only equipment 1 and 2 and the building. The other assets, excluding cash, can be sold for $24,000. The total cash received is thus $28,000 ($24,000 + $4,000 initial cash balance). Blake desires $50,000 for the entire business. Charles will therefore have to pay a total of $130,000, which is $80,000 in total liabilities and $50,000 for its owners. The actual net cash outlay is therefore $102,000 ($130,000 − $28,000). It is anticipated that the after-tax cash inflows from the new equipment will be $27,000 per year for the next 5 years. The cost of capital is 8%.

The net present value of the acquisition is:

Year	Present Value
0 (−$102,000 × 1)	−$102,000
1–5 (27,000 × 3.992710)	107,803
Net present value	$ 5,803

The positive net present value indicates that the acquisition should take place.

A company may be bought by exchanging stock in accord with a predetermined ratio. The acquirer typically offers more for each share of the acquired company than the current market price of stock. The *exchange ratio* equals

$$\frac{\text{Amount paid per share of the acquired company}}{\text{Market price of the acquiring company's shares}}$$

EXAMPLE 12.4

Travis Company buys Boston Company. Travis Company's stock sells for $75 per share while Boston's stock sells for $45. According to the merger negotiations, Travis offers $50 per share. The exchange ratio is 0.667 ($50/$75).

Travis exchanges 0.667 shares of its stock for 1 share of Boston.

IMPACT OF MERGER ON EARNINGS PER SHARE AND MARKET PRICE PER SHARE

A merger can have a positive or negative effect on net income and market price per share of common stock.

EXAMPLE 12.5

The following information applies:

	Company A	Company B
Net income	$50,000	$84,000
Outstanding shares	5,000	12,000
EPS	$10	$7
P–E ratio	7	10
Market price	$70	$70

Company B acquires Company A and exchanges its shares for A's shares on a one-for-one basis. The effect on EPS follows.

	B Shares Owned After Merger	EPS Before Merger	EPS After Merger
A stockholders	5,000	$10	$7.88[a]
B stockholders	12,000	$ 7	$7.88[a]
Total	17,000		

[a]Total net income is determined as:

5,000 shares × $10 $ 50,000
12,000 shares × $7   _84,000_
                      $134,000

$$\text{EPS} = \frac{\text{Net income} = \$134{,}000}{\text{Total shares} = 17{,}000} = \underline{7.88} \text{ (rounded)}$$

EPS goes down by $2.12 for A stockholders and up by $0.88 for B stockholders.

The effect on market price is not clear. Assuming the combined entity has the same P–E ratio as Company B, the market price per share will be $78.80 (10 × $7.88). The stockholders experience a higher market value per share. The increased market value arises because net income of the combined entity is valued at a P–E ratio of 10, the same as Company B, while prior to the merger Company A had a lower P–E multiple of 7. But if the combined entity is valued at Company A's multiplier of 7, the market value would be $55.16 (7 × $7.88). In this case, the stockholders in each firm experience a reduction in market value of $14.84 ($70.00 − $55.16).

Because the impact of the merger on market value per share is not clear, the key consideration is EPS.

EXAMPLE 12.6

The following situation exists:

Market price per share of acquiring company = $100
Market price per share of acquired company = $ 20
Price per share offered   = $ 24

The exchange ratio equals:

Shares $24/$100   = 0.24
Market price $24/$20   = 1.20

EXAMPLE 12.7

Mart Company wants to buy James Company by issuing its shares. Relevant data follow.

	Mart	James
Net income	$40,000	$26,000
Outstanding shares	20,000	8,000

The exchange ratio is 2 to 1. The EPS based on the original shares of each company follows.

$$\text{EPS of combined entity} = \frac{\text{Combined net income}}{\text{Total shares}}$$

$$\frac{\$66,000}{20,000 + (8,000 \times 2)} = \frac{\$66,000}{36,000 \text{ shares}}$$

$$= \$1.83 \text{ (rounded)}$$

EPS of Mart = $1.83

EPS of James = $1.83 × 2 = $3.66

EXAMPLE 12.8

O'Connor Corporation wants to buy Phil Corporation by exchanging 1.8 shares of its stock for each share of Phil. O'Connor expects to have the same P–E ratio subsequent to the merger as prior to it. Applicable data follow.

	O'Connor	Phil
Net income	$500,000	$150,000
Shares	225,000	30,000
Market price per share	$50	$60

The exchange ratio of market price equals:

$$\frac{\text{Offer price}}{\text{Market price of Phil}} = \frac{\$50 \times 1.8}{\$60} = \frac{\$90}{\$60} = 1.5$$

EPS and P–E ratios for each company are:

	O'Connor	Phil
EPS	$500,000/225,000 = $2.22 (rounded)	$150,000/30,000 = $5
P–E ratio	$50/$2.22 = 22.5 (rounded)	$60/$5 = 12

The P–E ratio used in obtaining Phil is:

$$\frac{1.8 \times \$50}{\$5} = \frac{\$90}{\$5} = \underline{18 \text{ times}}$$

The EPS of O'Connor subsequent to the acquisition is:

$$\frac{\$650,000}{225,000 + (30,000 \times 1.8)} = \frac{\$650,000}{279,000} \text{ shares} = \underline{\$2.33} \text{ (rounded)}$$

The expected market price per share of the combined entity is:

$$\$2.33 \times 22.5 \text{ times} = \underline{\$52.43} \text{ (rounded)}$$

RISK

In evaluating the risk associated with an acquisition, a *scenario analysis* may be used, looking at best case, worst case, and most likely case. Operating scenarios consider assumptions as to variables, including sales, volume, cost, competitive reaction, customer perception, and government interference. You derive the probability for each scenario on the basis of experience. *Sensitivity analysis* may also be used to indicate how sensitive the project's returns are to variances from expected values of essential variables. For instance, you may undertake a sensitivity analysis on selling prices assuming they are, for example, 8 or 12% higher or lower than expected. The theory behind sensitivity analysis is to adjust key variables from their expected values in the most likely case. The analysis can be performed assuming one purchase price or all possible purchase prices. What is the impact, for example, of a 2% change in the gross profit rate on projected returns?

What price should you pay for a target company? You should pay an amount resulting in a cutoff return given the most likely operating scenario.

Warning: It is difficult to accomplish successful unrelated diversification. Examples are General Electric's acquisition of Utah International and RCA's acquisition of CIP. Both firms have divested their acquisitions. *Recommendation*: Acquisition of companies operating in related fields usually have a higher success rate.

HOLDING COMPANY

A holding company is one whose only purpose is owning the stock of other businesses. To obtain voting control of a business, the holding company may make a direct market purchase or a tender offer. A company may decide to become a holding company if its basic business is in a state of decline and it decides to liquidate its assets and uses the funds to invest in companies with high growth potential.

Because the operating companies owned by the holding company are separate legal entities, the obligations of one are isolated from the others. If one goes bankrupt, no claim exists on the assets of the other companies. *Recommendation:* A loan officer lending to one company should attempt to obtain a guarantee by the other companies.

Advantages of a Holding Company

- Ability to obtain a significant amount of assets with a small investment. In essence, the holding company can control more assets than it could acquire through a merger.
- Risk protection, in that the failure of one company does not result in the failure of another or of the holding company. If the owned company fails, the loss of the holding company is limited to its investment in it.
- Ease of obtaining control of another company; all that is involved is buying sufficient stock in the marketplace. Unlike a merger, in which stockholder or management approval is required, no approval is necessary for a holding company.
- Ability to obtain a significant amount of control with a small investment by getting voting control in a company for a minimal amount and then using that firm to gain voting control in another, and so on.

Disadvantages of a Holding Company

- Multiple tax because the income the holding company receives is in the form of cash. Prior to paying dividends, the subsidiary must pay taxes on the earnings. When profit is distributed to the holding company as dividends, it must pay tax on the dividends received less an 80% dividend exclusion. But if the holding company owns 80% or more of the subsidiary's shares, a 100% dividend exemption exists. No multiple tax exists for a subsidiary that is part of a merged company.

- More costly to administer than a single company emanating from a merger because economies of scale are not achieved.
- Possibility that the U.S. Department of Justice will deem the holding company a near monopoly and require dissolution of some of the owned companies.
- Incurrence of increased debt because the acquisition may magnify variability in earnings, thus subjecting the holding company to greater risk.

EXAMPLE 12.9

A holding company owns 70% of another firm. Dividends received are $20,000. The tax rate is 46%. The tax paid on the dividends follows.

Dividend	$20,000
Dividend exclusion (80%)	16,000
Dividend subject to tax	$ 4,000
Tax rate	× 46%
Tax	$ 1,840

The effective tax rate is 9.2% ($1,840/$20,000).

METHODS OF ACCOUNTING FOR A BUSINESS COMBINATION

A business combination occurs when an incorporated business combines with another incorporated or unincorporated business. The two possible methods of accounting are pooling-of-interests and purchase. The pooling method is used when voting common stock is issued to effect a combination of common stock interests. It assumes that both companies were always combined. The purchase method is used when cash and other assets are distributed or liabilities are incurred to effect a combination. Note: An acquisition of a minority interest is always a purchase at a later date, even if the combination was originally treated as a pooling.

Pooling-of-Interests Method

There are 12 criteria that must be met for a business combination to be treated as a pooling. They are:

1. A combining company must be autonomous, meaning that it must not have been a subsidiary or division of any other company within two

Chapter 12: Techniques for Analyzing Mergers and Acquisitions 233

years prior to the initiation date. (Initiation date is the date that stockholders are notified in writing of the combination.)

2. Each of the combining companies must be independent, meaning that a combining company does not own 10% or more of another combining company's common stock at the initiation or consummation dates.
3. The combining units come together in a single transaction or within one year after initiation.
4. The acquiring company issues voting common stock in exchange for 90% or more of the voting common stock of the acquired company.
5. None of the combining companies change the equity interest of voting common stock in contemplation of the business combination within two years prior to the initiation date.
6. Treasury stock is acquired for normal business reasons and not because of the business combination.
7. The relative percentage ownership of each stockholder remains the same as a result of the combination.
8. Stockholders are not restricted in voting rights.
9. The combination is complete at the consummation date, with no pending provisions.
10. There must be no reacquisition of stock issued to effect the combination.
11. There must be no financial arrangements that benefit former combining stockholders.
12. The combining company may not dispose of a significant part of its assets within two years after the combination.

The accounting treatment for a pooling involves the following:

- Net assets of the acquired company are brought forth at book value.
- Retained earnings and paid-in-capital of the acquired company are brought forth.
- Net income of the acquired company is picked up for the entire year, regardless of the acquisition date.
- Expenses in connection with the transaction are immediately charged against earnings.

The mechanics of a pooling are as follows:

	Company A	Company B	Combined
Assets	$2,000	$500	$2,500
Liabilities	600	100	700
Equity	$1,400	$400	[a]

[a] Sum of:
- Capital stock of Company A before
- Capital stock issued to pool
- Retained earnings of both companies
- Paid-in-capital absorbs the difference

The footnote disclosures of a pooling are:

- Name and description of combined companies.
- The fact that the pooling method was used.
- Description and number of shares issued to effect the combination.
- Net income of the acquired company before the business combination.
- Adjustments of net assets to adapt the combining companies to the same accounting principles.

Purchase Method

If any one of the 12 criteria for the pooling-of-interests method is not satisfied, the purchase method must be used to account for the business combination.

The accounting requirements of a purchase follow.

- Net assets of the acquired company are brought forth at fair market value. The excess of cash paid over the fair market value of net assets represents goodwill. Goodwill is then amortized over the period benefited under the straight-line method, not exceeding 40 years. If the cash paid was less than the fair market value of the net assets, the credit would be used to reduce on a proportionate basis the noncurrent assets (except for long-term investments). Any remaining credit goes to a deferred credit account and is then amortized.
- Goodwill of the acquired company is not brought forth.

- Net income of the acquired company is recognized from the acquisition date to year-end.
- Direct costs of the purchase reduce the fair value of securities issued; indirect costs are expensed.

    Disclosures under a purchase follow.

- Name and brief description of combined companies.
- The fact that the purchase method was used.
- The period for which operating results of the acquired company are included.
- Operating results for the current and immediately preceding periods as though the companies had combined at the beginning of the period.
- The cost of the acquired company, the number of shares issued, and the amount assigned.
- The amortization period for goodwill.
- Contingencies remaining under the acquisition agreement and their proposed accounting treatments.

CONCLUSION

In analyzing a potential merger and acquisition, many considerations must be taken into account, such as the market price of stock, earnings per share, dividends, book value of assets, risk, and tax considerations. A detailed evaluation of the target company is necessary to ensure that the price paid is realistic given the particular circumstances. Two methods to account for a business combination are the pooling-of-interests and purchase. The former involves an exchange of voting common stock while the latter requires cash payment or the incurrence of a liability.

PART III:
Financial Forecasting

13 Forecasting and Financial Planning as Management Tools

Financial management in both private and public organizations typically operate under conditions of uncertainty or risk. Probably the most important function of business is *forecasting*. A forecast is a starting point for planning. In business, forecasts are the basis for capacity planning, production and inventory planning, manpower planning, planning for sales and market share, and financial planning and budgeting. Sales forecasts are especially crucial aspects of many financial management activities, including budgets, profit planning, capital expenditure analysis and acquisition, and merger analysis.

Figure 13.1 illustrates how sales forecasts relate to various managerial functions of business.

WHO USES FORECASTS?

Forecasts are needed for marketing, production, manpower, and financial planning. Also top management needs forecasts for planning and implementing long-term strategic objectives and planning for capital expenditures. More specifically, marketing managers use sales forecasts to (1) determine optimal sales force allocations, (2) set sales goals, and (3) plan promotions and advertising.

Production planners need forecasts in order to:

- Schedule production activities.
- Order materials.
- Plan shipments.

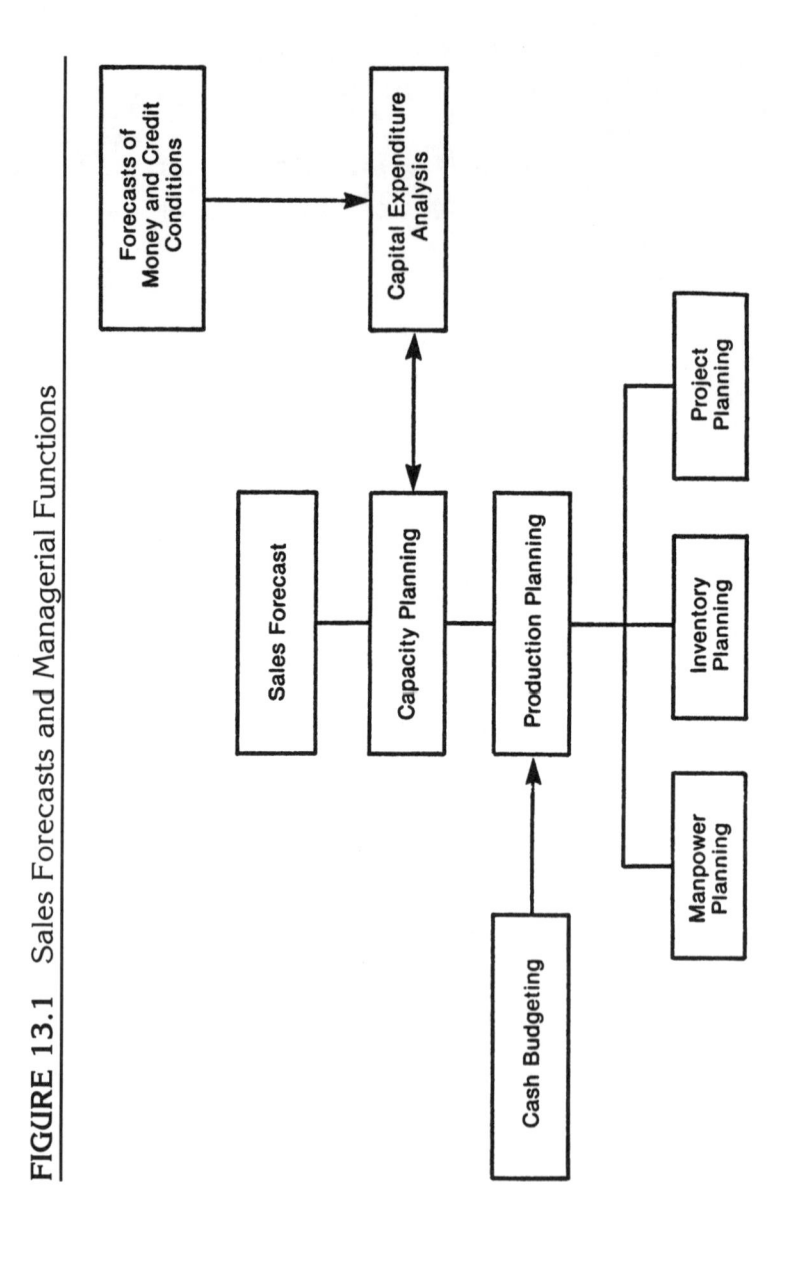

FIGURE 13.1 Sales Forecasts and Managerial Functions

As shown in Figure 13.1, as soon as the company is sure that it has enough capacity, the production plan is developed. If the company does not have enough capacity, planning and budgeting decisions will be required for capital spending to expand capacity.

On this basis, the financial manager must estimate the future cash inflow and outflow, and must plan cash and borrowing needs for the company's future operations. In planning for capital investments, predictions about future economic activity are required so that the returns, or cash inflows, accruing from the investment may be estimated. Forecasts must also be made of money and credit conditions and interest rates so that the cash needs of the firm may be met at the lowest possible cost. Long-term forecasts are needed in order to plan changes in the company's capital structure. Decisions as to whether to issue stock or debt in order to maintain the desired financial structure of the firm require forecasts of money and credit conditions.

Managers of nonprofit institutions and public administrators must also make forecasts. Hospital administrators face the problem of forecasting the health care needs of the community. In order to do this efficiently, a projection has to be made of

- The growth in absolute size of population
- The changes in the number of people in various age groupings
- The varying medical needs these different age groups will have

Universities forecast student enrollments, cost of operations, and in many cases, what level of funds will be provided by tuition and by government appropriations.

The service sector which today accounts for 57% of the U.S. gross national product and includes banks, insurance companies, restaurants, and cruise ships, need various projections for operational and long-term strategic planning. A bank, for example, has to forecast demands of various loans and deposits as well as money and credit conditions so that it can determine the cost of the money it lends.

FORECASTING METHODS

There is a wide range of forecasting techniques that a company may choose from. There are basically two approaches to forecasting: qualitative and quantitative. They are as follows:

1. Qualitative approach; forecasts based on judgment and opinion
   - Executive opinions
   - Sales-force polling
   - Techniques for eliciting experts' opinions—PERT derived
   - Consumer surveys
   - Delphi technique
2. Quantitative approach
   - Forecasts based on historical data
     — Naive methods
     — Moving averages
     — Exponential smoothing
     — Decomposition of time series
   - Associative forecasts
     — Regressions
     — Econometric modeling
   - Forecasts based on consumer behavior—Markov approach

Figure 13.2 summarizes the forecasting methods. The list presented in the Figure is neither comprehensive nor exhaustive. The qualitative method is discussed in this chapter, and various quantitative methods, along with their illustrations, are taken up in chapter 14.

SELECTION OF FORECASTING METHOD

Some of the abovementioned techniques are quite simple and are rather inexpensive to develop and use, whereas others are extremely complex, require significant amounts of time to develop, and may be quite expensive. Some are best suited for short-term projections, whereas others are better for intermediate- or long-term forecasts.

What technique or techniques to select depends on the following criteria:

- What is the cost associated with developing the forecasting model compared with potential gains resulting from its use? The choice is one of benefit–cost trade-off.
- How complicated are the relationships that are being forecasted?

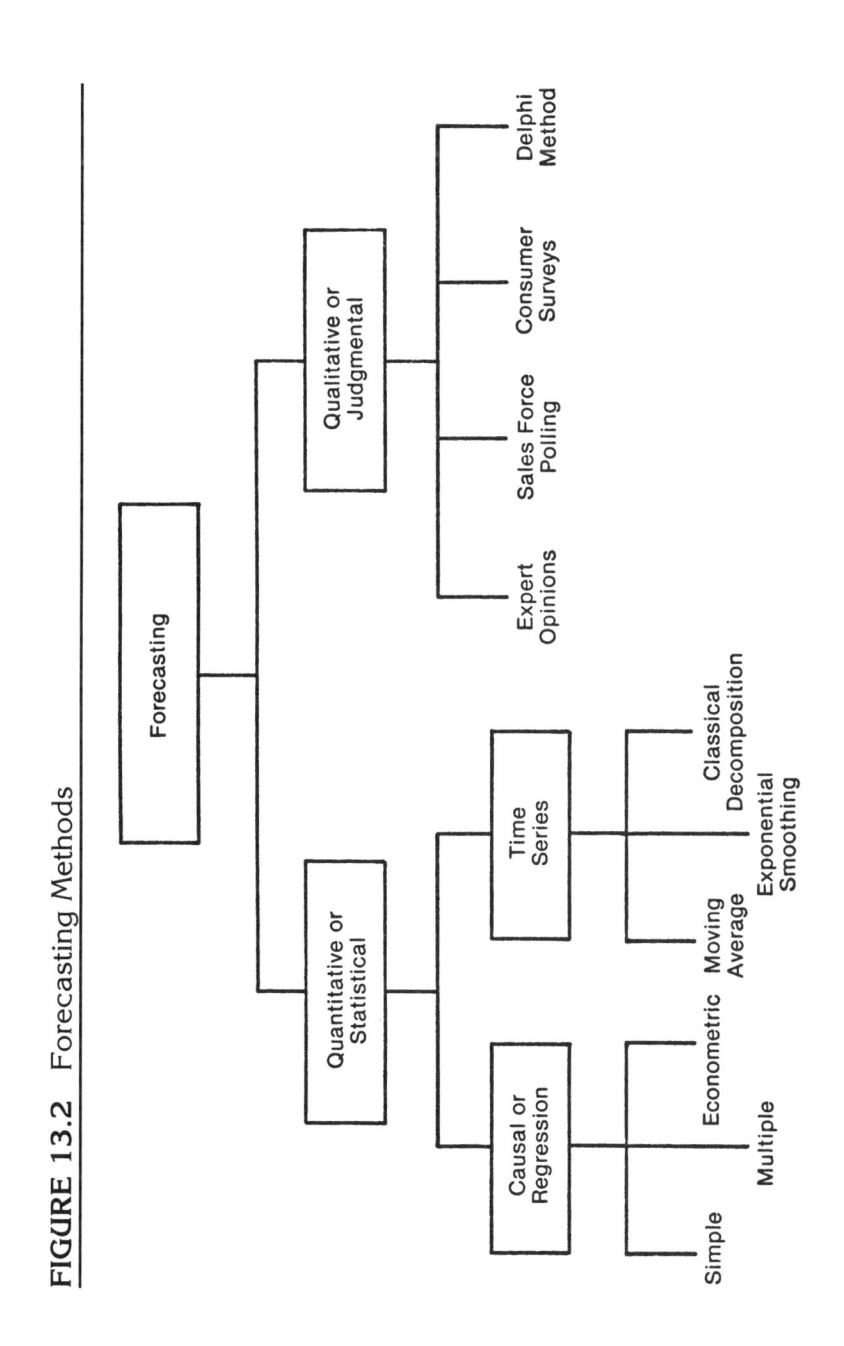

FIGURE 13.2 Forecasting Methods

```
                            Forecasting
                    ┌───────────┴───────────┐
          Quantitative or              Qualitative or
            Statistical                  Judgmental
        ┌───────┴───────┐        ┌───────┬───────┬───────┐
    Causal or        Time      Expert   Sales  Consumer  Delphi
   Regression       Series    Opinions  Force  Surveys   Method
    ┌───┴───┐      ┌───┴───┐            Polling
 Simple  Econometric Moving  Classical
         │         Average  Decomposition
      Multiple        Exponential
                      Smoothing
```

- Is it for short-run or long-run purposes?
- How much accuracy is desired?
- Is there a minimum tolerance level of errors?

THE QUALITATIVE APPROACH

The qualitative approach can be useful in formulating short-term forecasts and also can supplement projections based on any of the quantitative methods to be discussed in chapter 14.

Executive Opinions

The subjective views of executives or experts are averaged to generate a forecast about future sales. Usually this method is used in conjunction with some quantitative method, such as trend extrapolation. The management team modifies the resulting forecast on the basis of their expectations.

Sales-Force Polling

Some companies use as a forecast source salespeople who have continual contacts with customers. They believe that the sales force, which is closest to the ultimate customers, may have significant insights regarding the state of the future market. Forecasts based on sales-force polling may be averaged to develop a future forecast, or they may be used to modify other quantitative and/or qualitative forecasts that have been generated internally in the company.

PERT-Derived Forecasts

A technique known as PERT (Program Evaluation and Review Technique) has been useful in producing estimates based on subjective opinions, such as executive opinions or sales-force polling. The PERT methodology requires that the expert provide three estimates: pessimistic (a), the most likely (m), and optimistic (b). The theory suggests that these estimates combine to form an expected value, or forecast, as follows:

$$EV = (a + 4m + b)/6$$

with a standard deviation of

$$\sigma = (b - a)/6$$

where

EV = expected value (mean) of the forecast
σ = standard deviation of the forecast

For example, suppose that the management of a company believes that if the economy is in recession, the next year's sales will be $300,000 and if the economy is prosperous, sales will be $330,000. Their most likely estimate is $310,000. The PERT method generates an expected value of sales as follows:

$$EV = [\$300{,}000 + 4(\$310{,}000) + \$330{,}000]/6 = \$311{,}667$$

with a standard deviation of

$$\sigma = (\$330{,}000 - \$300{,}000)/6 = \$5{,}000$$

The advantages of this method are as follows:

- It is often easier and more realistic to ask the expert to give optimistic, pessimistic, and most likely estimates than a specific forecast value.
- The PERT method includes a measure of dispersion (the standard deviation), which makes it possible to develop probabilistic statements regarding the forecast. For example, in the above example the forecaster is 95% confident that the true value of the forecasted sales lies between plus or minus 2 standard deviations from the mean ($311,667). That is, the true value can be expected to fall between $301,667 and $321,667 [$311,667 ± 2($5,000)].

Consumer Surveys

Some companies conduct their own market surveys regarding specific consumer purchases. Surveys may consist of telephone contacts, personal interviews, or questionnaires. Extensive statistical analysis is usually applied to survey results in order to test hypotheses regarding consumer behavior.

The Delphi Method

This is a group technique in which several experts are individually questioned about their perceptions of future events. The experts do not meet as a group in order to reduce the possibility that consensus is reached because of dominant personality factors. Instead, the forecasts and accompanying arguments are summarized by an outside party and returned to the experts along with further questions. This continues until a consensus is reached by the group, especially after only a few rounds. This type of method is useful and quite effective for long-range forecasting. Table 13.1 shows how effective this method can be.

COMMON FEATURES AND ASSUMPTIONS INHERENT IN FORECASTING

As pointed out, forecasting techniques are quite different from each other, but there are certain features and assumptions that underlie the business of forecasting. They include the following:

- Forecasting techniques generally assume that the same underlying causal relationship that existed in the past will continue to prevail in the future. In other words, most of our techniques are based on historical data.
- Forecasts are very rarely perfect. Therefore, for planning purposes, allowances should be made for inaccuracies. For example, the company always maintains a safety stock in anticipation of stock-outs.

TABLE 13.1 An Example of the Delphi Method

1 Population (in Millions)	2 Midpoint	3 Number of Panelists	4 Probability Distribution of Panelists	5 Weighted Average (2×4)
30 and above	–	0	.00	0
20–30	25	1	.05	1.25
15–1	17	2	.10	1.70
10–14	12	2	.10	1.20
5–9	7	7	.35	2.45
2–4	3	8	.40	1.20
Less than 2	1	0	.00	0
Total		20	1.00	7.80

Case example: "In 1982, a panel of 20 representatives, with college educations, from different parts of the U.S.A., were asked to estimate the population of Bombay, India. None of the panelists had been to India since World War I. The population was estimated to be 7.8 million, which is very close to the actual population."
Source: Singhvi, Surendra. "Financial Forecast: Why and How?" *Managerial Planning*. March/April, 1984.

- Forecast accuracy decreases as the time period covered by the forecast (that is, the time horizon) increases. Generally speaking, long-term forecasts tend to be more inaccurate than short-term forecasts because of the greater uncertainty.
- Forecasts for groups of items tend to be more accurate than forecasts for individual items, since forecasting errors among items in a group tend to cancel each other. For example, industry forecasting is more accurate than individual firm forecasting.

STEPS IN THE FORECASTING PROCESS

There are six basic steps in the forecasting process. They are:

- Determine the what and why of the forecast and what will be needed. This will indicate the level of detail required in the forecast (for example, forecast by region, forecast by product, etc.), the amount of resources that can be justified (for example, computer hardware and software, manpower, etc.), and the level of accuracy desired.
- Establish a time horizon, short or long term. More specifically, determine whether projection will be made for the next year, next 5 years, etc.
- Select a forecasting technique. Refer to the criteria discussed before.
- Gather the data and develop a forecast.
- Identify any assumptions that had to be made in preparing and using the forecast.
- Monitor the forecast to see if it is performing in the manner desired. Develop an evaluation system for this purpose. If it is not performing as desired, return to the first step.

CONCLUSION

Financial management uses forecasts for planning purposes. A forecast aids in determining volume and dollar cost of production, inventory needs, labor hours required, and sales requirements. Cash requirements and financing needs can be formulated. The forecasting method used should be the one that portrays most realistically the particular circumstances given the constraints. However, consideration has to be given to cost, preparation time, accuracy, and time period involved. Some qualitative approaches to forecasting include executive opinions, polling the salespeople, PERT-based, consumer surveys, and Delphi technique. The assumptions that a particular forecast method is based on must be clearly understood by the financial executive to obtain maximum benefit.

14 Forecasting Methods for Financial Planning

This chapter discusses a variety of forecasting methods that fall in the *quantitative approach* category. Qualitative methods were described in the previous chapter.

NAIVE MODELS

Naive forecasting models are based exclusively on historical observation of sales or other variable, such as earnings or cash flows, to be forecast. They do not attempt to explain the underlying causal relationships that produce the variable being forecast. A simple example of a naive model type would be to use the actual sales of the current period as the forecast for the next period. Let us use the symbol $\hat{y}_{t+1}$ as the forecast value and the symbol y_t as the actual value. Then

$$\hat{y}_{t+1} = y_t$$

Advantages: It is inexpensive to develop, store data, and operate (i.e., they hardly need computer hardware and software). *Disadvantages:* It does not consider any possible causal relationships that underly the variable to be forecast.

SMOOTHING TECHNIQUES

Smoothing techniques are a higher form of naive model. There are two typical forms: moving average and exponential smoothing. *Note:* Moving averages are the simpler of the two.

Moving Averages

Moving averages are averages that are updated as new information is received. With the moving average, a manager simply employs the most recent observations to calculate an average, which is used as the forecast for the next period.

EXAMPLE 14.1

Assume that the marketing manager has the following sales data.

Date	Actual Sales (y_t)
Jan. 1	46
2	54
3	53
4	46
5	58
6	49
7	54

In order to predict the sales for the 7th and 8th days of January, the manager has to pick the number of observations for averaging purposes. Let us consider two cases: one is a 6-day moving average and the other is a 3-day average.

Case 1:

$$\hat{y}_7 = \frac{46 + 54 + 53 + 46 + 58 + 49}{6} = 51$$

$$\hat{y}_8 = \frac{54 + 53 + 46 + 58 + 49 + 54}{6} = 52.3$$

$\hat{y}$ = predicted

Case 2:

$$\hat{y}_7 = \frac{46 + 58 + 49}{3} = 51$$

$$\hat{y}_8 = \frac{58 + 49 + 54}{3} = 53.6$$

Date	Actual Sales (y_t)	Predicted Sales ($\hat{y}_t$) Case 1	Case 2
Jan. 1	46		
2	54		
3	53		
4	46		51
5	58		
6	49	53.6	
7	54	51	
8		52.3	

In terms of weights given to observations, in Case 1, the old data received a weight of 5/6, and our current observation got a weight of 1/6. In Case 2, the old data received a weight of only 2/3 while our current observation received a weight of 1/3.

Thus, the marketing manager's choice of the number of periods to use in a moving average is a measure of the relative importance attached to old versus current data.

Advantages and Disadvantages

The moving average is simple to use and easy to understand. But there are two shortcomings.

- It requires you to retain a great deal of data and carry it along with you from forecast period to forecast period.
- All data in the sample are weighted equally. If more recent data are more valid than older data, why not give it greater weight?

The forecasting method known as *exponential smoothing* gets around these disadvantages.

Exponential Smoothing

The exponential smoothing technique is popular among business forecasters for short-run forecasting. It uses a weighted average of past data as the basis for the forecast. The procedure gives the heaviest weight to more recent information and smaller weights to observations in the more distant past. The reason for this is that the future is more dependent upon the recent past than

252 Part III: Financial Forecasting

on the distant past. The method is known to be effective when there is random demand and no seasonal fluctuations in the sales data. One disadvantage of the method, however, is that it does not include industrial or economic factors, such as market conditions, prices, or the effects of competitors' actions.

The Model
The formula for exponential smoothing is

$$\hat{y}_{t+1} = \alpha y_t + (1 - \alpha)\hat{y}_t$$

or in words,

$$\hat{y}_{new} = \alpha y_{old} + (1 - \alpha)\hat{y}_{old}$$

where
$\hat{y}_{new}$ = Exponentially smoothed average to be used as the forecast
y_{old} = Most recent actual data
$\hat{y}_{old}$ = Most recent smoothed forecast
α = Smoothing constant

The higher the α, the higher the weight given to the more recent information.

EXAMPLE 14.2

Data on sales follow.

Time Period (t)	Actual Sales (y_t)
1	$60,000
2	64,000
3	58,000
4	66,000
5	70,000
6	60,000
7	70,000
8	74,000
9	62,000
10	74,000
11	68,000
12	66,000
13	60,000
14	66,000
15	62,000

To initialize the exponential smoothing process, we must have the initial forecast. The first smoothed forecast to be used can be

1. First actual observation
2. An average of the actual data for a few periods

For illustrative purposes, the manager uses a 6-year average as the initial forecast with a smoothing constant of 0.40 (the figures below are in thousands of dollars).

Then

$$\hat{y}_7 = \frac{y_1 + y_2 + y_3 + y_4 + y_5 + y_6}{6}$$

$$= \frac{60 + 64 + 58 + 66 + 70 + 60}{6}$$

$$= 63$$

Note that $y_7 = 70$. Then $\hat{y}_8$ is computed as follows:

$$\hat{y}_8 = \alpha y_7 + (1 - \alpha)\hat{y}_7$$
$$= (0.40)(70) + (0.60)(63)$$
$$= 28.00 + 37.80 = 65.80$$

Similarly,

$$\hat{y}_9 = \alpha y_8 + (1 - \alpha)\hat{y}_8$$
$$= (0.40)(74) + (0.60)(65.80)$$
$$= 29.60 + 39.48 = 69.08$$

and

$$\hat{y}_{10} = \alpha y_9 + (1 - \alpha)\hat{y}_9$$
$$= (0.40)(62) + (0.60)(69.08)$$
$$= 24.80 + 41.45 = 66.25$$

By using the same procedure, the values of $\hat{y}_{11}$, $\hat{y}_{12}$, $\hat{y}_{13}$, $\hat{y}_{14}$, and $\hat{y}_{15}$ can be calculated. Table 14.1 shows a comparison between the actual sales and predicted sales using the exponential smoothing method.

As a result of the negative and positive differences between actual sales and predicted sales, the forecaster can use a higher or lower smoothing constant in order to adjust the prediction as quickly as possible to large fluctuations in the data series. For example, if the forecast is slow in reacting to increased sales (that is, if the difference is negative), you might want to try a higher value. For practical purposes, the optimal α may be picked by minimizing what is known as the *mean squared error* (MSE):

Part III: Financial Forecasting

TABLE 14.1 Comparison of Actual Sales and Predicted Sales

Time Period (t)	Actual Sales (y_t)	Predicted Sales ($\hat{y}_t$)	Difference ($y_t - \hat{y}_t$)	Squared Difference ($y_t - \hat{y}_t)^2$
1	60.0			
2	64.0			
3	58.0			
4	66.0			
5	70.0			
6	60.0			
7	70.0	63.00	7.00	49.00
8	74.0	65.80	8.20	67.24
9	62.0	69.08	−7.08	50.13
10	74.0	66.25	7.75	60.06
11	68.0	69.35	−1.35	1.82
12	66.0	68.81	−2.81	7.90
13	60.0	67.69	−7.69	59.14
14	66.0	64.61	1.39	1.93
15	62.0	65.17	−3.17	10.05
				307.27

$$\text{MSE} = \frac{\sum_{t=1}^{n}(y_t - \hat{y}_t)^2}{n - i}$$

where i = the number of observations used to determine the initial forecast (in this example, $i = 6$).

In our example,

$$\text{MSE} = \frac{307.27}{15 - 6} = 307.27/9 = 34.14$$

The idea is to select the α that minimizes MSE, which is the average sum of the variations between the historical sales data and the forecast values for the corresponding periods.

THE COMPUTER AND EXPONENTIAL SMOOTHING

So far we have illustrated how to use the exponential smoothing method *manually*. As managers, we will have to deal with complex problems requiring large sample data and try different α values. To demonstrate how a computer can handle exponential smoothing, consider the following sales data:

Time Period	Actual Sales
1	$117,000
2	120,000
3	132,000
4	141,000
5	140,000
6	156,000
7	169,000
8	171,000
9	174,000
10	182,000

Figure 14.1 is the printout of the exponential smoothing program written by one of the authors. As can be seen, the procedure for data entry is straightforward, because the program is conversational.

FORECASTING USING DECOMPOSITION OF TIME SERIES

When sales exhibit seasonal or cyclical fluctuation, we use a method called *classical decomposition*, which deals with seasonal, trend, and cyclical components together. We assume that a time series is combined into a model that consists of four components: trend (*T*), cyclical (*C*), seasonal (*S*), and random (*R*). The model we assume is of a multiplicative type, i.e.,

$$y_t = T \times C \times S \times R$$

In this section, we illustrate, step by step, the classical decomposition method by working with the quarterly sales data.

The approach basically involves the following four steps:

1. Determine seasonal indexes, using a four-quarter moving average.
2. Deseasonalize the data.
3. Develop the linear least squares equation in order to identify the trend component of the forecast.
4. Forecast the sales for each of the four quarters of the coming year.

FIGURE 14.1   Printout of Exponential Smoothing Program

```
        PLEASE ENTER THE NUMBER OF OBSERVATIONS.
?10
        ENTER YOUR DATA NOW.
        THE DATA SHOULD BE SEPARATED BY COMMAS.

?117,120,132,141,140,156,169,171,174,182
        ENTER THE NUMBER OF PERIODS OVER WHICH YOU COMPUTE THE
        AVERAGE TO BE USED AS THE FIRST FORECAST VALUE.
?1
        **********EXPONENTIAL SMOOTHING PROGRAM-SINGLE
SMOOTHING**********
                        JAE K. SHIM
```

PERIOD	ACTUAL VALUE	ESTIMATED VALUE	ERROR
1	117.00	.00	
2	120.00	117.00	

THE VALUE OF THE EXPONENTIAL SMOOTHER IS .1

3	132.00	117.30	14.70
4	141.00	118.77	22.23
5	140.00	120.99	19.01
6	156.00	122.89	33.11
7	169.00	126.20	42.80
8	171.00	130.48	40.52
9	174.00	134.54	39.46
10	182.00	138.48	43.52

THE TOTAL ABSOLUTE ERROR IN ESTIMATE IS 255.34
THE MEAN SQUARED ERROR IS 1136.48

THE VALUE OF THE EXPONENTIAL SMOOTHER IS .2

3	132.00	117.60	14.40
4	141.00	120.48	20.52
5	140.00	124.58	15.42
6	156.00	127.67	28.33
7	169.00	133.33	35.67
8	171.00	140.47	30.53
9	174.00	146.57	27.43
10	182.00	152.06	29.94

THE TOTAL ABSOLUTE ERROR IN ESTIMATE IS 202.24
THE MEAN SQUARED ERROR IS 690.23

THE VALUE OF THE EXPONENTIAL SMOOTHER IS .3

3	132.00	117.90	14.10
4	141.00	122.13	18.87
5	140.00	127.79	12.21
6	156.00	131.45	24.55
7	169.00	138.82	30.18
8	171.00	147.87	23.13
9	174.00	154.81	19.19
10	182.00	160.57	21.43

THE TOTAL ABSOLUTE ERROR IN ESTIMATE IS 163.66

THE VALUE OF THE EXPONENTIAL SMOOTHER IS .4

3	132.00	118.20	13.80
4	141.00	123.72	17.28
5	140.00	130.63	9.37

Continued

FIGURE 14.1 (*Continued*)

6	156.00	134.38	21.62
7	169.00	143.03	25.97
8	171.00	153.42	17.58
9	174.00	160.45	13.55
10	182.00	165.87	16.13

THE TOTAL ABSOLUTE ERROR IN ESTIMATE IS 135.31
THE MEAN SQUARED ERROR IS 308.97

THE VALUE OF THE EXPONENTIAL SMOOTHER IS .5

3	132.00	118.50	13.50
4	141.00	125.25	15.75
5	140.00	133.12	6.88
6	156.00	136.56	19.44
7	169.00	146.28	22.72
8	171.00	157.64	13.36
9	174.00	164.32	9.68
10	182.00	169.16	12.84

THE TOTAL ABSOLUTE ERROR IN ESTIMATE IS 114.16
THE MEAN SQUARED ERROR IS 226.07

THE VALUE OF THE EXPONENTIAL SMOOTHER IS .6

3	132.00	118.80	13.20
4	141.00	126.72	14.28
5	140.00	135.29	4.71
6	156.00	138.12	17.88
7	169.00	148.85	20.15
8	171.00	160.94	10.06
9	174.00	166.98	7.02
10	182.00	171.19	10.81

THE TOTAL ABSOLUTE ERROR IN ESTIMATE IS 98.13
THE MEAN SQUARED ERROR IS 174.23

THE VALUE OF THE EXPONENTIAL SMOOTHER IS .7

3	132.00	119.10	12.90
4	141.00	128.13	12.87
5	140.00	137.14	2.86
6	156.00	139.14	16.86
7	169.00	150.94	18.06
8	171.00	163.58	7.42
9	174.00	168.77	5.23
10	182.00	172.43	9.57

THE TOTAL ABSOLUTE ERROR IN ESTIMATE IS 85.76
THE MEAN SQUARED ERROR IS 140.55

THE VALUE OF THE EXPONENTIAL SMOOTHER IS .8

3	132.00	119.40	12.60
4	141.00	129.48	11.52
5	140.00	138.70	1.30
6	156.00	139.74	16.26
7	169.00	152.75	16.25
8	171.00	165.75	5.25
9	174.00	169.95	4.05
10	182.00	173.19	8.81

THE TOTAL ABSOLUTE ERROR IN ESTIMATE IS 76.05
THE MEAN SQUARED ERROR IS 117.91

THE VALUE OF THE EXPONENTIAL SMOOTHER IS .9

3	132.00	119.70	12.30

Continued

258   Part 3: Financial Forecasting

FIGURE 14.1   (*Continued*)

```
      4            141.00              130.77              10.23
      5            140.00              139.88                .02
      6            156.00              140.00              16.00
      7            169.00              154.40              14.60
      8            171.00              167.54               3.46
      9            174.00              170.65               3.35
     10            182.00              173.67               8.33
THE TOTAL ABSOLUTE ERROR IN ESTIMATE IS 68.30
THE MEAN SQUARED ERROR IS 102.23
SUMMARY RESULTS


THE EXPONENTIAL SMOOTHER .1         WITH A MEAN SQUARED
                                    ERROR OF 1136.48
THE EXPONENTIAL SMOOTHER .2         WITH A MEAN SQUARED
                                    ERROR OF 690.23
THE EXPONENTIAL SMOOTHER .3         WITH A MEAN SQUARED
                                    ERROR OF 447.49
THE EXPONENTIAL SMOOTHER .4         WITH A MEAN SQUARED
                                    ERROR OF 308.97
THE EXPONENTIAL SMOOTHER .5         WITH A MEAN SQUARED
                                    ERROR OF 226.07
THE EXPONENTIAL SMOOTHER .6         WITH A MEAN SQUARED
                                    ERROR OF 174.23
THE EXPONENTIAL SMOOTHER .7         WITH A MEAN SQUARED
                                    ERROR OF 140.55
THE EXPONENTIAL SMOOTHER .8         WITH A MEAN SQUARED
                                    ERROR OF 117.91
THE EXPONENTIAL SMOOTHER .9         WITH A MEAN SQUARED
                                    ERROR OF 102.23
```

The data we are going to use are the quarterly sales data for the video set over the past 4 years (Table 14.2). We begin our analysis by showing how to identify the seasonal component of the time series.

Step 1: Use moving average to measure the combined trend–cyclical (TC) components of the time series. This way we eliminate the seasonal and random components, S and R. More specifically, Step 1 involves the following sequences of steps:

- Calculate the 4-quarter moving average for the time series, discussed previously. However, the moving average values computed do not correspond directly to the original quarters of the time series.
- This difficulty is resolved by using the midpoints between successive moving average values. For example, because 6.35 corresponds to the

TABLE 14.2 Sales Data for Video Set

Year	Quarter	Sales
1	1	5.8
	2	5.1
	3	7.0
	4	7.5
2	1	6.8
	2	6.2
	3	7.8
	4	8.4
3	1	7.0
	2	6.6
	3	8.5
	4	8.8
4	1	7.3
	2	6.9
	3	9.0
	4	9.4

first half of quarter 3 and 6.6 corresponds to the last half of quarter 3, (6.35 + 6.6)/2 = 6.475 is used as the moving average value of quarter 3. Similarly, (6.6 + 6.875)/2 = 6.7375 is associated with quarter 4. A complete summary of the moving average calculation is shown in Table 14.3.

- Next we calculate the ratio of the actual value to the moving average value for each quarter in the time series having a 4-quarter moving average entry. This ratio in effect represents the seasonal–random component, $SR = Y/TC$. The ratios calculated this way appear in Table 14.4.

- Arrange the ratios by quarter and then calculate the average ratio by quarter in order to eliminate the random influence.

    For example, for quarter 1

    $$(0.975 + 0.929 + 0.920)/3 = 0.941$$

- The final step, shown below, adjusts the average ratio slightly (for example, for quarter 1, 0.941 becomes 0.939), which will be the *seasonal index*.

TABLE 14.3 Moving Average Calculation for the Video Set Sales Time Series

Year	Quarter	Sales	4-Quarter Moving Average	Centered Moving Average
1	1	5.8		
	2	5.1		
			6.35	
	3	7		6.475
			6.6	
	4	7.5		6.7375
			6.875	
2	1	6.8		6.975
			7.075	
	2	6.2		7.1875
			7.3	
	3	7.8		7.325
			7.35	
	4	8.4		7.4
			7.45	
3	1	7		7.5375
			7.625	
	2	6.6		7.675
			7.725	
	3	8.5		7.7625
			7.8	
	4	8.8		7.8375
			7.875	
4	1	7.3		7.9375
			8	
	2	6.9		8.075
			8.15	
	3	9	0	
	4	9.4		

Step 2: After obtaining the seasonal index, we must first remove the effect of season from the original time series. This process is referred to as *deseasonalizing the time series*. For this we must divide the original series by the seasonal index for that quarter. This is illustrated in Table 14.5.

Step 3: Looking at the graph in Figure 14.2, we see that the time series seem to have an upward linear trend. To identify this trend, we

TABLE 14.4 Seasonal Random Factors for the Series

Year	Quarter	Sales	4-Quarter Moving Average	Centered Moving Average (TC)	Seasonal Random (SR = Y/TC)
1	1	5.8			
	2	5.1			
			6.35		
	3	7		6.475	1.081
			6.6		
	4	7.5		6.738	1.113
			6.875		
2	1	6.8		6.975	0.975
			7.075		
	2	6.2		7.188	0.863
			7.3		
	3	7.8		7.325	1.065
			7.35		
	4	8.4		7.400	1.135
			7.45		
3	1	7		7.538	0.929
			7.625		
	2	6.6		7.675	0.860
			7.725		
	3	8.5		7.763	1.095
			7.8		
	4	8.8		7.838	1.123
			7.875		
4	1	7.3		7.938	0.920
			8		
	2	6.9		7.950	0.868
			7.9		
	3	9			
	4	8.4			

develop the least-squares trend equation. This procedure is shown in Table 14.6. (The least-squares trend method is discussed in detail in Chapter 15.)

Step 4: Develop the forecast using the trend equation and adjust these forecasts to account for the effect of season. The quarterly forecast, as shown in Table 14.7, can be obtained by multiplying the forecast based on trend times the seasonal factor.

TABLE 14.5 Seasonal Component Calculations

Quarter	Seasonal Random (SR)	Seasonal Factor (S)	Adjusted S
1	0.975		
	0.929		
	0.920	0.941	0.939
2	0.863		
	0.860		
	0.868	0.863	0.862
3	1.081		
	1.065		
	1.095	1.080	1.078
4	1.113		
	1.135		
	1.123	1.124	1.121
		4.009	4.000

Video Set Sales

- Original
- Deseasonalized

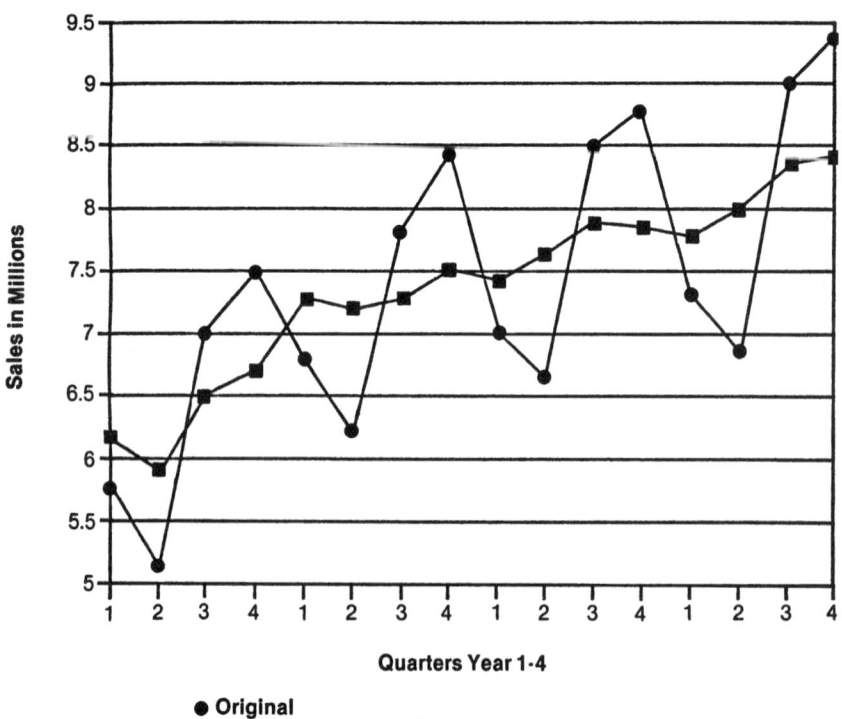

FIGURE 14.2 Actual versus Deseasonalized Data

TABLE 14.6 Deseasonalized Data

Year	Quarter	Sales	Seasonal Factor (S)	Deseasonalized Data	t	tY	t²
1	1	5.8	0.939	6.18	1	6.18	1
	2	5.1	0.862	5.92	2	11.84	4
	3	7	1.078	6.49	3	19.48	9
	4	7.5	1.121	6.69	4	26.75	16
2	1	6.8	0.939	7.24	5	36.21	25
	2	6.2	0.862	7.20	6	43.17	36
	3	7.8	1.078	7.24	7	50.65	49
	4	8.4	1.121	7.49	8	59.93	64
3	1	7	0.939	7.45	9	67.09	81
	2	6.6	0.862	7.66	10	76.60	100
	3	8.5	1.078	7.89	11	86.74	121
	4	8.8	1.121	7.85	12	94.18	144
4	1	7.3	0.939	7.77	13	101.06	169
	2	6.9	0.862	8.01	14	112.11	196
	3	9	1.078	8.35	15	125.23	225
	4	9.4	1.121	8.38	16	134.13	256
				117.81	136	1,051.34	1,496

$\bar{t}$ = 8.5
b_1 = 0.14693
b_o = 6.1143
$\bar{y}$ = mean

which means that $Y = 6.1143 + 0.14693t$ for the forecast periods

$t = 17$
18
19
20

TABLE 14.7 Sales Forecasts for Year 5

Year	Quarter	Trend Forecast	Seasonal Factor	Quarterly Forecast
5	1	8.6120[a]	0.939	8.0873
	2	8.7589	0.862	7.5470
	3	8.9058	1.078	9.6004
	4	9.0528	1.121	10.1508

[a] $\hat{y} = 6.1143 + 0.14693t = 6.1143 + 0.141693(17) = 8.6120$.

CONCLUSION

Various quantitative forecasting methods exist. Naive techniques are based solely on previous experience. Smoothing approaches include moving average and exponential smoothing. Moving averages are continually updated. Exponential smoothing, typically done by computer, employs a weighted average of past data as the means of deriving the forecast. The classical decomposition method is utilized for seasonal and cyclical situations.

15 How to Forecast with Regression and Markov Methods

REGRESSION ANALYSIS FOR SALES AND EARNINGS PROJECTION

A popularly used method to forecast sales and earnings is regression analysis, which is a statistical procedure for estimating mathematically the average relationship between the dependent variable y and the independent variable or variables. *Simple regression* involves one independent variable, whereas *multiple regression* involves two or more independent variables. (We will assume simple *linear* regression throughout this section, meaning that we will use the $y = a + bx$ relationship.)

The regression method attempts to find a *line of best fit* through a technique called the *method of least squares*.

Method of Least Squares

To explain the least-squares method, we define the error as the difference between the observed value and the estimated value of sales or earnings and denote it with u. Symbolically,

$$u = y - \hat{y}$$

where

y = observed value

$\hat{y}$ = estimated value based on $\hat{y} = a + bx$

The least-squares criterion requires that the line of best fit be such that the sum of the squares of the errors (or the vertical distance from the observed data points to the line in Figure 15.1) is a minimum; i.e.,

$$\text{Min } \Sigma u^2 = \Sigma(y - \hat{y})^2 = \text{the sum of the errors squared}$$

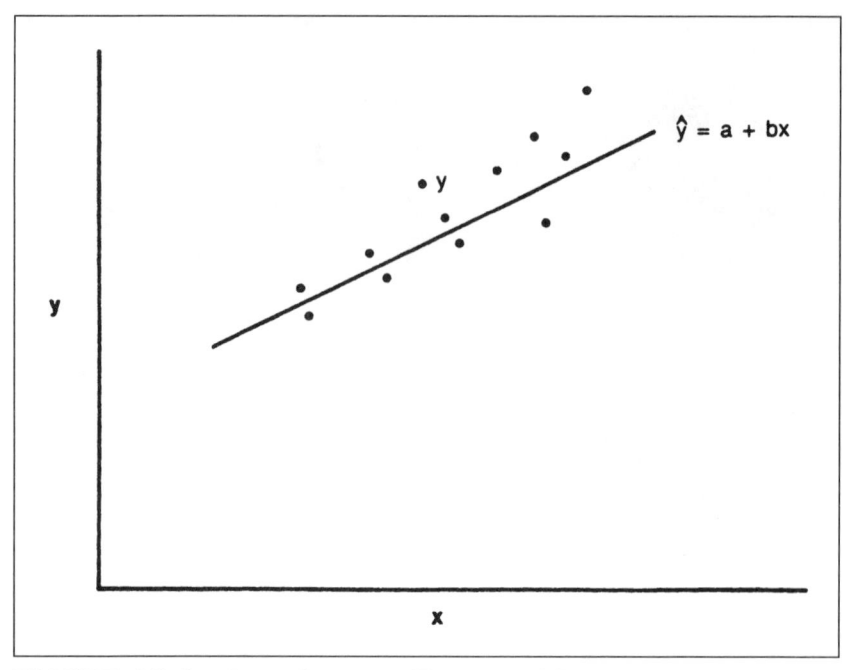

FIGURE 15.1 Actual versus Estimated Data

Using differential calculus we obtain the following formulas for *b* and *a*:

$$b = \frac{n \Sigma xy - (\Sigma x)(\Sigma y)}{n \Sigma x^2 - (\Sigma x^2)}$$

$$a = \bar{y} - b\bar{x} \text{ where } \bar{y} = y/n \text{ and } \bar{x} = x/n$$

The formula for *a* is a shortcut formula, which requires the computation of *b* first. This will save a considerable amount of time. If the data collected are too voluminous to fit into a calculator, *b* can be computed using the following formula:

$$b = \frac{\Sigma(x - \bar{x})(y - \bar{y})}{\Sigma(x - \bar{x})^2}$$

$$a = \text{the same as above}$$

EXAMPLE 15.1

To illustrate the computations of *b* and *a*, we will use the following data on sales and advertising expenses, which is of much concern to marketing managers. All the sums required are computed as follows:

Chapter 15: Forecast with Regression and Markov Methods 267

(00) Advertising (x)	(000) Sales (y)	xy	x^2	y^2
$ 9	$15	135	81	225
19	20	380	361	400
11	14	154	121	196
14	16	224	196	256
23	25	575	529	625
12	20	240	144	400
12	20	240	144	400
22	23	506	484	529
7	14	98	49	196
13	22	286	169	484
15	18	270	225	324
17	18	306	289	324
$174	$225	$3,414	$2,792	$4,359

From the preceding table:

$$\Sigma x = 174 \quad \Sigma y = 225$$
$$\Sigma xy = 3{,}414 \quad \Sigma x^2 = 2{,}792$$
$$\bar{x} = \Sigma x/n = 174/12 = 14.5$$
$$\bar{y} = \Sigma y/n = 225/12 = 18.75$$

Substituting these values into the formula for b first:

$$b = \frac{n\Sigma xy - (\Sigma x)(\Sigma y)}{n\Sigma x^2 - (\Sigma x)^2}$$

$$b = \frac{(12)(3{,}414) - (174)(225)}{(12)(2{,}792) - (174)^2} = \frac{1{,}818}{3{,}228} = 0.5632$$

$$a = \bar{y} - b\bar{x}$$
$$a = (18.75) - (0.5632)(14.5) = 18.75 - 8.1664 = 10.5836$$

Assume that the advertising of $10 is to be expended for next year. The projected sales for the next year would be computed as follows:

$$\hat{y} = \$10.5836 + \$0.5632x$$
$$= \$10.5836 + \$0.5632(10)$$
$$= \$10.5836 + \$5.632$$
$$= \$16.2156$$

Note that Σy^2 is not used here but rather is computed for future use.

Using Microsoft Excel® for Regression

Alternatively, you can use Microsoft Excel® to develop the model.

EXAMPLE 15.2

The following shows the data input and regression output.

Month	Advertising (in $00s)	Sales (in $000s)
1	9	15
2	19	20
3	11	14
4	14	16
5	23	25
6	12	20
7	12	20
8	22	23
9	7	14
10	13	22
11	15	18
12	17	18

Summary Output:

Regression Statistics	
Multiple R	0.7800
R Square	0.6084
Adjusted R Squ	0.5692
Standard Error	2.3436
Observations	12

ANOVA:

	df	SS	MS	F	Significance F
Regression	1	85.3243	85.3243	15.5345	0.0028
Residual	10	54.9257	5.4926		
Total	11	140.25			

	Coefficients	Standard Err	t Stat	P-Value[a]	Lower 95%	Upper 95%
Intercept	10.583643	2.1796	4.8558	0.0007	5.7272	15.4401
Advertising	0.563197	0.1429	3.9414	0.0028	0.2448	0.8816

[a]The P-value for X variable = .0028 indicates that there is a 0.28% chance that the true value of the X variable coefficient is equal to 0, implying a high level of accuracy about the estimated value of 0.563197.

At this juncture of our discussion, we only note from the output

$$a = 10.58364$$
$$b = 0.563197$$

That is, $\hat{y} = 10.58364 + 0.563197x$

Other statistics shown on the printout are discussed later in the chapter.

Trend Analysis

Another common method for forecasting sales or earnings by financial executives is trend analysis, which is a special type of regression analysis. This method involves a regression whereby a trend line is fitted to a time series of data. The trend line equation can be shown as

$$y = a + bx$$

The formulas for the coefficients a and b are essentially the same as the ones for simple regression. However, for regression purposes, a time period can be given a number so that $\Sigma x = 0$. When there is an odd number of periods, the period in the middle is assigned a zero value. If there is an even number, then -1 and $+1$ are assigned the two periods in the middle, so that again $\Sigma x = 0$.

With $\Sigma x = 0$, the formula for b and a reduces to the following:

$$b = \frac{n \Sigma xy}{n \Sigma x^2}$$
$$a = \Sigma y/n$$

EXAMPLE 15.3

Case 1 (Odd Number):

	2001	2002	2003	2004	2005
x =	−2	−1	0	+1	+2

Case 2 (Even Number):

	2001	2002	2003	2004	2005	2006
x =	−3	−2	−1	+1	+2	+3

EXAMPLE 15.4

Consider TDK company, whose historical earnings per share (EPS) follows:

Year	EPS
2001	$1.00
2002	1.20
2003	1.30
2004	1.60
2005	1.70

Since the company has 5 years' data, which is an odd number, the year in the middle is assigned a zero value.

Year	x	EPS (y)	xy	x^2	y^2
2001	−2	$1.00	−2.00	4	1.00
2002	−1	1.20	−1.20	1	1.44
2003	0	1.30	0	0	1.69
2004	+1	1.60	1.60	1	2.56
2005	+2	1.70	3.40	4	2.89
	0	$6.80	1.80	10	9.58

$$b = \frac{(5)(1.80)}{(5)(10)} = \frac{9}{50} = \$0.18$$

$$a = \frac{\$6.80}{5} = \$1.36$$

Therefore, the estimated trend equation is

$$\hat{y} = \$1.36 + \$0.18x$$

where

$$\hat{y} = \text{estimated EPS}$$
$$x = \text{year index value}$$

To project 2006 sales, we assign +3 to the *x* value for the year 2006. Thus,

$$\hat{y} = \$1.36 + \$0.18(+3)$$
$$= \$1.36 + \$0.54$$
$$= \$1.90$$

Note that Σy^2 was not used in this example; it was reserved for a future purpose.

Table 15.1 contains a summary of the more commonly used forecasting methods discussed in this chapter.

REGRESSION STATISTICS

Regression analysis is a statistical method. It uses a variety of statistics that tell us about the accuracy and reliability of the regression results. They include:

- Correlation coefficient (r) and coefficient of determination (r^2)
- Standard error of the estimate (s_e)
- Standard error of the regression coefficient (s_b) and *t*-statistic

Correlation Coefficient and Coefficient of Determination

The correlation coefficient, r, measures the degree of correlation between *y* and *x*. The range of values it takes on is between −1 and +1. More widely used, however, is the coefficient of determination, r^2. Simply put, r^2 tells us how good the estimated regression equation is. In other words, it is a measure of "goodness of fit" in the regression. Therefore, the higher the r^2, the more confidence we can have in our estimated equation.

More specifically, the coefficient of determination represents the proportion of the total variation in *y* that is explained by the regression equation. It has a range of value between 0 and 1.

TABLE 15.1 Summary of Commonly Used Forecasting Methods

Technique	Moving Average	Exponential Smoothing	Trend Analysis	Regression Analysis
Description	Each point of a moving average of a time series is the arithmetic or weighted average of a number of consecutive points of the series, where the number of data points is chosen so that the effects of seasons or irregularity or both are eliminated.	Similar to moving average, except that more recent data points are given more weight. Descriptively, the new forecast is equal to the old one plus some proportion of the past forecasting error. Effective when there is random demand and no seasonal fluctuation in the data series.	Fits a trend line to a mathematical equation and then projects it into the future by means of this equation. There are several variations: the slope-characteristic method, polynomials, logarithms, and so on.	Functionally relates sales to other economic, competitive, or internal variables and estimates an equation using the least-squares technique. Relationships are primarily analyzed statistically, although any relationship could be selected for testing on a rational ground.
Accuracy				
Short-term (0–3 months)	Poor to good	Fair to very good	Very good	Good to very good
Medium-term (3 months–2 years)	Poor	Poor to good	Good	Good to very good

Long-term (2 years and over)	Very poor	Very poor	Good	Poor
Typical application	Inventory control for low-volume items	Production and inventory control, forecasts of sales, and financial data	New product forecasts (particularly intermediate and long-term)	Forecasts of sales by product classes, forecasts of income and other financial data.
Data required	A minimum of two years of sales history if seasonals are present. Otherwise, fewer data. (Of course, the more history the better.) The moving average must be specified.	The same as for a moving average	Varies with the technique used. However, a good rule of thumb is to use a minimum of five years' annual data to start. Thereafter, the complete history.	Several years' quarterly history to obtain good, meaningful relationships. Mathematically necessary to have two more observations than there are independent variables.
Cost of forecasting with a computer	Very minimal	Minimal	Minimal	Varies with application.
Time required to develop an application and make forecasts	1 day	1 day	1 day	Depends on ability to identify relationships.

274 Part III: Financial Forecasting

EXAMPLE 15.5

The statement "Sales is a function of advertising with $r^2 = 70\%$" can be interpreted as "70% of the total variation of sales is explained by the regression equation or the change in advertising and the remaining 30% is accounted for by something other than advertising (for example, price or income)."

The coefficient of determination is computed as follows:

$$r^2 = 1 - \frac{\Sigma(y - \hat{y})^2}{\Sigma(y - \bar{y})^2}$$

In a simple regression situation, however, a shortcut method is available.

$$r^2 = \frac{[n \cdot \Sigma xy - (\Sigma x)(\Sigma y)]^2}{[n\Sigma x^2 - (\Sigma x)^2] \cdot [n\Sigma y^2 - (\Sigma y)^2]}$$

Comparing this formula with one for b in Example 15.1, we see the only additional information we need in order to compute r^2 is Σy^2.

EXAMPLE 15.6

From the table in Example 15.1, $\Sigma y^2 = 4{,}359$. Using the shortcut method for r^2,

$$r^2 = \frac{(1{,}818)^2}{(3{,}228) \cdot [(12)(4{,}359) - (225)^2]}$$

$$= \frac{3{,}305{,}124}{(3{,}228)(52{,}308 - 50{,}625)} = \frac{3{,}305{,}124}{(3{,}228)(1{,}683)}$$

$$= \frac{3{,}305{,}124}{5{,}432{,}724} = 0.6084 = 60.84\%$$

This means that about 60.84% of the variation in total sales is explained by advertising, and the remaining 39.16% is still unexplained. A relatively low r^2 indicates that there is a lot of room for improvement in our estimated forecast equation ($y' = \$10.5836 + \$0.5632x$). Income or a combination of income and advertising might improve r^2.

In Example 15.4,

$$r^2 = \frac{(9)^2}{(50)[(5)(9.58) - (6.80)^2]}$$

$$= \frac{81}{(50)(47.9 - 46.24)}$$

$$= \frac{81}{(50)(1.66)} = \frac{81}{83} = 0.9759 = 97.59\%$$

The very high r^2 (97.59%) indicates that the trend line is an excellent fit and there is a growing trend in EPS over time.

Standard Error of the Estimate and Confidence Interval

The standard error of the estimate, s_e, is defined as the standard deviation of the regression. It is computed as follows:

$$s_e = \sqrt{\frac{\Sigma(y - \hat{y})^2}{n - 2}} = \sqrt{\frac{\Sigma(y^2 - a\Sigma y - b\Sigma xy)}{n - 2}}$$

Tip: The statistics can be used to gain some idea of the accuracy of management predictions.

EXAMPLE 15.7

Going back to Example 15.1, s_e is calculated as follows:

$$s_e = \sqrt{\frac{(4{,}359) - (10.5836)(225) - (0.5632)(3{,}414)}{12 - 2}}$$

$$s_e = \sqrt{\frac{(4{,}359) - (10.5836)}{1}}$$

If a manager wants the prediction to be 95% confident, the *confidence interval* would be the *estimated sales* ± 2(2.3436). More specifically, the confidence interval for the prediction, given an advertising expense of $10, would be

$$\$16.2156 \pm 2(2.3436)$$
$$= \$16.2156 \pm 4.6872, \text{ which means}$$
$$\$16.2156 - \$20.9028$$

Standard Error of the Regression Coefficient and *t*-Statistic

The standard error of the coefficient s_b and the *t*-statistic are closely related. The value of s_b is calculated as follows:

$$s_b = \frac{s_e}{\sqrt{\Sigma(x - \bar{x})^2}}$$

or, in shortcut form,

$$s_b = \frac{s_e}{\sqrt{\Sigma x^2 - \bar{x}\Sigma x}}$$

The standard error of the coefficient gives an estimate of the range in which the true coefficient actually is. The *t*-statistic shows the statistical significance of x in explaining y. It is developed by dividing the estimated coefficient b by its standard error s_b. That is

$$t\text{-statistic} = b/s_b$$

Thus, the *t*-statistic really measures how many standard errors the coefficient is away from zero. Generally, any *t* value greater than +2 or less than −2 is acceptable. The higher the *t*-value, the more significant the b is, and therefore the greater confidence we have in the coefficient as a predictor.

EXAMPLE 15.8

The s_b for our example is (note that $s_e = 2.3436$, $\Sigma x^2 = 2{,}792$, $\bar{x} = 14.5$, $\Sigma x = 174$)

$$s_b = \frac{2.3436}{\sqrt{2{,}792 - (14.5)(174)}}$$

$$= \frac{2.3436}{\sqrt{2{,}792 - 2{,}523}} = \frac{2.3436}{\sqrt{269}}$$

$$= \frac{2.3436}{16.40} = 0.143$$

Thus, *t*-statistic = b/s_b = 0.5632/0.143 = 3.94.

Because $t = 3.94 > 2$, we conclude that the b coefficient is statistically significant.

STATISTICS TO LOOK FOR IN MULTIPLE REGRESSIONS

In multiple regressions that involve more than one independent (explanatory) variable, managers must look for the following statistics:

- *t*-statistic
- *r*-bar squared ($\bar{r}^2$) and *F*-statistic
- Multicollinearity
- Autocorrelation (or serial correlation)

t-Statistic

The *t*-statistic was discussed earlier, but is taken up again here because it is more valid in multiple regressions than in simple regressions. The *t*-statistic shows the significance of each explanatory variable in predicting the dependent variable. It is desirable to have as large (either positive or negative) a *t*-statistic as possible for each independent variable. Generally, a *t*-statistic greater than +2.0 or less than −2.0 is acceptable. Explanatory variables with low *t*-value can usually be eliminated from the regression without substantially decreasing r^2 or increasing the standard error of the regression. In a multiple regression situation, the *t*-statistic is defined as

$$t\text{-statistic} = \frac{b_i}{s_{b_i}}$$

where
 $i = i$th independent variable

r-Bar Squared ($\bar{r}^2$) and *F*-Statistic

A more appropriate test for goodness of fit for multiple regressions is *r*-bar squared ($\bar{r}^2$):

$$\bar{r}^2 = 1 - (1 - r^2)\frac{n - 1}{n - k}$$

where
 n = the number of observations
 k = the number of coefficients to be estimated

An alternative test of the overall significance of a regression equation is the *F*-test. Virtually all computer programs for regression analysis show an *F*-statistic.

The *F*-statistic is defined as:

$$F = \frac{\Sigma(\hat{y}' - \bar{y})^2/k}{\Sigma(y - \hat{y}')^2/n - k - 1} = \frac{\text{Explained variation}/k}{\text{Unexplained variation}/n - k - 1}$$

If the *F*-statistic is greater than the table value, it is concluded that the regression equation is statistically significant in overall terms.

Multicollinearity

When using more than one independent variable in a regression equation, there is sometimes a high correlation between the independent variables themselves. Multicollinearity occurs when these variables interfere with each other. It is a pitfall because the equations with multicollinearity may produce spurious forecasts.

Multicollinearity can be recognized when:

- The *t*-statistics of two seemingly important independent variables are low.
- The estimated coefficients on explanatory variables have the opposite sign from that which would logically be expected.

There are two ways to get around the problem of multicollinearity:

- One of the highly correlated variables may be dropped from the regression.
- The structure of the equation may be changed using one of the following methods:
  — Divide both the left- and right-hand side variables by some series that will leave the basic economic logic but remove multicollinearity.
  — Estimate the equation on a first-difference basis.
  — Combine the collinear variables into a new variable, which is their weighted sum.

Autocorrelation (Serial Correlation)

Autocorrelation is another major pitfall often encountered in regression analysis. It occurs where there is a correlation between successive errors. The Durbin–Watson statistic provides the standard test for autocorrelation.

Table 15.2 provides the values of the Durbin–Watson statistic for specified sample sizes and explanatory variables. The table gives the significance points for d_L and d_U for tests on the autocorrelation of residuals (when no explanatory variable is a lagged endogenous variable). The number of explanatory variables, K', *excludes* the constant term.

Generally speaking,

Durbin–Watson Statistic	*Autocorrelation*
Between 1.5 and 2.5	No autocorrelation
Below 1.5	Positive autocorrelation
Above 2.5	Negative autocorrelation

Autocorrelation usually indicates that an important part of the variation of the dependent variable has not been explained. *Recommendation:* The best solution to this problem is to search for other explanatory variables to include in the regression equation.

EVALUATION OF FORECASTS

Forecasters must always look for ways to improve their forecasts, meaning that they might want to examine some objective evaluations of alternative forecasting techniques. This section presents the necessary guidelines via two evaluation techniques. The first is in the form of a checklist. A forecaster could use it to evaluate either a new model or an existing model. The second method is a statistical technique for evaluating a model.

Checklist

Two main items to be checked are the data and the model with its accompanying assumptions. The questions to be raised are:

- Is the source reliable and accurate?
- In the case of use of more than one source that is reliable and accurate, is the source that is used the best one?
- Are the data the most recent available?
- If the answer to the previous question is yes, are the data subject to subsequent revision?
- Is there any known systematic bias in the data that can be dealt with?

TABLE 15.2 Values of the Durbin–Watson d for Specified Samples Sizes (T) and Explanatory Variables (Significance level = 0.01)

Number of Residuals T	$K=1$ d_L	$K=1$ d_U	$K=2$ d_L	$K=2$ d_U	$K=3$ d_L	$K=3$ d_U	$K=4$ d_L	$K=4$ d_U	$K=5$ d_L	$K=5$ d_U
15	1.08	1.36	0.95	1.54	0.82	1.75	0.69	1.97	0.56	2.21
16	1.10	1.37	0.98	1.54	0.86	1.73	0.74	1.93	0.62	2.15
17	1.13	1.38	1.02	1.54	0.90	1.71	0.78	1.90	0.67	2.10
18	1.16	1.39	1.05	1.53	0.93	1.69	0.82	1.87	0.71	2.06
19	1.18	1.40	1.08	1.53	0.97	1.68	0.86	1.85	0.75	2.02
20	1.20	1.41	1.10	1.54	1.00	1.68	0.90	1.83	0.79	1.99
21	1.22	1.42	1.13	1.54	1.03	1.67	0.93	1.81	0.83	1.96
22	1.24	1.43	1.15	1.54	1.05	1.66	0.96	1.80	0.86	1.94
23	1.26	1.44	1.17	1.54	1.08	1.66	0.99	1.79	0.90	1.92
24	1.27	1.45	1.19	1.55	1.10	1.66	1.01	1.78	0.93	1.90
25	1.29	1.45	1.21	1.55	1.12	1.66	1.04	1.77	0.95	1.89
26	1.30	1.46	1.22	1.55	1.14	1.65	1.06	1.76	0.98	1.88
27	1.32	1.47	1.24	1.56	1.16	1.65	1.08	1.76	1.01	1.86
28	1.33	1.48	1.26	1.56	1.18	1.65	1.10	1.75	1.03	1.85
29	1.34	1.48	1.27	1.56	1.20	1.65	1.12	1.74	1.05	1.84
30	1.35	1.49	1.28	1.57	1.21	1.65	1.14	1.74	1.07	1.83
31	1.36	1.50	1.30	1.57	1.23	1.65	1.16	1.74	1.09	1.83
32	1.37	1.50	1.31	1.57	1.24	1.65	1.18	1.73	1.11	1.82

33	1.38	1.51	1.32	1.58	1.26	1.65	1.19	1.73	1.13	1.81
34	1.39	1.51	1.33	1.58	1.27	1.65	1.21	1.73	1.15	1.81
35	1.40	1.52	1.34	1.58	1.28	1.65	1.22	1.73	1.16	1.80
36	1.41	1.52	1.35	1.59	1.29	1.65	1.24	1.73	1.18	1.80
37	1.42	1.53	1.36	1.59	1.31	1.66	1.25	1.72	1.19	1.80
38	1.43	1.54	1.37	1.59	1.32	1.66	1.26	1.72	1.21	1.79
39	1.43	1.54	1.38	1.60	1.33	1.66	1.27	1.72	1.22	1.79
40	1.44	1.54	1.39	1.60	1.34	1.66	1.29	1.72	1.23	1.79
45	1.48	1.57	1.43	1.62	1.38	1.67	1.34	1.72	1.29	1.78
50	1.50	1.59	1.46	1.63	1.42	1.67	1.38	1.72	1.34	1.77
55	1.53	1.60	1.49	1.64	1.45	1.68	1.41	1.72	1.38	1.77
60	1.55	1.62	1.51	1.65	1.48	1.69	1.44	1.73	1.41	1.77
65	1.57	1.63	1.54	1.66	1.50	1.70	1.47	1.73	1.44	1.77
70	1.58	1.64	1.55	1.67	1.52	1.70	1.49	1.74	1.46	1.77
75	1.60	1.65	1.57	1.68	1.54	1.71	1.51	1.74	1.49	1.77
80	1.61	1.66	1.59	1.69	1.56	1.72	1.53	1.74	1.51	1.77
85	1.62	1.67	1.60	1.70	1.57	1.72	1.55	1.75	1.52	1.77
90	1.63	1.68	1.61	1.70	1.59	1.73	1.57	1.75	1.54	1.78
95	1.64	1.69	1.62	1.71	1.60	1.73	1.58	1.75	1.56	1.78
100	1.65	1.69	1.63	1.72	1.61	1.74	1.59	1.76	1.57	1.78

(Continued)

TABLE 15.2 (*Continued*) (Significance level = 0.05)

Number of Residuals	K = 1		K = 2		K = 3		K = 4		K = 5	
T	d_L	d_U	d_L	d_U	d_L	d_U	d_L	d_U	d_L	d_U
15	0.81	1.07	0.70	1.25	0.59	1.46	0.49	1.70	0.39	1.96
16	0.84	1.09	0.74	1.25	0.63	1.44	0.53	1.66	0.44	1.90
17	0.87	1.10	0.77	1.25	0.67	1.43	0.57	1.63	0.48	1.85
18	0.90	1.12	0.80	1.26	0.71	1.42	0.61	1.60	0.52	1.80
19	0.93	1.13	0.83	1.26	0.74	1.41	0.65	1.58	0.56	1.77
20	0.95	1.15	0.86	1.27	0.77	1.41	0.68	1.57	0.60	1.74
21	0.97	1.16	0.89	1.27	0.80	1.41	0.72	1.55	0.63	1.71
22	1.00	1.17	0.91	1.28	0.83	1.40	0.75	1.54	0.66	1.69
23	1.02	1.19	0.94	1.29	0.86	1.40	0.77	1.53	0.70	1.67
24	1.04	1.20	0.96	1.30	0.88	1.41	0.80	1.53	0.72	1.66
25	1.05	1.21	0.98	1.30	0.90	1.41	0.83	1.52	0.75	1.65
26	1.07	1.22	1.00	1.31	0.93	1.41	0.85	1.52	0.78	1.64
27	1.09	1.23	1.02	1.32	0.95	1.41	0.88	1.51	0.81	1.63
28	1.10	1.24	1.04	1.32	0.97	1.41	0.90	1.51	0.83	1.62
29	1.12	1.25	1.05	1.33	0.99	1.42	0.92	1.51	0.85	1.61
30	1.13	1.26	1.07	1.34	1.01	1.42	0.94	1.51	0.88	1.61
31	1.15	1.27	1.08	1.34	1.02	1.42	0.96	1.51	0.90	1.60
32	1.16	1.28	1.10	1.35	1.04	1.43	0.98	1.51	0.92	1.60

33	1.17	1.29	1.11	1.36	1.05	1.43	1.00	1.51	0.94	1.59
34	1.18	1.30	1.13	1.36	1.07	1.43	1.01	1.51	0.95	1.59
35	1.19	1.31	1.14	1.37	1.08	1.44	1.03	1.51	0.97	1.59
36	1.21	1.32	1.15	1.38	1.10	1.44	1.04	1.51	0.99	1.59
37	1.22	1.32	1.16	1.38	1.11	1.45	1.06	1.51	1.00	1.59
38	1.23	1.33	1.18	1.39	1.12	1.45	1.07	1.52	1.02	1.58
39	1.24	1.34	1.19	1.39	1.14	1.45	1.09	1.52	1.03	1.58
40	1.25	1.34	1.20	1.40	1.15	1.46	1.10	1.52	1.05	1.58
45	1.29	1.38	1.24	1.42	1.20	1.48	1.16	1.53	1.11	1.58
50	1.32	1.40	1.28	1.45	1.24	1.49	1.20	1.54	1.16	1.59
55	1.36	1.43	1.32	1.47	1.28	1.51	1.25	1.55	1.21	1.59
60	1.38	1.45	1.35	1.48	1.32	1.52	1.28	1.56	1.25	1.60
65	1.41	1.47	1.38	1.50	1.35	1.53	1.31	1.57	1.28	1.61
70	1.43	1.49	1.40	1.52	1.37	1.55	1.34	1.58	1.31	1.61
75	1.45	1.50	1.42	1.53	1.39	1.56	1.37	1.59	1.34	1.62
80	1.47	1.52	1.44	1.54	1.42	1.57	1.39	1.60	1.36	1.62
85	1.48	1.53	1.46	1.55	1.43	1.58	1.41	1.60	1.39	1.63
90	1.50	1.54	1.47	1.56	1.45	1.59	1.43	1.61	1.41	1.64
95	1.51	1.55	1.49	1.57	1.47	1.60	1.45	1.62	1.42	1.64
100	1.52	1.56	1.50	1.58	1.48	1.60	1.46	1.63	1.44	1.65

Note: K = number of explanatory variables excluding the constant term.

Measuring Accuracy of Forecasts

The performance of a forecast should be checked against its own record or against that of other forecasts. There are various statistical techniques that can be used to measure performance of the model. Of course, the performance is measured in terms of forecasting error, where error is defined as the difference between a predicted value and the actual result.

$$\text{Error } (e) = \text{Actual } (A) - \text{Forecast } (F)$$

MAD and MSE

Two commonly used measures for summarizing historical errors are the mean absolute deviation (MAD) and the mean squared error (MSE). The formulas used to calculate MAD and MSE are:

$$\text{MAD} = \Sigma | A - F | / n$$
$$\text{MSE} = \Sigma (A - F)^2 / (n - 1)$$

Example 15.9 illustrates the computation of MAD and MSE.

EXAMPLE 15.9

Sales data of a microwave oven manufacturer follow:

Period	A	F	Error (A − F)	|Error|	Error²
1	217	215	2	2	4
2	213	216	−3	3	9
3	216	215	1	1	1
4	210	214	−4	4	16
5	213	211	2	2	4
6	219	214	5	5	25
7	216	217	−1	1	1
8	212	216	−4	4	16
			−2	22	76

Using these figures

$$\text{MAD} = \Sigma\, e/n = 22/8 = 2.75$$
$$\text{MSE} = \Sigma e^2/(n-1) = 76/8 - 1 = 10.86$$

One way in which these measures are used is to evaluate forecasting ability of alternative forecasting methods. For example, using either MAD or MSE, a forecaster could compare the results of exponential smoothing with alphas and elect the one that performed best in terms of the lowest MAD or MSE for a given set of data. Also, it can help select the best initial forecast value for exponential smoothing.

U-Statistic and Turning-Point Errors

There are still a number of statistical measures for measuring accuracy of the forecast. Two standards may be identified. First, one could compare the forecast being evaluated with a naive forecast to see if there are vast differences. The naive forecast can be anything, such as the same as last year's, a moving average, or the output of an exponential smoothing technique. In the second case, the forecast may be compared against the actual outcome. The comparison may be against the actual level of the variable forecasted, or the change observed may be compared with the change forecast. Other evaluation techniques consider the number of turning-point errors correctly forecast.

The Theil U-statistic is based upon a comparison of the predicted change with the observed change. It is calculated as follows:

$$U = 1/n\, \Sigma\, (A - F)^2 / [(1/n)\, \Sigma F^2 + (1/n) \Sigma A^2]$$

As can be seen, $U = 0$ is a perfect forecast, since the forecast would equal actual and $A - F = 0$ for all observations. At the other extreme, $U = 1$ would be a case of all incorrect forecasts.

Most computer software packages routinely compute the U-statistic.

Control of Forecasts

It is important to monitor forecast errors to ensure that the forecast is performing well. If the model is performing poorly based on some criteria, the forecaster might reconsider the use of the existing model or switch to

286   Part III: Financial Forecasting

another forecasting model or technique. *Tip:* The forecasting control can be accomplished by comparing forecasting errors to predetermined values, or limits. Errors that fall within the limits would be judged acceptable, while errors outside the limits would signal that corrective action is desirable. Forecasts can be monitored using either *tracking signals* or *control charts.*

A tracking signal is based on the ratio of cumulative forecast error to the corresponding value of MAD.

$$\text{Tracking signal} = \Sigma(A - F)/\text{MAD}$$

The resulting values are compared to predetermined limits. These are based on experience and judgment, and often range from + or − 3 to + or − 8. Values within the limits suggest that the forecast is performing adequately.

The control chart approach involves setting upper and lower limits for individual forecasting errors instead of cumulative errors. The limits are multiples of the square root of MSE. *Recommendation:* It is always a good idea to plot the errors so that the forecaster can visualize the process and determine if the method being used is in control.

EXAMPLE 15.10

For the sales data below, using the naive forecast, we will determine whether the forecast is in control. For illustrative purposes, we will use two sigma control limits.

Year	Sales	Forecasts	Error	Error^2
1	320	—	—	—
2	326	320	6	36
3	310	326	−16	256
4	317	310	7	49
5	315	317	−2	4
6	318	315	3	9
7	310	318	−8	64
8	316	310	6	36
9	314	316	−2	4
10	317	314	3	9
			−3	467

First compute the standard deviation of forecast errors:

$$\sqrt{\Sigma e^2/(n-1)} = \sqrt{467/(9-1)} = 7.64$$

Two sigma limits are then + or − 2 (7.64) = −15.28 to + 15.28.

Note that the forecast error for year 3 (i.e., −16) is below the lower bound, so the forecast is not in control. *Note:* Using other methods, such as moving average, exponential smoothing, or even regression, might achieve a better forecast.

CHECKLISTS—HOW TO CHOOSE THE BEST FORECASTING EQUATION

Choosing among alternative forecasting equations basically involves two steps. The first step is to eliminate the obvious losers. The second is to select the winner from among the remaining contenders.

How to Eliminate Losers

- Does the equation make sense? Equations that do not make sense intuitively or from a theoretical standpoint must be eliminated.
- Does the equation have explanatory variables with low *t*-statistics? These equations should be reestimated or dropped in favor of equations in which all independent variables are significant. This test will eliminate equations where multicollinearity is a problem.
- How about a low $\bar{r}^2$? The $\bar{r}^2$ can be used to rank the remaining equations in order to select the best candidates. A low $\bar{r}^2$ could mean:
  — A wrong functional was fitted.
  — An important explanatory variable is missing.
  — Other combinations of explanatory variables might be more desirable.

How to Choose the Best Equation

- Best Durbin–Watson statistic. Given equations that survive all previous tests, the equation with the Durbin–Watson statistic closest to 2.0 can be a basis for selection.
- Best forecasting accuracy. Examining the forecasting performance of the equations is essential for selecting one equation from those that have not been eliminated. The equation whose prediction accuracy is best in terms of MAD or MSE generally provides the best basis for forecasting.

USE OF A COMPUTER STATISTICAL PACKAGE FOR MULTIPLE REGRESSION

Example 15.11 demonstrates how a computer program handles multiple regression.

EXAMPLE 15.11

Cypress Consumer Products Corporation wishes to develop a forecasting model for its dryer sales by using multiple regression analysis. The marketing department prepared the following sample data.

Month	Sales of Washers (x_1)	Disposable Income (x_2)	Savings (x_3)	Sales of Dryers (y)
January	$45,000	$16,000	$71,000	$29,000
February	42,000	14,000	70,000	24,000
March	44,000	15,000	72,000	27,000
April	45,000	13,000	71,000	25,000
May	43,000	13,000	75,000	26,000
June	46,000	14,000	74,000	28,000
July	44,000	16,000	76,000	30,000
August	45,000	16,000	69,000	28,000
September	44,000	15,000	74,000	28,000
October	43,000	15,000	73,000	27,000

The computer statistical package called SPSS for Windows, which is one of the easiest programs to use, was employed to develop the regression model. Figure 15.2 contains the input data and output that resulted using three explanatory variables. To help you understand the listing, illustrative comments are added whenever applicable.

1. *The forecasting equation.* From the SPSS output we see that

$$\hat{y} = -45.796 + 0.597x_1 + 1.177x_2 + 0.405x_3$$

Suppose that in November the company expects:

x_1 = sales of washers = $43,000
x_2 = disposable income = $15,000
x_3 = savings = $75,000

Chapter 15: Forecast with Regression and Markov Methods 289

Then the forecast sales for the month of November would be

$$\hat{y} = -45.796 + 0.597(43) + 1.177(15)$$
$$+ 0.405(75) = -45.796 + 25.671 + 17.655$$
$$+ 30.375 = 27.905 \text{ or } \$27,905$$

2. *The coefficient of determination.* From the output we see that:

$$r^2 = 0.983$$

FIGURE 15.2 SPSS Regression Output

VARIABLES ENTERED/REMOVED[a]:

Model	Variables Entered	Variables Removed	Method
1	Savings, sales, Income[b]		Enter

[a]Dependent Variable: SALESDRY.
[b]All requested variables entered.

MODEL SUMMARY[a]:

Model	R	R Square (r^2)	Adjusted R Square (r^{-2})	Standard Error of the Estimate (s_e)	Durbin-Watson
1	.992[b]	.983	.975	.2861	2.094

[a]Dependent Variable: SALESDRY.
[b]Predictors: (Constant), SAVINGS, sales, INCOME.

ANOVA[a]:

Model		Sum of Squares	df	Mean Square	F	Sig.
1	Regression	29.109	3	9.703	118.517	.000[b]
	Residual	.491	6	8.187E-02		
	Total	29.600	9			

[a]Dependent Variable: SALESDRY.
[b]Predictors: (Constant), SAVINGS, sales, INCOME.

(Continued)

FIGURE 15.2 (continued)

Coefficients[a]**:**

Model		Unstandardized Coefficients B	Std. Error	Standardized Coefficients Beta	t	Sig.
1	(Constant)	−45.796	4.878		−9.389	.000
	sales wash	.597	.081	.394	7.359	.000
	Income	1.177	.084	.752	13.998	.000
	Savings	.405	.042S_b	.508	9.592	.000

[a]Dependent Variable: SALESDRY.

Residuals Statistics[a]**:**

	Minimum	Maximum	Mean	Std. Deviation	N
Predicted Value	24.1098	30.0881	27.2000	1.7984	10
Residual	−.2908	.4445	−7.11E-16	.2336	10
Std. Predicted Value	−1.718	1.606	.000	1.000	10
Std. Residual	−1.016	1.554	.000	.816	10

[a]Dependent Variable: SALESDRY.

In the case of multiple regression, $\bar{r}^2$ is more appropriate, as was discussed previously.

$$\bar{r}^2 = 0.975$$

This tells us that 97.5% of total variation in sales of dryers is explained by the three explanatory variables. The remaining 2.5% was unexplained by the estimated equation.

3. *The standard error of the estimate (s_e).* This is a measure of dispersion of actual sales around the estimated equation. The output shows $s_e = 0.28613$.

4. *Computed t.* We read from the output

	t-Statistic
x_1	7.359
x_2	13.998
x_3	9.592

All t values are greater than a rule-of-thumb table t value of 2.0. (Strictly speaking, with $n - k - 1 = 10 - 3 - 1 = 6$ degrees of freedom and a level of significance of, say, 0.01, we see from Table 15.3 that the table t value is 3.707.) For two-sided test, the level of significance to look up was .005. In any case, we conclude that all three explanatory variables we have selected were statistically significant.

5. *F-test*. From the output, we see that

$$F = 118.517$$

At a significance level of 0.01, our F-value is far above the value of 9.78 (which is circled in Table 15.4), so we conclude that the regression as a whole is highly significant.

6. *Durbin–Watson test*. The output shows 2.094 which is between 1.5 and 2.5. No autocorrelation exists.
7. *Conclusion*. Based on statistical considerations, we see that:

- The estimated equation had a good fit.
- All three variables are significant explanatory variables.
- The regression as a whole is highly significant.
- The model developed can be used as a forecasting equation with a great degree of confidence.
- No autocorrelation exists.

MODELS BASED ON LEARNED BEHAVIOR— MARKOV MODEL

The forecasting methods discussed so far are for the most part based on the use of historical data. They do not consider aspects of consumer behavior in making purchase decisions in the marketplace. In this section we present a model based on learned behavior, called the *Markov model*. We operate on the thesis that consumption is a form of learned behavior; that is, consumers tend to repeat their past consumption activities. Some consumers become loyal to certain product types as well as to specific brands. Others seek other brands and products. In general, there is a great degree of regularity about such behavior. The Markov model is used to predict market share by considering consumer brand loyalty and switching behavior.

TABLE 15.3 Values of t_p for Specified Probabilities P and Degrees of Freedom ($v = n - k - 1$)

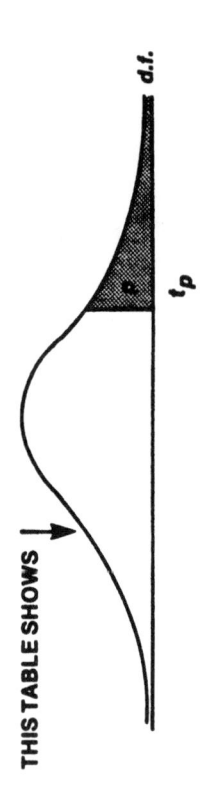

Degrees of Freedom v	0.45	0.40	0.35	0.30	0.25	0.20	0.15	0.10	0.05	0.025	0.01	0.005	0.0005
1	0.158	0.325	0.510	0.727	1.000	1.376	1.963	3.078	6.314	12.706	31.821	63.657	636.692
2	0.142	0.289	0.445	0.617	0.816	1.061	1.386	1.886	2.920	4.303	6.965	9.925	31.598
3	0.137	0.277	0.424	0.584	0.765	0.978	1.250	1.638	2.353	3.182	4.541	5.841	12.924
4	0.134	0.271	0.414	0.569	0.741	0.941	1.190	1.533	2.132	2.776	3.747	4.604	8.610
5	0.132	0.267	0.408	0.559	0.727	0.920	1.156	1.476	2.015	2.571	3.365	4.032	6.869
6	0.131	0.265	0.404	0.553	0.718	0.906	1.134	1.440	1.943	2.447	3.143	3.707	5.959
7	0.130	0.263	0.402	0.549	0.711	0.896	1.119	1.415	1.895	2.365	2.998	3.499	5.408
8	0.130	0.262	0.399	0.546	0.706	0.889	1.108	1.397	1.860	2.306	2.896	3.355	5.041
9	0.129	0.261	0.398	0.543	0.703	0.883	1.100	1.383	1.833	2.262	2.821	3.250	4.781
10	0.129	0.260	0.397	0.542	0.700	0.879	1.093	1.372	1.812	2.228	2.764	3.169	4.587
11	0.129	0.260	0.396	0.540	0.697	0.876	1.088	1.363	1.796	2.201	2.718	3.106	4.437
12	0.128	0.259	0.395	0.539	0.695	0.873	1.083	1.356	1.782	2.179	2.681	3.055	4.318
13	0.128	0.259	0.394	0.538	0.694	0.870	1.079	1.350	1.771	2.160	2.650	3.012	4.221
14	0.128	0.258	0.393	0.537	0.692	0.868	1.076	1.345	1.761	2.145	2.624	2.977	4.140

Level of Significance P for One-Sided Statements

15	0.128	0.258	0.393	0.536	0.691	0.866	1.074	1.341	1.753	2.131	2.602	2.947	4.073
16	0.128	0.258	0.392	0.535	0.690	0.865	1.071	1.337	1.746	2.120	2.583	2.921	4.015
17	0.128	0.257	0.392	0.534	0.689	0.863	1.069	1.333	1.740	2.110	2.567	2.898	3.965
18	0.127	0.257	0.392	0.534	0.688	0.862	1.067	1.330	1.734	2.101	2.552	2.878	3.922
19	0.127	0.257	0.391	0.533	0.688	0.861	1.066	1.328	1.729	2.093	2.539	2.861	3.883
20	0.127	0.257	0.391	0.533	0.687	0.860	1.064	1.325	1.725	2.086	2.528	2.845	3.850
21	0.127	0.257	0.391	0.532	0.686	0.859	1.063	1.323	1.721	2.080	2.518	2.831	3.819
22	0.127	0.256	0.390	0.532	0.686	0.858	1.061	1.321	1.717	2.074	2.508	2.819	3.792
23	0.127	0.256	0.390	0.532	0.685	0.858	1.060	1.319	1.714	2.069	2.500	2.807	3.767
24	0.127	0.256	0.390	0.531	0.685	0.857	1.059	1.318	1.711	2.064	2.492	2.797	3.745
25	0.127	0.256	0.390	0.531	0.684	0.856	1.058	1.316	1.708	2.060	2.485	2.787	3.725
26	0.127	0.256	0.390	0.531	0.684	0.856	1.058	1.315	1.706	2.056	2.479	2.779	3.707
27	0.127	0.256	0.389	0.531	0.684	0.855	1.057	1.314	1.703	2.052	2.473	2.771	3.690
28	0.127	0.256	0.389	0.530	0.683	0.855	1.056	1.313	1.701	2.048	2.467	2.763	3.674
29	0.127	0.256	0.389	0.530	0.683	0.854	1.055	1.311	1.699	2.045	2.462	2.756	3.659
30	0.127	0.256	0.389	0.530	0.683	0.854	1.055	1.310	1.697	2.042	2.457	2.750	3.646
40	0.126	0.255	0.388	0.529	0.681	0.851	1.050	1.303	1.684	2.021	2.423	2.704	3.551
60	0.126	0.254	0.387	0.527	0.679	0.848	1.046	1.296	1.671	2.000	2.390	2.660	3.460
120	0.126	0.254	0.386	0.526	0.677	0.845	1.041	1.289	1.658	1.980	2.358	2.617	3.373
∞	0.126	0.253	0.385	0.524	0.674	0.842	1.036	1.282	1.645	1.960	2.326	2.576	3.291

t_p is the value of the student's t random variable such that the probability of obtaining a sample t value at least as large as t_p is P. The value of P must be doubled if two-sided statements are made using the same t_p value.

Source: This table is taken from Table III of Fisher and Yates, *Statistical Tables for Biological, Agricultural and Medical Research*, published by Oliver and Boyd, Edinburgh, and by permission of the authors and publishers.

TABLE 15.4 Values of F_p for Specified Probabilities P and Degrees of Freedom in the Numerator n_1 and Degrees of Freedom in the Denominator n_2

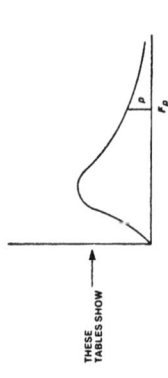

F_p is the value of the Snedecor F random variable such that the probability of obtaining a sample F value at least as large as F_p is P. In the first comprehensive table, the level of significance P is 0.05 *for all lightface entries* and 0.01 *for all boldface entries*. This table continues on four pages with the degrees of freedom in the numerator specified across the top and the degrees of freedom in the denominator specified along the side. The areas are shown in the illustration above. For example, given $n_1 = 4$ and $n_2 = 9$, the value of F is 3.63 when 5% of the total area is in the right tail of the distribution.

F Distribution

	n_1 = degree of freedom for numerator = k								n_2 = degrees of freedom for denominator = $n - k - 1$			
	1	2	3	4	5	6	7	8	9	10	11	12
1	161	200	216	225	230	234	237	239	241	242	243	244
	4,052	**4,999**	**5,408**	**5,625**	**5,764**	**5,559**	**5,928**	**5,981**	**6,023**	**6,054**	**6,082**	**6,106**
2	18.51	19.00	19.16	19.25	19.30	19.33	19.36	19.37	19.38	19.39	19.40	19.41
	98.49	**99.01**	**99.17**	**99.25**	**99.30**	**99.33**	**99.34**	**99.36**	**99.38**	**99.40**	**99.41**	**99.42**
3	10.13	9.55	9.28	9.12	9.01	8.94	8.88	8.84	8.81	8.78	8.76	8.74
	34.12	**30.81**	**29.46**	**28.71**	**28.24**	**27.91**	**27.67**	**27.49**	**27.34**	**27.23**	**27.13**	**27.06**
4	7.71	6.94	6.59	6.39	6.26	6.16	6.09	6.04	6.00	5.96	5.93	5.91
	21.20	**18.00**	**16.69**	**15.98**	**15.52**	**15.21**	**14.98**	**14.80**	**14.66**	**14.54**	**14.45**	**14.37**
5	6.61	5.79	5.41	5.19	5.05	4.95	4.88	4.82	4.78	4.74	4.70	4.68
	16.26	**13.27**	**12.06**	**11.39**	**10.37**	**10.67**	**10.45**	**10.27**	**10.15**	**10.05**	**9.96**	**9.89**
6	5.99	5.14	4.76	4.53	4.39	4.28	4.21	4.15	4.10	4.06	4.03	4.00
	13.74	**10.92**	**9.78**	**9.15**	**8.76**	**8.47**	**8.26**	**8.10**	**7.98**	**7.87**	**7.79**	**7.72**
7	5.59	4.74	4.35	4.12	3.97	3.87	3.79	3.73	3.68	3.63	3.60	3.57
	12.25	**9.55**	**8.45**	**7.85**	**7.44**	**7.19**	**7.00**	**6.84**	**6.71**	**6.62**	**6.54**	**6.47**
8	5.32	4.48	4.07	3.84	3.69	3.58	3.50	3.44	3.39	3.34	3.31	3.28

9	11.26	8.64	7.69	7.01	6.63	6.37	6.19	6.03	5.91	5.82	5.74	5.67
	5.12	4.26	3.86	3.63	3.48	3.37	3.29	3.23	3.18	3.13	3.10	3.07
10	10.66	8.02	6.99	6.42	6.06	5.30	5.62	5.47	5.35	5.26	5.18	5.11
	4.96	4.10	3.71	3.48	3.33	3.22	3.14	3.07	3.02	2.97	2.94	2.91
11	10.04	7.54	6.55	5.99	5.64	5.39	5.21	5.06	4.95	4.85	4.78	4.71
	4.84	3.98	3.59	3.36	3.20	3.09	3.01	2.95	2.90	2.86	2.82	2.79
12	9.65	7.20	6.22	5.67	5.32	5.07	4.88	4.74	4.63	4.54	4.46	4.40
	4.75	3.88	3.49	3.26	3.11	3.00	2.92	2.85	2.80	2.76	2.72	2.69
13	9.33	6.93	5.95	5.41	5.04	4.82	4.65	4.50	4.39	4.30	4.22	4.16
	4.67	3.80	3.41	3.18	3.02	2.92	2.84	2.77	2.72	2.67	2.63	2.60
14	9.07	6.70	5.74	5.20	4.86	4.62	4.44	4.30	4.19	4.10	4.02	3.96
	4.60	3.74	3.34	3.11	2.96	2.85	2.77	2.70	2.65	2.60	2.56	2.53
15	8.86	6.51	5.56	5.03	4.69	4.46	4.28	4.14	4.03	3.94	3.86	3.80
	4.54	3.68	3.29	3.06	2.90	2.79	2.70	2.64	2.59	2.55	2.51	2.48
16	8.62	6.36	5.42	4.89	4.56	4.32	4.14	4.00	3.89	3.80	3.73	3.67
	4.49	3.63	3.24	3.01	2.85	2.74	2.66	2.59	2.54	2.49	2.45	2.42
17	8.53	6.23	5.29	4.77	4.44	4.20	4.03	3.89	3.78	3.69	3.61	3.55
	4.45	3.59	3.20	2.96	2.81	2.70	2.62	2.55	2.50	2.45	2.41	2.38
18	8.40	6.11	5.18	4.67	4.34	4.10	3.93	3.79	3.68	3.59	3.52	3.45
	4.41	3.55	3.16	2.93	2.77	2.66	2.58	2.51	2.46	2.41	2.37	2.34
19	8.26	6.01	5.09	4.58	4.25	4.01	3.86	3.71	3.60	3.51	3.44	3.37
	4.38	3.52	3.13	2.90	2.74	2.63	2.55	2.48	2.43	2.38	2.34	2.31
20	8.18	5.98	5.01	4.50	4.17	3.94	3.77	3.63	3.52	3.43	3.36	3.30
	4.35	3.49	3.10	2.87	2.71	2.60	2.52	2.45	2.40	2.35	2.31	2.28
21	8.10	5.86	4.94	4.43	4.10	3.87	3.71	3.56	3.45	3.37	3.30	3.23
	4.32	3.47	3.07	2.84	2.68	2.57	2.49	2.42	2.37	2.32	2.28	2.25
22	8.02	5.78	4.87	4.37	4.04	3.81	3.65	3.51	3.40	3.31	3.24	3.17
	4.30	3.44	3.05	2.82	2.66	2.55	2.47	2.40	2.35	2.30	2.26	2.23
23	7.94	5.72	4.82	4.31	3.99	3.76	3.69	3.45	3.35	3.26	3.18	3.12
	4.28	3.42	3.03	2.80	2.64	2.53	2.45	2.38	2.32	2.28	2.24	2.20
24	7.88	5.64	4.76	4.28	3.94	3.71	3.54	3.41	3.30	3.21	3.14	3.07
	4.26	3.40	3.01	2.78	2.62	2.51	2.43	2.36	2.30	2.26	2.22	2.18
25	7.82	5.61	4.72	4.22	3.90	3.67	3.50	3.36	3.25	3.17	3.09	3.03
	4.24	3.38	2.99	2.76	2.60	2.49	2.41	2.34	2.28	2.24	2.20	2.16
26	7.77	5.57	4.68	4.13	3.86	3.63	3.46	3.32	3.21	3.13	3.05	2.99
	4.22	3.37	2.98	2.74	2.59	2.47	2.39	2.32	2.27	2.22	2.18	2.15
	7.72	5.83	4.64	4.14	3.82	3.59	3.42	3.29	3.17	3.09	3.02	2.96

(Continued)

TABLE 15.4 (continued)

	n_1 = degrees of freedom for numerator = k								n_2 = degrees of freedom for denominator = $n - k - 1$						
	14	16	20	24	30	40	50	75	100	250	500	∞
1	245 6,142 19.42 99.43	246 6,169 19.43 99.44	248 6,208 19.44 99.45	249 6,234 19.45 99.46	250 6,258 19.46 99.47	251 6,286 19.47 99.48	252 6,302 19.47 99.48	253 6,323 19.48 99.49	253 6,334 19.49 99.49	254 6,352 19.49 99.49	254 6,361 19.50 99.50	254 6,364 19.50 99.50
2	8.71 26.92	8.69 26.83	8.66 26.69	8.64 26.60	8.62 26.50	8.60 26.41	8.58 26.35	8.57 26.27	8.56 26.23	8.54 26.18	8.54 26.14	8.53 26.12
3	5.87 14.24	5.84 14.15	5.80 14.02	5.77 13.93	5.74 13.83	5.71 13.74	5.70 13.69	5.68 13.61	5.66 13.57	5.65 13.52	5.64 13.48	5.63 13.46
4	4.64 9.77	4.60 9.68	4.56 9.55	4.53 9.47	4.50 9.38	4.46 9.29	4.44 9.24	4.42 9.17	4.40 9.13	4.38 9.07	4.37 9.04	4.36 9.02
5	3.96 7.60	3.92 7.52	3.87 7.39	3.84 7.31	3.81 7.23	3.77 7.14	3.75 7.09	3.72 7.02	3.71 6.99	3.69 6.94	3.68 6.90	3.67 6.88
6	3.52 6.35	3.49 6.27	3.44 6.15	3.41 6.07	3.38 5.98	3.34 5.90	3.32 5.85	3.29 5.78	3.28 5.75	3.25 5.70	3.24 5.67	3.23 5.65
7	3.23 5.56	3.20 5.48	3.15 5.36	3.12 5.28	3.08 5.20	3.05 5.11	3.03 5.06	3.00 5.00	2.98 4.96	2.96 4.91	2.94 4.88	2.93 4.86
8	3.02 5.00	2.98 4.92	2.93 4.80	2.90 4.73	2.86 4.64	2.82 4.56	2.80 4.51	2.77 4.45	2.76 4.41	2.73 4.36	2.72 4.33	2.71 4.31
9	2.86 4.60	2.82 4.52	2.77 4.41	2.74 4.33	2.70 4.25	2.67 4.17	2.64 4.12	2.61 4.05	2.59 4.01	2.56 3.96	2.55 3.93	2.54 3.91
10	2.74 4.29	2.70 4.21	2.65 4.10	2.61 4.02	2.57 3.94	2.53 3.86	2.50 3.80	2.47 3.74	2.45 3.70	2.42 3.66	2.41 3.62	2.40 3.60
11	2.64 4.50	2.60 3.98	2.54 3.86	2.50 3.78	2.46 3.70	2.42 3.61	2.40 3.56	2.36 3.49	2.35 3.46	2.32 3.41	2.31 3.38	2.30 3.36
12	2.55 3.85	2.51 3.78	2.46 3.67	2.42 3.59	2.38 3.51	2.34 3.42	2.32 3.37	2.28 3.30	2.26 3.27	2.24 3.21	2.22 3.18	2.21 3.16
13	2.48 3.70	2.44 3.62	2.39 3.51	2.35 3.43	2.31 3.34	2.27 3.26	2.24 3.21	2.21 3.14	2.19 3.11	2.16 3.06	2.14 3.02	2.13 3.00

15	2.43	2.39	2.33	2.29	2.25	2.21	2.18	2.15	2.12	2.10	2.08	2.07
	3.56	**3.48**	**3.36**	**3.29**	**3.20**	**3.12**	**3.07**	**3.00**	**2.97**	**2.92**	**2.89**	**2.87**
16	2.37	2.33	2.28	2.24	2.20	2.16	2.13	2.09	2.07	2.04	2.02	2.01
	3.45	**3.37**	**3.25**	**3.18**	**3.10**	**3.01**	**2.96**	**2.89**	**2.86**	**2.80**	**2.77**	**2.75**
17	2.33	2.29	2.23	2.19	2.15	2.11	2.08	2.04	2.02	1.99	1.97	1.96
	3.35	**3.27**	**3.16**	**3.08**	**3.00**	**2.92**	**2.86**	**2.79**	**2.76**	**2.70**	**2.67**	**2.65**
18	2.29	2.25	2.19	2.15	2.11	2.07	2.04	2.00	1.98	1.95	1.93	1.92
	3.27	**3.19**	**3.07**	**3.00**	**2.91**	**2.83**	**2.78**	**2.71**	**2.68**	**2.62**	**2.59**	**2.57**
19	2.26	2.21	2.15	2.11	2.07	2.02	2.00	1.96	1.94	1.91	1.90	1.88
	3.19	**3.12**	**3.00**	**2.92**	**2.84**	**2.76**	**2.70**	**2.63**	**2.60**	**2.54**	**2.51**	**2.49**
20	2.23	2.18	2.12	2.08	2.04	1.99	1.96	1.92	1.90	1.87	1.85	1.84
	3.13	**3.05**	**2.94**	**2.86**	**2.77**	**2.69**	**2.63**	**2.56**	**2.53**	**2.47**	**2.44**	**2.42**
21	2.20	2.15	2.09	2.05	2.00	1.96	1.93	1.89	1.87	1.84	1.82	1.81
	3.07	**2.99**	**2.88**	**2.80**	**2.72**	**2.63**	**2.58**	**2.51**	**2.47**	**2.42**	**2.38**	**2.36**
22	2.18	2.13	2.07	2.03	1.98	1.93	1.91	1.87	1.84	1.81	1.80	1.78
	3.02	**2.94**	**2.83**	**2.75**	**2.67**	**2.58**	**2.53**	**2.46**	**2.42**	**2.37**	**2.33**	**2.31**
23	2.14	2.10	2.04	2.00	1.96	1.91	1.88	1.84	1.82	1.79	1.77	1.76
	2.97	**2.89**	**2.78**	**2.70**	**2.62**	**2.53**	**2.48**	**2.41**	**2.37**	**2.32**	**2.28**	**2.26**
24	2.13	2.09	2.02	1.98	1.94	1.89	1.86	1.82	1.80	1.76	1.74	1.73
	2.93	**2.85**	**2.74**	**2.66**	**2.58**	**2.49**	**2.44**	**2.36**	**2.33**	**2.27**	**2.23**	**2.21**
25	2.11	2.06	2.00	1.96	1.92	1.87	1.84	1.80	1.77	1.74	1.72	1.71
	2.89	**2.81**	**2.70**	**2.62**	**2.54**	**2.45**	**2.40**	**2.32**	**2.29**	**2.23**	**2.19**	**2.17**
26	2.10	2.05	1.99	1.95	1.90	1.85	1.82	1.78	1.76	1.72	1.70	1.69
	2.86	**2.77**	**2.66**	**2.58**	**2.50**	**2.41**	**2.36**	**2.28**	**2.25**	**2.19**	**2.15**	**2.13**

TABLE 15.5 Flow of Customers

Company	Jan. 1 Customers	From	Gains A	B	C	To	Losses A	B	C	Feb. 1 Customers
A	300		0	45	35		0	30	30	320
B	600		30	0	20		45	0	15	590
C	400		30	15	0		35	20	0	390

The model has the following objectives:

- Predict the market share that a firm will have at some point in the future.
- Predict whether or not some constant or level market share will obtain in the future. Most Markov models will result in a final constant market share where changes in market share will no longer result with the passage of time.
- Investigate the impact of the company's marketing strategies and promotional efforts such as advertising on gain or loss in market share.

To answer these questions, we need to compute what is called *transition probabilities* for all the companies involved in the market. Transition probabilities are nothing more than the probability that a certain seller will retain, gain, and lose customers. To develop this, we need sample data of past consumer behavior. Let us assume that there are three battery manufacturers, A, B, and C. All of the firms know that consumers switch from one firm to another over time because of advertising, dissatisfaction with service, and sales promotion efforts. We assume that each firm maintains records of consumer movements for a specified time period; 1 month, for example. We further assume that no new customers enter and no old customers leave the market during this period. Table 15.5 provides data on the flows among all the firms.

This table can be converted into a matrix form, as shown in Table 15.6.

TABLE 15.6 Retention, Gain, and Loss of Customers

	Company	Retention and Loss to A	B	C	Total
Retention	A	240	30	30	300
and	B	45	540	15	600
Gain	C	35	20	345	400
	Total	320	590	390	

Table 15.7 is a matrix of the same size as the one above illustrating exactly how each probability was determined.

TABLE 15.7   Transition Probability Matrix

Probability of Customers Being Retained or Gained (Rows)	Probability of Customers Being Retained or Lost (Columns)		
	A	B	C
A	240/300 = 0.8	30/300 = 0.1	30/300 = 0.1
B	45/600 = 0.075	540/600 = 0.9	25/600 = 0.025
C	35/400 = 0.0875	20/400 = 0.05	345/400 = 0.8625

The rows in this matrix show the probability of the retention of customers and the loss of customers; the columns represent the probability of retention of customers and the gain of customers. For example, the first row indicates that A retains 0.8 of its customers (240), loses 0.1 of its customers (30) to B, and loses 0.1 of its customers (30) to C. The first column indicates that A retains 0.8 of its customers (240), gains 0.075 of B's customers (45), and gains 0.0875 of C's customers (35).

The original market share at January 1 was:

(300A   600B   400C) = (0.2308A   0.4615B   0.3077C)

With this, we will be able to calculate market share using the transition matrix we developed in the above.

To illustrate, Company A held 23.08% of the market at January 1. Of this, 80% was retained. Company A gained 10% of Company B's 46.15% of the market, and another 10% of Company C's 30.77%.

The February 1 market share of A is therefore calculated to be:

Retention	$0.8 \times 0.2308 = 0.1846$
Gain from B	$0.1 \times 0.4615 = 0.0462$
Gain from C	$0.1 \times 0.3077 = \underline{0.0308}$
	0.2616*

---

*These numbers do not add up to exactly 100% because of rounding.

Similarly, B's market share is as follows:

Gain from A	0.075 × 0.2308 = 0.0173
Retention	0.9 × 0.4615 = 0.4154
Gain from C	0.025 × 0.3077 = 0.0077
	0.4404*

C's market share is:

Gain from A	0.0875 × 0.2308 = 0.0202
Gain from B	0.05 × 0.4615 = 0.0231
Retention	0.8625 × 0.3077 = 0.2654
	0.3087*

In summary, the February 1 market share came out to be approximately 26% for A, 44% for B, and 30% for C. This market share forecast may then be used to generate a specific forecast of sales. For example, if industry sales are forecast to be, say, $10,000,000, obtained through regression analysis, input–output analysis, or some other technique, the forecast of sales for A is $2,600,000 ($10,000,000 × 0.26).

If the company wishes to forecast the market share for March, then, the procedure is the same as before, except the February 1 forecasted market share is used as a basis. *Caution:* The forecaster must be careful when using the Markov model, since the model is generally successful only for forecasting market shares in the near future. Distant forecasts, after many time periods, are generally not very reliable forecasts by this method. Even in short-term forecasts, constant updating of the transition matrix is needed for accuracy of projection.

At least in theory, most Markov models will result in a final constant market share that will no longer change with passage of time. However, this market share and its derivation will not be discussed here. In effect, this result has very little practical value because the constant or level condition assumes no changes in competitive efforts of the firms within the industry.

---

*These numbers do not add up to exactly 100% because of rounding.

CONCLUSION

Regression analysis is the examination of the effect of a change in independent variables on the dependent variable. For example, various financial ratios bear upon a company's market price of stock. This analysis is performed with the aid of a computer, which computes the coefficient of determination, which reflects the degree to which the independent variables as a whole explain the change in the dependent variable, and the regression coefficient, which indicates the extent that one particular explanatory variable can explain the dependent variable. The means of appraising the reliability and suitability of a particular forecasting approach involves many considerations, such as whether bias exists and information is timely. The Markov model can be used to take into account learned behavior, such as consumer spending patterns.

16 Financial Forecasting, Planning, and Budgeting Techniques

FINANCIAL FORECASTING

Financial forecasting, an essential element of planning, is the basis for budgeting activities. It is also needed where future financing needs are being estimated. Basically, forecasts of future sales and their related expenses provide the information needed to project a firm's future financing needs. The basic steps involved in projecting those financing needs are:

- Project the firm's sales. The sales forecast is initially the most important step. Most other forecasts (budgets) follow the sales forecast. (The methods of forecasting sales are discussed in Chapters 13, 14, and 15.)
- Project additional variables, such as expenses.
- Estimate the level of investment in current and fixed assets that are required to support the projected sales.
- Calculate the firm's financing needs.

Percent-of-Sales Method of Financial Forecasting

Traditional financial forecasting takes the sales forecast as given and makes forecasts of its impact on the firm's various expenses, assets, and liabilities. The most widely used method for making these projections is the *percent-of-sales method*. This method involves estimating the various expenses, assets, and liabilities for a future period as a percent of the sales forecast and then using these percentages, together with the projected sales, to construct *pro forma* (planned or projected) balance sheets.

EXAMPLE 16.1

(In millions of dollars)

	Present (20X1)	Percent of Sales (20X1 sales = $20)	Projected (20X2 sales = $24)
Assets			
Current assets	$2.0	10	$24 × 10% = $2.4
Fixed assets	4.0	20	4.8
Total	$6.0		$7.2
Liabilities and stockholders' equity			
Current liabilities	$2.0	10	$2.4
Long-term debt	2.5	n.a.[a]	2.5
Total liabilities	$4.5		$4.9
Common stock	$0.1	n.a.	0.1
Paid-in-capital	0.2	n.a.	0.2
Retained earnings	1.2		1.92[b]
Total equity	$1.5		$2.22
Total	$6.0	Total financing provided	$7.12
		External financing needed	0.08[c]
		Total	$7.2

Notes:

[a] Not applicable. These figures are assumed not to vary with sales.

[b] 20X2 retained earnings = 20X1 retained earnings + projected net income − cash dividends paid. Assume that net income = 5% of sales and the dividend payout ratio = 40%. Therefore, 20X2 retained earnings = $1.2 + 5% ($24) − 0.4 [5%($24)] = $1.2 + $1.2 − 0.4($1.2) = $1.92

[c] External financing needed = projected total assets ($7.2) − projected total liabilities ($4.9) − projected equity ($2.22) = $0.08

The steps for the computations are outlined as follows:

- *Step 1.* Express those balance sheet items *that vary directly with sales* as a percentage of sales. Any item such as long-term debt that does not vary directly with sales is designated n.a., "not applicable."
- *Step 2.* Multiply these percentages by the 20X2 projected sales = $24 to obtain the projected amounts as shown in the last column.
- *Step 3.* Simply insert figures for long-term debt, common stock, and paid-in-capital from the 20X1 balance sheet.
- *Step 4.* Compute 20X2 retained earnings as shown in note b.

- *Step 5.* Sum the asset accounts, obtaining a total projected assets figure of $7.2, and also add the projected liabilities and equity to obtain $7.12, the total financing provided. Since liabilities and equity must total $7.2, but only $7.12 is projected, we have a shortfall of $0.08 "external financing needed."

Although the forecast of additional funds required can be made by setting up pro forma balance sheets as described previously, it is often easier to use the following simple formula:

$$\text{EFN} = \begin{bmatrix} \text{Required} \\ \text{increase} \\ \text{in assets} \end{bmatrix} - \begin{bmatrix} \text{Spontaneous} \\ \text{increase in} \\ \text{liabilities} \end{bmatrix} - \begin{bmatrix} \text{Increase in} \\ \text{retained} \\ \text{earnings} \end{bmatrix}$$

$$\text{EFN} = \left(\frac{A}{S}\right) \Delta S - \left(\frac{L}{S}\right) \Delta S - (PM)(PS)(1 - d)$$

where

- EFN = External funds needed
- A/S = Assets that increase spontaneously with sales as a percentage of sales
- L/S = Liabilities that increase spontaneously with sales as a percentage of sales
- ΔS = Change in sales
- PM = Profit margin on sales
- PS = Projected sales
- d = Dividend payout ratio

EXAMPLE 16.2

In Example 16.1:

- A/S = $6/$20 = 30%
- L/S = $2/$20 = 10%
- ΔS = ($24 − $20) = $4
- PM = 5% on sales
- PS = $24
- d = 40%

Plugging these figures into the formula yields:

$$\text{EFN} = 0.3(\$4) - 0.1(\$4) - (0.05)(\$24)(1 - 0.4)$$
$$= \$1.2 - \$0.4 - \$0.72 = \$0.08$$

This $800,000 in external financing can be raised by issuing notes payable, bonds, stocks, or any combination of these financing sources.

The major advantage of the percent-of-sales method of financial forecasting is that it is simple and inexpensive to use. To obtain a more precise projection of the firm's future financing needs, however, the preparation of a cash budget is required, which is discussed later in the chapter.

One important assumption behind the use of the percent-of-sales method is that the firm is operating *at full capacity*. This means that the firm has no sufficient productive capacity to absorb a projected increase in sales and thus requires additional investment in assets.

BUDGETING AND FINANCIAL PLANNING

A comprehensive (master) budget is a formal statement of management's expectation regarding sales, expenses, volume, and other financial transactions of an organization for the coming period. Simply put, a budget is a set of pro forma (projected or planned) financial statements. It consists basically of a pro forma income statement, pro forma balance sheet, and cash budget. A budget is a tool for both planning and control. At the beginning of the period, the budget is a plan or standard; at the end of the period, it serves as a control device to help management measure its performance against the plan so that future performance may be improved.

It is important to realize that with the aid of computer technology, budgeting can be used as an effective device for evaluation of "what if" scenarios. This way management should be able to move toward finding the best course of action among various alternatives through simulation. If management does not like what it sees on the budgeted financial statements for various financial ratios such as liquidity, activity (turnover), leverage, profit margin, and market value ratios, it can always alter its contemplated decision and planning set.

The budget is classified broadly into two categories:

1. Operating budget, reflecting the results of operating decisions
2. Financial budget, reflecting the financial decisions of the firm

The operating budget consists of:

- Sales budget
- Production budget
- Direct materials budget
- Direct labor budget

- Factory overhead budget
- Selling and administrative expense budget
- Pro forma income statement

The financial budget consists of:

- Cash budget
- Pro forma balance sheet

The major steps in preparing the budget are:

1. Prepare a sales forecast.
2. Determine expected production volume.
3. Estimate manufacturing costs and operating expenses.
4. Determine cash flow and other financial effects.
5. Formulate projected financial statements.

Figure 16.1 shows a simplified diagram of the various parts of the comprehensive (master) budget, the master plan of the company.

HOW THE BUDGET WORKS: AN EXAMPLE

To illustrate how all these budgets are put together, we will focus on a *manufacturing* company called the Putnam Company, which produces and markets a single product. We will make the following assumptions:

- The company uses a single material and one type of labor in the manufacture of the product.
- It prepares a master budget on a *quarterly* basis.
- Work in process inventories at the beginning and end of the year are negligible and are ignored.
- The company uses a single cost driver—direct labor hours (DLH)—as the allocation base for assigning all factory overhead costs to the product.

The Sales Budget

The sales budget (Schedule 1) is the starting point in preparing the master budget, because estimated sales volume influences nearly all other items appearing throughout the master budget. The sales budget should show total

308   Part III: Financial Forecasting

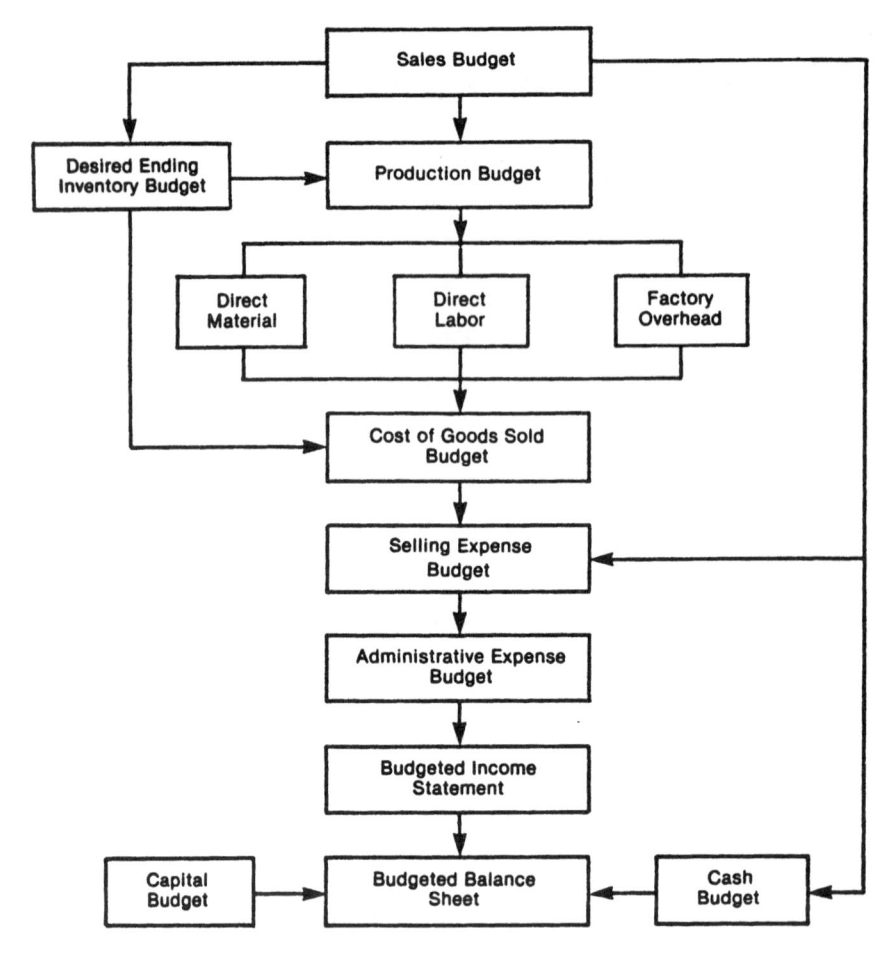

FIGURE 16.1   Master Budget

sales in quantity and value. The expected total sales can be breakeven or target income sales or projected sales. It may be analyzed further by product, by territory, by customer, and, of course, by seasonal pattern of expected sales.

Generally, the sales budget includes a computation of expected cash collections from credit sales, which will be used later for cash budgeting.

Monthly Cash Collections from Customers

Frequently, there are time lags between monthly sales made *on account* and their related monthly cash collections. For example, in any month,

SCHEDULE 1

THE PUTNAM COMPANY
Sales Budget
For the Year Ended December 31, 20X2

	Quarter 1	Quarter 2	Quarter 3	Quarter 4	Year as a Whole
Expected sales in units[a]	1,000	1,800	2,000	1,200	6,000
Unit sales price[a]	× $150	× $150	× $150	× $150	× $150
Total sales	$150,000	$270,000	$300,000	$180,000	$900,000

[a] Given.

Schedule of Expected Cash Collections

	Q1	Q2	Q3	Q4	Total
Accounts receivable, 12/31/20X1	100,000[a]				$100,000
1st quarter sales ($150,000)	60,000[b]	$90,000[c]			150,000
2d quarter sales ($270,000)		108,200	$162,000		270,000
3d quarter sales ($300,000)			120,000	$180,000	300,000
4th quarter sales ($180,000)				72,000	72,000
Total cash collections	$160,000	$198,000	$282,000	$252,000	$892,000

[a] All of the $100,000 accounts receivable balance is assumed to be collectible in the 1st quarter.
[b] 40% of a quarter's sales are collected in the quarter of sale.
[c] 60% of a quarter's sales are collected in the quarter following.

credit sales are collected as follows: 15% in month of sale, 60% in the following month, 24% in the month after, and the remaining 1% are uncollectible.

	April-Actual	May-Actual	June-Bugeted	July-Budgeted
Credit Sales	$320	200	300	280

The budgeted cash receipts for June and July are computed as follows:

For June:

From April sales	$320 × .24	$ 76.80
From May sales	200 × .6	120.00
From June sales	300 × .15	45.00
Total budgeted collections in June		$241.80

For July:

From May sales	$200 × .24	$ 48
From June sales	300 × .6	180
From July sales	280 × .15	42
Total budgeted collections in July		$270

The Production Budget

The production budget can be determined after sales are budgeted (Scheddule 2). It is a statement of the output by product and is generally expressed in units. It should take into account the sales budget, plant capacity, whether stocks are to be increased or decreased, and outside purchases. The number of units expected to be manufactured to meet budgeted sales and inventory requirements is set forth in the production budget.

$$\text{Expected production volume} = \text{Planned sales} + \text{Desired ending inventory} - \text{Beginning inventory}$$

The production budget is illustrated as follows:

SCHEDULE 2

THE PUTNAM COMPANY
Production Budget
For the Year Ended December 31, 20X2

	Quarter 1	Quarter 2	Quarter 3	Quarter 4	Year as a Whole
Planned sales (Sch. 1)	1,000	1,800	2,000	1,200	6,000
Desired ending inventory[a]	180	200	120	300[b]	300
Total needs	1,180	2,000	2,120	1,500	6,300
Less: Beginning inventory	200[b]	180[c]	200	120	200
Units to be produced	980	1,820	1,920	1,380	6,100

[a] 10% of the next quarter's sales. (For example, 180 = 10% × 1,800).
[b] Given.
[c] The same as the previous quarter's ending inventory.

Inventory Purchases—Merchandising Firm

The Putnam Company is a manufacturing firm, so it prepares a production budget, as shown in Schedule 2. If it were a *merchandising* (retailing or wholesaling) firm, then instead of a production budget, it would develop a *merchandise purchase budget* showing the amount of goods to be purchased from its suppliers during the period. The merchandise purchases budget is in the same basic format as the production budget, except that it shows *goods to be purchased* rather than goods to be produced, as shown below:

Budgeted cost of goods sold (in units or dollars)	$500,000
Add: Desired ending merchandise inventory	120,000
Total needs	$620,000
Less: Beginning merchandise inventory	(90,000)
Required purchases (in units or in dollars)	$530,000

The Direct Material Budget

When the level of production has been computed, a direct material budget (Schedule 3) should be constructed to show how much material will be required for production and how much material must be purchased to meet this production requirement.

The purchase will depend on both expected usage of materials and inventory levels. The formula for computation of the purchase is:

$$\text{Purchase in units} = \text{Usage} + \text{Desired ending material inventory units} - \text{Beginning inventory units}$$

The direct material budget is usually accompanied by a computation of expected cash payments for materials.

The Direct Labor Budget

The production requirements as set forth in the production budget also provide the starting point for the preparation of the direct labor budget (Schedule 4). To compute direct labor requirements, expected production volume for each period is multiplied by the number of direct labor hours required to produce a single unit. The direct labor hours to meet production requirements is then multiplied by the (standard) direct labor cost per hour to obtain budgeted total direct labor costs.

SCHEDULE 3

THE PUTNAM COMPANY
Direct Material Budget
For the Year Ended December 31, 20X2

	Quarter 1	Quarter 2	Quarter 3	Quarter 4	Year as a Whole
Units to be produced (Sch. 2)	980	1,820	1,920	1,380	6,100
Material needs per unit (lbs)[a]	× 2	× 2	× 2	× 2	× 2
Production needs (usage)	1,960	3,640	3,840	2,760	12,200
Desired ending inventory of materials[b]	910	960	690	520[c]	520
Total needs	2,870	4,600	4,530	3,280	12,720
Less: Beginning inventory of materials	490	910[d]	960	690	490
Materials to be purchased	2,380	3,690	3,570	2,590	12,230
Unit price[a]	× $5	× $5	× $5	× $5	× $5
Purchase cost	$11,900	$18,450	$17,850	$12,950	$61,150

Schedule of Expected Cash Disbursements

	Q1	Q2	Q3	Q4	Total
Accounts payable, 12/31/20X1	$ 6,275[e]				$ 6,275
1st quarter purchases ($11,900)	5,950[f]	5,950[f]			11,900
2d quarter purchases ($18,450)		9,225	9,225		18,450
3d quarter purchases ($17,850)			8,925	8,925	17,850
4th quarter purchases ($12,950)				6,475	6,475
Total disbursements	$12,225	$15,175	$18,150	$15,400	$60,950

[a] Given.
[b] 25% of the next quarter's units needed for production. For example, the 2nd quarter production needs are 3,640 lbs. Therefore, the desired ending inventory for the 1st quarter would be 25% × 3,640 lbs = 910 lbs.
[c] Assume that the budgeted production needs in lbs for the 1st quarter of 20X2 = 2,080 lbs. So, 25% x 2,080 lbs = 520 lbs.
[d] The same as the prior quarter's ending inventory.
[e] All of the $6,275 accounts payable balance (from the balance sheet, 20X1) is assumed to be paid in the first quarter.
[f] 50% of a quarter's purchases are paid for in the quarter of purchase; the remaining 50% are paid for in the following quarter.

SCHEDULE 4

THE PUTNAM COMPANY
Direct Labor Budget
For the Year Ended December 31, 20X2

	Quarter 1	Quarter 2	Quarter 3	Quarter 4	Year as a Whole
Units to be produced (Sch. 2)	980	1,820	1,920	1,380	6,100
Direct labor hours per unit[a]	× 5	× 5	× 5	× 5	× 5
Total hours	4,900	9,100	9,600	6,900	30,500
Direct labor cost per hour[a]	$10	× $10	× $10	× $10	× $10
Total direct labor cost	$49,000	$91,000	$96,000	$69,000	$305,000

[a]Both are given.

The Factory Overhead Budget

The factory overhead budget (Schedule 5) should provide a schedule of all manufacturing costs other than direct materials and direct labor. The contribution approach to budgeting requires a cash budget; remember that depreciation does not entail a cash outlay and therefore must be deducted from the total factory overhead in computing cash disbursement.

Schedule 5 illustrates the factory overhead budget, and assumes that:

- Total factory overhead budgeted = $18,300 fixed (per quarter), plus $2 per hour of direct labor. This is one example of a cost–volume (or flexible budget) formula ($y = a + bx$), developed via the regression (*least-squares*) *method* with a high R^2.
- Depreciation expenses are $4,000 each quarter.
- Overhead costs involving cash outlays are paid for in the quarter incurred.

The Ending Finished Goods Inventory Budget

The ending finished goods inventory budget (Schedule 6) provides the information required for the construction of budgeted financial statements. After completing Schedules 1–5, sufficient data will have been generated to compute the per-unit manufacturing cost of finished product. This com-

SCHEDULE 5

THE PUTNAM COMPANY
Factory Overhead Budget
For the Year Ended December 31, 20X2

	Quarter 1	Quarter 2	Quarter 3	Quarter 4	Year as a Whole
Budgeted direct labor hours (Sch. 4)	4,900	9,100	9,600	6,900	30,500
Variable overhead rate	× $2	× $2	× $2	× $2	× $2
Variable overhead budgeted	9,800	18,200	19,200	13,800	61,000
Fixed overhead budgeted	18,300	18,300	18,300	18,300	73,200
Total budgeted overhead	28,100	36,500	37,500	32,100	134,200
Less: Depreciation[a]	4,000	4,000	4,000	4,000	16,000
Cash disbursements for factory overhead	$24,100	$32,500	$33,500	$28,100	$118,200

[a] Depreciation does not require a cash outlay.

putation is required for two reasons: (1) to help compute the cost of goods sold on the budgeted income statement, and (2) to give the dollar value of the ending finished goods inventory to appear on the budgeted balance sheet.

SCHEDULE 6

THE PUTNAM COMPANY
Ending Finished Goods Inventory Budget
For the Year Ended December 31, 20X2

Ending Inventory Units	Unit Product Cost	Total
300 units (Sch. 2)	$82[a]	$24,600

[a] The unit product cost of $82 is computed as follows:

	Unit Cost	Units	Total
Direct materials	$5 per lb	2 lbs	$10
Direct labor	10 per hr	5 hrs	50
Factory overhead[b]	$4.40 per hr	5 hrs	22
Unit product cost			$82

[b] Predetermined factory overhead applied rate = Budgeted annual factory overhead/budgeted annual activity units = $134,200/30,500 DLH = $4.40.

The Selling and Administrative Expense Budget

The selling and administrative expense budget (Schedule 7) lists the operating expenses involved in selling the products and in managing the business. Just as in the case of the factory overhead budget, this budget can be developed using the cost–volume (*flexible budget*) formula in the form of $y = a + bx$.

If the number of expense items is very large, separate budgets may be needed for the selling and administrative functions.

The Cash Budget

The cash budget (Schedule 8) is prepared for the purpose of cash planning and control. It presents the expected cash inflow and outflow for a desig-

SCHEDULE 7

THE PUTNAM COMPANY
Selling and Administrative Expense Budget
For the Year Ended December 31, 20X2

	Quarter 1	Quarter 2	Quarter 3	Quarter 4	Year as a Whole
Expected sales in units	1,000	1,800	2,000	1,200	6,000
Variable selling and administrative expense per unit[a]	× $3	× $3	× $3	× $3	× $3
Budgeted variable expense	$3,000	$5,400	$6,000	$3,200	$18,000
Fixed selling and administrative expense:[b]					
Advertising	20,000	20,000	20,000	20,000	80,000
Insurance		12,600			12,600
Office salaries	40,000	40,000	40,000	40,000	160,000
Taxes				7,400	7,400
Total budgeted selling and administrative expenses[c]	$63,000	$78,000	$66,000	$71,000	$278,000

[a] Assumed. It includes sales agents' commissions, shipping, and supplies.
[b] Scheduled to be paid.
[c] Paid for in the quarter incurred.

SCHEDULE 8

THE PUTNAM COMPANY
Cash Budget
For the Year Ended December 31, 20X2

	From Schedule	1	2	Quarter 3	4	Year as a Whole
Cash balance, beginning		$19,000[a]	10,675	10,000	10,350	19,000
Add: Receipts:						
Collections from customers	1	160,000	198,000	282,000	252,000	892,000
Total cash available (a)		179,000	208,675	292,000	262,350	911,000
Less: Disbursements:						
Direct materials	3	12,225	15,175	18,150	15,400	60,950
Direct labor	4	49,000	91,000	96,000	69,000	305,000
Factory overhead	5	24,100	32,500	33,500	28,100	118,200
Selling and admin.	7	63,000	78,000	66,000	71,000	278,000
Equipment purchase	Given	30,000	12,000	0	0	42,000
Dividends	Given	5,000	5,000	5,000	5,000	20,000
Income tax	10	15,000	15,000	15,000	15,000	60,000
Total disbursements (b)		198,325	248,675	233,650	203,500	884,150
Minimum cash balance		10,000	10,000	10,000	10,000	10,000
Total cash needed (c)		208,325	258,675	243,650	213,500	894,150

Cash surplus (deficit) (a) − (c)	(29,325)	(50,000)	48,350	48,850	16,850
Financing:					
Borrowing	30,000[b]	50,000	0	0	80,000
Repayment	0	0	(45,000)	(35,000)	(80,000)
Interest	0	0	(3,000)[c]	(2,625)[d]	(5,625)
Total effects of financing (d)	30,000	50,000	(48,000)	(37,625)	(5,625)
Cash balance, ending [(a) − (b) + (d)]	$ 10,675	10,000	10,350	21,225	$21,225

[a] $19,000 (from the balance sheet 20X1).

[b] The company desires to maintain a $10,000 minimum cash balance at the end of each quarter. Therefore, borrowing must be sufficient to cover the cash shortfall of $19,325 and to provide for the minimum cash balance of $10,000, for a total of $29,325.

[c] The interest payments relate only to the principal being repaid at the time it is repaid. For example, the interest in quarter 3 relates only to the interest due on the $30,000 principal being repaid from quarter 1 borrowing and on the $15,000 principal being repaid from quarter 2 borrowing. Total interest being paid is $3,000, shown as follows:

$30,000 × 10% × 3/4 = $2,250
$15,000 × 10% × 2/4 =   750

[d] $35,000 × 10% × 3/4 = $2,625.

nated time period. The cash budget helps management keep cash balances in reasonable relationship to its needs. It aids in avoiding unnecessary idle cash and possible cash shortages. The cash budget consists typically of five major sections:

1. The *cash receipts* section, which is cash collections from customers and other cash receipts such as royalty income and investment income.
2. The *cash disbursements* section, which comprises all cash payments made by purpose.
3. The *cash surplus* or *deficit* section, which simply shows the difference between the total cash available and the total cash needed including a *minimum cash balance* if required. If there is surplus cash, loans may be repaid or temporary investments made.
4. The *financing* section, which provides a detailed account of the borrowings, repayments, and interest payments expected during the budgeting period.
5. The *investments* section, which encompasses investment of excess cash and liquidation of investment of surplus cash.

To illustrate, we will make the following assumptions:

- The Putnam Company has an open line of credit with its bank, which can be used as needed to bolster the cash position.
- The company desires to maintain a $10,000 minimum cash balance at the end of each quarter. Therefore, borrowing must be sufficient to cover the cash shortfall and to provide for the minimum cash balance of $10,000.
- All borrowings and repayments must be in multiples of $1,000 amounts, and interest is 10% per annum.
- Interest is computed and paid on the principal as the principal is repaid.
- All borrowings take place at the beginning of a quarter, and all repayments are made at the end of a quarter.
- No investment option is allowed in this example. The loan is *self-liquidating* in the sense that the borrowed money is used to obtain resources that are combined for sale, and the proceeds from sales are used to pay back the loan.

Note: To be useful for cash planning and control, the cash budget (Schedule 8) must be prepared on a *monthly basis*.

Note the following:

Cash balance, beginning
Add Receipts:
  Total cash available before financing (a)

Deduct Disbursements:
  Total cash disbursements (b)

+ Minimum cash balance desired:
  Total cash needed (c)

Cash surplus or deficit (a) – (c)
Financing:
  Borrowing (at beginning)
  Repayment (at end)
  Interest
Total effects of financing (d)
Cash balance, ending [(a) – (b) + (d)]

The Budgeted Income Statement

The budgeted income statement (Schedule 9) summarizes the various component projections of revenue and expenses for the budgeting period. However, for control purposes the budget can be divided into quarters or even months depending on the need.

The Budgeted Balance Sheet

The budgeted balance sheet is developed by beginning with the balance sheet for the year just ended and adjusting it, using all the activities that are expected to take place during the budgeting period. Some of the reasons why the budgeted balance sheet must be prepared are:

- It could disclose some unfavorable financial conditions that management might want to avoid.
- It serves as a final check on the mathematical accuracy of all the other schedules.
- It helps management perform a variety of ratio calculations.

SCHEDULE 9

THE PUTNAM COMPANY Budgeted Income Statement For the Year Ended December 31, 20X2			
	From Schedule		
Sales (6,000 units @ $150)	1		$900,000
Less: Cost of goods sold			
Beginning finished goods inventory	10	$ 16,400	
Add: Cost of goods manufactured			
(6,100 units @$82)	6	500,200	
Cost of goods available for sale		516,600	
Less: Ending finished goods			
inventory	6	(24,600)	$492,000
Gross margin			$408,000
Less: Selling and administrative			
expense	7		278,000
Operating income			130,000
Less: Interest expense	8		5,625
Net income before taxes			124,375
Less: Income taxes			60,000[a]
Net income after taxes			$64,375
[a]Estimated.			

- It highlights future resources and obligations.

We can construct the budgeted balance sheet by using:

- The December, 20X1 balance sheet (Schedule 10)
- The cash budget (Schedule 8)
- The budgeted income statement (Schedule 9)

Putnam's budgeted balance sheet for December 31, 20X2, is presented below. Supporting calculations of the individual statement accounts are also provided.

To illustrate, we will use the following balance sheet for the year 20X1.

SCHEDULE 10

THE PUTNAM COMPANY
Balance Sheet
December 31, 20X1

Assets

Current assets:		
Cash	$ 19,000	
Accounts receivable	100,000	
Materials inventory (490 lbs)	2,450	
Finished goods inventory (200 units)	16,400	
Total current assets		$137,850
Plant and equipment:		
Land	30,000	
Buildings and equipment	250,000	
Accumulated depreciation	(74,000)	
Plant and equipment, net		206,000
Total assets		$343,850

Liabilities and Stockholders' Equity

Current liabilities		
Accounts payable (raw materials)	$ 6,275	
Income tax payable	60,000	
Total current liabilities		$ 66,275
Stockholders' equity:		
Common stock, no par	$200,000	
Retained earnings	77,575	
Total stockholders' equity		277,575
Total liabilities and stockholders' equity		$343,850

THE PUTNAM COMPANY
Balance Sheet
December 31, 20X2

Assets

Cash	$ 21,225	(a)	
Accounts receivable	108,000	(b)	
Materials inventory (520 lbs)	2,600	(c)	
Finished goods inventory (300 units)	24,600	(d)	
Total curent assets			$156,425

(Continued)

SCHEDULE 10 (*Continued*)

Plant and equipment:				
Land		30,000	(e)	
Buildings and equipment		292,000	(f)	
Accumulated depreciation		(90,000)	(g)	
Plant and equipment, net				232,000
Total assets				$388,425
Current liabilities				
Accounts payable (raw materials)		$ 6,475	(h)	
Income tax payable		60,000	(i)	
Total current liabilities				$66,475
Stockholders' equity:				
Common stock, no par		$200,000	(j)	
Retained earnings		121,950	(k)	
Total stockholders' equity				321,950
Total liabilities and stockholders' equity				$388,425

Supporting computations:

(a) From Schedule 8 (cash budget).

(b) $100,000 (Accounts receivable, 12/31/20X1) + $900,000 (Credit sales from Schedule 1) − $892,000 (Collections from Schedule 1) = $108,000, *or* 60% of 4th quarter credit sales, from Schedule 1 ($180,000 *or* 60% = $108,000).

(c) Direct materials, ending inventory = 520 lbs × $5 = $2,600 (from Schedule 3).

(d) From Schedule 6 (Ending finished goods inventory budget).

(e) From the 20X1 balance sheet and Schedule 8 (no change).

(f) $250,000 (Building and equipment, 12/31/20X1) + $42,000 (Purchases from Schedule 8) = $292,000.

(g) $74,000 (Accumulated depreciation, 12/31/20X1) + $16,000 (Depreciation expense from Schedule 5) = $90,000.

(h) Note that all accounts payable relate to material purchases. $6,275 (Accounts payable, 12/31/20X1) + $61,150 (Credit purchases from Schedule 3) = $6,475, *or* 50% of the 4th quarter purchases = 50% ($12,950) = $6,475.

(i) From Schedule 9.

(j) From the 20X1 balance sheet and Schedule 8 (no change).

(k) $77,575 (Retained earnings, 12/31/20X1) + $64,375 (net income for the period, Schedule 9) − $20,000 (cash dividends from Schedule 8) = $121,950.

Some Financial Calculations

To see what kind of financial conditions the Putnam Company is expected to be in for the budgeting year, a sample of financial ratio calculations are in order. (Assume 20X1 after-tax net income was $45,000.)

	20X1	*20X2*
Current ratio:		
(Current assets/Current liabilities)	$137,850/$66,275 = $2.08	$156,425/$66,475 = $2.35
Return on total assets:		
(Net income after taxes / Total assets)	$45,000/$343,850 = $13.08%	$64,375/$388,425 = $16.57%

Sample calculations indicate that the Putnam Company is expected to have better liquidity as measured by the current ratio. Overall performance will be improved as measured by return on total assets. This could be an indication that the contemplated plan may work out well.

A SHORTCUT APPROACH TO FORMULATING THE BUDGET

Although we went through a detailed procedure for formulating the budget using a comprehensive example, use of a shortcut approach is a common practice. This approach can be summarized as follows:

- A pro forma income statement is developed using past percentage relationships between certain expense and cost items and the firm's sales and applying these percentages to the firm's forecasted sales. This is a version of the percent-of-sales method discussed previously.
- A pro forma balance sheet is estimated by determining the desired level of certain balance sheet items and letting additional financing act as a balancing, or plug, figure.

The following basic assumptions underlie this approach:

- The firm's past financial condition is an accurate predictor of its future condition.
- The value of certain variables, such as cash, inventory, and accounts receivable, can be forced to take on certain "desired" values.

This approach is discussed in greater detail in the subsequent chapters.

COMPUTER-BASED MODELS AND SPREADSHEET PROGRAM MODELS FOR BUDGETING

More and more companies are developing computer-based models for financial planning and budgeting, using powerful, yet easy-to-use, financial modeling languages such as *Comshare's Interactive Financial Planning System (IFPS)* and *Up Your Cash Flow*. The models help build a budget for profit planning, and also answer a variety of "what if" scenarios. The resultant calculations provide a basis for choice among alternatives under conditions of uncertainty. Furthermore, budget modeling can also be accomplished using spreadsheet programs such as Microsoft's Excel®. (This is covered in greater detail in Chapter 21.)

ZERO-BASE BUDGETING

Zero-base budgeting (ZBB) is employed by some entities. Under this approach, budgeted figures for particular product lines, functions, or activities are started at minimum funding levels. Anything above that minimum level must be justified. For example, if a manager wants to manufacture product A, he or she must be able to justify its value. If this is not possible, that product will not be funded. ZBB is in effect starting fresh each accounting year, basically ignoring what happened in the past. The emphasis is on the current and future feasibility of the item. ZBB is like "cleaning house." A key feature of ZBB is looking at the relationship between inputs and outputs, therefore resources are reallocated more efficiently.

Managers engage in the following steps:

- Determine objectives and costs for all activities.
- Evaluate alternative means of accomplishing a task.
- Appraise alternative budget levels for different activity volumes.
- Derive workload and performance measures.

The procedure for zero-base budgeting follows.

A decision package is made up for each product that a manager wants the department to produce. Assuming 50 possible products (old and new), there will be 50 decision packages. The decision package indicates the manager's recommended way of accomplishing a given product in terms of dollar cost and time, plus alternative means of producing the product in dollars and time. For example, lowering quality can reduce the cost. Shortening the time period may increase the cost because of overtime. An illustrative decision package for product A to be manufactured in Department X follows:

Product A
Decision Package

Alternative A	$ 8,000,	5 months
Recommended Way	$10,000,	3 months
Alternative B	$11,000,	$3\frac{1}{2}$ months

Each of the decision packages for all 50 products are then submitted to upper management. Upper management then evaluates the decision packages coming from all the departments of the company, including that from Department X. Upper management then sets a priority ranking of all packages along with a cutoff. The decision package for product A may be rejected because it does not pass the cutoff. If it is accepted, upper management will give permission to the department manager to either produce the product in the recommended way or in an alternative fashion. An alternative approach may be chosen because it is cheaper.

While zero-base budgeting seems to be efficient, an important shortcoming must be taken into account. The cost–benefit relationship probably will be one in which the cost to undertake ZBB outweighs the benefits derived. It is a very time-consuming process. If it is done, we recommend long intervals (e.g., every 5 years). To do it on an annual basis is probably not justified. *Note:* ZBB is much more common in nonprofit organizations than in commercial enterprises because the former have larger portions of discretionary costs. Very few public companies are practicing it.

THE CPA'S INVOLVEMENT AND RESPONSIBILITY WITH PROSPECTIVE FINANCIAL STATEMENTS

There are three types of functions that CPAs (Certified Public Accountants) can perform with respect to *prospective financial statements* that will be relied upon by third parties: examination, compilation, and application of agreed-upon procedures. CPAs must prepare prospective financial statements according to AICPA standards. There must be disclosure of the underlying assumptions.

Prospective financial statements may be for general use or limited use. *General use* is for those not directly dealing with the client. The general user may take the deal or leave it. *Limited use* is for those having a direct relationship with the client.

Prospective financial statements may be presented as a complete set of financial statements (balance sheet, income statement, and statement of changes in financial position). However, in most cases it is more practical to present them in summarized or condensed form. At a minimum, the financial statement items to be presented are:

- Sales
- Gross margin
- Nonrecurring items
- Taxes
- Income from continuing operations
- Income from discontinued operations
- Net income
- Primary and fully diluted earnings per share
- Material change in financial position

Not considered prospective financial statements are pro forma financial statements and partial presentations.

The American Institute of CPAs' Code of Professional Ethics includes the following guidelines regarding prospective financial statements:

- Cannot vouch for the achievability of prospective results
- Must disclose assumptions
- Accountant's report must state the nature of the work performed and the degree of responsibility assumed

CPAs are not permitted to furnish services on prospective financial statements if the statements are solely appropriate for limited use but are distributed to parties not involved directly with the issuing company. They are not allowed to use plain-paper services on prospective financial statements for third-party use.

A prospective financial statement may be classified as either a forecast or a projection.

Financial Forecast

A *financial forecast* presents management's expectations, and there is an expectation that all assumptions will take place. *Note:* A financial forecast encompasses a presentation that management *expects* to occur but that is *not* necessarily most probable. A financial forecast may be most useful to general users, since it presents the client's expectations. A financial forecast and not a financial projection may be issued to *passive users*, or those not negotiating directly with the client.

A financial forecast may be given in a single monetary amount based on the best estimate, or as a reasonable range. *Caution:* This range must *not* be chosen in a misleading manner.

Irrespective of the accountant's involvement, management is the only one who has responsibility for the presentation because only management knows how it plans to run the business and accomplish its plans.

Financial Projection

A *financial projection* presents a "what if" scenario that management does not necessarily expect to occur. However, a given assumption may actually occur if management moves in that direction. A financial projection may be most beneficial for limited users, since they may seek answers to hypothetical questions based on varying assumptions. These users may wish to alter their scenarios based on anticipated changing situations. A financial projection, like a forecast, may contain a range.

A financial projection may be presented to general users *only* when it *supplements* a financial forecast. Financial projections are not permitted in tax shelter offerings and other general-use documents.

Types of Engagements

The following five types of engagements may be performed by the CPA in connection with prospective financial statements.

Plain Paper
The CPA's name is *not associated* with the prospective statements. This service can only be conducted if *all* of the following conditions are satisfied:

- The CPA is *not* reporting on the presentation.
- The prospective statements are on paper not identifying the accountant.
- The prospective financial statements are not shown with historical financial statements that have been audited, reviewed, or compiled by the CPA.

Internal Use

The prospective financial statements are only *assembled*, meaning mathematical and clerical functions are performed. Assembling financial data is permitted if the following two criteria exist:

- Third parties will not use the statements.
- The CPA's name is associated with the statement.

Note that assembling prospective financial statements is limited only to internal use. Appropriate language on the statements might be "For Internal Use Only."

Compilation

This is the lowest level of service performed for prospective financial statements directed for third parties. The compilation engagement involves:

- Assembling prospective data
- The conduct of procedures to ascertain whether the presentation and assumptions are appropriate
- Preparation of a compilation report

With a compilation, no assurance is given regarding the presentation or assumptions, but rather serves to identify obvious matters to be investigated further. *Note:* Working papers have to be prepared to show there was proper planning and supervision of the work, as well as compliance with required compilation procedures. The CPA must also obtain a management letter from the client regarding representations provided.

Warning: A compilation should not be made when the forecasted financial statements exclude disclosure of the significant assumptions or when the financial projections exclude the hypothetical assumptions.

Agreed-Upon Procedures

This relates to applying procedures agreed to or requested by *specific* users, and issuing a report. The report identifies the procedures undertaken, gives the accountant's finding, and restricts distribution of the report to the particular parties. The specified users have to participate in establishing the nature and scope of the engagement and assume responsibility for the adequacy of the procedures. Also, the procedures undertaken must be more than just reading the prospective data.

Examination
The CPA appraises the preparation underlying the supporting assumptions and the presentation of prospective financial information in accordance with AICPA standards. A report is then issued on whether AICPA guidelines have been adhered to and whether the assumptions are reasonable. It is the highest level of assurance. An adverse opinion must be given if there is a failure to disclose a material assumption or if disclosed assumptions are unreasonable. For example, there may be no reasonable expectation that the actual figure will fall within the range of assumptions presented in a forecast having a range. A disclaimer opinion is necessary in the event of a scope limitation, such as when a required examination procedure cannot be performed because of client restrictions or inappropriate circumstances.

CONCLUSION

A financial forecast is needed to predict future fund requirements and sources of financing. The percent-of-sales method estimates expenses, assets, and obligations based on a relationship to sales. Budgets aid financial executives in planning and controlling operations. Budgeted and actual figures are compared for variance analysis. Types of budgets include those for sales, costs, production, inventory, cash, profit, and balance sheet position. Zero-base budgeting can also be used where activity must be justified in order to be funded. A decision package is prepared specifying alternative ways of accomplishing an objective. A CPA's involvement with prospective financial statements may be in the form of an examination, compilation, or agreed-upon procedures.

17 How to Forecast Cash Inflows for Budgeting

A forecast of cash collections and potential writeoffs of accounts receivable is essential in *cash budgeting* and in judging the appropriateness of current credit and discount policies. The critical step in making such a forecast is estimating the cash collection and bad debt percentages to be applied to sales or accounts receivable balances. This chapter discusses methods of estimating cash collection rates (or payment proportions) and illustrates how these rates are used for cash budgeting purposes.*

The first approach, which was developed more than 15 years ago, involves the use of a probability matrix based on the estimates of what is referred to as transition probabilities. This method is described on a step-by-step basis using an illustrative example. The second approach, empirically tested and improved by the author, offers a more pragmatic method of estimating collection and bad debt percentages by relating credit sales and collection data. This method employs regression analysis. By using these approaches, a financial planner should be able to

- Estimate future cash collections from accounts receivable.
- Establish an allowance for doubtful accounts.
- Provide a valuable insight into better methods of managing accounts receivable.

---

*For further reference on forecasting cash receipts, please see:
    Cyert, R. M., H. J. Davidson, and G. L. Thompson, "Estimation of the Allowance for Doubtful Accounts by Markov Chains," *Management Science*, August 1962, pp. 287–303.
    Shim, Jae K., "Estimating Cash Collection Rates from Credit Sales: A Lagged Regression Approach," *Financial Management*, Vol. 10, No. 5, Winter 1981.
    Shim, Jae K., "An Econometric Investigation on Cash Inflows for Budgeting," *Advances in Accounting*. Vol. 2, 1986.

PROBABILITY MATRIX APPROACH

The probability matrix (or Markov) approach has been around for a long time. This approach has been successfully applied by Cyert and others to accounts receivable analysis, specifically to the estimation of that portion of the accounts receivable that will eventually become uncollectible. The method requires classification of outstanding accounts receivable according to age categories that reflect the stage of account delinquency, e.g., current accounts, accounts one month past due, accounts two months past due, and so forth. Consider the following example. XYZ department store divides its accounts receivable into two classifications: 0 to 60 days old and 61 to 120 days old. Accounts that are more than 120 days old are declared uncollectible by XYZ. XYZ currently has $10,000 in accounts receivable: $7,000 from the 0–60-day-old category and $3,000 from the 61–120-day-old category. Based on an analysis of its past records, it provides us with what is known as the matrix of transition probabilities. The matrix is given as shown in Table 17.1.

Transition probabilities are nothing more than the probability that an account receivable moves from one age stage category to another. We note three basic features of this matrix. First, notice the squared element, 0 in the matrix. This indicates that $1 in the 0–60-day-old category *cannot* become a bad debt in one month's time. Now look at the two circled elements. Each of these is 1, indicating that, in time, all the accounts receivable dollars will either be paid or become uncollectible. Eventually, all the dollars do wind up either as collected or uncollectible, but XYZ would be interested in knowing the probability of a dollar from a 0–60-day-old or a 61–120-day-old receivable eventually finding its way into either paid bills or bad debts. It is convenient to partition the matrix of transition probabilities into four submatrices, as follows.

TABLE 17.1 Probability Matrix

From \ To	Collected	Uncollectible	0–60 Days Old	61–120 Days Old
Collected	①	0	0	0
Uncollectible	0	①	0	0
0–60 days old	.3	[0]	.5	.2
61–120 days old	.5	.1	.3	.1

Chapter 17: How to Forecast Cash Inflows for Budgetging

$$\begin{bmatrix} I & O \\ \hline R & Q \end{bmatrix}$$

so that

$$I = \begin{bmatrix} 1 & 0 \\ 0 & 1 \end{bmatrix} \qquad O = \begin{bmatrix} 0 & 0 \\ 0 & 0 \end{bmatrix}$$

$$R = \begin{bmatrix} .3 & 0 \\ .5 & .1 \end{bmatrix} \qquad Q = \begin{bmatrix} .5 & .2 \\ .3 & .1 \end{bmatrix}$$

Now we are able to illustrate the procedure used to determine:

- Estimated collection and bad debt percentages by age category
- Estimated allowance for doubtful accounts

Step-by-step, the procedure is as follows:

- *Step 1:* Set up the matrix $[I - Q]$.

$$[I - Q] = \begin{bmatrix} 1 & 0 \\ 0 & 1 \end{bmatrix} - \begin{bmatrix} .5 & .2 \\ .3 & .1 \end{bmatrix} = \begin{bmatrix} .5 & -.2 \\ -.3 & .9 \end{bmatrix}$$

- *Step 2:* Find the inverse of this matrix, denoted by N.

$$N = [I - Q]^{-1} = \begin{bmatrix} 2.31 & .51 \\ .77 & 1.28 \end{bmatrix}$$

- *Step 3:* Multiply this inverse by matrix R.

$$NR = \begin{bmatrix} 2.31 & .51 \\ .77 & 1.28 \end{bmatrix} \begin{bmatrix} .3 & 0 \\ .5 & .1 \end{bmatrix} = \begin{bmatrix} .95 & .05 \\ .87 & .13 \end{bmatrix}$$

NR gives us the probability that an account will eventually be collected or become a bad debt. Specifically, the top row in the answer is the probability that $1 of XYZ's accounts receivable in the 0–60-day-old category will end up in the collected and bad debt categories. There is a .95 probability that $1 currently in the 0–60-day-old category will be paid, and a .05 probability that it will eventually become a bad debt. Turning to the second row, the two entries represent the probability that $1 now in the 61–120-day-old category will end up in the collected and bad debt categories. We can see from this row that there is a .87 probability that $1 currently in the 61–120-day-category will be collected and a .13 probability that it will eventually become uncollectible.

If XYZ wants to estimate the future of its $10,000 accounts receivable ($7,000 in the 0–60 day category and $3,000 in the 61–120 day category), it must set up the following matrix multiplication:

$$[7{,}000 \quad 3{,}000] \begin{bmatrix} .95 & .05 \\ .87 & .13 \end{bmatrix} = [9{,}260 \quad 740]$$

Hence, of its $10,000 in accounts receivable, XYZ expects to collect $9,260 and to lose $740 to bad debts. Therefore, the estimated allowances for uncollectible accounts is $740.

The variance of each component is equal to:

$$A = be(cNR - (cNR)_{sq})$$

where

$$c_i = b_i / \sum_{1=i}^{2} b_i \text{ and } e \text{ is the unit vector.}$$

In our example,

$$b = (7{,}000 \quad 3{,}000), c = (.7 \quad .3).$$

Therefore,

$$A = [7{,}000 \quad 3{,}000] \begin{bmatrix} 1 \\ 1 \end{bmatrix} \left[[.7 \quad .3] \begin{bmatrix} .95 & .05 \\ .87 & .13 \end{bmatrix} \right.$$

$$- [.7 \quad .3] \begin{bmatrix} .95 & .05 \\ .87 & .13 \end{bmatrix}_{sq} \left. \right] = 10{,}000 \begin{bmatrix} [.926 & .074] \end{bmatrix}$$

$$- [.857476 \quad .005476] \Big] = [685.24 \quad 685.24]$$

which makes the standard deviation equal to $26.18 ($\sqrt{\$685.24}$). If we want to be 95% confident about our estimate of collections, we would set the interval estimate at $9,260 ± 2(26.18), or $9,207.64 − $9,312.36, assuming $t = 2$ as a rule of thumb. We would also be able to set the allowance to cover the bad debts at $740 + 2(26.18), or $792.36.

REGRESSION APPROACH

There is a time lag between the point of a credit sale and realization of cash. More specifically, the lagged effect of credit sales and cash inflows is distributed over a number of periods, as follows:

$$C_t = b_1 S_{t-1} + b_2 S_{t-2} + \ldots b_i S_{t-i}$$

where

C_t = cash collections

S_t = credit sales made in period t

$b_1, b_2, \ldots b_i$ = collection percentages, and

i = number of periods lagged

By using the regression method discussed previously, we will be able to estimate these collection rates (or payment proportions). We can utilize Regression of Excel or special packages such as Minitab and SPSS.

It should be noted that the cash collection percentages, $(b_1, b_2, \ldots b_i)$ may not add up to 100% because of the possibility of bad debts. Once we estimate these percentages by using the regression method, we should be able to compute the bad debt percentage with no difficulty.

Table 17.2 shows the regression results using actual monthly data on credit sales and cash inflows for a real company. Equation 1 can be written as follows:

$$C_t = 60.6\% \ (S_{t-1}) + 24.3\% \ (S_{t-2}) + 8.8\% \ (S_{t-3})$$

This result indicates that the receivables generated by the credit sales are collected at the folllowing rates: first month after sale, 60.6%; second month after sale, 24.3%; and third month after sale, 8.8%. The bad debt percentage is computed as 6.3% (100 − 93.7%).

TABLE 17.2 Regression Results for Cash Collection (C_t)

Independent Variables	Equation 1	Equation 2
S_{t-1}	0.606[a]	0.596[a]
	(0.062)[b]	(0.097)
S_{t-2}	0.243[a]	0.142
	(0.085)	(0.120)
S_{t-3}	0.088	0.043
	(0.157)	(0.191)
S_{t-4}		0.136
		(0.800)
$\bar{R}^2$	0.754	0.753
Durbin–Watson	2.52[c]	2.48[c]
Standard Error of the estimates (s_e)	11.63	16.05
Number of monthly observations	21	20
Bad debt percentages	0.063	0.083

[a]Statistically significant at the 5% significance level.
[b]This figure in the parentheses is the standard error of the estimate for the coefficient (s_b).
[c]No autocorrelation present at the 5% significance level.

It is very important to note, however, that these collection and bad debt percentages are probabilistic variables; that is, variables whose values cannot be known with precision. However, the standard error of the regression coefficient and the *t*-value permit us to assess the probability that the true percentage is between specified limits. The confidence interval takes the following form:

$$b \pm ts_b$$

where

$$t \cdot s_b = \text{standard error of the coefficient.}$$

EXAMPLE 17.1

To illustrate, assuming $t = 2$ as rule of thumb at the 95% confidence level, the true collection percentage from the prior month's sales will be

$$60.6\% \pm 2(6.2\%)$$

$$= 60.6\% + 12.4\%$$

Turning to the estimation of cash collections and allowance for doubtful accounts, the following values are used for illustrative purposes:

$S_{t-1} = \$77.6, S_{t-2} = \$58.5, S_{t-3}$
$= \$76.4$, and forecast average monthly net credit sales = \$75.2

Then, (a) the forecast cash collection for period t would be

$$C_t = 60.6\% \, (77.6) + 19.3\% \, (58.5) + 8.8\% \, (76.4) = \$65.04$$

If the financial planner wants to be 95% confident about this forecast value, then the interval would be set as follows:

$$C_t \pm t \cdot s_e \text{(standard error of the estimate)}$$

where

$$s_e = \text{standard error of the estimate.}$$

To illustrate, using $t = 2$ as a rule of thumb at the 95% confidence level, the true value for cash collections in period t will be

$$\$65.04\% \pm 2 \, (11.63\%)$$
$$= \$65.04\% \pm 23.26$$

(b) The estimated allowance for uncollectible accounts for period t will be

$$6.3\% \, (\$75.2) = \$4.73$$

By using the limits discussed so far, financial planners can develop flexible (or probabilistic) cash budgets, where the lower and upper limits can be interpreted as pessimistic and optimistic outcomes, respectively. They can also simulate a cash budget in an attempt to determine both the expected change in cash collections for each period and the variation in this value.

In preparing a conventional cash inflow budget, the financial manager considers the various sources of cash, including cash on account, sale of assets, incurrence of debt, and so on. Cash collections are emphasized, since that is the greatest problem in this type of budget. For example, assume that the accounts receivable balance on October 1 is $70,000, of which $40,000 is attributable to sales made in August and $30,000 applies to sales made in September. Assume the pattern of collection is as follows: Month of sale, 35%; second month, 40%; third month, 20%; and uncollectible, 5%. This, of course, equals 100%. Credit sales for October are $120,000. Cash collections for October are as follows:

August sales $40,000 × 20%/25%	$32,000
September sales $30,000 × 40%/65%	18,462
October sales $120,000 × 35%	42,000
Total	$92,462

EXAMPLE 17.2

Cash Collections
The following data are given for Erich Stores:

	September Actual	October Actual	November Estimated	December Estimated
Cash sales	$ 7,000	$ 6,000	$ 8,000	$ 6,000
Credit sales	50,000	48,000	62,000	80,000
Total sales	57,000	54,000	70,000	86,000

Past experience indicates net collections normally occur in the following pattern:

- No collections are made in the month of sale.
- 80% of the sales of any month are collected in the following month.
- 19% of sales are collected in the second following month.
- 1% of sales are uncollectible.

Compute the following:

(1) Total cash receipts for November and December
(2) Accounts receivable balance at November 30 if the October 31 balance is $50,000

Chapter 17: How to Forecast Cash Inflows for Budgetging

(1)	November	December
Cash receipts		
Cash sales	$ 8,000	$ 6,000
Cash collections		
September sales		
50,000 (19%)	9,500	
October sales		
48,000 (80%)	38,400	
48,000 (19%)		9,120
November sales		
62,000 (80%)		49,600
Total cash receipts	$55,900	$64,720

(2) Accounts Receivable Balance

$50,000 + $62,000 − $9,500 − $38,400 = $64,100

EXAMPLE 17.3

Cash Collections and Discount Policy

The treasurer of John Loyde Co. plans for the company to have a cash balance of $91,000 on March 1. Sales during March are estimated at $900,000. February sales amounted to $600,000, and January sales amounted to $500,000. Cash payments for March have been budgeted at $580,000. Cash collections have been estimated as follows:

- 60% of the sales for the month are to be collected during the month.
- 30% of the sales for the preceding month are to be collected during the month.
- 8% of the sales for the second preceding month are to be collected during the month.

The treasurer plans to accelerate collections by allowing a 2% discount for prompt payment. With the discount policy, the company expects to collect 70% of the current sales and will permit the discount reduction on these collections. Sales of the preceding month will be collected to the extent of 15% with no discount allowed, and 10% of the sales of the second preceding month will be collected with no discount allowed. This pattern of collection can be expected in subsequent months. During the transitional month of March, collections may run somewhat higher. However, the treasurer prefers to estimate collections on the basis of the new pattern so that the estimates will be somewhat conservative.

340   Part III: Financial Forecasting

(1) Estimate cash collections for March and the cash balance at March 31 under the present policy.
(2) Estimate cash collections for March and the cash balance at March 31 according to the new policy of allowing discounts.
(3) Is the discount policy desirable?

(1) and (2)	Under the Present Policy	Under the Discount Policy
Balance, March 1	$ 91,000	$ 91,000
Collections		
From March sales	540,000 ($900,000 × 60%)	617,400[a]
From February sales	180,000 ($600,000 × 30%)	90,000 ($600,000 × 15%)
From January sales	40,000 ($500,000 × 8%)	50,000 ($500,000 × 10%)
Total cash available	$851,000	$848,400
Less disbursements	580,000	580,000
Balance, March 31	$271,000	$268,400

[a]$900,000 × 70% × 98% = $617,400

(3)
No, because under the discount policy, the March 31 cash balance will be smaller as indicated above ($268,400 as compared to $271,000 under the present policy).

EXAMPLE 17.4

Cash Forecast Model
Over the past several years the Program Corporation has encountered difficulties in estimating its cash flows. The result has been a rather strained relationship with its banker.

Program's controller would like to develop a means by which the firm's monthly operating cash flows can be forecasted. The following data were gathered to facilitate the development of such a forecast.

- Sales have been increased and are expected to increase at 0.5% each month.
- 30% of each month's sales are for cash; the other 70% are on open account.

Chapter 17: How to Forecast Cash Inflows for Budgetging   341

- Of the credit sales, 80% are collected in the first month following the sale and the remaining 20% are collected in the second month. There are no bad debts.
- Gross margin on sales averages 25%.
- Program purchases enough inventory each month to cover the following month's sales.
- All inventory purchases are paid for in the month of purchase at a 2% cash discount.
- Monthly expenses are: payroll, $1,500; rent, $400; depreciation, $120; other cash expenses, 1% of that month's sales. There are no accruals.
- Ignore the effects of corporate income taxes, dividends, and equipment acquisitions.

Using these data, we develop a mathematical model the controller can use for calculations. Your model should be capable of calculating the monthly operating cash inflows and outflows for any specified month.

Let S = current month's sales

t = number of months in the future the forecast is desired

Sales t months from now

$$= S (1.005)^t$$

Collections t months from now

$$= 0.3S(1.005)^t + (0.8)(0.7)S(1.005)^{t-1}$$
$$+ (0.2)(0.7)S(1.005)^{t-2}$$
$$= 0.3S (1.005)^t + 0.56S (1.005)^{t-1} + 0.14S(1.005)^{t-2}$$

Purchases t months from now

$$= 0.75S (1.005)^{t+1}$$

Cash payments t months from now*

$$= (0.98)(0.75)S (1.005)^{t+1} + 0.015 (1.005)^t + 1,900$$
$$= 0.735S (1.005)^{t+1} + .01S (1.005)^t + 1,900$$

---

*If it is assumed that the discounts were included to arrive at the 25% gross margin, then the (0.98) in the first expression would not appear.

IS CASH FLOW SOFTWARE AVAILABLE?

Computer software allows for day-to-day cash management, determining cash balances, planning and analyzing cash flows, finding cash shortages, investing cash surpluses, accounting for cash transactions, automating accounts receivable and payable, and dial-up banking. Computerization improves availability, accuracy, timeliness, and monitoring of cash information at minimal cost. Daily cash information aids in planning how to use cash balances. It enables the integration of different kinds of related cash information such as collections on customer accounts and cash balances, and the effect of cash payments on cash balances.

Spreadsheet program software such as Microsoft's Excel, Lotus 1-2-3, and Quattro Pro can assist you in developing cash budgets and answering a variety of "what if" questions. For example, you can see the effect on cash flow from different scenarios (e.g., the purchase and sale of different product lines).

There are computer software packages specially designed for cash management. Three popular ones are briefly described below.

1. *Quicken (Intuit, Inc., 800-246-8848, www.quicken.com)*.This program is a fast, easy-to-use, inexpensive accounting program that can help a small business manage its cash flow. Bills can be recorded as postdated transactions when they arrive; the program's *Billminder* feature automatically reminds the payer when bills are due. Then, checks can be printed for due bills with a few mouse and/or keystrokes. Similarly, invoices can be recorded and aged receivables tracked. Together, these features help maximize cash on hand.

2. *Up Your Cash Flow (Granville Publications Software, 10960 Wilshire Blvd., Suite 826, Los Angeles, CA 90024, 800-873-7789).* This program contains automatically prepared spreadsheets for profit/loss forecasts, cash flow budgets, projected balance sheet, payroll analysis, term loan amortization schedule, sales/cost of sales by product, ratio analysis, and graphs. It is a menu-driven system and can be customized to forecasting needs.

3. *Cash Flow Analysis (Superior Software, 16055 Ventura Blvd., Suite 725, Encino, CA 91436, 800-421-3264).* This software provides projections of cash inflow and cash outflow. Data are input into eight categories: sales, cost of sales, general and administrative expenses, long-term debt, other cash receipts, inventory build-up/reduction, cap-

ital expenditures (acquisition of long-term assets such as store furniture), and income tax. The program allows changes in assumptions and scenarios and provides a complete array of reports.

Telecommunications software may be used to link up your personal computer via modem and telephone lines to the bank to execute cash payments and transfers between accounts, and to obtain current cash balance information. Software available from banks aids in managing cash collections, payments, investment, and borrowing. An example is Chase Manhattan Bank's InfoCash software package which includes modules for:

- *Cash Reporter* (provides account information up to the close of the previous day; information available includes checks cleared and money transfers)
- *Current Day Reporter* (provides information on current-day transactions)
- *Regional Bank Reporter* (provides information on checking accounts held at other banks)
- *Money Transfer Input* (enables the transfer of funds between accounts)

CONCLUSION

Two methods of estimating the expected collectible and uncollectible patterns were presented. One advantage of the Markov model is that the expected value and standard deviation of these percentages can be determined, thereby making it possible to specify probabilistic statements about these figures. We have to be careful about these results, however, since the model makes some strong assumptions. A serious assumption is that the matrix of transition probabilities is constant over time. We do not expect this to be perfectly true. Updating of the matrix may have to be done, perhaps through the use of such techniques as exponential smoothing and time series analysis.

The regression approach is relatively inexpensive to use in the sense that it does not require a lot of data. All it requires is data on cash collections, and credit sales. Furthermore, credit sales values are all predetermined; we use previous months' credit sales to forecast cash collections, and there is no need to forecast credit sales. The model also allows us to make all kinds of statistical inferences about the cash collection percentages and forecast value.

Extensions of these models can be made toward setting credit and discount policies. Corresponding to a given set of policies, there are:

- An associated transition matrix in the Markov model
- Associated collection percentages in the regression model

By computing long-term collections and bad debts for each policy, an optimal policy can be chosen that maximizes expected long-run profits per period.

Part IV:

Financial Modeling

18 Using Corporate Planning Models

Today more and more companies are using, developing, or experimenting with some form of corporate planning model. This is primarily a result of the planning and modeling software packages now available that make it possible to develop a model without much knowledge of computer coding and programming. For the accountant and financial analyst, the attractive features of corporate modeling are the formulation of budgets, budgetary planning and control, and financial analyses that can be used to support management decision making. However, corporate modeling involves much more than the generation of financial statements and budgets. Depending on the structure and breadth of the modeling activity, a variety of capabilities, uses, and analyses are available.

A corporate planning model is an integrated business planning model in which marketing and production models are linked to the financial model. More specifically, a corporate model is a description, explanation, and interrelation of the functional areas of a firm (accounting, finance, marketing, production, and others) expressed in terms of a set of mathematical and logical relationships so as to produce a variety of reports, including financial statements. The ultimate goals of a corporate planning model are to improve quality of planning and decision making, reduce the decision risk, and, more important, influence or even shape the future environment favorably.

Generally speaking, a corporate model can be used to

- Simulate an alternative strategy by evaluating its impact on profits.
- Help establish corporate and divisional goals.
- Measure the interactive effect of parts with the firm.
- Help management better understand the business and its functional relationships and help improve decision-making ability.

347

- Link the firm's goals and strategies to its master budgets.
- Assess critically the assumptions underlying environmental constraints.

TYPES OF ANALYSIS

The choice of a corporate model depends on what types of analysis management wishes to perform. There are typically three types of model investigations.

The first type of investigation involves "what is" or "what has been" questions, such as the relationship between variables of the firm and external macroeconomic variables such as GNP or inflation. The goal of this type of model investigation is to obtain a specific answer based on the stipulated relationship. For example, what is or what has been the firm's profit when the price of raw material was $12.50?

The second type of investigation focuses on "what if" questions. This is done through simulation or sensitivity analysis. This analysis often takes the following form: "What happens under a given set of assumptions if a decision variable is changed in a prescribed manner?" For example, "What is going to happen to the company's cash flow and net income if it reduces the price by 10% and increases the advertising budget by 25%?"

The third type of question that can be addressed takes the following form: "What has to be done in order to achieve a particular objective?" This type of analysis is often called "goal seeking." It usually requires the use of optimization models, such as linear programming and goal programming.

TYPICAL QUESTIONS ABOUT CORPORATE MODELING

The following is a list of questions management addresses using corporate modeling.*

- What are the effects of different pricing policies?
- What is the effect of different interest rates and current exchange rates on the income statement and balance sheet of the firm?

---

*For greater detail, see F. Rosenkranz, *An Introduction to Corporate Modeling*. Duke University Press, Durham, NC, 1979.

- What will be the demand for the end products of the firm at various locations and different times?
- What is and will be the unit contribution margin for certain production, transportation, and sales allocations?
- What will the absence and turnover rates of the employees of the firm be and what effect will they have?
- What is the effect of advertising and distribution expenditures on sales?
- What marketing strategy can and should the firm follow?
- What do price–demand or supply relations on the output or input side of the firm look like? What are the effects of price and cost changes on sales?
- How do certain states of the national or world economy influence sales of the firm on the one side and purchase price of the production factors on the other?
- What is the nature of the conditions that must be fulfilled if the total sales of the firm at a certain firm are supposed to be higher than a certain budget value?
- Should the firm produce and sell a certain product, purchase and sell the product, or not get involved at all?
- In what range will the return on investment on various projects and units lie?
- How will the income statement, the balance sheet, and the cash flow statement develop for several operating divisions? What will their contributions be?
- What effects with respect to the financial position of the firm could an acquisition or merger with another firm have?

Benefits derived from the corporate planning models include:

- The ability to explore more alternatives
- Better quality decision making
- More effective planning
- A better understanding of the business
- Faster decision making
- More timely information
- More accurate forecasts
- Cost savings

TYPES OF MODELS

Corporate planning models can be categorized according to two approaches: simulation and optimization. Simulation models are attempts to mathematically represent the operations of the company or of the conditions in the external economic environment. By adjusting the values of controllable variables and assumed external conditions, the future implications of present decision making can be estimated. *Note:* Probabilistic simulation models incorporate probability estimates into the forecast sequence, while deterministic models do not. Optimization models are intended to identify the best decision, given specific constraints. Both simulation and optimization models are discussed and illustrated in Chapters 19 and 20, respectively.

HISTORY OF MODELS

The rudiments of corporate modeling go back to the early 1960s with the large, cumbersome simulation models developed by major corporations, such as AT&T, Wells Fargo Bank, Dow Chemical, IBM, Sun Oil, and Boise Cascade. Most of the models were written in one of the general programming languages (GPLs) such as Fortran, and were used for generating pro forma financial statements. The models typically required several years to develop and, in some cases, never provided benefits sufficient to outweigh the costs of development. Planning models were considered an untested concept, suitable only for those corporations large enough to absorb the costs and risks of development.

Important advancements in computer technology in the early 1970s provided the means for greater diversity and affordability in corporate modeling. Interactive computing facilities allowed for faster and more meaningful input–output sequences for modelers; trial-and-error adjustments of inputs and analyses were possible while on-line to the central computer or to an outside timesharing service. The advent of corporate simulation languages enabled analysts with little experience with GPLs to write modeling programs in an English-like programming language—for example, IFPS, Compete, and Encore Plus. In addition, a number of spreadsheet programs such as Microsoft's Excel became available for use by corporate planning modelers. Currently, virtually every *Fortune* 1000 company is using a corporate simulation model. This statistic will definitely increase to cover small- and medium-sized firms.

As companies gained experience in developing basic, deterministic simulations, renewed effort was directed toward consolidating and integrating smaller models into the larger corporate models first attempted in the 1960s.

Furthermore, certain companies were attempting the more difficult optimization models and were increasing predictive power by using econometric models to link their simulations with product markets and the external economy. Early successes with the simpler models led to a boom in modeling, but an increasing number of failures in more ambitious projects soon moderated the general enthusiasm. As the economy entered a recession and became more unstable (less predictable), the weaknesses in the rationale underlying many corporate models were revealed. Managers realized that the purpose of a model must be well defined and that the end users should be involved in its development. Although the bad experiences of the mid 1970s have prejudiced some executives against models to the present day, most veterans of the period have developed a realistic attitude toward the capabilities of models and are employing recent advancements in techniques to construct more serviceable models.

CURRENT TRENDS IN MODELING

Surveys of Corporations

Several surveys of financial model-making in U.S. and U.K. firms have been conducted over the past 15 years. The firms represented a broad cross section of industries and services, with sales ranging from $1 million to over $1 billion annually. The specific purposes of the surveys varied somewhat among researchers, but each was designed to estimate the general acceptance and development of corporate modeling. While different sample sizes and populations prevent pooling the results, it is instructive to discuss important issues and common findings.

Surveys by McLean and Neale (1980) and by Klein (1982) indicated that 85% of companies surveyed (410 and 204, respectively) were using some type of financial model. The results indicate that corporate modeling has become a common tool in U.S. business firms (Table 18.1).

TABLE 18.1 Results of Surveys for the Use of Corporate Models

Author	Sample Size (Responses)	Companies Using or Developing Models
McLean and Neale (1980)	410	245 (60%)
Brightman and Harris (1982)	237	126 (53%)
Klein (1982)	204	175 (86%)

Among the reasons cited by corporations for using planning models were:

- Economic uncertainty
- Shortages of resources
- Diminishing increase in productivity
- International competition
- Tight money and inflation
- Political upheavals (affecting foreign operations)
- Environmental problems
- New business opportunities

There was general agreement that models enabled managers to run alternative analyses and to adjust decision variables, while reducing the time needed for report writing. The many possible applications of corporate planning models are listed in Table 18.2. Financial forecasting and pro forma balance sheet statements were the most common applications at most companies. The models proved to be useful tools in "what if" analysis, sensitivity analysis, simulations, best/worst case scenarios, goal seeking, optimization, and report preparation.

A consistent finding among the surveys was the involvement of top management in successful modeling efforts. Klein (1982) found that in 50 to 90% of the companies using models, upper managers (e.g., president; vice president, finance; controller; treasurer; executive vice president) participated in the definition and implementation of the model. The background of the participants in Klein's survey was predominantly in finance, followed by computer science and accounting.

TABLE 18.2 Applications of Corporate Planning Models

Financial forecasting	Construction scheduling
Pro forma financial statements	Tax planning
Capital budgeting	Energy requirements
Market decision making	Labor contract negotiation fees
Merger and acquisition analysis	Foreign currency analysis
Lease versus purchase decisions	Utilities:
Production scheduling	Load forecasting
New venture evaluation	Rate cases
Manpower planning	Generation planning
Profit planning	
Sales forecasting	
Investment analysis	

ATTITUDES AND PROBLEMS

The reluctance of many firms to experiment with corporate planning models derives chiefly from a fear of the unknown. Confusion over what models are and how they are used precludes serious investigation of their potential benefits. Myths that discourage managers from considering models include the following:

- *Myth*: Models are complicated. *Fact*: On the contrary, most effective models are fairly simple structures, incorporating only the essential processes of the problem under investigation. The math involved is often basic algebra, and modeling languages reduce complex terminology.
- *Myth*: The company is not large enough. *Fact*: Models do not consist solely of comprehensive simulations. Some of the most frequently used models center on a limited number of key relationships.
- *Myth*: We do not own a mainframe computer. *Fact*: Models are being designed for use on inexpensive personal computers, and outside time-sharing services are available.
- *Myth*: We do not have any modelers. *Fact*: Modern planning languages have so simplified the modeling process that even a novice quickly becomes competent. Outside consultants are also available for assistance.

Attitudes toward modeling have progressed from the rather deteriorated outlook of the mid-1970s to today's more optimistic viewpoint. The past trend probably explains the general negativity of earlier results reported by Higgins and Finn (1976) in their literature review of top management attitudes toward modeling in the United Kingdom. In summarizing the activities making up the senior executive's role, the authors concluded that most of the manager's duties involved behavioral, interpersonal communication problems requiring his direct ministering. The majority view of managers emphasized that models could not capture the essential complexity of the organization and ignored the political and behavioral issues. In the few areas where a model could prove useful, the executive had insufficient time to learn how to apply it. At that time, the picture of an executive seated at a computer and engaged in problem analysis was unrealistic. The ultimate finding, however, was not a wholesale abandonment of corporate planning models among managers, but the delegation of modeling analysis to lower managers. Thus, models seemed destined to become strictly a middle management tool.

At about the same time, Grinyer and Wooler's survey showed the importance of obtaining top management's support to ensure success in any model-making project. However, top managers in over 50% of the companies sampled believed their models had improved forecasts; 31% were undecided. More encouraging results followed. Wagner (1979) reported that upper management in his survey not only requested that models be built but participated in their development. The finished products received a high average utility rating of 3.9 out of a total of 5. A similar evaluation in 1980 by top management at 410 U.S. firms (annual sales exceeding $100 million) yielded a 4.95 rating out of 7 for their computer-based planning models. None of the CEOs considered the models useless. Klein (1982) found evidence of significant cost savings through modeling, with one vice president of finance reporting a $600,000 savings through use of a financial planning model.

The growing acceptance of planning models has enabled managers and technicians to identify areas requiring improvement and to formulate criteria for success. Optimization models are one technique in need of refinement. *Note:* Optimization models are inscrutable "black boxes" to those managers who have had no part in the modeling effort (Powers, 1975). Naturally, top management has little confidence in forecasts produced by a model they cannot understand. The need to monitor several financial and nonfinancial variables precludes the construction of simple optimization models.

No serious limitations in modeling were noted by respondents in Naylor's 1975 survey. The criticisms were directed at the inflexibility of some models, poor documentation by the model builder, and excessive input data requirement. Aggarwal and Khera (1980) identified several points of inflexibility in most models. Models usually simulate only one cause-and-effect relationship, whereas multiple effects are often present. Similarly, the intended results of a control action may be accompanied by unintended results. In that instance, the desirability of the two consequences must be compared on a common utility scale. When several consequences of a decision are separated in time, a means for making comparisons among them is required, similar to a discount rate in capital budgeting. Such techniques are rarely available in practice.

The reasons for discontinuation of corporate planning models in 31 of the largest U.S. corporations were reported by Ang and Chua (1980). The majority of firms sampled were industries, followed by retailers, transporters, utilities, banks, and finance and insurance institutions. The 31 firms having discontinued models comprised only 27% of the total sample of 113 corporations. Twenty-nine of the 31 models were designed for producing pro forma financial statements, and were discontinued within three years of construction. The various reasons for the rejections are listed in Table 18.3. The common justifications were model deficiencies and human problems in implementation. Three of the prevalent reasons (inflexibility, lack of management support, excessive input data requirements) are familiar shortcomings, as discussed earlier. The need for management's support for successful model making cannot be overemphasized; its role as champion of the effort is essential for compa-

TABLE 18.3 Reasons for Discontinued Models

Lack of sufficient flexibility
Lack of adequate management support
Excessive amounts of input data required
Replaced by a better model
The need no longer existed
The model did not perform as expected
New management de-emphasized planning
Poor documentation
Lack of user interest
Excessive development costs
Excessive operating costs
Excessive development time required

nywide acceptance of the final product. It is interesting to note that excessive development time and costs were not often a basis for rejection.

A novel insight on success factors in modeling was provided by Simon et al. (1976). The authors asserted that the modeler must understand that management's expressed need for a particular model may be specious; the modeler must perceive from the manager's behavior, rather than from merely the verbal request, the type of model needed. If an incorrect determination is made, the model may never be implemented. Two of the five categories of uses for models outlined in the study were legitimate and straightforward: Type I models are simulation/optimization techniques, and Type II models condition data for easier utilization. When the modeler perceives that management's objectives are not consistent with those of Type I or II models, one of three alternative choices is implied:

- *Type III*: Merely a subterfuge for establishing a data link, forcing one part of the organization to channel information to another.
- *Type IV*: A means of supplying a formal rationale for decisions reached in the past.
- *Type V*: A means of establishing a manager's reputation—simply a remake of a previously successful model.

A table of management behavior was provided by the authors as a guide for modelers in determining the type of model implied in the original request and in subsequent feedback.

State-of-the-Art and Recommended Practice

The acceptance of corporate planning models has resulted in many firms establishing planning departments responsible for developing and implementating planning models. The structure of the typical corporate financial model is an integration of smaller modules used by each department or business unit for planning purposes. Figure 18.1 shows that marketing, production, and financial models from each business unit can be consolidated to drive a comprehensive model used by upper management.

Optimal procedures for assembling effective models are still largely at the discretion of the individual planning department, but useful guidelines have been published. The modeling effort could be divided into ten stages of activities:

```
┌──────────┐      ┌──────────┐
│Marketing │      │Production│
│  Model   │      │  Model   │
└────┬─────┘      └────┬─────┘
     │                 │
     └────────┬────────┘
              │
         ┌────▼─────┐
         │Financial │
         │  Model   │
         └────┬─────┘
              │
              ▼
    ┌───────────────────┐
    │Integrated Corporate│
    │  Planning Model   │
    └───────────────────┘
```

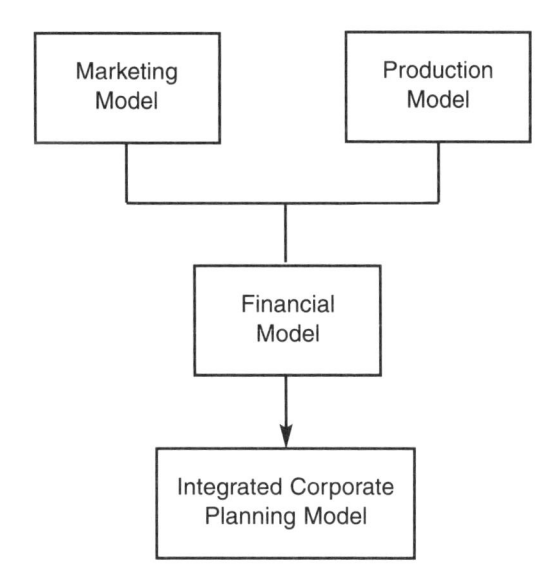

FIGURE 18.1 Typical Structure of an Integrated Planning Model

1. Determine which process(es) can be modeled effectively.
2. Decide whether to use a model.
3. Formalize the specifications of the model (e.g., inputs and outputs, structure, etc.).
4. Prepare a proposal.
5. Conduct modeling and data gathering concurrently.
6. Debug the model.
7. Educate the prospective users.
8. Have users validate the model.
9. Put model into use.
10. Update and modify the model as needed.

Table 18.4 lists prerequisites for modeling and control factors for success.

The anatomy of the contemporary financial model is composed of five parts: the documentation supporting the calculations; input assump-

358   Part IV: Financial Modeling

TABLE 18.4   Success Factors in Modeling

Uncontrollable Prerequisites

Operations understood, data plentiful
Relevant data accessible
Budgets, plans, and control systems are well defined, understood
Modelers have management's support
Management scientists accept responsibility for implementation
Similar innovative techniques used in the past
Manager and modeler share status and background

Controllable Factors

Involve potential users in development process
Define model's goals explicitly
Input and output are in familiar formats
Company procedures are modified little at first
Look for common management problems to model
Start simple and keep it simple
Allow for ample judgmental inputs
Be realistic about planning time and expected results
Put a manager (not a modeler) in charge
Define roles clearly
Demonstrate part of model early on
Build model within users' organization
Develop expertise to manage and update model
Provide ample documentation

---

tions regarding future periods; the projections and decision points leading to the forecasted values; managerial (financial) ratios; and graphics displaying information from decision points. The forecasting systems utilized depend upon the breadth and planning horizon of the model; typical methods include market research and Delphi method, time trends, moving averages, Box–Jenkins, and various causal methods, such as leading indicators, life cycle analysis, and regression.

Forecasting methods should be reviewed periodically by an independent party to ensure that the techniques have not become outdated. This can be determined only by maintaining a current management information system (MIS), which provides data to econometric models of the external environment. *Note:* The critical importance of external data in determining company strategy is the central theorem of MIS. Thus, planners make assumptions about the business environment for a particular planning horizon, based upon the output from the MIS. The information is combined with internal data to prepare demand forecasts, and the results can be input to a planning model or used to check the validity of forecasts produced by current techniques.

Planning and modeling languages (PMLs) have been a major incentive in involving higher management in modeling. General programming languages, such as Fortran, are seldom used in current models; oddly, Cobol, the "business language," has never been used extensively in modeling. The advantages of PMLs are steadily edging out GPLs: with PMLs, models are built more easily, with shorter development and data processing times, are more easily understood by upper management, and are periodically updated with enhancements from the vendor.

Today more than 70 PMLs are available at reasonable cost, including IFPS, Encore Plus, and Venture. A further convenience is premade planning packages sold by software vendors. The packages have often been criticized for their inflexibility, but the newer models allow for more user specificity. Analytical portfolio models are commercial packages that tell a conglomerate how to distribute resources across the portfolio of profit centers. Boston Consulting Group, Arthur D. Little, and McKinsey have developed models that categorize investments into a matrix of profit potentials and recommended strategies.

A model for Profit Impact of Market Strategy (PIMS) is offered by the Strategic Planning Institute. The package is a large multiple regression model used to identify the optimal strategy in a given business environment. Similar packages will likely proliferate in the future as more companies are forced to use decision models to remain competitive. Furthermore, more spreadsheet-based *add-ins* and *templates* for budgeting are being developed for Lotus 1-2-3, Microsoft's Excel, and Quattro Pro.

MIS, DSS, EIS, AND PERSONAL COMPUTERS

The analytic and predictive capabilities of corporate planning models depend in large part upon the supporting data base. Information technology has advanced to the point that data bases consist of logic–mathematical models and highly integrated collections of data, derived from both inside and outside the firm. The data bases are now called *Management Information Systems* (MISs), *Decision Support Systems* (DSSs), or *Executive Information Systems* (EISs). They store the data and decision tools utilized by management.

A primary value of the MIS, DSS, and EIS and their large storage capacity for data is the potential to more accurately model the external economy and to forecast business trends. Managers are finding that effective long-range planning depends primarily upon a thorough understanding of their competitors and the forces at work in the marketplace. A considerable body of data is required to develop insight into the competitive environment. *Note*: Information derived from within the company has little strategic value for those purposes, thus the collection of external data should be emphasized.

As a result, the relevance of information to future conditions is the standard by which input of data to the MIS is controlled.

Once the strategic data have been stored in the mainframe computer system, managers need quick access to the data base and a means for inputting alternative data sets and/or scenarios into the econometric models. Only recently have such activities been made possible by the development of communication links between mainfame systems and PCs. Many of the applications of the mainframe–PC connection involve rather basic analyses, such as accounts payable, receivables, general ledger, and the like. However, internal financial planning packages (e.g., IFPS) are currently available, as are external timesharing services, such as Dow Jones and The Source.

The outlook for the next few years indicates increasing integration of the PC with the mainframe. A recent survey of more than 1,000 organizations showed that 67% of middle management and 22% of top management of non–data-processing departments were using personal computers. The results indicate significant momentum at the top of corporate management for the use of PCs which should intensify the need for mainframe connections.

Corporate planning software packages for PCs are already proliferating. Applications now available range from cash flow analysis and budget projections to regressions, time series analysis, and probabilistic analysis.

PC World listed 116 software packages for financial and business analysis on the IBM PC; many were suitable as corporate planning models. The trend in PC technology is aimed toward incorporating as many mainframe, analytical capabilities into the microcomputer as the market will support.

THE FUTURE OF CORPORATE PLANNING MODELS

The interest in obtaining corporate models is likely to continue. The concept of the strategic business unit (SBU) as an object of analysis may prove not to be viable. There has been no consistent definition of an SBU, and most models treat them as independent of one another, even though this may not be accurate. The SBU is typically forced into short-term profit making (rather than long-term development), eventually sapping its vitality. Consequently, an improved rationale may cause models to be built around a different grouping of profit centers.

We can expect to see an increased linking of portfolio models with corporate simulation and optimization models. Modeling software will become more modular in order to perform limited analyses or comprehensive projections. More software will be written for microcomputers, graphics will improve, and modeling languages will become more user friendly. The future of modeling is somewhat assured because it is intimately linked with the continued expansion of the computer market. Though shakeouts may frequently occur among hardware manufacturers, planning models will always have a market, as software writers improve their understanding of the planner's needs and produce more efficient decision-making tools.

CONCLUSION

In the face of uncertainty about the future, management is particularly interested in following the best possible course of action under a given circumstance. The corporate planning model is used as a tool to help minimize risk and uncertainty and to develop the best course of action for the company. For example, management is able to examine the effects of proposed mergers and acquisitions with much less uncertainty and to estimate with more confidence the potential profits from new markets.

BIBLIOGRAPHY AND ADDITIONAL READINGS

Ang, J. and J. Chua. "Corporate planning models that failed," *Managerial Planning* 29(4): 34–38, 1980.
Baxendale, Sidney J. "Integrated operational and financial modeling at a public utility." *Public Utilities Fortnightly*, February 1987, 39–45.
Brightman, H. J. and S. E. Harris. "The planning and modeling language revolution: A managerial perspective," *Business* 32(4): 15–21, 1982.
Buckerley, William M. "PC networks begin to oust mainframe in some companies," *The Wall Street Journal*, May 23, 1990, 1.
Gantt, J. D. and C. M. Beise. "The public reacts to GDSS," *Byte*, March, 1993, 118.
Kador, John. "The software that changed decision making at Xerox." *Business Software Review*, January 1987, 20–22.
Kennedy, J. "Financial applications," *PC World—Annual Software Review*, pp. 324–340, 1983.

Klein, R. "Computer-based financial modeling," *Journal of Systems Management* 33(5): 6–13, 1982.

Leibowitz, J. *Expert Systems for Business and Management*. Englewood Cliffs, NJ: Yourdon Press, 1990.

McLean, E. R. and G. L. Neale. "Computer-based planning models come of age," *Harvard Business Review* 58: 46–54, 1980.

Naylor, T. H. "Strategic planning models," *Managerial Planning* 30(1): 3–11, 1983.

———. (ed.) *Simulation in Business Planning and Decision Making*, The Society for Computer Simulation (Simulation Councils, Inc.), La Jolla, CA 1981.

Shim, Jae K. and R. McGlade. "Current trends in the use of corporate planning models," *Journal of Systems Management*, September 34(9), 1984.

19 Financial Modeling—Simulation

This section introduces financial modeling. We begin with a review.

- What is a financial model?
- What are some typical uses of a financial model?
- What are the types of financial modeling?
- How widespread is the use of financial modeling in practice?
- How do we go about building a financial model?

FINANCIAL MODEL

A financial model is a system of mathematical equations, logic, and data that describes the relationships among financial and operating variables. It can be viewed as a subset of broadly defined corporate planning models or a stand-alone functional system that attempts to answer a particular financial planning problem. A financial model is one in which:

- One or more financial variables appear (expenses, revenues, investment, cash flow, taxes, earnings, etc.).
- The model user can manipulate (set and alter) the value of one or more financial variables.
- The purpose is to influence strategic decisions by revealing to the decision maker the implications of alternative values of these financial variables.

Types of Financial Models

Financial models fall into two types: *simulation*, better known as "what if" models, and *optimization* models. "What if" models are those that attempt to simulate the effects of alternative management policies and assumptions about the firm's external environment. They are basically a tool for management's laboratory. Optimization models are those in which the goal is to maximize or minimize an objective, such as present value of profit or cost. *Note*: Multiobjective techniques such as goal programming are under experimentation. Models can be deterministic or probabilistic. Deterministic models do not include any random or probabilistic variables, whereas probabilistic models incorporate random numbers and/or one or more probability distributions for variables such as sales and costs. A financial model can be solved and manipulated computationally to derive from it the current and projected implications and consequences. Due to technological advances in computers (such as spreadsheets, financial modeling languages, graphics, data base management systems, and networking), more and more companies are using modeling.

APPLICATIONS AND USES OF FINANCIAL MODELS

Basically, a financial model is used to generate projected financial statements, such as the income statement, balance sheet, and cash flow statement. Such a model can be called a budgeting model, because we are essentially developing a master budget with it. Applications and uses of the model are numerous, including:

- Projection of financial statements and development of budgets
- Financial forecasting and analysis
- Cash budgeting
- Capital expenditure analysis
- Tax planning
- Exchange rate analysis
- Analysis for mergers and acquisitions
- Labor contract negotiations
- Capacity planning
- Cost–volume–profit analysis

- New venture analysis
- Lease–purchase analysis
- Evaluation of performance by segments
- Market analysis
- New product analysis
- Development of long-term strategy
- Planning for financial requirements
- Risk analysis
- Cash flow analysis
- Cost and price projections

PUTTING FINANCIAL MODELING INTO PRACTICE

The use of financial modeling, especially computer-based financial modeling systems, is rapidly growing. The reason is quite simple: the growing need for improved and quicker support for management decisions, and wide and easy availability of computer hardware and software.

Some of the functions currently served by financial models, as described by the users, are as follows:

- Projecting financial results under any given set of assumptions, evaluating the financial impact of various assumptions and alternative strategies, and preparing long-range financial forecasts
- Computing income and cash flow and ratios for 5 years by month; calculating energy sales, revenue, and power generation requirements, operating and manufacturing expenses, manual or automatic financing, and rate structure analysis
- Providing answers and insights into financial "what if" questions, and producing financial scheduling information
- Preparing forecasts of balance sheets and income statements with emphasis on alternatives for the investment portfolio
- Projecting operating results and various financing needs, such as plant and property levels and financing requirements
- Computing manufacturing profit given sales forecasts and processing sequence through the manufacturing facilities; simulating effect on profits of inventory policies

366   Part IV: Financial Modeling

- Generating reports concerning profitability of various cost centers
- Projecting financial implications of capital investment programs
- Showing effect of various volume and activity levels on budget and cash flow
- Forecasting corporate sales, costs, and income by division and by month
- Providing sales revenue for budget, a basis for evaluating actual sales department performance, and other statistical comparisons
- Determining pro forma cash flow for alternative development plans for real estate projects
- Analyzing impact of acquisition on company earnings
- Determining economic attractiveness of new ventures; e.g., products, facilities, and acquisitions
- Evaluating alternatives of leasing or buying types of computer equipment
- Determining corporate taxes as a function of changes in prices
- Evaluating investments in additional capacity at each major refinery
- Generating net income statements, cash flow, present value, and discounted rate of return for potential mining ventures, based on production and sales forecasts

Supported by the expanded capabilities provided by models, many companies are increasingly successful in including long-term strategic considerations in their business plans, thus enabling them to investigate the possible impact of their current decisions on long-term welfare of the company.

QUANTITATIVE TECHNIQUES USED IN FINANCIAL MODELS

In view of the development of sophisticated quantitative models for analysis in business planning and decision making, there is a rapidly growing trend for their use, certainly with the aid of computer technology. Here is a list of techniques used by model builders today:

- Econometric and statistical methods
  —Simple and multiple regressions
  —Econometric models

- —Time series models
- —Exponential smoothing
- —Risk analysis
- —Simulation
- Optimization models
  - —Linear programming
  - —Goal programming
  - —Integer programming
  - —Dynamic programming

DEVELOPING FINANCIAL MODELS

Development of financial models essentially involves two steps: (1) the definition of variables and input parameters and (2) model specification. As far as model specification goes, we will concentrate only on simulation-type models in this section. (Optimization models will be discussed in the next chapter.) Generally speaking, the simulation model consists of three important ingredients:

- Variables
- Input parameter values
- Definitional and/or functional relationships

Definition of Variables and Input Parameters

Fundamental to the specification of a financial model is the definition of the variables to be included in the model. There are basically three types of variables: policy variables (Z), external variables (X), and performance variables (Y).

Policy Variables

The policy variables are those over which management can exert some degree of control. They are often called control variables. Among these we may list such variables as cash management policy, working capital policy, debt management policy, depreciation policy, tax policy, merger–acquisition decisions, the rate and direction of the firm's capital investment programs, the extent of its equity and external debt financing and the financial leverage represented thereby, and the size of its cash balances and liquid assets position. Policy variables are denoted by the symbol Z in Figure 19.1.

External Variables

The external variables are those that influence the firm's decisions from outside the firm. Generally speaking, the firm is embedded in an industry environment. This industry environment, in turn, is influenced by overall general business conditions. General business conditions exert influences upon particular industries in several ways. Total volume of demand, product prices, labor costs, material costs, money rates, and general expectations are among the industry variables affected by the general business conditions. The symbol X represents the external variables in Figure 19.1.

Performance Variables

The performance variables measure the firm's economic and financial performance. They are represented by a Y in the diagram. The Ys are often called "output variables." The output variables of a financial model would

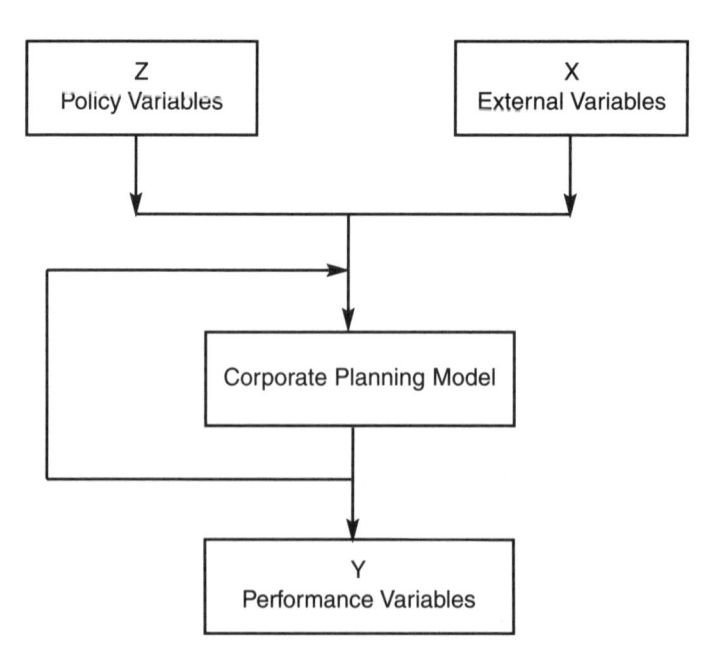

FIGURE 19.1 Flowchart of Variables in a Corporate Model

be the line items of the balance sheet, cash budget, income statement, or statement of changes in financial position. How to define the output variables of the firm will depend on the goals and objectives of the management. They basically indicate how management measures the performance of the organization or some segments of it. Management is likely to be concerned with the firm's level of earnings, growth in earnings, projected earnings, growth in sales, and cash flow.

Frequently when we attempt to set up a financial model we face risk or uncertainty associated with particular projections. In a case such as this, we treat some of these variables, such as sales, as *random variables* with given probability distributions. The inclusion of random variables in the model transforms it from a *deterministic* model to a *risk analysis* model. However, the use of the risk analysis model in practice is rare because of the difficulty involved in modeling and computation.

Input Parameter Values

The model includes various input parameter values. For example, in order to generate a balance sheet, the model needs to input beginning balances of various asset, liability, and equity accounts. These input and parameter values are supplied by management. The ratio between accounts receivable and sales and financial decision variables, such as the maximum desired debt–equity ratio, would be good examples of parameters.

The general process involved in a corporate financial model is presented in Figure 19.2.

MODEL SPECIFICATION

Once we define various variables and input parameters for our financial model, we must specify a set of mathematical and logical relationships linking the input variables to the performance variables. The relationships usually fall into two types of equations: definition equations and behavioral equations. Definitional equations take the form of accounting identities. Behavioral equations involve theories or hypotheses about the behavior of certain economic and financial events. They must be empirically tested and validated before they are incorporated into the financial model.

370   Part IV: Financial Modeling

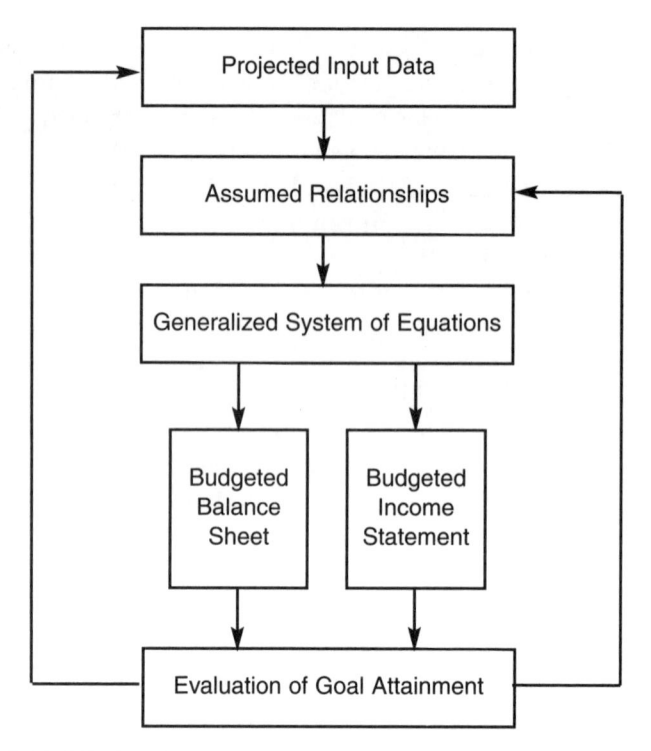

```
Projected Input Data
        ↓
Assumed Relationships
        ↓
Generalized System of Equations
        ↓
Budgeted Balance Sheet  |  Budgeted Income Statement
        ↓
Evaluation of Goal Attainment
```

FIGURE 19.2   Corporate Financial Model

Definitional Equations

Definitional equations are mathematical or accounting definitions. For example,

$$\text{Assets} = \text{Liabilities} + \text{Equity}$$

$$\text{Net income} = \text{Revenues} - \text{Expenses}$$

These definitional equations are fundamental definitions in accounting for the balance sheet and income statement, respectively. Two more examples follow.

$$\text{CASH} = \text{Cash}(-1) + \text{CC} + \text{OCR} + \text{Debt} - \text{CD} - \text{LP}$$

This equation is a typical cash equation in a financial model. It states that ending cash balance (CASH) is equal to the beginning cash balance

[CASH(– 1)] plus cash collections from customers (CC) plus other cash receipts (OCR) plus borrowings (DEBT) minus cash disbursements (CD) minus loan payments (LP).

$$INV = INV(-1) + MAT + DL + OVER - CGS$$

This equation states that ending inventory (INV) is equal to the beginning inventory [INV(– 1)] plus cost of materials used (MAT) plus cost of direct labor (DL) plus manufacturing overhead (OVER) minus the cost of goods sold (CGS).

Behavioral Equations

Behavioral equations describe the behavior of the firm with respect to the specific activities that are subject to empirical testing and validation. The classical demand function in economics is

$$Q = f(P) \text{ or more specifically } Q = a - bP$$

It simply says that the quantity demanded is negatively related to the price. That is, the higher the price, the lower the demand.

However, the firm's sales are more realistically described as follows:

$$SALES = f(P, ADV, I, GNP, Pc, \text{etc.})$$

or, assuming a linear relationship among these variables, we can specify the model as follows:

$$SALES = a + bP + cADV + dI + eGNP + fPc + u$$

which says that the sales are affected by such factors as price (P), advertising expenditures (ADV), consumer income (I), gross national product (GNP), prices of competitive goods (Pc), etc., u is the error term.

With the data on SALES, P, ADV, I, GNP, and Pc, we will be able to estimate parameter values a, b, c, d, e, and f using linear regression. We can test the statistical significance of each of the parameter estimates and evaluate the overall explanatory power of the model, measured by the t-statistic and r^2, respectively.

372   Part IV: Financial Modeling

This way we will be able to identify most influential factors that affect the sales of a particular product. With the best model chosen, management can simulate the effects on sales of alternative pricing and advertising strategies. We can also experiment with alternative assumptions regarding the external economic factors, such as GNP, consumer income, and prices of competitive goods.

Model Structure

A majority of financial models that have been in use are recursive and/or simultaneous models. *Recursive models* are those in which each equation can be solved one at a time by substituting the solution values of the preceding equations into the right-hand side of each equation. An example of a financial model of recursive type follows.

$$
\begin{aligned}
(1)\ \text{SALES} &= A - B*\text{PRICE} + C*\text{ADV} \\
(2)\ \text{REVENUE} &= \text{SALES}*\text{PRICE} \\
(3)\ \text{CGS} &= 0.70*\text{REVENUE} \\
(4)\ \text{GM} &= \text{SALES} - \text{CGS} \\
(5)\ \text{OE} &= \$10{,}000 + 0.2*\text{SALES} \\
(6)\ \text{EBT} &= \text{GM} - \text{OE} \\
(7)\ \text{TAX} &= 0.46*\text{EBT} \\
(8)\ \text{EAT} &= \text{EBT} - \text{TAX}
\end{aligned}
$$

In this example, the selling price (PRICE) and advertising expenses (ADV) are given. A, B, and C are parameters to be estimated, and

$$
\begin{aligned}
\text{SALES} &= \text{Sales volume in units} \\
\text{REVENUE} &= \text{Sales revenue} \\
\text{CGS} &= \text{Cost of goods sold} \\
\text{GM} &= \text{Gross margin} \\
\text{OE} &= \text{Operating expenses} \\
\text{EBT} &= \text{Earnings before taxes} \\
\text{TAX} &= \text{Income taxes} \\
\text{EAT} &= \text{Earnings after taxes}
\end{aligned}
$$

Simultaneous models are frequently found in econometric models that require a higher level of computational methods, such as matrix inversion. An example of a financial model of this type follows.

(1) INT   = 0.10*DEBT
(2) EARN = REVENUE − CGS − OE − INT − TAX − DIV
(3) DEBT = DEBT(−1) + BOW
(4) CASH = CASH(−1) + CC + BOW + EARN − CD − LP
(5) BOW   = MBAL − CASH

Note that earnings (EARN) in equation (2) is defined as sales revenue minus CGS, OE, interest expense (INT), TAX, and dividend payment (DIV). But INT is a percentage interest rate on total debt in equation (1). Total debt in equation (3) is equal to the previous period's debt [DEBT(− 1)] plus new borrowings (BOW). New debt is the difference between a minimum cash balance (MBAL) minus cash. Finally, the ending cash balance in equation (5) is defined as the sum of the beginning balance [(CASH(− 1)], cash collection, new borrowings and earnings *minus* cash disbursements and loan payments of the existing debt (LP). Even though the model presented here is a simple variety, it is still simultaneous in nature, which requires the use of a method capable of solving simultaneous equations. Very few of the financial modeling languages, which are discussed in Chapter 22, have the capability to solve this kind of system.

Decision Rules

The financial model may include basic decision rules specified in a very general form. The decision rules are not written in the form of conventional equations. They are described algebraically using *conditional operators*, which consist of statements of the type: "IF . . . THEN . . . ELSE." For example, suppose that we wish to express the following decision rule: "IF X is greater than 0, then Y is set equal to X multiplied by 5. Otherwise, Y is set equal to 0." We can express this rule as follows:

$$Y = \text{IF } X \text{ GT } 0 \text{ THEN } X*5 \text{ ELSE } 0$$

Suppose the company wishes to develop a financing decision problem that is based upon alternative sales scenarios. To determine an optimal financing alternative, financial managers might want to incorporate some decision rules into the model for a what-if or sensitivity analysis. Some examples of these decision rules are

- The amount of dividends paid are determined on the basis of targeted earnings available to common stockholders and a maximum dividend payout ratio as specified by management.
- After calculating the external funds needed to meet changes in assets as a result of increased sales, dividends, and maturing debt, the amount of long-term debt to be floated is selected on the basis of a prespecified leverage ratio.
- The amount of equity financing (e.g., common stock, preferred stock) to be raised is determined on the basis of funds needed which are not being financed by debt (e.g., bonds payable), but is constrained by the responsibility to meet minimum dividend payments.

In the model we have just described, *simultaneity* is quite evident. A sales figure is used to generate earnings, and this in turn leads to, among other items, the level of long-term debt required. Yet the level of debt affects the interest expense incurred within the current period, and therefore earnings. Furthermore, as earnings are affected, so are the price at which new shares are issued, the number of shares to be sold, and thus earnings per share. Earnings per share then "feeds back" into the stock price calculation.

Lagged Model Structure

Lagged model structure is common in financial modeling. Virtually all balance sheet equations or identities are of this type. For example,

Capital = Capital(−1) + Net income + Contributions − Cash dividends

More interestingly,

$$CC = a*SALES + b*SALES(-1) + c*SALES(-2)$$

where CC = cash collections from customers

a = percent received within the current period

b = percent received with 1-period lag

c = percent received with 2-period lag

The model discussed in Chapter 17 indicates that the realization of cash lags behind credit sales.

COMPREHENSIVE FINANCIAL MODEL

A comprehensive corporate financial model is illustrated in Example 19.1.

EXAMPLE 19.1

A Corporate Financial Model

Balance Sheet Equations

$$\text{Cash}_t = \text{Cash}_{t-1} + \text{Cash receipts}_t - \text{Cash disbursements}_t$$

$$\text{Accounts receivable}_t = (1-a)\,\text{Sales}_t + (1-b-a)\,\text{Sales}_{t-1}$$
$$+ (1-c-b-a)\,\text{Sales}_{t-2}$$

$$\text{Inventory}_t = \text{Inventory}_{t-1} + \text{Inventory purchase}_t$$
$$- \text{Variable cost per unit}) \left(\frac{\text{Sales}_t}{\text{Selling price per unit}}\right)$$

$$\text{Plant} = \text{Initial value}$$

$$\text{Accounts payable}_t = (m)\text{Variable selling/administrative expenses}_{t-1}$$
$$+ (n)\text{Variable selling/administrative expenses}_t$$
$$+ \text{Inventory purchase}_t + \text{Fixed expenses}_t$$

$$\text{Bank loan}_t = \text{Bank loan}_{t-1} + \text{Loan}_t - \text{Loan repayment}_t$$

$$\text{Common stock} = \text{Initial value}$$

$$\text{Retained earnings}_t = \text{Retained earnings}_{t-1} + \text{Net income}_t$$

Income Statement and Cash Flow Equations

$$\text{Cash receipts}_t = (a)\,\text{Sales}_t + (b)\,\text{Sales}_{t-1}$$
$$+ (c)\,\text{Sales}_{t-2} + \text{Loan}_t$$

$$\text{Cash disbursements}_t = \text{Accounts payable}_{t-1} + \text{Interest}_t$$
$$+ \text{Loan payments}_t$$

$$\text{Inventory purchase}_t\,[\geq 0] = \text{Variable cost per unit}$$
$$\left(\frac{\text{Sales}_t + \text{Sales}_{t-1} + \text{Sales}_{t-2} + \text{Sales}_{t-3}}{\text{Selling price per unit}}\right) - \text{Inventory}_{t-1}$$

$$\text{Interest}_t = (i)\,\text{Bank loan}_t$$

$$\text{Variable cost of sales}_t = \text{Sales}_t \left(\frac{\text{Variable cost per unit}}{\text{Selling price per unit}}\right)$$

Variable selling/
administrative expenses$_t$ = (x) Sales$_t$

Net income before taxes$_t$ = Sales$_t$ − Interest$_t$
  + Variable cost of sales$_t$
  + Variable selling/administrative expenses$_t$
  − Fixed expenses$_t$ − Depreciation$_t$

Tax expense$_t$ (≥0) = (r) Net income before taxes$_t$

Net income$_t$ = Net income before taxes$_t$ − Tax expense$_t$

Input Variables (Dollars)

Sales$_{t-1, t-2, t-3}$

Loan$_t$

Loan repayment$_t$

Fixed expense$_t$

Depreciation$_t$

Selling price per unit

Variable cost per unit

Input Parameters

Accounts receivable collection patterns
a—Percent received within current period
b—Percent received with one-period lag
c—Percent received with two-period lag
$a + b + c < 1$

Lag in accounts payable cash flow
m—Percent paid from previous period
n—Percent paid from current period
$m + n = 1$

r = Tax rate

i = Interest rate

x = Ratio of variable selling/administrative expense to sales

---

Initial Values (Dollars)

Plant

Common stock

Cash$_{t-1}$

Sales$_{t-1, t-2}$

Inventory$_{t-1}$

Retained earnings$_{t-1}$

Bank loan$_{t-1}$

Variable selling/administrative expenses$_{t-1}$

Accounts payable$_{t-1}$

Assumptions: time interval equals one month; accounts payable paid in full in next period; no lag between inventory purchase and receipt of goods; and no dividends paid.

CONCLUSION

Financial models are mathematical equations describing financial variables that are used in solving a financial management problem. Simulation models solve "what-if" scenarios indicating the outcome of various alternative policies. Optimization models maximize revenue and minimize cost. In using a model, the variables must be clearly identified and measured. Variables may be controllable or noncontrollable by the financial executive.

20 Techniques to Use to Develop Optimal Budgets

In this chapter we discuss how *optimization* techniques, such as linear programming or goal programming, can be used in developing an optimal budget. For this purpose, we will illustrate with a simple example.

LINEAR PROGRAMMING

Linear programming (LP) is a mathematical technique for finding an optimal resource allocation plan. There are numerous applications of this technique to business planning and decision problems. For our purposes, we will use this technique first to find the optimal product mix and then to develop the budget on the optimal program.

EXAMPLE 20.1

The CSU Company produces and sells two products: snowmobiles (A) and outboard motors (B). The sales price of A is $900 per unit, and that of B is $800 per unit. Production department estimates, based on standard cost data, are that the capacity required for manufacturing one unit of A is 10 hours, while one unit of product B requires 20 hours. The total available capacity for the company is 160 hours. The variable manufacturing cost of A is $300 per unit, and it is paid in cash at the same rate at which the production proceeds. The variable manufacturing cost of B is $600 per unit. These costs are also paid in cash. For simplicity we assume no variable selling costs. Demand forecasts have been developed: The maximum amount of product A that can be sold is six units, whereas that of B is 10 units. Product A is sold with one period of credit, while one half of the sales of product B are received in the same period in which the sales are realized. Additional information:

- The company has existing loans that require $2,100 in payment.
- The company plans to maintain a minimum balance of $500.
- The accounts payable balance of $900 must be paid in cash in this period.

The balance sheet and the fixed overhead budget are given below:

Balance Sheet

Assets				Liabilities		
Current assets				Current liabilities		
Cash	$1,000			Accounts payable		900
Accounts receivable	6,800			Short-term loan		10,000
Inventory	6,000	13,800				10,900
Fixed assets		4,500		Equity		7,400
Total assets		$18,300		Liabilities and equity		$18,300

Fixed Overhead Budget

Expenses involving cash	$1,900
Accruals	800
Depreciation	500
	$3,200

Formulation of the LP Model

We begin the formulation of the model by setting up the objective function, which is to maximize the company's total contribution margin (CM). By definition, CM per unit is the difference between the unit sales price and the variable cost per unit.

	Product	
	A	B
Sales price	$900	$800
Variable cost	300	600
CM per unit	$600	$200

Let us define A to mean the number of units of product A to be produced, and B as the number of units of product B to be produced.

Chapter 20: Techniques to Use to Develop Optimal Budgets   381

Then the total CM is

$$TCM = 600A + 200B$$

Remember that demand forecasts show that there were upper limits of the demand of each product as follows:

$$A \leq 6,\ B \leq 10$$

The planned use of capacity must not exceed the available capacity. Specifically, we need the restriction:

$$10A + 20B \leq 160$$

We also need the cash constraint. The funds tied up in the planned operations must not exceed the available funds. The initial cash balance plus the cash collections of accounts receivable are available for the financing of operations. On the other hand, we need some cash to pay for expenses and maintain a minimum balance. The cash constraint we are developing involves two stages. In the first stage, we observe the cash receipts and disbursements that can be considered fixed regardless of the planned production and sales:

Funds initially available		
Beginning cash balance	$1,000	
Accounts receivable	6,800	7,800
Funds to be disbursed		
Accounts payable	$ 900	
Repayment of loans	2,100	
Fixed cash expenses	1,900	4,900
Difference		2,900
Minimum cash balance required		500
Funds available for the financing of operations		$2,400

In the second stage, we observe the cash receipts and disbursements caused by the planned operations.

First, the total sales revenues:

Product A   900A
Product B   800B

The cash collections from:

Product A (0) 900A = 0
Product B (0.5) 800B = 400B

The variable manufacturing costs are

Product A 300A
Product B 600B

Therefore, the cash disbursements for each are

Product A (1) 300A = 300A
Product B (1) 600B = 600B

Then, the cash constraint is formulated by requiring that the cash disbursements for planned operations must not exceed the cash available plus the cash collections resulting from the operations:

$$300A + 600B \leq 2{,}400 + 0 + 400B$$

This can be simplified to form the following:

$$300A + 200B \leq 2{,}400$$

Using a widely used LP program known as LINDO (Linear Interactive and Discrete Optimization) program (see Figure 20.1), we obtain the following optimal solution:

$$A = 6, B = 3, \text{ and } CM = \$4{,}200$$

Generation of Budgets on the Basis of Optimal Mix

The sales budget would look like this:

Product	Price	Quantity	Revenues
A	$900	6	$5,400
B	800	3	2,400
			$7,800

FIGURE 20.1 LINDO Output

```
: MAX 600A + 200B
> ST
> A<6
> B<10
> 10A+20B<160
> 300A + 200B<2400
> END
: LOOK ALL

MAX     600 A + 200 B
SUBJECT TO
   2)    A < = 6
   3)    B< = 10
   4)    10 A + 20 B < = 160
   5)    300 A + 200 B < = 2400
:GO
   LP OPTIMUM FOUND     AT STEP   2

   OBJECTIVE FUNCTION VALUE

   1)     4200.00000

   VARIABLE    VALUE              REDUCED COST
       A       6.000000             .000000
       B       3.000000             .000000

   ROW           SLACK OR SURPLUS   DUAL PRICES
   2)                 .000000        300.000000
   3)                7.000000          .000000
   4)               40.000000          .000000
   5)                 .000000          1.000000

   NO. ITERATIONS = 2

   DO RANGE (SENSITIVITY) ANALYSIS?    >
   4)                40.000000          .000000
   5)                  .000000         1.000000

   NO. ITERATIONS = 2

     DO RANGE (SENSITIVITY) ANALYSIS? > YES

     RANGES IN WHICH THE BASIS IS UNCHANGED

                OBJ COEFFICIENT RANGES
   VARIABLE    CURRENT      ALLOWABLE     ALLOWABLE
               COEF         INCREASE      DECREASE
       A       600.000000   INFINITY      300.000000
       B       200.000000   200.000000    200.000000

               RIGHTHAND SIDE RANGES
   ROW         CURRENT      ALLOWABLE     ALLOWABLE
               RHS          INCREASE      DECREASE
     2         6.000000     2.000000      2.000000
     3        10.000000     INFINITY      7.000000
     4       160.000000     INFINITY     40.000000
     5      2400.000000   400.000000    600.000000
```

Continued

384 Part IV: Financial Modeling

FIGURE 20.1 (Continued)

Cash Budget

Beginning cash balance			$1,000
Accounts receivable		6,800	
Cash collections from credit sales			
A: (0) 900A = (0) (900) (6)	0		
B: (.5) 800B = 400B = 400 (3)	1,200	1,200	8,000
Total cash available			9,000
Cash disbursements			
Production			
A: 300A = 300 (6)	1,800		
B: 600B =600 (3)	1,800	3,600	
Fixed cash expenses			
Accounts payable balance	900		
Repayment of loan	2,100		
Fixed expenses	1,900	4,900	8,500
Ending cash balance			$ 500

Budgeted Income Statement

Sales	$7,800 (1)	
Less variable costs	3,600 (2)	
Contribution margin (CM)	4,200	
Less fixed expenses		
Depreciation	500	
Payables in cash	1,900	
Accruals	800	3,200
Operating income		$1,000

Supporting calculations:

	A	B	Total
(1)	900 (6) = 5,400	800 (3) = 2,400	7,800
(2)	300 (6) = 1,800	600 (3) = 1,800	3,600

Budgeted Balance Sheet

Assets
Current assets
  Cash $500 (1)
  Accounts receivable   6,600 (2)
  Inventories   6,000 (3)
Total current assets   13,100

Continued

FIGURE 20.1 (Continued)

```
Fixed assets
    Beginning balance                    4,500
    Less accumulated depreciation        (500)      4,000
                                                   $17,100

Liabilities
Current liabilities
    Accounts payable                     800 (4)
    Short-term debt                    7,900 (5)    8,700
Equity                                              8,400 (6)
                                                   $17,100
```

Supporting calculations:

(1) From the cash budget
(2) A: 900 (6) = 5,400
    B: 400 (3) = 1,200
                 6,600
(3) Production and sales were assumed to be equal. This implies there is no change in inventories.
(4) Accrual of fixed costs.
(5) Beginning balance − Repayment = $10,000 − 2,100 = 7,900.
(6) Beginning balance + Net income = $7,400 + 1,000 = 8,400.

Similarly, production and cost budgets can be developed easily. The cash budget, budgeted income statement, and budgeted balance sheet are given in Figure 20.1.

GOAL PROGRAMMING

In the previous section we saw how we can develop a budget based on an optimal program (or product mix), using linear programming. LP, however, has one important drawback; that is, it is limited primarily to solving problems where the objectives of management can be stated in a single goal, such as profit maximization or cost minimization. But management must now deal with multiple goals, which are often incompatible and conflicting with each other. Goal programming (GP) gets around this difficulty. In GP, unlike LP, the objective function may consist of multiple, incommensurable, and conflicting goals. Rather than maximizing or minimizing the objective criterion, the deviations from these set goals are minimized, often based on the priority factors assigned to each goal. The fact that the management will have multiple goals that are in conflict with each other means that instead of attempting to maximize or minimize, management attempts to "satisfize." In other words, they will look for a satisfactory solution rather than an optimal solution.

To illustrate how we can use a GP model to develop an optimal—or, more exactly, satisfactory—budget, we will use the same data as in the linear programming problem.

EXAMPLE 20.2

We will further assume that fixed cash receipts include (a) a new short-term loan amount of $1,200; (b) a dividend payment of $700; and (c) a capital expenditure of $500.

Now the company has two goals, income and working capital. In other words, instead of maximizing net income or contribution margin, the company has a realistic, satisfactory level of income to achieve. On the other hand, the company wants to have a healthy balance sheet, with working capital at least at a given level. (For example, a lending institution might want to see that before approving a line of credit.)

For illustrative purposes, we will make the following specific assumptions:

- The company wants to achieve a return of 20% on equity. That means 20% of $7,400 = $1,480, which translates into a CM of $1,480 + $3,200 (fixed expenses) = $4,680.
- The company wants its working capital balance to be at least $3,000. Currently, it is $2,900 (current assets of $13,800 − current liabilities of $10,900 = $2,900).

These two goals are clearly in conflict. The reason is that we can increase the working capital by increasing cash funds or the inventory. However, the funds in the form of idle cash and the goods in the form of unsold inventories will not increase profits. The first goal can be set up as follows:

$$600A + 200B + d^- - d^+ = \$4{,}680$$

Note that:
Working capital balance = Beginning balance + Net income + Depreciation − Dividends − Capital expenditures = Beginning Balance + (Sales − Variable costs − Fixed costs) − Dividend − Capital Expenditure.

Using this definition, the second goal can be set up as follows:

$$\underbrace{2{,}900 + 900A + 800B}_{\text{Sales}} - \underbrace{300A - 600B}_{\text{Variable costs}} - \underbrace{2{,}700 - 700 - 500}_{\text{Fixed expenses}} \geq 3{,}000$$

This can be simplified to form an inequality:

$$600A + 200B \geq 4{,}000$$

Then our GP model is as follows:

$$\text{Min } D = d^- + d^+$$

subject to:
$$\begin{aligned}
A &&&\leq 6 \\
&& B &\leq 10 \\
10A &+& 20B &\leq 160 \\
300A &+& 200B &\leq 2{,}400 \\
600A &+& 200B &\geq 4{,}000 \\
600A &+& 200B + d^- - d^+ &= 4{,}680 \\
\end{aligned}$$
all variables > 0

This particular problem can be easily solved by LINDO. Figure 20.2 shows the optimal GP solution. Note that in the LINDO output, d^- and d^+ are D_1 and D_2, respectively,

The GP solution is:

$$A = 6,\ B = 3,\ d^- = 480,\ d^+ = 0,$$

which means that the income target was underachieved by $480. Just as in the case of LP, financial executives will be able to develop the budget using this optimal solution in exactly the same manner as presented in the previous section. More sophisticated GP models can be developed with "preemptive" priority factors assigned to multiple goals, which is beyond the scope of this book. (For an advanced treatment of this technique for financial modeling, see James Mao, *Quantitative Analysis of Financial Decisions*, Macmillan Publishing Co., New York, 1969.)

FIGURE 20.2 LINDO Output Showing the GP Solution

```
MIN     D1 + D2
SUBJECT TO
   2)      A < = 6
   3)      B < = 10
   4)      10 A + 20 B < = 160
   5)      300 A + 200 B < = 2400
   6)      600 A + 200 B > = 4000
   7)      D1 - D2 + 600 A + 200 B = 4680
END

:GO
   LP OPTIMUM FOUND AT STEP     4

            OBJECTIVE FUNCTION VALUE
   1)     480.000000

   VARIABLE            VALUE           REDUCED COST
        D1           480.000000             .000000
        D2             .000000             2.000000
         A            6.000000              .000000
         B            3.000000              .000000

   ROW       SLACK OR SURPLUS       DUAL PRICES
    2)             .000000           300.000000
    3)            7.000000              .000000
    4)           40.000000              .000000
    5)             .000000             1.000000
    6)          200.000000              .000000
    7)             .000000            - 1.000000

   NO. ITERATIONS =     4

   DO RANGE (SENSITIVITY) ANALYSIS? >
   NO. ITERATIONS= 4

   DO RANGE (SENSITIVITY) ANALYSIS? > YES

      RANGES IN WHICH THE BASIS IS UNCHANGED
                    OBJ COEFFICIENT RANGES
   VARIABLE    CURRENT      ALLOWABLE      ALLOWABLE
                COEF        INCREASE       DECREASE
        D1    1.000000      INFINITY       1.000000
        D2    1.000000      INFINITY       2.000000
         A     .000000      300.000000     INFINITY
         B     .000000      200.000000     200.000000
                    RIGHTHAND SIDE RANGES
   ROW       CURRENT       ALLOWABLE      ALLOWABLE
              RHS          INCREASE       DECREASE
    2       6.000000       1.600000        .666667
    3      10.000000       INFINITY       7.000000
    4     160.000000       INFINITY      40.000000
    5    2400.000000      400.000000    200.000000
    6    4000.000000      200.000000      INFINITY
    7    4680.000000       INFINITY
```

Continued

FIGURE 20.2 (*Continued*)

ROW	CURRENT RHS	ALLOWABLE INCREASE	ALLOWABLE DECREASE
		RIGHTHAND SIDE RANGES	
2	6.000000	1.600000	.666667
3	10.000000	INFINITY	7.000000
4	160.000000	INFINITY	40.000000
5	2400.000000	400.000000	200.000000
6	4000.000000	200.000000	INFINITY
7	4680.000000	INFINITY	480.000000

CONCLUSION

Thus far we have seen how optimization techniques such as LP and GP can help develop an overall optimal plan for the company. However, in the Naylor study it was found that only 4% of the users of corporate planning models employed an optimization-type model. The disadvantage with using optimization models to develop optimal plans for a firm as a whole is that problems are difficult to define and the firm has multiple objectives.

It is not easy to develop an optimization model that incorporates performance variables such as ROI, profits, market share, and cash flow as well as the line items of the income statement, balance sheet, and cash flow statement. Despite the availability of goal programming that handles multiple objectives, the possibility of achieving global optimization is very rare at the corporate level. The usage tends to be limited to submodels and suboptimization within the overall corporate level. Thus, the use of these models in corporate modeling will probably continue to be focused at the operational level. Production planning and scheduling, advertising, resource allocation, and many other problem areas will continue to be solved with huge success by these techniques.

21
How to Use Spreadsheet and Financial Modeling Languages

Financial forecasting and planning can be done using a personal computer with a powerful spreadsheet program, such as Microsoft Excel, or it can be done using a specific financial modeling language such as IFPS (Interactive Financial Planning System), usually done at a terminal hooked up to a mainframe. Below is a list of the programs that are widely available for use by financial planners.

Spreadsheet Programs

- Lotus 1-2-3
- Quattro Pro
- Microsoft Excel

Financial Modeling Languages

- IFPS
- SIMPLAN
- EXPRESS
- Venture
- Encore! Plus
- Micro FCS

In this chapter we illustrate how to use the more popular programs.

USE OF A SPREADSHEET PROGRAM FOR FINANCIAL MODELING

In this section we discuss how we can use spreadsheet programs such as Excel to develop a financial model. The following problems are illustrated:

- Two examples of projecting an income statement:
  —Contribution format
  —Traditional format
- Projecting balance sheet—the percent-of-sales method
- Forecasting financial distress with Z score

EXAMPLE 21.1

Projecting Income Statement—Contribution Format
Sales for 1st month = $60,000
Cost of sales = 42% of sales, all variable
Operating expenses = $10,000 fixed plus 5% of sales
Taxes = 46% of net income
Sales increase by 5% each month

Based on this information, we will create a spreadsheet for the contribution income statement for the next 12 months and in total.

EXAMPLE 21.2

Forecasting Income Statement—Traditional Format
Your client, the Sigma Company, has asked you to prepare a 3-year projection of net income using the following information:

1. 2000 base year amounts are as follows:

Sales revenues	$4,500,000
Cost of sales	2,900,000
Selling and administrative expenses	800,000
Net income before taxes	800,000

2. Use the following assumptions:
   - Sales revenues increase by 6% in 2001, 7% in 2002, and 8% in 2003.
   - Cost of sales increase by 5% each year.
   - Selling and administrative expenses increase only 1% in 2001 and will remain at the 200 level thereafter.
   - The income tax rate is 46%.

Spreadsheet Solution

	1	2	3	4	5	6	7	8	9	10	11	12	Total	Percent
Sales	$60,000	$63,000	$66,150	$69,458	$72,930	$76,577	$80,406	$84,426	$88,647	$93,080	$97,734	$102,620	$955,028	100%
Less: VC														
Cost of sales	$25,200	$26,460	$27,783	$29,172	$30,631	$32,162	$33,770	$35,459	$37,232	$39,093	$41,048	$43,101	$401,112	42%
Operating ex.	$ 3,000	$ 3,150	$ 3,308	$ 3,473	$ 3,647	$ 3,829	$ 4,020	$ 4,221	$ 4,432	$ 4,654	$ 4,887	$ 5,131	$ 47,751	5%
CM	$31,800	$33,390	$35,060	$36,812	$38,653	$40,586	$42,615	$44,746	$46,983	$49,332	$51,799	$54,389	$506,165	53%
Less: FC Op. expenses	$10,000	$10,000	$10,000	$10,000	$10,000	$10,000	$10,000	$10,000	$10,000	$10,000	$10,000	$10,000	$120,000	13%
Net income	$21,800	$23,390	$25,060	$26,812	$28,653	$30,586	$32,615	$34,746	$36,983	$39,332	$41,799	$44,389	$386,165	40%
Less: Tax	$10,028	$10,759	$11,527	$12,334	$13,180	$14,069	$15,003	$15,983	$17,012	$18,093	$19,227	$20,419	$177,636	19%
NI after tax	$11,772	$12,631	$13,532	$14,479	$15,473	$16,516	$17,612	$18,763	$19,971	$21,239	$22,571	$23,970	$208,529	22%

A spreadsheet for the income statement for the next 3 years follows.

Sigma Company
3-Year Income Projections
2000–2003

	2000	2001	2002	2003
Sales	4,500,000	4,770,000	5,103,900	5,512,212
Cost of sales	2,900,000	3,045,000	3,197,250	3,357,113
Gross profit	1,600,000	1,725,000	1,906,650	2,155,100
S & A	800,000	808,000	816,080	824,241
Net income before tax	800,000	917,000	1,090,570	1,330,859
Tax	368,000	421,820	501,662	612,19S
Net income after tax	432,000	495,180	588,908	718,664

EXAMPLE 21.3

Projecting Balance Sheet—Percent-of-Sales Method

To illustrate how Excel can be used to determine the amount of external financing needed using the percent-of-sales method, we will use the same example discussed in Chapter 16. The completed spreadsheet solution follows.

Pro-Forma Balance Sheet
(in Millions of Dollars)

	Present (20X1)	Percent of Sales (20X1) Sales = $20	Projected (20X2) Sales = $24
Assets			
Current assets	2	10	2.4
Fixed assets	4	20	4.8
Total assets	6		7.2
Liabilities and Stockholders' Equity			
Current liabilities	2	10	2.4 •
Long-term debt	2.5	n.a.	2.5
Total liabilities	4.5		4.9
Common stock	0.1	n.a.	0.1
Paid-in-capital	0.2	n.a.	0.2
Retained earnings	1.2		1.92[a]

Total equity	1.5		2.22
Total liabilities and stockholders' equity	6	7.12	Total financing provided
			External financing needed
		0.08	needed[b]
		7.2	Total

[a] 20X2 Retained earnings = 20X1 Retained earnings + Projected net income − Cash dividends paid

$$= \$1.2 + 5\%(\$24) - 40\%[5\%(\$24)]$$
$$= \$1.2 + \$1.2 - \$0.48 = \$2.4 - \$0.48 = \$1.92$$

[b] External financing needed-projected total assets − (Projected total liabilities + Projected equity) = $7.2 − ($4.9 + $2.22) = $7.2 − $7.12 = $0.08

FORECASTING BUSINESS FAILURES WITH Z SCORES

There is an increasing number of bankruptcies. Will the company of the stock you own be among them? Will your major customers or suppliers go bankrupt? What are the warning signs and what can be done to avoid corporate failure?

Bankruptcy for a particular company is the final declaration of the inability to sustain current operation given the current debt obligations. The majority of firms require loans and therefore increase their liabilities during their operations in order to expand, improve, or even just survive. The "degree" to which a firm has current debt in excess of assets is the most common factor in bankruptcy.

If you can predict with reasonable accuracy ahead of time (a year or two) that the company you are interested in is developing financial distress, you could better protect yourself. For example, loan institutions face a major difficulty in calculating the "degree of debt relative to assets" or the likelihood of bankruptcy, yet this is precisely what these institutions must accomplish prior to issuing a financial loan to a firm.

Need of Prediction

Various groups of business people can reap significant rewards and benefits from a *predictive* model for their own purposes. For example:

1. *Merger analysis.* The predictive model can help identify potential problems with a merger candidate.
2. *Loan credit analysis.* Bankers and lenders can use it to determine if they should extend a loan. Other creditors such as vendors have used it to determine whether to extend credit.
3. *Investment analysis.* The model can help an investor selecting stocks of potentially troubled companies.
4. *Auditing analysis.* External CPA auditors are able to use this type of model to assess whether the client will continue as a going concern.
5. *Legal analysis.* Those investing or giving credit to your company may sue for losses incurred. The model can help in your company's defense.

Are there early warning systems to detect the likelihood of bankruptcy? Investment bankers, financial analysts, security analysts, auditors, and others have used financial ratios as an indication of the financial strength of a company. However, financial ratio analysis is limited because the methodology is basically *univariate*. Each ratio is examined in isolation and it is up to the financial analyst to use professional judgment to determine whether a set of financial ratios are developing into a meaningful analysis.

In order to overcome the shortcomings of financial ratio analysis, it is necessary to combine mutually exclusive ratios into groups to develop a meaningful predictive model. *Regression analysis* and *multiple discriminant analysis (MDA)* are two statistical techniques that have been used to predict the financial strength of a company.

Using a blend of the traditional financial ratios and multiple discriminant analysis, Altman* developed a bankruptcy prediction model that produces a Z score as follows:

$$Z = 1.2*X_1 + 1.4*X_2 + 3.3*X_3 + 0.6*X_4 + 0.999*X_5$$

where
X_1 = Working capital/Total assets
X_2 = Retained earnings/Total assets
X_3 = Earnings before interest and taxes (EBIT)/Total assets
X_4 = Market value of equity/Book value of debt
  (or Net worth for *private firms*)
X_5 = Sales/Total assets

---

*Edward I. Altman, *Corporate Financial Distress* (New York: John Wiley & Sons, 1983).

Altman established the following guideline for classifying firms:

Z score	Probability of Short-term Illiquidity
1.8 or less	Very high
1.81–2.99	Not sure
3.0 or higher	Unlikely

The Z score is known to be about 90% accurate in forecasting business failure 1 year in the future and about 80% accurate in forecasting it 2 years in the future. It has been found that with the many important changes in reporting standards since the late 1960s, the Z-score model is somewhat out of date for the 2000s. A second-generation model known as *Zeta Analysis* adjusts for these changes, primarily the capitalization of financial leases. The resulting Zeta discriminant model is extremely accurate for up to 5 years before failure. Because this analysis is a proprietary one, the exact weights for the model's seven variables cannot be specified here. The new study resulted in the following variables explaining corporate failure:

X_1 = Return on assets: Earnings before interest and taxes to total assets.

X_2 = Stability of earnings: Measure by the "normalized measure of the standard error of estimate around a 10-year trend in X_1."

X_3 = Debt service: Earnings before interest and taxes to total interest payments.

X_4 = Cumulative profitability: Retained earnings to total assets.

X_5 = Liquidity: Current assets to current liabilities.

X_6 = Capitalization: Equity to total capital.

X_7 = Size measured by the firm's total assets.

Example

A spreadsheet model has been developed to calculate the Z model prediction of bankruptcy using data extracted from *Moody's* and *Standard & Poor's*. Navistar International (formerly International Harvester) has been trying to recover from previous bankruptcy and is used for illustrative purposes. Financial data have been collected for the period 1979 through 1998. Table 21.1 shows a spreadsheet of the 20-year financial history and the Z scores of Navistar International. Figure 21.1 displays a Z score graph for the company.

The graph shows that Navistar International performed at the edge of the ignorance zone ("unsure area") for the year 1979. Since 1980,

TABLE 21.1 Navistar International–NAV (NYSE) Z Score: Prediction of Financial Distress

	Balance Sheet					Income Statement		Stock Data	Calculation					Miscellaneous		
Year	Current Assets (CA)	Total Assets (TA)	Current Liability (CL)	Total Liability (TL)	Retained Earnings (RE)	Working Capital (WC)	Sales	EBIT	Market Value or Net Worth (MKT-NW)	WC/TA (X1)	RE/TA (X2)	EBIT/TA (X3)	MKT-NW/TL (X4)	Sales/TA (X5)	Z Score	Graph Top Gray	Graph Bottom Gray
---	---	---	---	---	---	---	---	---	---	---	---	---	---	---	---	---	---
1979	3266	5247	1873	3048	1505	1393	8426	719	1122	0.2655	0.2868	.1370	0.3681	1.6059	3.00	2.99	1.81
1980	3427	5843	2433	3947	1024	994	6000	−402	1147	0.1701	0.1753	−0.0688	0.2906	1.0269	1.42	2.99	1.81
1981	2672	5346	1808	3864	600	864	7018	−16	376	0.1616	0.1122	−0.0030	0.0973	1.3128	1.71	2.99	1.81
1982	1656	3699	1135	3665	−1078	521	4322	−1274	151	0.1408	−0.2914	−0.3444	0.0412	1.1684	−0.18	2.99	1.81
1983	1388	3362	1367	3119	−1487	21	3600	−231	835	0.0062	−0.4423	−0.0687	0.2677	1.0708	0.39	2.99	1.81
1984	1412	3249	1257	2947	−1537	155	4861	120	575	0.0477	−0.4731	0.0369	0.1951	1.4962	1.13	2.99	1.81
1985	1101	2406	988	2364	−1894	113	3508	247	570	0.0470	−0.7872	0.1027	0.2411	1.4580	0.89	2.99	1.81
1986	698	1925	797	1809	−1889	−99	3357	163	441	−0.0514	−0.9813	0.0847	0.2438	1.7439	0.73	2.99	1.81
1987	785	1902	836	1259	−1743	−51	3530	219	1011	−0.0268	−0.9164	0.1151	0.8030	1.8559	1.40	2.99	1.81
1988	1280	4037	1126	1580	150	154	4082	451	1016	0.0381	0.0372	0.1117	0.6430	1.0111	1.86	2.99	1.81
1989	986	3609	761	1257	175	225	4241	303	1269	0.0623	0.0485	0.0840	1.0095	1.1751	2.20	2.99	1.81
1990	2663	3795	1579	2980	81	1084	3854	111	563	0.2856	0.0213	0.0292	0.1889	1.0155	1.60	2.99	1.81
1991	2286	3443	1145	2866	332	1141	3259	232	667	0.3314	0.0964	0.0674	0.2326	0.9466	1.84	2.99	1.81
1992	2472	3627	1152	3289	93	1320	3875	−145	572	0.3639	0.0256	−0.0400	0.1738	1.0684	1.51	2.99	1.81
1993	2672	5060	1338	4285	−1588	1334	4696	−441	1765	0.2636	−0.3138	−0.0872	0.4119	0.9281	0.76	2.99	1.81
1994	2870	5056	1810	4239	−1538	1060	5337	158	1469	0.2097	−0.3042	0.0313	0.3466	1.0556	1.19	2.99	1.81
1995	3310	5566	1111	4696	−1478	2199	6342	262	966	0.3951	−0.2655	0.0471	0.2057	1.1394	1.52	2.99	1.81
1996	2999	5326	820	4410	−1431	2179	5754	105	738	0.4091	−0.2687	0.0197	0.1673	1.0804	1.36	2.99	1.81
1997	3203	5516	2416	4496	−1301	787	6371	272	1374	0.1427	−0.2359	0.0439	0.3055	1.1550	1.32	2.99	1.81
1998	3715	6178	3395	5409	−1160	320	7885	410	1995	0.0518	−0.1878	0.0664	0.3688	1.2763	1.51	2.99	1.81

Note: (1) To calculate "Z" score for private firms, enter Net Worth in the MKT-NW column. (For public-held companies, enter Market Value of Equity).
(2) EBIT = Earnings Before Interest and Taxes.

398

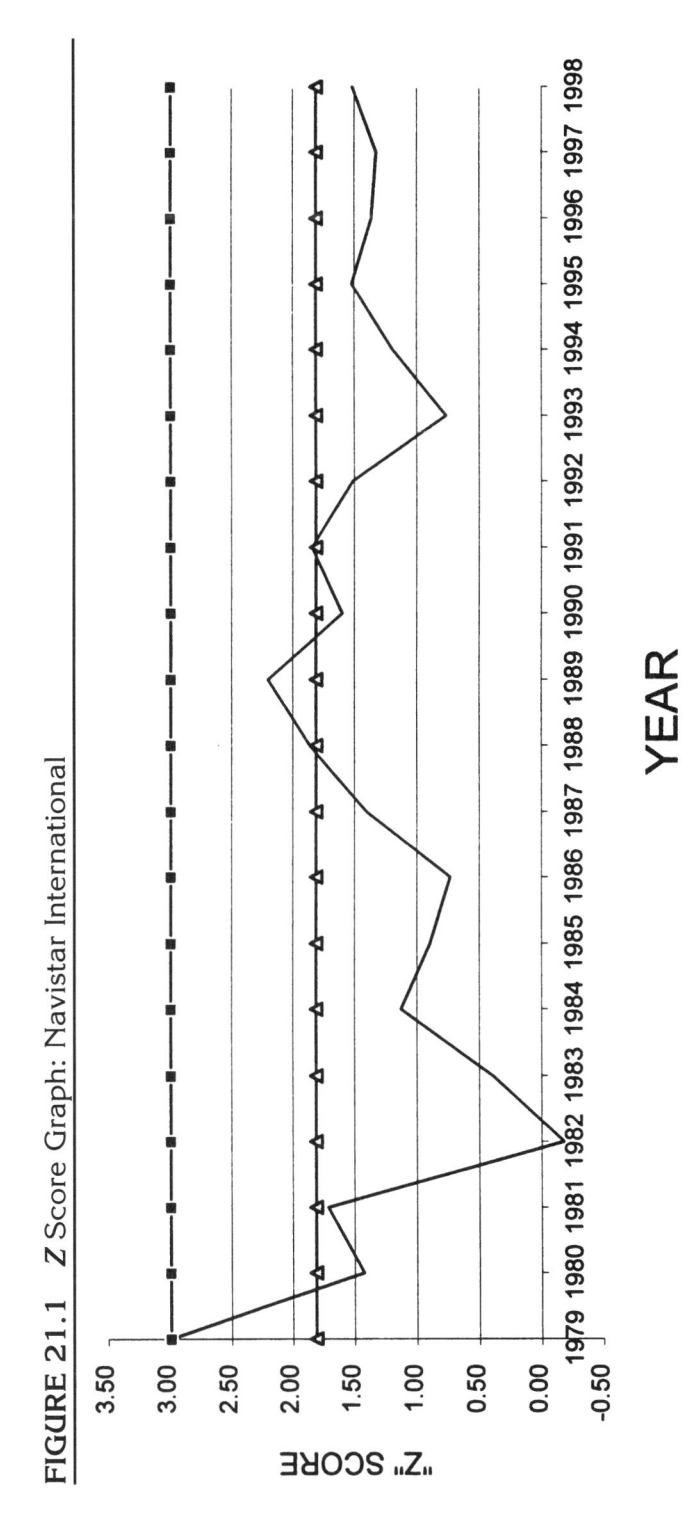

FIGURE 21.1 Z Score Graph: Navistar International

though, the company started signaling a sign of failure. By selling stock and assets, however, the firm managed to survive. Since 1983, the company showed an improvement in its Z scores, although the firm continually scored on the danger zone.

We note, however, that the 1994 Z score of 1.19 is in the high probability range of < 1.81, and yet it is above the firm's norm or average over the past decade. Based on this assumption, it seems unlikely that Navistar will go bankrupt by 1995. This is not to say that if their financial position erodes below the firm's norm that the prediction for beyond 1995 might change. However, the 1995–1998 Z scores appear to be on the rise, indicating that Navistar is improving its financial position and becoming a more viable business.

FINANCIAL MODELING LANGUAGES

There are many user-oriented modeling languages specifically designed for corporate planners, controllers, treasurers, budget preparers, managerial accountants, and business managers. These languages do not require any knowledge of computer programming languages (such as Basic, Fortran, Pascal, and Cobol) on the part of the financial officer; they are all English-like languages. Among the well-known system packages are:

- IFPS (Interactive Financial Planning System)
- SIMPLAN
- EXPRESS
- Encore! Plus
- Budget Maestro
- Micro FCS

In the following sections, each of the two more widely used languages (IFPS and SIMPLAN) are discussed and illustrated. Then the next most popular (EXPRESS and Encore! Plus) are covered briefly.

INTERACTIVE FINANCIAL PLANNING SYSTEM (IFPS)

IFPS is a multipurpose interactive financial modeling system that supports and facilitates building, solving, and asking "what if" questions of financial mod-

Chapter 21: Spreadsheet and Financial Modeling Languages   401

els. The output from an IFPS model is in the format of a spreadsheet, that is, a matrix or table in which:

- The rows represent user-specified variables, such as market share, sales, growth in sales, unit price, gross margin, variable cost, contribution margin, fixed cost, net income, net present value, internal rate of return, and earnings per share.
- The columns designate a sequence of user-specified time periods, such as month, quarter, year, and total, and percentages or divisions.
- The entries in the body of the table display the values taken by the model variable *over time* or *by segments* of the firm, such as divisions, product lines, sales territories, and departments.

IFPS offers the following key features:

- Like other special-purpose modeling languages, IFPS is like English. That means that without an extensive knowledge of computer programming, the financial officer can build financial models and use them for "what if" scenarios and managerial decisions.
- IFPS has a collection of built-in financial functions that perform the calculations, such as net present value (NPV), internal rate of return (IRR), loan amortization schedules, and depreciation alternatives.
- IFPS also has a collection of built-in mathematical and statistical functions, such as regression, linear interpolation, polynomial autocorrelation, and moving average functions.
- IFPS supports use of leading and/or lagged variables that are commonly used in financial modeling. For example, cash collections lag behind credit sales of prior periods.
- IFPS also supports deterministic and probabilistic modeling. It offers a variety of functions for sampling from probability distributions, such as uniform, normal, bivariate normal, and user-described empirical distributions.
- IFPS is nonprocedural in nature. This means that the relationships, logic, and data used to calculate the various values in the output do not have to be arranged in any particular top-to-bottom order in an IFPS model. IFPS automatically detects and solves a system of two or more linear or nonlinear equations.
- IFPS has extensive editing capabilities that include adding statements to and deleting statements from a model, making changes in existing statements, and making copies of parts or all of a model.

- IFPS supports sensitivity analysis by providing the following solution options:

  —What if. The IFPS lets you specify one or more changes in the relationships, logic, data, and/or parameter values in the existing model and recalculates the model to show the impact of these changes on the performance measures.

  —Goal seeking. In the goal-seeking mode, the IFPS can determine what change would have to take place in the value of a specified variable in a specified time period to achieve a specified value for another variable. For example, the user can ask the system to answer the question, "What would the unit sales price have to be for the project to achieve a target return on investment of 20%?"

  —Sensitivity. This command is employed to determine the effect of a specified variable on one or more other variables. The sensitivity command is similar to the what-if command, but it produces a convenient, model-produced tabular summary for each new alternative value of the specified variable.

  —Analyze. The analyze command examines in detail those variables that have contributed to the value of a specified variable and their values.

  —Impact. The impact command is used to determine the effect on a specified variable of a series of percentage changes in one or more specified variables.

  —IFPS/optimum. The IFPS/optimum routine is employed to answer questions of the "What is the best?" type rather than "What if."
- Routine graphic output.
- Interactive color graphics.
- Data files that can contain both data and relationships.
- A consolidation capability that lets the user produce composite reports from two or more models.
- Extraction of data from existing non-IFPS data files and placement of them in IFPS-compatible data files.
- Operates on all major mainframes and microcomputers.

Prospective users of IFPS are encouraged to refer to the following sources from Comshare (Ann Arbor, Michigan):

Chapter 21: Spreadsheet and Financial Modeling Languages 403

- *IFPS Cases and Models*
- *IFPS Tutorial*
- *IFPS User's Manual*
- *IFPS/Personal User's Manual*
- *IFPS University Seminar*
- *Comprehensive Fundamentals of IFPS*
- *Papers Available from the Comshare University Support Programs*

In the following section we present step-by-step instructions on how to build a model using IFPS.

EXAMPLE 21.4

The following case illustrates the use of IFPS.*

The MCL Corporation is considering diversifying and wishes to evaluate the profitability of the new venture over the next 2 years. A quarterly profit picture is desired. Marketing research has provided the following information: (1) The total market for the product will be 7,000 units at the start of production and will grow at the rate of 1% per quarter; (2) MCL's initial share of the market is 11%, and this is expected to grow at the rate of 0.5% per quarter if intense marketing efforts are maintained; (3) the selling price is expected to be $2.50 per unit the first year and $2.65 the following year; (4) the standard cost system has produced the following estimates: (a) selling expenses, $0.233 per unit; (b) labor cost, $0.61 per unit; and (c) raw materials, $0.42 per unit; (5) general and administrative expenses are estimated to be $450 in the first quarter, with a quarterly growth rate of 1%; and (6) setup costs for the line are $3,500.

First, log on to your computer and access IFPS.

1. To establish the model:

INTERACTIVE PLANNING SYSTEM

ENTER NAME OF FILE CONTAINING MODELS AND REPORTS
? PROFIT

FILE PROFIT NOT FOUND - NEW FILE WILL BE CREATED
READY FOR EXECUTIVE COMMAND
? MODEL EXAMPLE

---

*This example was adapted from Comshare, IFPS University Seminar, 1984, pp. 7–18 with permission.

404 Part IV: Financial Modeling

BEGIN ENTERING NEW MODEL
? AUTO 10, 5

10? (Model is entered)

2. The model is entered as listed here (from 10 on down):

```
10 COLUMNS 1-8,2001,2004, GROWTH
15 *EXAMPLE OF IFPS
20 *
25 **
30 PERIODS 4
35 * SALES DATA AND PROJECTIONS
40 PRICE=2.5 FOR 4, 2.65
45 MARKET SHARE = .11,PREVIOUS MARKET SHARE + .005
50 TOTAL MARKET = 7000, PREVIOUS TOTAL MARKET*1.01
55 SALES VOLUME = L45*L50
60 * PREVIOUS CALCULATIONS
65 SALES REVENUE = SALES VOLUME*PRICE
70 NET INCOME = SALES REVENUE – TOTAL EXPENSES
75 * COSTS
80 UNIT SELLING COSTS = .233
85 UNIT LABOR COST = .61
90 UNIT MATERIAL COST = .42
95 UNIT COST = SUM(UNIT SELLING COST THRU UNIT MATERIAL COST)
100 VARIABLE COST = UNIT COST*SALES VOLUME
105 ADMIN EXPENSES=450,PREVIOUS ADMIN EXPENSES*1.01
110 TOTAL EXPENSES=VARIABLE COST+ADMIN EXPENSES
115 *PERFORMANCE MEASURES
120 INITIAL INVESTMENT= 3500,0
125 DISCOUNT RATE =.12
130 PRESENT VALUE=NPVC(NET INCOME, DISCOUNT RATE, INITIAL
    INVESTMENT)
14O RATE OF RETURN=IRR(NET INCOME, INITIAL INVESTMENT)
145 *
150 COLUMN 2000 FOR L55,L65,L70,L100,L105,L110,L120= '
155                    SUM(C1 THRU C4)
160 COLUMN 2004 FOR L55,L65,L70,L100,L105,L110,L120= '
165                    SUM(CD5 THRU C8)
170 COLUMN GROWTH FOR L55,L65,L70,L100,L105,L110,L120='
175                    100*(C10-C9)/C9
END OF MODEL
?
```

3. The model is displayed:

Once the model is complete, the solution can be displayed by using a sequence of commands like the ones that follow. A brief discussion of each command follows the illustration.

180? SOLVE

MODEL NEWPROD VERSION OF 12/20/00 16 38 — 11 COLUMNS 17 VARIABLES

ENTER SOLVE OPTIONS

? COLUMNS 1 2000,5-8, 2001,GROWTH

? WIDTH 72, 16, 8

? ALL

ALL instructs IFPS to print the values of all variables.

```
                                    IFPS Output
                         2000      5        6        7        8       2001    GROWTH
EXAMPLE OF IFPS
*
   SALES DATA AND PROJECTIONS
PRICE                              2.650    2.650    2.650    2.650
MARKET SHARE                       .1300    .1350    .1400    .1450
TOTAL MARKET                       7284     7357     7431     7505
SALES VOLUME             3341      946.9    993.2    1040     1088    4069    21.76
   PREVIOUS CALCULATIONS
SALES REVENUE            8354      2509     2632     2757     2884    10782   29.07
NET INCOME               2306      845.1    904.6    965.2    1027    3742    62.25
   COSTS
UNIT SELLING COST                  .2330    .2330    .2330    .2330
UNIT LABOR COST                    .6100    .6100    .6100    .6100
UNIT MATERIAL COST                 .4200    .4200    .4200    .4200
UNIT COST                          1.263    1.263    1.263    1.263
VARIABLE COST            4220      1196     1254     1314     1374    5139    21.76
ADMIN EXPENSES           1827      468.3    473.0    477.7    482.5   1901    4.060
TOTAL EXPENSES           6047      1664     1727     1792     1857    7040    16.41
   PERFORMANCE MEASURES
INITIAL                  3500      0        0        0        0       0       -100
   INVESTMENT
DISCOUNT RATE                      .1200    .1200    .1200    .1200
PRESENT VALUE                      −623.5   139.7    931.3    1750
RATE OF RETURN                              .1676    .3988    .5812
```

4. "What if" analysis:

Instead of merely solving a model as it is, WHAT IF command can be used to determine the effect of changes in the definitions of variables in the model. The examples that follow show how these questions can be answered.

Case	Question
1	What if the total market size starts out at 6,000 units instead of 7,000, but grows by 5% per quarter instead of 1%?
2	What if the selling price is $2.70 in the second year instead of $2.65 (and total market follows the original assumptions)?
3	What if, in addition to price being $2.70 in 2001, unit material cost is 3 cents higher than expected in both years?

406   Part IV: Financial Modeling

Note that Cases 1 and 2 are independent, while Case 3 builds on the changes made in Case 2. To handle both kinds of situations, two different WHAT IF commands are available:

WHAT IF Enables the user to modify temporarily as many individual model statements as desired to determine the effect on the solution. Each WHAT IF erases the assumptions made by the previous one.

WHAT IF CONTINUE Since each WHAT IF normally starts from the base case, this command makes possible successive, cumulative, WHAT IF statements.

In the printout that follows, the user has asked to see only selected variables. In Case 1, individual variable names, separated by commas, are used. In Case 2, model line numbers have been used instead. Case 3 illustrates the use of THRU to print an inclusive list of variables.

The SOLVE OPTIONS entered earlier to specify columns and page layout remain in effect through the modeling session.

?WHAT IF

WHAT IF CASE 1
ENTER STATEMENTS

? TOTAL MARKET = 6000, PREVIOUS TOTAL MARKET * 1.05
? SOLVE

ENTER SOLVE OPTIONS

? NET INCOME, PRESENT WORTH, RATE OF RETURN

***** WHAT IF CASE 1 *****

1 WHAT IF STATEMENT PROCESSED

	2000	5	6	7	8	2001	GROWTH
NET INCOME	1941	846.7	960.9	1084	1215	4107	111.5
PRESENT WORTH		−966.3	−155.6	733.1	1702		
RATE OF RETURN			.0703	.3240	.5318		

ENTER SOLVE OPTIONS

? WHAT IF

WHAT IF CASE 2

ENTER STATEMENTS

? PRICE = 2.5 FOR 4, 2.70

? SOLVE

ENTER SOLVE OPTIONS

? L70, L130, L140

***** WHAT IF CASE 2 *****

1 WHAT IF STATEMENT PROCESSED

	2000	5	6	7	8	2001	GROWTH
NET INCOME	2306	892.5	954.3	1017	1081	3945	71.07
PRESENT WORTH		−582.4	−222.7	1057	1919		
RATE OF RETURN			.1952	.4333	.6198		

ENTER SOLVE OPTIONS

? WHAT IF CONTINUE

WHAT IF CASE 3

ENTER STATEMENTS

? UNIT MATERIAL COST = UNIT MATERIAL COST + .03

? SOLVE

ENTER SOLVE OPTIONS

? UNIT MATERIAL COST THRU VARIABLE COST

***** WHAT IF CASE 3 *****

2 WHAT IF STATEMENTS PROCESSED

	2000	5	6	7	8	2001	GROWTH
UNIT MATERIAL COST		.4500	.4500	.4500	.4500		
UNIT COST		1.293	1.293	1.293			
VARIABLE COST	4320	1224	1284	1345	1407	5261	21.76

Summary of What if Analysis

Case 1	If the total market size starts out at 6,000 units and grows by 5% per quarter, then net income will go up by 111.5%.
Case 2	If the selling price is $2.70 in the second year, then the net income will go up by 71.07%.
Case 3	If, in addition to price being $2.70 in 2001, unit material cost is 3 cents higher than expected in both years, then the variable cost will go up by 21.76%.

5. Goal-seeking analysis:

The GOAL SEEKING command allows the user to work backward. That is, the user tells IFPS what assumption can be adjusted and what objective is to be sought. IFPS then solves the model repetitively until it finds the value that yields the desired objective. To illustrate the use of this command, consider the following two situations.

408   Part IV: Financial Modeling

Case	Question
1	Market share estimates could be less than originally expected. How low could it be and still provide first-quarter net income of $700 and 3% more in each subsequent quarter?
2	The required initial investment might be larger than originally expected. How much larger could it be and still permit a 25% return over the 8-quarter horizon?

The first question is really asking what market share would have to be in each column in order to achieve a certain net income in the same column. The second question asks what investment has to be in column 1 to produce a certain rate of return in column 8.

As shown in the following example, the second question is handled by enclosing the column number in parentheses after the variable name. The variable is then said to be "subscripted."

The command BASE MODEL is issued before GOAL SEEKING. Without this command, modifications made by the last WHAT IF command would still be in effect.

ENTER SOLVE OPTIONS

? BASE MODEL
? GOAL SEEKING

GOAL SEEKING CASE 1
ENTER NAME OF VARIABLE TO BE ADJUSTED TO ACHIEVE PERFORMANCE
? MARKET SHARE

ENTER COMPUTATIONAL STATEMENT FOR PERFORMANCE

? NET INCOME = 700, PREVIOUS NET INCOME * 1.03

***** GOAL SEEKING CASE 1 *****

	2000	5	6	7	8	2001	GROWTH
MARKET SHARE		.1243	.1259	.1274	.1291		

ENTER SOLVE OPTIONS

? NET INCOME, PRESENT WORTH, RATE OF RETURN

	2000	5	6	7	8	2001	GROWTH
NET INCOME	2929	787.9	811.5	835.8	860.9	3296	12.55
PRESENT WORTH		−89.41	595.2	1281	1967		
RATE OF RETURN		.0822	.3446	.5494	.7073		

ENTER SOLVE OPTIONS

? GOAL SEEKING

GOAL SEEKING CASE 2
ENTER NAME OF VARIABLE TO BE ADJUSTED TO ACHIEVE PERFORMANCE

```
? INITIAL INVESTMENT(1)

ENTER COMPUTATIONAL STATEMENT FOR
PERFORMANCE

? RATE OF RETURN(8) = 25%

***** GOAL SEEKING CASE 2 *****
                        2000    5     6     7     8     2001 GROWTH
INITIAL INVESTMENT     4595    0 0   0     0     0     -100
ENTER SOLVE OPTIONS
? RATE OF RETURN
                        2000    5     6     7     8     2001 GROWTH
RATE OF RETURN                              .0835 .2500
ENTER SOLVE OPTIONS
?
```

Summary of Goal-Seeking Analysis

Case 1	The market share could be as low as 0.1243 in the first quarter and still provide first-quarter net income of $700 and 3% more in each subsequent quarter.
Case 2	The initial investment would have to be $4,595 to permit a 25% return over the 8-quarter horizon.

SIMPLAN: A PLANNING AND MODELING SYSTEM

SIMPLAN is more than a financial modeling package. In fact, it is an integrated, multipurpose, planning, budgeting, and modeling system. SIMPLAN is a system developed by Social Systems, Inc. (Chapel Hill, North Carolina 27514). The system is extremely powerful and flexible. In addition to the general financial modeling function, the system has the capability to perform (1) sales forecasting and time series analysis and (2) econometric modeling. Thus, sophisticated users can really take advantage of the package. For forecasting sales, interest rates, material supplies, factor input prices, and other key variables, SIMPLAN offers a variety of time series forecasting models. These include time trends, exponential smoothing, and adaptive forecasting. Forecasts developed by any of these methods may be incorporated directly into SIMPLAN models and reports. As for econometric modeling capability, SIMPLAN offers models for sales, market share, and industry, which can, with SIMPLAN, be specified, estimated, validated, simulated, and linked directly to division financial and production models or corporate financial models. SIMPLAN can be used to estimate single-equation and simultaneous-equation linear and nonlinear models to simulate the effects of alternative marketing strategies and economic conditions on market share and industry demand. Note: Direct access from SIMPLAN to all series of the NBER (National Business and Economic Research) macroeconomic data base is available on several time-sharing networks.

With SIMPLAN, 16 major functions are integrated into a single planning and modeling system. These functions include:

- Data base creation
- Data base manipulation
- Consolidation
- Model specification
- Model changes
- Report formulation
- Report changes
- Statistical analysis
- Forecasting
- Econometrics
- Model solution
- Validation
- Policy simulation
- Report generation
- Security
- Graphical display

SIMPLAN contains a number of commands to facilitate logical operations. For example, if the cash balances (CASH) fall below some minimum level (MBAL), the company's line of credit may be automatically increased by the amount of cash shortfall. The SIMPLAN commands to accomplish this task would be as follows:

$$\text{IF CASH<MBAL}$$
$$\text{DEBT} = \text{DEBT}(-1) + \text{MBAL} - \text{CASH}$$
$$\text{CASH} = \text{MBAL}$$

SIMPLAN utilizes a set of logical comparison operations, as well as IF and GO TO commands.

Chapter 21: Spreadsheet and Financial Modeling Languages   411

For a complete instruction about the system, refer to R. Britton Mayo and Social Systems, Inc., *Corporate Planning and Modeling with SIMPLAN*, Addison-Wesley Publishing Company, 1979.

EXAMPLE 21.5

The model we develop using SIMPLAN is designed to calculate the current asset portion of a typical balance sheet. First, Table 21.2 shows a list of data records or variables to use. Table 21.3 presents a sample model on SIMPLAN. The definitional equations, behavioral equations, and decision rules (using, for example, IF-ELSE statements) constructed here are pretty much self-explanatory. The first simulation for the period 2001–2004 is given in Table 21.4. To give the reader an idea of policy simulation, suppose that we want to determine the effects of an increase in the sales growth rate from 7 to 8.5%. Basically, all we needed to do is replace statement 3 with

3 GROWTHRATE = 8.5

TABLE 21.2 Data Records and Variables

Name	Abbreviation	Units
Accounts payable	AP	$000
Accounts receivable (net)	AR	$000
Cash	CASH	$000
Cost of goods sold	COGS	$000
Accounts receivable collected	COLLECTION	$000
Total current assets	CURASSETS	$00
Dollar value of sales	DOLLARSALE	$000
Fixed costs	FIXEDCOST	$000
Sales growth rate	GROWTHRATE	%
Cost of labor	LABOR	$/unit
Raw material cost	MATCOST	$/unit
Raw material inventory	MATERIALS	000 lbs.
Current value of inventory	MATVALUE	$000
Reduction of accounts payable	PAYMENTS	$000
Selling price	PRICE	$/unit
Production volume	PRODUCTION	000 units
Additions to inventory	PURCHASES	000 lbs.
Inventory reorder point	REORDER	000 lbs.
Sales	SALES	000 units
Production cost per unit	UNITCOST	$/unit
Variable costs	VARCOST	$000
Production payroll	WAGES	$000

TABLE 21.3 The Complete SIMPLAN Model

3	GROWTHRATE = 7
5	PRICE= 1.2
10	MATCOST = .6
15	REORDER = 3000
20	LABOR = .285
30	UNITCOST = LABOR + MATCOST
40	PRODUCTION=SALES(- 1)
50	MATERIALS = MATERIALS(- 1) - PRODUCTION
60	WAGES = LABOR*PRODUCTION
70	SALES=SALES(- 1)*(1 + GROWTHRATE/100)
80	FIXEDCOST = 50
90	VARCOST = UNITCOST*SALES
100	COGS = FIXEDCOST + VARCOST
110	DOLLARSALE = SALES*PRICE
120	IF MATERIALS<REORDER
130	PURCHASES = REORDER + 2*PRODUCTION - MATERIALS
140	MATERIALS = MATERIALS + PURCHASES
145	ELSE
146	PURCHASES=0
150	END
160	COLLECTLON = 3/4*AR(- 1)
170	AR = AP(- 1) - COLLECTION + DOLLARSALE
180	PAYMENTS = .6*AP(- 1)
190	AP= AP(- 1) - PAYMENTS + (PURCHASES*MATCOST)
200	CASH = CASH(- 1) + COLLECTION - PAYMENTS - WAGES
210	MATVALUE = MATERIALS*MATCOST
220	CURASSETS = CASH + AR + MATVALUE

With this new policy assumption, Table 21.5 shows the simulated results. We note that total current assets grow at an annual rate of 13.44% as opposed to 12.61%. The result indicates that a change in the assumed growth rate does not produce so large a change in the company's assets. In this case, a 1.5% increase in the growth rate causes cash and accounts receivable to rise by 0.67% and 1.4%, respectively. Thus the company's financial position in terms of liquidity and working capital appears to be relatively inelastic with respect to the assumed growth rate in sales.

EXPRESS

EXPRESS, which was developed by Management Decision Systems, provides the standard set of financial planning and analysis features, including

TABLE 21.4 The Initial SIMPLAN Result

Policy Assumptions

	2001	2002	2003	2004	Average
Sales growth rate (%)	7.00	7.00	7.00	7.00	7.00
Selling price ($/unit)	1.20	1.20	1.20	1.20	1.20
Raw material price ($/unit)	0.60	0.60	0.60	0.60	0.60
Cost of labor ($/unit)	0.28	0.28	0.28	0.28	0.28
Inventory reorder point (000 lbs)	3,000	3,000	3,000	3,000	3,000

Results (All in $000 Unless Otherwise Noted)

	2001	2002	2003	2004	Percent Growth
Cash	1,432	1,997	1,860	2,346	17.88
Accounts receivable (net)	1,527	1,481	1,546	1,645	2.51
Current value of inventory	1,920	2,827	2,278	2,976	15.73
Total current assets	4,879	6,306	5,684	6,967	12.61
Sales (000 units)	856	916	980	1,049	7.00
Variable costs	758	811	867	928	7.00
Fixed costs	50	50	50	50	
Cost of goods sold	808	861	917	978	6.59
Dollar value of sales	1,027	1,099	1,176	1,258	7.00
Accounts receivable collected	(1,500)	(1,145)	(1,111)	(1,160)	(8.22)
Accounts receivable (net)	1,527	1,481	1,546	1,645	2.51
Reduction of accounts payable	840	336	987	395	(22.25)
Accounts payable	560	1,645	658	1,550	40.39
Production payroll	228	244	261	279	7.00
Production cost per unit ($/unit)	0.885	0.885	0.885	0.885	
Production volume (000 units)	(800)	(856)	(916)	(980)	7.00
Additions to inventory (000 lbs)		2,368		2,144	
Raw material inventory (000 lbs)	3,200	4,712	3,796	4,960	15.73

the generation of pro forma financial statements, budgeting, analysis, projections, target analysis, and consolidations. One of the special modeling features of the system is risk analysis (including a Monte Carlo simulation). EXPRESS contains a variety of analytical and statistical features. Besides the standard mathematical capabilities, the system has the following automatic built-in calculations: sorting, percent difference, lags and leads, maximum/minimum of a set of numbers, year-to-date, and rounding. The statistical features include a number of time-series analysis and forecasting routines, such as exponential smoothing, linear extrapolation, deseasonalization, multiple regression, cluster analysis, and factor analysis. EXPRESS contains the report generator and display features for the system. All the dis-

TABLE 21.5 The Simulated Result with Policy Assumption

Policy Assumptions

	2001	2002	2003	2004	Average
Sales growth rate (%)	8.50	8.50	8.50	8.50	8.50
Selling price ($/unit)	1.20	1.20	1.20	1.20	1.20
Raw material price ($/unit)	0.60	0.60	0.60	0.60	0.60
Cost of labor ($/unit)	0.28	0.28	0.28	0.28	0.28
Inventory reorder point (000 lbs)	3,000	3,000	3,000	3,000	3,000

Results (All in $000 Unless Otherwise Noted)

	2001	2002	2003	2004	Percent Growth
Cash	1,432	2,005	1,873	2,386	18.55
Accounts receivable (net)	1,542	1,516	1,605	1,732	3.95
Current value of inventory	1,920	2,842	2,277	3,026	16.38
Total current assets	4,894	6,362	5,755	7,144	13.44
Sales (000 units)	868	942	1,022	1,109	8.50
Variable costs	768	833	904	981	8.50
Fixed costs	50	50	50	50	
Cost of goods sold	818	883	954	1,031	8.02
Dollar value of sales	1,042	1,130	1,226	1,330	8.50
Accounts receivable collected	(1,500)	(1,156)	(1,137)	(1,204)	(7.07)
Accounts receivable (net)	1,542	1,516	1,605	1,732	3.95
Reduction of accounts payable	840	336	1,000	400	(21.91)
Accounts payable	560	1,666	667	1,629	42.76
Production payroll	228	247	268	291	8.50
Production cost per unit ($/unit)	0.885	0.885	0.885	0.885	
Production volume (000 units)	(800)	(868)	(942)	(1,022)	8.50
Additions to inventory (000 lbs)		2,404		2,271	
Raw material inventory (000 lbs)	3,200	4,736	3,794	5,044	16.38

play capabilities are integrated with the system's data management, analysis, and modeling routine. The system has full graphic display capabilities.

ENCORE! PLUS

This package was developed by Ferox Microsystems. The analytical functions are similar to IFPS, but Encore has more model-building capability. For example, it is stronger in its risk analysis than IFPS, and even includes a Monte Carlo Simulator. Because Encore! Plus is more powerful at the application development level than, say, IFPS, it requires a higher level of programming ability.

BUDGET MAESTRO

Planet's Budget Maestro is probably the best answer to distributed budgeting, strategic planning, and financial control. Budget Maestro shortens your budgeting cycle and puts you in control of the process. Its information-driven environment guides you through budgeting, planning, modeling, forecasting, resource management, consolidation, analysis, and reporting.

CFOs and budget managers can plan, analyze, and manage in ways never before possible. You can look at a user's screen and make changes directly without ever being there, and deliver budget models and deploy reconfigured software updates to many users at once. Plus you can manage budgetary information, even enterprise-wide information systems, with a single consistent interface. Planet's Budget Maestro is designed to put CFOs and financial managers in control of all aspects of managing budgets, creating financial models, and building and deploying financial plans. Budget Maestro allows business managers unparalleled flexibility in analyzing cash flow and business performance throughout the enterprise. It significantly shortens your budgeting and planning cycles; eliminates rekeying, formatting of data; and increases your data accuracy and integrity, allowing you time to manage and analyze your business. Budget Maestro is available in both Desktop and Enterprise Editions. The Maestro Enterprise Edition enables multiple independent budgets and plans to be consolidated into a unified enterprise model. The Desktop Edition can be upgraded to the Enterprise Edition at any time.

CONCLUSION

There are a number of software packages for financial and corporate modeling. Companies just entering the modeling arena must keep in mind that the differences between the software packages available in the market can be substantial. A comparison should be made by examining the software in light of the planning system, the information system, and the modeling activities. The companies should also consider making effective use of in-house computer hardware and data bases. An effective modeling system does not necessarily imply an outside time-sharing system or an external economic data base. A checklist for factors to consider in the evaluation of modeling software follows.

Factors to Consider in the Evaluation of Modeling Software

- Main application area
  —Corporate modeling
  —Financial modeling
  —Marketing modeling
  —Production modeling
- Type of system
  —Fixed structure
  —Flexible, modular structure
- Hardware requirements
  —Main storage
  —Input–output facilities
- Software requirements
  —Compilers and source languages
  —Interfaces
  —File organization, data access methods
- Mode of operation
  —Batch
  —Real time
  —In-house
  —Service bureau
- Costs of system
  —Purchasing, leasing
  —Consulting, training
  —Storage
  —Operation
- Type of language
  —Free format–fixed format
  —Compiler–interpreter
  —Restrictions
  —English-like or symbolic text
- Flexibility of input and output
  —Choice and number of formats
  —Sequence
  —Graphics and histograms
- Type of data base
  —File and data set structure
  —Internal, external data base
  —Connection and hierarchies of data bases and files
- Basic time intervals
  —Maximum number
  —Specific periods
  —Interval transformations
- Maximum size of model
  —Statements
  —Number and size of arrays, matrices and tables, and files and number of data
- Arithmetic
  —Operators
  —Column arithmetic
  —Line arithmetic
  —Table arithmetic
  —Built-in functions
- Systems logic
  —Linear sequential
  —Logical branching
  —Index calculations
  —IF, GOTO
  —DO loop, END
  —Labels
  —Subroutines
  —Table access methods
- Handling of nonnumeric data
  —Character string operations
  —List and tree processing
  —Set statements

- Macroinstructions
  - Practitioner methods; e.g., interpolation and extrapolation; financial indicators
  - Short-term forecasting
  - Trend forecasting
  - Econometric methods
  - Specification and verification testing
  - Random numbers and stochastic simulation
  - Matrix algebra and linear programming
  - Nonlinear solution and optimization methods
  - Sensitivity analysis
  - Experimental designs
  - Graph analysis
- Security system
  - Physical security of data base, model and CSPS
  - Authorization codes and passwords for data base, files, models—privacy
- Documentation and support
  - User and system manuals
  - Debugging and error tracing
  - Menu programs, prompting, and "help" explanations
  - Computer-aided instruction
  - Consulting support

22 How to Use and Apply Management Games for Executive Training

Management games offer a unique means of teaching business managers and financial executives financial and managerial concepts and of developing their strategic abilities. More and more companies as well as virtually all MBA programs across the nation are using management games as a basic teaching tool for industrial training programs. Games have also found their way into university and corporate executive development programs.

The management game is a form of simulation. The distinction between a game and a simulation is subtle. Both are mathematical models, but they differ in purpose and mode of use. As discussed in previous chapters, simulation models are designed to simulate a system and to generate a series of quantitative and financial results regarding system operations. Games are a form of simulation, except that in games human beings play a significant part. In games, participants make decisions at various stages; games are therefore distinguished by the idea of play. The major goals of game play can be summarized as follows:

- Improve decision-making and analytical skills.
- Facilitate participants' understanding of the external environment simulated.
- Integratively apply the knowledge, concepts, and skills acquired in various business courses.
- Develop awareness of the need to make decisions without complete information.
- Improvise appropriately and adapt constructively from previously learned concepts, theories, and techniques.

- Develop ability to recognize the need for additional factual material.
- Develop an understanding of the interrelationships of the various functions within the firm and how these interactions affect overall performance.
- Teach the effects of present decisions on future decisions.
- Develop an understanding of the fact of uncertainty and the impact of the competitive environment on the firm.
- Develop an understanding of the necessity for good communications, teamwork, and leadership.
- Develop an ability to function cooperatively and effectively in a group situation.

Management games generally fall into two categories: executive games and functional games. Executive games are general management games and cover all functional areas of business and theory interactions and dynamics. Executive games are designed to train general executives. Functional games, on the other hand, focus on middle management decisions and emphasize particular functional areas of the firm. They cover such areas as:

- Resource allocation in general
- Production planning and scheduling
- Manpower requirements and allocation
- Logistics systems
- Material management
- Maintenance scheduling
- Sales management
- Advertising and promotion
- Stock transactions
- Investment analysis
- Research and development management

The objective in functional games is usually to minimize cost by achieving efficient operations or to maximize revenues by allocating limited resources efficiently. With emphasis on efficiency in specific functional areas, rather than on competition in a marketplace, which is the case in executive management games, there is no or little interaction in many functional games between player decisions. From that standpoint, functional games are very similar to simulation models. Here is a partial list of some well-known functional games:

Names of Functional Games	Areas They Cover
Worldwide Simulation Exercise The Multinational Game—Micro Version Multinational Management Game Multinational Business Game International Operations Simulation The Business Policy Game	International
Management Accounting Game	Accounting
COMPETE MARKSTRAT Marketing Game	Marketing
MICROSIM	Economics
The Westinghouse Plant Scheduling Warehouse Simulation Exercise	Distribution and logistics

Green and Sisson's:
  Materials Inventory Management Game
  Production Scheduling
  Scheduling Management Game
  X-Otol
	
	Inventory planning
	
	Production scheduling
	Distribution

Interpretive Software:
  PharmaSim
  AutoSim
  ServiceSim
	
	Brand management simulation
	Marketing laboratory
	Managing customer satisfaction

IBM Production Manpower Decision Model	Production and manpower scheduling decisions
FINASIM Simulation	Financial management
PERT-SIM	Project planning and control

Part IV: Financial Modeling

A partial list of some well-known executive management games follows:

- PriSim Business War Games and Business Simulations (PriSim; (http://www.prisim.com)
- The Business Policy Game: An International Simulation (Richard V. Cotter and David J. Fritzsche)
- StratSim: The Strategy Simulation (Interpretive Software, Inc.; 1-800-SIMUL8R; http://www.interpretive.com; http://www.execpc.com/~isi)
- The Executive Game (XGAME) (R.C. Henshaw, Jr. and J.R. Jackson)
- MICROMATIC (A. Strickland)
- TEMPOMATIC IV (O. Embry)
- DECIDE (T. Pary)
- The Business Management Laboratory (Ronald L. Jensen)
- Decision Making Exercise (John E. Van Tassel)
- Electronic Industry Game (James Francisco)
- Executive Decision Making Through Simulation (P.R. Cone et al.)
- The Executive Simulation (Bernard Keys)
- Integrated Simulation (W.N. Smith et al.)
- The IMAGINIT MANAGEMENT GAME (R. Barton)
- COGITATE (Carnegie Mellon University)
- Top Management Decision Game (R. Schrieber)
- Harvard Business Game (Harvard University)
- AIRLINE: A Business Simulation
- Alacrity Team Simulation Exercise
- BusSim: An Integrated Business Instruction System
- CEO: A Business Simulation for Policy and Strategic Management
- Collective Bargaining Simulated
- COMPETE: A Dynamic Marketing Simulation
- The Global Business Game
- Corporation: A Global Business Simulation
- DEAL: An Entrepreneurship Gaming Simulation
- Entrepreneur: A Business Simulation in Retailing

- GEO: An International-Business Gaming Simulation
- The Human Resources Management Simulation
- INFOGAME: Game for Research and Education in Information Systems
- INTOPIA: International Operations Simulation/Mark 2000
- MAGEUR: A General Business Game
- MANAGEMENT 500: A Business Simulation for Production and Operations Management
- Manager: A Simulation Game
- Marketer: A Simulation Game
- Marketplace
- The Multinational Management Game
- Threshold Competitor: A Management Simulation

EXECUTIVE MANAGEMENT GAMES

Executive (general management) games* offer a unique means of teaching management concepts and developing strategic abilities. Executive games involve sequential decision making in which the problems at any point in the decision process are at least partly dependent upon a participant's prior actions.

The game environment is an oligopolistic industry composed of the participating players who represent companies in the industry. A single product is made by the companies, and this product is sold in a single market. The period of operations covered by the game is usually assumed to be one quarter of a year.

Tip: To be successful, participating managers need to adopt the top management viewpoint. That is to say, they need to first define the goals and objectives of the firm they represent. *Caution*: They must always keep in mind that they are competing with the management teams of other firms in their industry. The game simulation model is designed to include general relationships that might exist in any competitive industry (or, more precisely, any oligopolistic industry). Participants need to use, in a small-group setting, their knowledge and experience in order to make

---

*For more detail, refer to Shim, Jae K., "Management Game Simulations: Survey and New Directions," *Michigan Business Review*, Vol. 30, No. 3, May 1978, and Shim, Jae K., "A Conversational Game," *Simulation and Games*, Vol. 111, No. 4, December 1977.

certain deductions about the economy in which they are operating and about general relationships within the game. These deductions must be combined with knowledge and experience about the specific relationships and with the team's belief about what action the competitors are likely to take.

A set of quarterly decisions designed to meet the organization's goals and objectives ideally will be apparent after data are analyzed and forecasting methods are applied. Figure 22.1 is a flowchart of a variety of activities to be performed by the teams involved in preparing quarterly decisions.

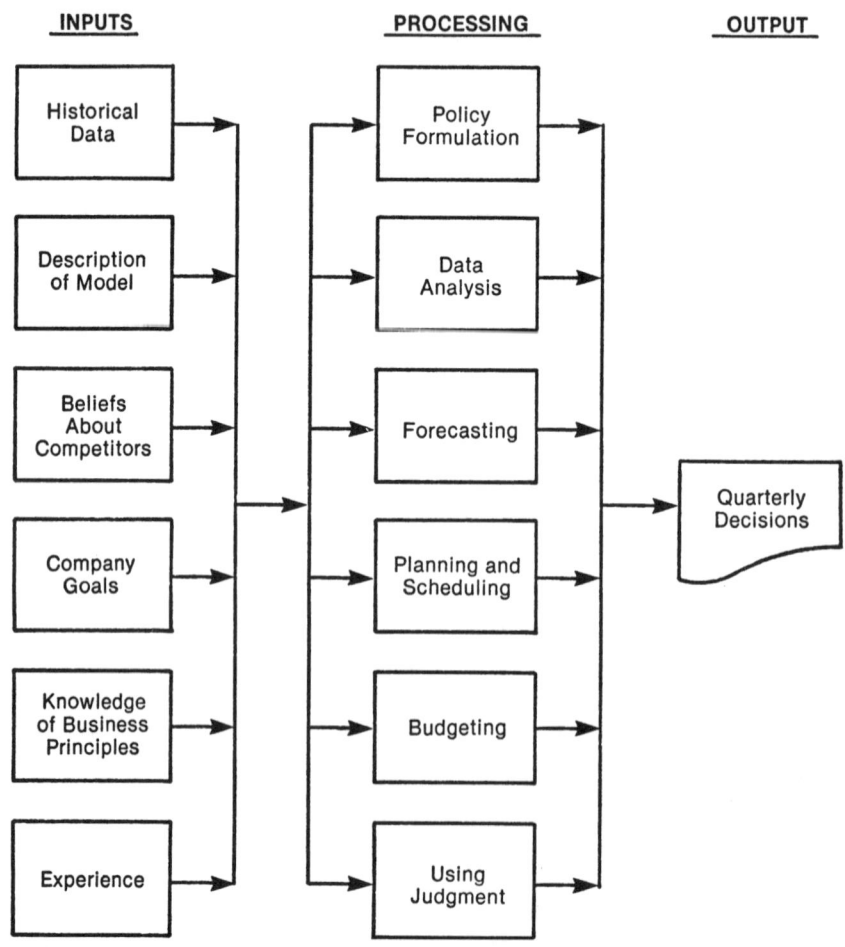

FIGURE 22.1 Flowchart for Quarterly Decisions

In the course of playing the game, players will encounter a variety of business situations. It will be necessary to undertake business forecasting, sales forecasting, and profit planning. Cash and capital budgets will have to be formulated. Production planning, scheduling, cost analysis, formulation of pricing policies, and development of marketing and advertising programs must all be done. The potential effects of investment and financing decisions on the capital structure must be investigated. In addition, players must prepare and analyze financial statements, cash flow statements, cost and sales data, and general informational reports regarding their competitors, industry, and economic conditions.

The Executive Game (XGAME) is typical of such top management games. The game environment is an oligopolistic industry composed of the participating players or teams who represent companies in the industry. A single product is made by the companies, and this product is sold in a single market.

The teams manage their companies by making the following quarterly decisions:

- Price of product
- Marketing budget
- Research and development budget
- Maintenance budget
- Production volume scheduled
- Investment in plant and equipment
- Purchase of materials
- Dividends declared

After decisions have been made they are transmitted to a computer, along with historical data summarizing the condition of the firms at the end of the preceding quarter. The computer, programmed to simulate the industry's operations, generates historical data and prints the following reports for each firm:

- General economic information
- Information on competitors
- Market potential
- Sales volume

- Percent share of industry sales
- Production this quarter
- Inventory, finished goods
- Plant capacity next quarter
- Income statement
- Cash flow statement
- Balance sheet

For the next quarter, a new set of decisions is made. This set, together with operating results of the preceding quarter and external economic conditions, are given as input data to the computer program, which then calculates results of play for the next quarter. The program prepares a new set of reports, which are returned to the players, and the cycle continues until the end of the game.

Figure 22.2 illustrates the basic structure of a typical executive game. For each play, data inputs for team decisions, current economic index, status of the game from preceding plays, and parameters of the model functions are built into the game model. Teams' decisions include price, marketing expenditures, R&D expenditures, production rate, investment in plant and equipment, and the like. The model then simulates interactions between the simulated environment and the decisions of the participants. At the end of each simulated period of play:

- Financial statements and summary reports for each company are prepared and printed (Figure 22.3).
- Historical game data for input to the next play are generated.
- Data needed for performance evaluation purposes are stored so that the game administrator is able to rate them, as shown in Figure 22.4.

This process is repeated for each firm in the industry.

ADVANTAGES AND DISADVANTAGES OF EXECUTIVE GAMES

Executive games are most useful to individuals seeking expanded business background. With this goal as a basis for participation, the individuals playing executive games will receive valuable insight into decision-making

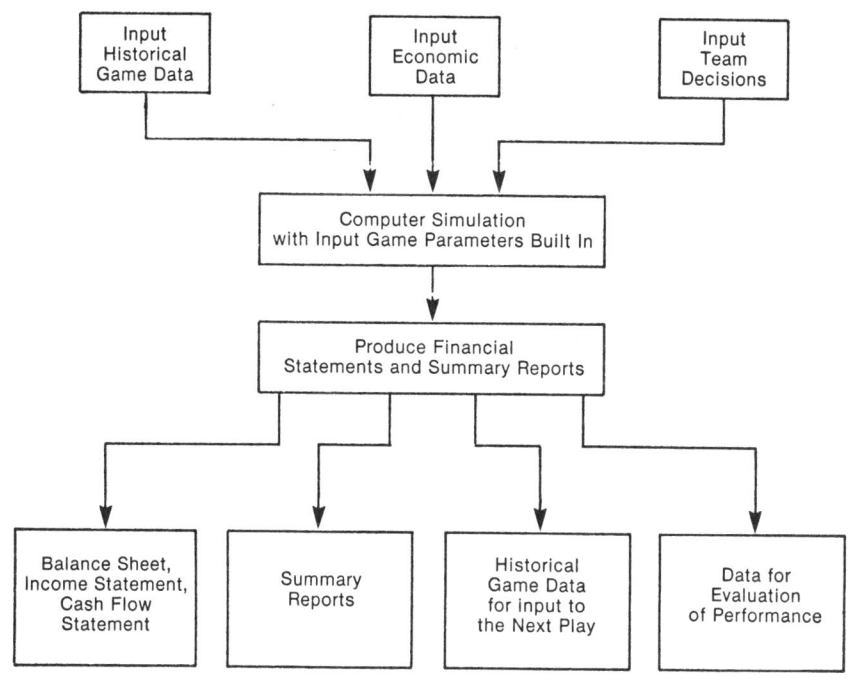

FIGURE 22.2 Structure of a Typical Executive Game

FIGURE 22.3 Company Financial Statement and Summary Report

```
MODEL 1 PERIOD   3 JFM PRICE INDEX 104.0 FORECAST ANNUAL CHANGE   4.3
0/0 SEAS.INDEX 90. NEXT QTR. 100. ECON.INDEX 91. FORECAST,NEXT QTR. 90.
                     INFORMATION ON COMPETITORS
              PRICE      DIVIDEND     SALES VOLUME    NET PROFIT
    FIRM 1   $ 25.75    $200000.        145215.      $    99384.
    FIRM 2   $ 25.75    $ 20000.        108796.      $     1342.
    FIRM 3   $ 26.00    $100000         113323.      $  -455219.
    FIRM 4   $ 26.00    $     0         106000.      $    67275.
    FIRM 5   $ 25.70    $ 75000.        106559.      $   -48419.
    FIRM 6   $ 25.75    $ 55000.         68550.      $  -355738.
                            FIRM   7  2
                       OPERATING STATEMENTS
    MARKET POTENTIAL                       108796.
    SALES VOLUME                           108796.
    PERCENT SHARE OF INDUSTRY                  17.
    PRODUCTION,THIS QUARTER                120000.
    INVENTORY,FINISHED GOODS                11204.
    PLANT CAPACITY,NEXT QUARTER            114192.
                       INCOME STATEMENT
```

(*Continued*)

FIGURE 22.3 *Continued*

```
                    INCOME STATEMENT
RECEIPTS,SALES REVENUE                              $ 2801489.
EXPENSES,MARKETING                  $  275000.
  RESEARCH AND DEVELOPMENT             350000.
  ADMINISTRATION                       351332.
  MAINTENANCE                           80000.
  LABOR(COST/UNIT EX.OVERTIME          723186.
    $ 5.82)
  MATERIALS CONSUMED(COST/UNIT         723127.
    6.03)
  REDUCTION,FINISHED GOODS INV.       -137769.
  DEPRECIATION (3.125 O/O)             242460.
  FINISHED GOODS CARRYING               22961.
    COSTS
  RAW MATERIALS CARRYING                40753.
    COSTS
  ORDERING COSTS                        51234.
  SHIFTS CHANGE COSTS                       0
  PLANT INVESTMENT EXPENSES             16000.
  FINANCING CHARGES AND                     0
    PENALITIES
  SUNDRIES                              92595.       2830879.
PROFIT BEFORE INCOME TAX                             -29390.
INCOME TAX(IN.TX.CR. 10.                             -30732.
  O/O,SURTAX  0 O/O)
NET PROFIT AFTER INCOME TAX                            1342.
DIVIDENDS PAID                                        20000.
ADDITION TO OWNERS EQUITY                            -18658.
                        CASH FLOW
RECEIPTS,SALES REVENUE                              $ 2801489.
DISBURSEMENTS,CASH EXPENSE          $ 2003061.
  INCOME TAX                           -30732.
  DIVIDENDS PAID                        20000.
  PLANT INVESTMENT                     400000.
  MATERIALS PURCHASED                  750000.       3142329.
ADDITION TO CASH ASSETS                             -340840.
                    FINANCIAL STATEMENT
NET ASSETS,CASH                                     $  736478.
  INV. VALUE,FINISHED GOODS                            137769.
  INVENTORY VALUE,MATERIALS                            841939.
  PLANT BOOK                                          7916256.
    VALUE(REPLACE.VAL.$ 8516087.)
  OWNERS EQUITY(ECONOMIC EQUITY                       9632442.
    $10232273.)
```

environments. The effectiveness of these games is dependent upon the trade-off between simplicity in model formulation and the maintenance of realism. *Warning*: As the complexity of the system grows, the participating audience loses its attentiveness with the game. It is for these reasons

Chapter 22: Management Games for Executive Training 429

EXECUTIVE GAME
END OF FISCAL YEAR 1.

FIRM NO.	NET CASH ASSETS ($)	INVENTORY VALUE FIN. GOODS ($)	INVENTORY VALUE MATERIALS ($)	PLANT REPLACE. VALUE ($)	OWNERS ECONOMIC EQUITY ($)
7 1	868469.	0.	1344725.	7724297.	9937491.
7 2	492619.	225250.	814990.	8695345.	10228204.
7 3	830205.	0.	228009.	8433799.	9492013.
7 4	1757777.	0.	918532.	7735186.	10411495.
7 5	684679.	127477.	1087781.	8160278.	10060215.
7 6	745705.	0.	907815.	7953408.	9606928.

AVERAGES PER QUARTER FOR FISCAL YEAR 1. ONLY

FIRM NO.	MARKETING ($)	R AND D ($)	SALES VOLUME (UNITS)	NET PROFIT ($)	RATE OF RETURN* (0/0)	RANK*
7 1	403125.	500000.	138107.	45644.	8.81	1
7 2	306250.	387500.	109953.	−29567.	5.76	4
7 3	387500.	625000.	129138.	−69184.	4.19	5
7 4	350000.	375000.	112732.	25584.	7.85	2
7 5	300000.	462500.	114301.	−21617.	5.96	3
7 6	251250.	775000.	123015.	−136277.	1.32	6

*RANK AND ANNUAL RATE OF RETURN ARE BASED UPON DIVIDEND PAY-OUT FOR ALL 4 PERIODS AND OWNERS ECONOMIC EQUITY AT THE END OF FISCAL YEAR 1.

FIGURE 22.4 Performance Evaluation Data

that simplicity is of major importance in designing an effective and informative executive game. Ease of understanding, playing, and administration are the factors that should be of utmost consideration to the designer. With this in mind, an optimal model can be designed for the use intended.

The intended use of executive games is for the participants to draw a basic understanding of the complexity of a modern-day concern. Players attempt to determine the effects of various decisions on the specific environment being simulated. The interaction of several endogenous variables (marketing budget, research and development budget, plant maintenance budget, scheduled production volume, plant investment, purchase of raw materials, declaration of cash dividends, selected by the players with exogenous variables (economic index, general price index, seasonal demand) formulated by the administrator to portray prevailing market and economic conditions, allows for excellent simulation of actual conditions found in today's business world.

VALIDATING THE GAME

A good executive game should be a valid one. Fortunately, the users of simulators are seldom concerned with proving the truth of a model. *Recommendation*: A model should be established on the basis that no one excellent decision or combination of poor decisions by others should permit one team to capture an overwhelming portion of the market. Built into the system should be parameters that prohibit high degrees of elasticity from affecting any one decision. The executive game previously discussed has implemented these controlling factors along with the controls maintained by the game administrator. The administrator can change or revise any of the exogenous variables or goals of the game to facilitate proper play by the participating teams. This executive game uses these controls to magnify its intended purpose for practical business applications. Removal of controlling factors might enhance realism, but at the same time would interfere with competition and finally destroy the executive lessons to be learned.

It is the learning process that the simple executive game wishes to portray, although for significantly large problems, realism makes the simulation technique highly preferable to others. Many decisions are made on the basis of simulation results, and these decisions can only prove to be as good as the data employed in the simulation. Thus, strong statistical inference should be made to test the validity of the data.

While models of this type offer adequate feedback to beginning executives, the more advanced find drawbacks to an oversimplified model because they lack detailed relationships in functional areas. The lack of competitive interaction among players is the prime reason for the deficient descriptiveness in functional areas. Those seeking these descriptive relationships should make use of functional games that focus their attention on efficiency rather than competition. It is this competitive nature of executive games that enhances their appeal to participate. *Recommendation*: The interaction and competition of players can be increased by allowing these individuals to actually operate computers.

Benefits of Game Play

- Ability to explore more alternatives
- Better understanding of the interaction of functional areas in business
- Facilitates group interaction
- Provides immediate feedback
- Develops decision-making skills
- Better learning device than case methods

A NEW ROLE FOR COMPUTERIZED EXECUTIVE GAMES

An additional purpose has been found for executive games—researchers are using the games to assess the effectiveness of teaching using computerized games, and the effectiveness of changing behaviors, performance, and analytical skills.

CONCLUSION

Management games are useful in instructing financial managers on how to make good decisions in various operating scenarios and circumstances. Financial executives should make decisions in various stages of the process so they can modify their policies as appropriate. The two types of games are executive games, covering the overall strategic plan of the firm, and functional games, concentrating on specific aspects of the business. Executive games require adjustment and changes in expectations given the variety of assumed business situations experienced. Functional games try to reduce cost via efficient operations or maximize revenue through properly allocating resources.

BIBLIOGRAPHY AND ADDITIONAL READINGS

The Association for Business Simulation and Experiential Learning (http://www.towson.edu/absel/) has the following links to a variety of games:

- AIRLINE: A Business Simulation
- Alacrity Team Simulation Exercise
- The Business Management Laboratory
- The Business Policy Game
- BusSim: An Integrated Business Instruction System
- CEO: A Business Simulation for Policy and Strategic Management
- Collective Bargaining Simulated
- COMPETE: A Dynamic Marketing Simulation
- The Global Business Game
- Corporation: A Global Business Simulation
- DEAL: An Entrepreneurship Gaming Simulation
- Entrepreneur: A Business Simulation in Retailing
- GEO: An International-Business Gaming Simulation
- The Human Resources Management Simulation
- INFOGAME: Game for Research and Education in Information Systems
- INTOPIA: International Operations Simulation/Mark 2000
- MAGEUR: A General Business Game
- MANAGEMENT 500: A Business Simulation for Production and Operations Management
- The Management Accounting Simulation
- Manager: A Simulation Game
- Marketer: A Simulation Game
- Marketplace
- The Multinational Management Game
- Threshold Competitor: A Management Simulation

Barker, J. R., C. S. Temple, and H. M. Sloan III. *Worldwide Simulation Exercise: User's Manual.* (Available from the authors, 33 Hayden Street, Lexington, MA), 1976.

Biggs, W. D. "Functional business games," *Simulation & Games*, 18, 242–267, 1987.

Burgess, T. F. "The use of computerized business games in business studies." *Educational and Training Technology International.* 26(3), 226–238, 1989.

———. "The use of computerized management and business simulations in the United Kingdom." *Simulation & Games*, 22, 174–195, 1991.

Carvalho, Gerard F. "Evaluating computerized business simulators for objective learning validity," *Simulation & Games*, 22, 328–349, 1990.

Cotter, R. and D. Fritzsche. *Modern Business Decisions*. Englewood Cliffs, NJ: Prentice-Hall, 1985.

Cotter, Richard V. and David S. Fritzsche. *Business Policy Game-Player's Manual*, Second Edition. Englewood Cliffs, NJ: Prentice-Hall, 1986.

Edge, A. G., B. Keys and W. Remus. *Multinational Management Game: User Manual*. Dallas, TX: Business Publications, Inc., 1979.

———. *The Multinational Game–MicroVersion*. Homewood, IL: Irwin, 1989.

Elgood, C. *Handbook of Management Games,* Fourth Edition. Aldershot, CA: Gower,, 1988.

Embry, O., A. Strickland and C. Scott *TEMPOMATIC IV: A Management Simulation.* Boston: Houghton Mifflin, 1974.

Faria, A. J. "A survey of the use of business games in academia and business," *Simulation & Games*. 18, 207–224, 1987.

Faria, A., R. Nulsen and D. Roussos. *COMPETE: A Dynamic Marketing Simulation,* Third Edition. Dallas, TX: Business Publications, Inc., 1984.

Gold, S., T. Pray and T. Dennis. *MICROSIM: A Computerized Microeconomics Simulation.* New York: Macmillan, 1984.

Goosen, Kenneth. *Introduction to Management Accounting: A Business Game.* Glenview, IL: Scott Foresman, 1994.

Hemmasi, M., L. A. Graf and C. E. Kellogg. "A comparison of the performance behaviors, and analysis strategies of MBA versus BBA students in a simulation environment," *Simulation & Games*, 20, 15–30, 1989.

Henshaw, Richard C. and James R. Jackson. *The Executive Game.* New York: Richard D. Irwin, Inc., 1986.

Horn, R. E. and A. Cleaves. *The Guide to Simulation/Games for Education and Training.* London: Sage, 1989.

Hoskins, W. R. *Multinational Business Game: User Manual.* Phoenix, AZ: American Graduate School of Business, 1983.

Interpretive Software, Inc. (http://www.execpc.com/~isi), *StratSim: The Business Strategy Simulation.* Charlottesville, Virginia, 1997–99.

———. *PharmaSim: A Brand Management Simulation.* Charlottesville, Virginia, 1997-99.

———. *AutoSim: The Marketing Laboratory.* Charlottesville, Virginia, 1997–99.

———. *ServiceSim: Managing Customer Satisfaction.* Charlottesville, Virginia, 1997–99.

Jensen, R. and D. Cherrington. *The Business Management Laboratory.* Dallas, TX: Business Publications, Inc., 1977.

Keys, B. "Total enterprise business games," *Simulation & Games*, 18, 225–241, 1987.

Klein, Ronald D. and Robert A. Fleck, Jr. "International business simulation/gaming: An assessment and review," *Simulation & Games,* 21, 147–165, 1990.

Larreche, J. and H. Gatignon, *MARKSTRAT: A Marketing Strategy Game.* Mass: Scientific Press, 1977.

Mehreg, A. A., A. Reichel and R. Olami. "The business game versus reality," *Simulation & Games,* 18, 488–500, 1987.

Mills, L. and D. McDowell. *The Business Game.* Boston: Little Brown, 1985.

Parasuraman, A. "Assessing the worth of business simulation games: Problems and prospects," *Simulation & Games,* 12, 189–200, 1981.

Pray, T. and D. Strang. *DECIDE: A Management Decision Making Simulation.* New York: Random House, 1980.

Pray, T. F. "Management training: It's all in the game," *Personnel Administrator,* 32, 68–72, 1987.

Pray, T. F. and David T. Methe. "Modeling radical changes in technology within strategy-oriented business simulations," *Simulation & Games,* 22, 19–35, 1991.

Remus, W. and S. Jenner. "Playing business games: Expectations and realities," *Simulation & Games,* 12, 480–488, 1981.

Robinson, J. N. "Games and simulation in management and economics: A survey," *Economics, 21* (Winter), 163–171, 1985.

Segev, E. "Strategy, strategy-making, and performance in the business game," *Strategic Management Journal,* 8, 565–577, 1987.

Strickland, A. and T. Scott. *MICROMATIC—A Management Simulation.* Boston: Houghton Mifflin, 1985.

Thorelli, H. B. and R. L. Graves. *International Operations Simulation: User's Manual.* New York: Free Press and Macmillan, 1999.

Wolfe, J. "The teaching effectiveness of games in collegiate business courses: A 1973–1983 update," *Simulation & Games,* 16, 251–288, 1985.

Wolfe, J. and C. R. Roberts. "The external validity of a business management game: A five-year longitudinal study," *Simulation & Games,* 17, 45–59, 1986.

23 Corporate Valuations

Corporate valuation—or broadly *business valuation*—involves estimating the worth or price of a company, one of its operating units, or its ownership shares. There are many reasons for the valuation: the purchase or sale of the business, mergers and acquisitions, buy-back agreements, expanding the credit line, or tax matters (Table 23.1). The buying and selling of businesses are not the only reasons for conducting business valuations. Tough economic times result in increased litigation involving partner disputes and dissenting shareholder actions. Economies of scale encourage mergers and acquisitions to help maintain market share and ensure economic stability in a recessing economy.

A valuation might be important for establishing an asking or offering price when buying or selling a business. But what is the value of the business? Is it the value of the company's assets? Or is it the value of the company's earnings? Is it the value of the company's loyal customers and good reputation? Or is it something else? The answer is that it might be any or all of these things. Additionally, you must consider the type of business and its major activities, industry conditions, competition, marketing requirements, management possibilities, risk factors, earning potential, and financial health of the business.

Usually, *value* is determined by an interested party. Although there is usually no single value (or "worth") that can be associated with a business in all situations, there is usually a defendable value that can be assigned to a business in most situations. To be a proficient valuation analyst, a CFO requires analytical and writing skills. More specifically, one must be adept at financial analysis, economic forecasts, accounting and audit fundamentals, income taxes, and legal and economic research.

TABLE 23.1 Business Valuation Opportunities

Buy–sell agreements	Allocation of acquisition price
Mergers, acquisitions, and spinoffs	Adequacy of life insurance
Liquidation or reorganization of a business	Litigation
Initial public offering	Divorce action
Minority shareholder interests	Compensatory damage cases
Employee stock ownership plans	Insurance claims
Financing	Estate and gift taxes
Return-on-investment (ROI) analysis	Incentive stock options
Government actions	Charitable contributions

Source: National Association of Certified Valuation Analysts.

The valuation process is an art and not a science because everyone's perception is slightly different. This chapter provides the basic steps involved in valuation and gives various ways to determine what a business is worth. Further, various Internal Revenue Service Revenue Rulings are presented recommending specific valuation measures especially with regard to income tax issues.

To determine a company's value, the purpose of the valuation and an appropriate perspective must be specified. The perspective might be that of a buyer, a seller, the IRS, or a court. A business appraisal can be performed when these are known. Generally, the appraisal process determines the value of the business based on an asset, earnings (or cash flows), and/or market approach. In valuing the business, the following factors should be considered:

- History of the business
- Nature of the company
- Economic and political conditions
- Health of the industry
- Distribution channels and marketing factors
- Financial position
- Degree of risk
- Growth potential
- Trend and stability of earnings
- Competition
- Employee relationships

- Location
- Customer base
- Quality of management
- Ease of transferability of ownership

STEPS IN VALUATION

As an initial step in valuation, the key financial information must be accumulated and analyzed including historical financial statements, projected financial statements, and tax returns. There must be familiarity with the business, including the company's strategic position in the industry. Further, the major assumptions of the valuation must be clearly spelled out. A variety of "what-if" scenarios must be investigated to reduce valuation errors. Figure 23.1 summarizes the basic steps in business valuations.

Analyze historical performance
- Accumulate and analyze key financial information such as earnings and invested capital.
- Develop an integrated historical perspective.
- Analyze financial health.

Project future performance
- Understand strategic position.
- Develop performance scenarios.
- Forecast financial statement line items.
- Check overall forecast for reasonableness.

Estimate rate of capitalization
- Develop target market value weights.
- Estimate capitalization rate (cost of capital).

Estimate valuation
- Select proper valuation method.
- Choose forecast horizon.
- Discount future value to present.

Compute and interpret results
- Incorporate market and control discounts.
- Compute and test results with major assumptions.
- Interpret results within decision context.

FIGURE 23.1 Steps in Valuation

Definitions of "Value"

Various individuals will have different ideas of how much a business is worth and how its value should be determined. Various individuals and groups might define "value" differently.

Fair Market Value

Fair market value is generally defined as the price at which property would change hands between a willing buyer and a willing seller, when neither is compelled to act and both have a reasonable knowledge of the relevant facts. With the asset approach, assets are valued at fair (i.e., appraised) market value.

Fair market value is often an important valuation definition in estate, gift, and other federal tax-related valuations. It is a well-accepted IRS and tax court concept. Generally, these groups will consider that a company's value is equivalent to its fair market value. Accordingly, a financial manager will need to consider this definition when performing valuations that may have the IRS as an interested party.

Replacement Value

Replacement value is the cost of replacing something. This definition might be applicable for establishing "damages" in antitrust suits, in condemnation proceedings, and in similar situations. At times, the definition could be used in a federal or state court. In some situations, replacement value might be determined to be a company's fair market value.

Liquidation Value

The lowest value associated with a business is its liquidation value. Liquidation value is, in effect, the value of an item (a business) sold to the highest available bidder. Typically, the seller is compelled to sell and the buyer knows of the seller's need to sell. Liquidation value is a depressed value. For a business, assets might be sold piecemeal. Usually, liquidation value is defined as the amount received by the seller after selling and administrative expenses are paid. At times, a company's liquidation value could be its fair market value.

"Going Concern" Value

"Going concern" value is the opposite of liquidation value. It is the value of a business based on the presumption that the business will continue as an operating entity; that is, the company will not be liquidated. A company's going concern value will usually be its fair market value.

Matching Value Definitions and Valuation Reasons

An initial step in the business valuation process is to match the reason and perspective of the valuation with an appropriate definition of value. Note that each definition of "value" is not mutually exclusive. In a given situation, several definitions might concurrently apply. Table 23.2 shows valuation reasons and value definitions that might be connected with them.

General Approaches to Business Valuation

When a company is not publicly traded, willing buyers and willing sellers capable of establishing an independent and objective value for a business usually will not exist when the valuation is needed. Accordingly, an estimate of the price at which the company might change hands between a willing buyer and a willing seller must be made. To do this, one or more of three approaches to valuation might be used.

Market Comparison

Values of comparable companies in the industry may provide useful norms. The idea is to establish the company's value based on actual sales that are indicative of the company's current value.

A basic requirement for using prior sales of a firm's ownership interests in the appraisal of its current value is that each prior sale be indicative of the existing circumstances of the company. If prior sales were made in the too distant past, or were of a form or substance not indicative of the subject company's current situation, the use of the sale(s) may not be appropriate for establishing the company's current worth. In particular,

TABLE 23.2 Definition of Value

Valuation Reason	Fair Market Value	Liquidation Value	Replacement Value	Going Concern Value
Purchase of business	x		x	x
Sale of business	x			x
Shareholder litigation	x			x
Bankruptcy, dissolution		x		
Recapitalization	x			x

small sales of non-controlling interests and sales between related parties might not indicate the value of the company and its related ownership interests at the time of the sale. They would not be indicative of the company's current value either.

The requirements are greater when comparable company sales are evaluated. Comparable company sales should only be used when the sales have occurred in the recent past and are of a sufficient size to appropriately establish a supportable value. They should be in the same industry and similar in products and services offered, competitive positions, financial structures, and historical financial performance. Unfortunately, finding comparable companies is difficult because closely held company operating performance and sale information are frequently unavailable. *Note:* Refer to John Sanders's, *Biz-Comps Business Sale Statistics,* published by BizComps (P.O. Box 711777, San Diego, CA 92171, www.bizcomps.com). This is the annual report compiling information for 1,600 businesses in many industries.

Earnings (or Cash Flows)

A second approach for business valuations is based on earnings. The earnings approach considers a company's value to be equivalent to its ability to create income (or cash flow). The concept is to associate the firm's income with a rate of return commensurate with the company's investment risk.

Assets

A third approach for establishing the value of a business is to consider the company's value to be equivalent to the value of its net tangible assets. For the dissolution of the business, the company's value might be based on the liquidated value of the company's assets. If the company is to be "duplicated," the company's value might be based on asset replacement values. If the company will continue as a going concern, the company's value might be based on the fair market value of the company's assets.

Performing a General Analysis of the Company Being Valued

For appraisal purposes, the determination of a company's value is usually based on a market, earnings, and/or assets approach to value. There are various business valuation methods associated with each. To analyze and apply the methods, one needs to understand various attributes about the company being valued, especially, understanding of the company's:

- industry
- customers and markets
- products and services
- employees and management
- assets
- historical and projected financial performance

Each of these areas will significantly affect the valuation of the business and the use of various valuation methods.

Industry Outlook

In assessing a company's industry, a CFO should evaluate the economic outlook for the industry, barriers to entry, government controls, and similar items. If the industry is expected to grow, firms in the industry might be perceived as being increasingly valuable. Further, you will need to consider competition. In a highly competitive industry, companies might be reduced in value because of competitive pressures, price discounting, etc.

Customers and Markets

In assessing a company's customers and markets, you should evaluate the company's key customers and the strength of the customers. If the company has many customers, and none of the customers represent a significant percentage of the sales of the company, the company might be increasingly stable. The company may have a lower associated investment risk. If a company has only a few large customers, you will need to weigh carefully the implications and the likelihood of its losing the customers.

Products and Services

In evaluating a company's products and services, you should look at their quality. You should compare the company's products and services with competitive products and services. Evaluate the company's investments in research and development, and historical trends in sales and expenses of important products and services. Consider the number of products and services the company offers and the extent to which the company relies on one or several products or services for most of its sales and profits. When a company has only one or a few products or services, the competitive risks associated with the products and services become a factor. Generally, diverse and stable product lines might be associated with a stable company. Limited product lines might imply an increased investment risk.

Employees and Management

Qualified management usually means that the company is stable, and might enhance the value of the company. If a firm has had significant turnover in its management (and/or employees), the company might be considered a risky investment. In general, inexperienced management and a high turnover rate are indicative of a high-risk company.

Assets

Typically, the value of a company's tangible assets is a minimum value associated with the business. For valuation purposes, you should judge a company's assets to ensure that the assets are indeed valuable and scrutinize in detail such items as obsolete inventory, old fixed assets, bad debts in accounts receivable, and capitalized expenses. For some assets, specific evaluations may be necessary.

Historical and Projected Financial Performance

Evaluating a company's historical and projected financial performance can be time consuming and complex. A CFO needs to establish the reliability of the company's historical financial statements and assess the implications of sales, expenses, and profits. Typically, for determining the value of a company, you evaluate the company's operating performance. Accordingly, you may have to remove the implications of nontypical and nonoperating transactions included in the company's financial statements.

A company's historical financial statements might include excess compensation and significant perks to owners. Frequently, the CFO must add back to the company's income any excess compensation paid to owners to fully understand the profitability of the company. Adjustments might also be made to the financial statements to convert cash basis statements to accrual basis statements. In particular, cash basis statements might not display accounts receivable, accounts payable, and accrued liabilities.

In evaluating a company's financial performance, the CFO will want to review various expense ratios as a percent of sales and various sales, income, and expense trends. In particular, the CFO would assess the financial statements for purposes of making assumptions about the future profitability of the company. Evaluate various company ratios and compare them with other companies in the industry. You might also develop projected financial statements for the company for three or more years.

BUSINESS VALUATION METHODS

There are numerous ways of determining the value of the business. Further, there are many possible combinations of these various methods. Nine popular valuation methods are illustrated below.

Adjusted Net Assets Method

The adjusted net assets valuation method presumes the value of a company is equivalent to the value of its net tangible assets. Asset values are often based on fair market values when the company is expected to continue as a going concern, liquidated values when the company is not expected to continue as a going concern, and replacement values when the costs of duplicating the company are being assessed.

The fair market value of the net tangible assets of the company may be based on independent appraisal. An addition is made for goodwill. An investment banking firm that handles the purchase and sale of businesses may be hired to appraise the tangible property. Usually, the fair market value of the assets exceeds their book value.

An advantage of the adjusted net assets valuation method is that it is frequently easy to determine the value of a company's tangible net assets. A disadvantage is that it ignores the important implications of company earnings. In many instances, an adjusted net assets valuation is a conservative valuation. It might be a minimum value associated with a business.

EXAMPLE 23.1

Net tangible assets (at fair market value)	$12,000,000
Plus goodwill	6,000,000
Valuation	$18,000,000

Gross Revenue Multiplier Method

The value of the company may be determined based on the revenue-generating capacity of the company. For example, many Internet stocks that lose money in the short run and yet have great future earnings potential tend to derive their value from their revenue-generating capacity or registered member subscriptions. The formula for this method is as follows:

$$\text{Value of the business} = \text{Revenue} \times \text{Gross revenue multiplier}$$

The gross revenue multiplier used is the one customary in the industry. The industry norm gross multiplier is based on the average ratio of market price to sales typical in the industry. *Note: Business Week* magazine publishes a special weekly edition each year called *Corporate Scorecard*, containing average industry ratios, www.businessweek.com).

If reported earnings are suspect, this method may also be advisable.

EXAMPLE 23.2

Gross revenue	$32,500,000
× Gross revenue multiplier	.4
Valuation	$13,000,000

Capitalization of Earnings Method

The capitalization of earnings valuation method is in many ways the opposite of the adjusted net assets valuation method. It uses income, as opposed to assets, to value the business. A variation of the method incorporates *cash flows* as opposed to earnings.

The capitalization of earnings valuation method is based on the notion that the investors will only acquire stock in a company if they can earn a rate of return that is high enough to offset the risks associated with the investment. The trade-off is the risk of the loss of the investment with the rate of return that might be realized. In general, high-risk companies need to yield high rates of return to stimulate equity investments. Low-risk companies can produce lower rates of return and still attract equity investors.

The formula for the capitalization of earnings method follows:

Value of the business = Earnings (or Cash flow)/Capitalization rate

Frequently, earnings or cash flow for this method is the current year's earnings (or cash flow), a simple average of 2 to 5 prior years, a weighted-average adjusted historical earnings, or the company's projected profit for the following year. The method presumes the earnings value used in the method is indicative of future earnings expectations on an ongoing basis. In this method, earnings can be any one of the following:

- Before-tax earnings
- After-tax earnings
- Earnings before interest and taxes (EBIT)

The capitalization rate is the rate of return an investor would expect to receive for investing in the company based on the company's perceived risk. It is typically a weighted cost of capital, weights being target mix of different sources of financing, equity or nonequity.

Two examples for this method are presented below.

EXAMPLE 23.3

Earnings (simple average)	$1,250,000
÷ Capitalization rate	10%
Valuation	$12,500,000

The following example uses weighted-average historical earnings, in which more weight is given to the most recent years. This is more representative than a simple average. Weighted-average makes sense because current earnings reflect current prices and recent business activity. In the case of a five-year weighted average, the current year is assigned a weight of 5 while the initial year is assigned a weight of 1. The multiplier is then applied to the weighted-average 5-year adjusted historical earnings to derive a valuation.

EXAMPLE 23.4

Year	Historical Earnings	Weight	Total
20X0	$2,780,000	5	$13,900,000
20X1	$1,670,000	4	$ 6,680,000
20X2	$1,350,000	3	$ 4,050,000
20X3	$1,780,000	2	$ 3,560,000
20X4	$2,100,000	1	$ 2,100,000
		15	$30,290,000

Weighted average 5-year earnings:
$30,290,000/15 = $2,019,333

Weighted average 5-year earnings	$ 2,019,333
÷ Capitalization rate (20%)	20%
Valuation	$10,096,667

Note:

- In cases where cash flow is used instead of earnings, we use *distributable* or *free cash flow*—a term gaining increasing popularity among financial analysts. *Free cash flow* is defined as the company's operating cash flows (before interests) *minus* cash outlays for the replacement of existing operating capacity such as buildings, equipment, and furnishings. It is the amount available to finance planned expansion of operating capacity, to reduce debt, to pay dividends, or to repurchase stock.

- Many analysts prefer to use accrual accounting earnings rather than cash flows, however, on the belief that *current* accrual accounting earnings are more useful than measures of *current* cash flows in predicting *future* cash flows.

Price–Earnings Ratio Method

For publicly traded stocks, stock trading prices are often directly proportional to earnings. Often, within industries, there is a consistency between companies. The price–earnings ratio method is predicated on the notion that price–earnings ratios (P/Es) of publicly traded stocks might be indicative of a closely held company's value. The notion is this: If the closely held company were publicly traded, it would trade at a price similar to the price at which comparable companies trade.

The formula for this method is as follows:

Value of the business =
    Earnings per share (EPS)/Price–earnings (P/E) ratio or multiplier

Typically, earnings for this method is the most recent year's earnings per share (EPS) or an average of 2 to 5 prior years. The P/E multiplier is usually an historical average based on comparable, actively traded stocks. Some use a P/E ratio based on the most current period rather than an average of prior years. For more information see Chapter 24.

EXAMPLE 23.5

Earnings after taxes	$ 1,000,000
Outstanding shares	250,000
Earnings per share (EPS)	$ 4
P/E ratio	15
Estimated market price per share	$ 60
× Number of shares outstanding	250,000
Valuation	$15,000,000

Dividend Payout (or Dividend Paying Capacity) Method

The dividend payout (or dividend paying capacity) valuation method presumes that the "compensation" for stock ownership is dividends. The method is based on the notion that a stock's value is related to the company's ability to pay dividends and the yield investors expect.

The dividend payout method involves the following steps:

- Company's dividend paying capacity = Earnings × Dividend payout percentage
- Value of business = Company's dividend paying capacity ÷ Dividend yield rate

Typically, earnings for this method is an average of 2 to 5 prior years. Some use before-tax profits; others use after-tax profits. The dividend payout percentage and dividend yield rate are established with reference to comparable, publicly traded stocks. A variation of the method would establish the company's dividend paying capacity to be monies received by the owners of the closely held company as dividends, excess compensation, and perks.

Although the method is in infrequent use, the method incorporates some of the most defendable valuation principles of all methods.

EXAMPLE 23.6

Earnings after taxes	$ 1,000,000
Dividend payout percentage	40%
Dividend paying capacity	$ 400,000
÷ Dividend yield rate	4%
Valuation	$10,000,000

Excess Earnings Return on Assets Method

The excess earnings return on assets valuation method implies that within an industry, a given level of company assets will generate a particular level of earnings. To the extent a company has earnings above the expected level of earnings, the company is presumed to have an enhanced value. The enhanced value is attributed to goodwill (or intangible assets). The addition of the value of the goodwill and the fair market value of the net tangible assets equals the total valuation.

The excess earnings return on assets method involves the following steps:

- Industry expected earnings = Company assets × Industry expected return on assets

- Excess earnings = Company earnings − Industry expected earnings
- Goodwill (intangible assets) = Excess earnings/Capitalization rate
- Value of the business = Goodwill + Fair market value of net tangible assets

This method has several variations. Gross assets or net assets and book values or fair market values might be used to calculate industry earnings and excess earnings.

As per IRS Revenue ruling 59-60 (to be discussed later), the IRS recommends this method to value a business for tax purposes.

EXAMPLE 23.7

Year	Net Tangible Assets	Weight	Total
20X0	$10,000,000	1	$ 10,000,000
20X1	$14,000,000	2	$ 28,000,000
20X2	$18,000,000	3	$ 54,000,000
20X3	$19,000,000	4	$ 76,000,000
20X4	$18,500,000	5	$ 92,500,000
		15	$260,500,000

Weighted average net tangible assets
$260,500,000/15 = $17,366,667

Weighted average earnings (5 years)—assumed	$ 1,800,000
Minus industry rate of return on weighted-average Net tangible assets ($17,366,667 × 10%)	1,736,667
Excess earnings	$ 63,333
÷ Capitalization factor (20%)	0.2
Plus goodwill (intangibles) $	316,667
Plus fair market value of net tangible assets	$ 16,000,000
Valuation	$ 16,316,667

Excess Earnings Return on Sales Method

The excess earnings return on sales valuation method values a company based on sales, earnings, and assets. Generally, the method implies that within an industry, a given level of sales will generate a given level of earnings. When a company has earnings above the industry's expected level of earnings, the company is considered to have goodwill (or intangible assets). The value of goodwill plus the fair market value of the net tangible assets is considered to be the value of the company.

The excess earnings return on sales method involves the following steps:

- Industry expected earnings = Company sales × Industry expected return on sales
- Excess earnings = Company earnings − Industry expected earnings
- Goodwill (intangible assets) = Excess earnings/Capitalization rate
- Value of the business = Goodwill + Fair market value of net tangible assets

Variations in this method include the use of the company's current year's sales or a 2- to 5-year average for computing the industry-expected profits.

EXAMPLE 23.8

Year	Sales	Weight	Total
20X0	$11,100,000	1	$ 11,100,000
20X1	$12,500,000	2	$ 25,000,000
20X2	$20,000,000	3	$ 60,000,000
20X3	$21,000,000	4	$ 84,000,000
20X4	$24,200,000	5	$121,000,000
		15	$301,100,000

Weighted average sales
$301,100,000/15 = $802,933

Weighted average earnings (5 years)—assumed	$ 1,800,000
Minus industry rate of return on weighted-average sales ($20,073,333 × 4%)	802,933
Excess earnings	$ 997,067
÷ Capitalization factor (20%)	0.2
Valuation of goodwill (intangibles)	$ 4,985,333
Plus fair market value of net tangible assets	$ 16,000,000
Valuation	$ 20,985,333

Discounted Cash Flow Method

The discounted cash flow (DCF) method equates the value of a business with the cash flows the business is expected to create.

The discounted cash flow method presumes that the purpose of a company is to generate cash flow (or earnings) and, therefore, assets, distribution channels, etc., have a value related to the cash flows they are able to create. Conceptually, the method is similar to the capitalization of earnings valuation method except that in the discounted cash flow method *projected* earnings (or cash flows) as opposed to historical earnings (or cash flows) are assessed. If the growth rate is used to project future earnings, the rate may be based on prior growth rate, future expectations, and the inflation rate. The discount rate may be based on the market interest rate of a low-risk asset investment.

The formula for the discounted cash flow method follows:

Value of the business =
    Present value of the earnings (or Cash flow) projection
       + Present value of terminal value (selling price)

Typically, cash flows are projected for at least 5 years and a terminal value (or selling price) is established for the value of the business at the end of the term.

EXAMPLE 23.9

Year	Cash Flows (7% Growth Rate)	Present Value (PV) Factor at a 10% Discount Rate	Total PV
20X0	$500,000	0.909	$ 454,500
20X1	$535,000	0.826	$ 441,910
20X2	$572,450	0.751	$ 429,910
20X3	$612,522	0.683	$ 418,352
20X4	$655,398	0.621	$ 407,002
Present value of future earnings			$ 2,151,674

If the anticipated selling price at the end of year 20X4 is $15,000,000, the valuation of the business equals:

Present value of future earnings	$ 2,151,674
Present value of selling price 18,000,000 × .621	$11,178,000
Valuation	$13,329,674

The Abnormal Earnings Approach

The abnormal earnings approach is based on the notion that value is driven not by the level of earnings themselves but by the level of earnings *relative to some benchmark*, i.e., the cost of capital (or a minimum required rate of return). The rationale is that investors are willing to pay a premium for those firms that earn more than the cost of capital—i.e., firms that produce *positive abnormal earnings*. The formula is

Value of the business = Book value of assets
  + Present value of expected future abnormal earnings
   (Actual earnings minus required earnings)

EXAMPLE 23.10

Suppose a firm's book value of assets at the beginning of the year is $100 per share, and the cost of capital is 13%. Investors therefore require earnings of at least $13 per share ($100 × 13%). If the market expects the company to report earnings equal to the benchmark earnings but if it actually earns $23 per share for the year—thus exceeding the benchmark—the value of the company (stock price) will reflect the firm's superior performance.

Combination Valuation Method

The combination valuation method is not really a method; it's a combination of other methods. Often, the use of a combination method establishes a more reasonable value for a business than any single method. In particular, in a combination method earnings, assets, comparable companies, prior sales of company stock, and other important valuation concepts might be accounted for.

Further, the valuation of the company may be estimated based on a weighted-average value of several methods. The most weight should typically be placed on the earnings method and the least on the asset approaches.

EXAMPLE 23.11

Method	Valuation Amount	Weight	Total
Adjusted net assets	$18,000,000	1	$18,000,000
Excess earnings on rate of return	$20,985,333	2	$41,970,666
		3	$59,970,666
Total/3 = $69,970,666/3 = $19,990,222			
Valuation			$19,990,222

Generally, before a combination method is used, it should be established that the combination method results in a better valuation than any method individually, and that the use of each method in the combination supports the final valuation.

Earnings Surprises

Many valuation methods require estimates of future earnings. But estimates can (and usually do) prove to be off target. When this transpires, an "earnings surprise" results. For example, a *positive* earnings surprise—i.e., reported earnings exceeding market expectations—tend to have a upward rift in stock value. Earnings estimates are reported by such companies as *Zacks* (www.zacks.com), *First Call* (www.firstcall.com), *IBES,* and *Nelson's*, which are the leading trackers of analysis earnings projections. These firms constantly poll brokerages for their earnings estimates. From that survey, these companies publish a compilation that includes the high, low, and mean prediction for a company's upcoming quarterly and fiscal year results.

Marketability Discounts

Generally, a business ownership interest that can be sold quickly will be worth more than a similar ownership interest that cannot be sold quickly. In various business valuation methods, this implication may or may not be considered. When it is not, a marketability discount might be associated with the value of the ownership interest otherwise determined. A marketability discount is the reduction in the value of a company (or ownership interest) because the company (or ownership interest) might take considerable time to sell.

There are differences of opinion about marketability discounts. The IRS objects to them and will argue that the implications of marketability will have been accounted for elsewhere in the valuation process. Many believe that statistics prove there is in fact a depressed value for closely held company ownership interests, and they might assign discounts as high as 25% to 45% to account for this.

In assigning a marketability discount, some analysts compute the cost of taking the company public and deduct the amount from the value of the company otherwise determined. The presumption is that if the company is taken public, its ownership interests will be marketable.

Control Premiums and Discounts

A business valuation does not have to be restricted to the valuation of an entire company. Frequently, partial ownership interests are valued for purchase or sale, divorce proceedings, estate planning, and other reasons.

When a partial ownership interest is appraised, it is not necessarily true that its value is equivalent to its ownership percentage times the value of the company. Generally, to the extent the ownership interest can control the activities of the business, the ownership interest may have an enhanced value. To the extent the ownership interest has little control over the operations of the company, the ownership interest might have a reduced value. Practitioners frequently account for this with control premiums and lack of control discounts.

For closely held companies, noncontrolling ownership interests can have a depressed value. The company might not be particularly marketable, and the noncontrolling interests might have an even greater lack of appeal because of their inability to influence the payment of dividends and the general operations of the company.

In developing control premiums and lack of control discounts, the circumstances of the ownership interests must be considered. Before a discount or premium is assigned, it should be determined that in fact an ownership interest has an increased or decreased value based on control/lack of control implications. For example, in a company where the father is the controlling owner and two children are the noncontrolling owners, circumstances might indicate that the noncontrolling owners are in fact receiving dividends, etc., commensurate with the value of their ownership percentages. Accordingly, depending on the purpose of the valuation, the assignment of a discount to the noncontrolling interests might not be appropriate. Before assigning premiums or discounts, it is very important to ensure that the control/lack of control implications were not accounted for in some other way in the valuation process.

CONCLUSION

Performing a business valuation is not a simple task. Although a business valuation might seem overwhelming at first, valuation concepts are in fact very logical and intuitive. The major issue is to clearly understand the concepts of valuation and how the concepts are used by the interested party. The next step is to fully investigate the company being valued, its industry, and various implications that might affect its value. Financial forecasting, analytical reviews, sales forecasting, financial analysis, and various planning activities are an important part of the business valuation process.

ADDITIONAL READINGS

Copeland, T., T. Koller, and J. Murrin. *Valuation: Measuring and Managing the Value of Companies*, New York: Wiley, 1994.

Palepu, K., V. Bernard and P. Healy. *Business Analysis and Valuation.* Cincinnati, OH: South-Western Publishing, 1996.

Sanders, John. *Biz-Comps Business Sale Statistics, 1999.* San Diego, CA: BizComps, http://www.bizcomps.com

Yegge, Wilber. *Basic Guide for Buying and Selling a Company*, New York: Wiley, 1999.

24

Security Valuation

Valuation is the process of determining the worth (or value) of an asset. Just like a company's investors, the company's financial managers must have a good understanding of how to value its stocks, bonds, and other securities to judge whether or not they are a "good buy." The failure to understand the concepts and computational procedures in valuing a security may preclude sound financial decisions. This fact is evident in the company's objective of maximizing the value of its common stock. We will use the concept of the time value of money to analyze the values of bonds and stocks. Basic bond valuation and stock valuation models under varying assumptions are discussed. In all cases, bond and stock values are found to be the present value of the future cash flows expected from the security.

In this chapter, you will learn:

- The key inputs and concepts underlying the security valuation process
- How to value bonds
- The various methods of common stock valuation
- A pragmatic approach to stock valuation

HOW TO VALUE A SECURITY

The process of determining security valuation involves finding the present value of an asset's expected future cash flows using the investor's required rate of return. Thus, the basic security valuation model can be defined mathematically as follows:

$$V = \sum_{t=1}^{n} \frac{C_t}{(1+r)^t}$$

where

V = intrinsic value or present value of a security
C_t = expected future cash flows in period $t = 1, \ldots, n$
r = the investor's required rate of return

HOW TO VALUE BONDS

The valuation process for a bond requires knowledge of three basic elements: (1) the amount of the cash flows to be received by the investor, which is equal to the periodic interest to be received and the par value to be paid at maturity; (2) the maturity date of the loan; and (3) the investor's required rate of return.

Incidentally, the periodic interest can be received annually or semiannually. The value of a bond is simply the present value of these cash flows. Two versions of the bond valuation model are presented below.

If the interest payments are made annually, then

$$V = \sum_{t=1}^{n} \frac{I}{(1+r)^t} + \frac{M}{(1+r)^n} = I \times T_4(r,n) + M \times T_3(r,n)$$

where

I = interest payment each year = coupon interest rate × par value

M = par value, or maturity value, typically $1,000

r = the investor's required rate of return

n = number of years to maturity

T_4 = present value interest factor of an annuity of $1 (which can be found in Table 2.4 in Chapter 2)

T_3 = present value interest factor of $1 (which can be found in Table 2.3 in Chapter 2)

Chapter 24: Security Valuation   457

Both T_4 and T_3 were discussed in detail in Chapter 2 (Applying Discounting and Compounding Analysis Techniques).

EXAMPLE 24.1

Consider a bond, maturing in 10 years and having a coupon rate of 8%. The par value is $1,000. Investors consider 10% to be an appropriate required rate of return in view of the risk level associated with this bond. The annual interest payment is $80 (8% × $1,000). The present value of this bond is:

$$V = \sum_{t=1}^{n} \frac{I}{(1+r)^t} + \frac{M}{(1+r)^n}$$

$$= I \times T_4(r,n) + M \times T_3(r,n)$$

$$= \sum_{t=1}^{10} \frac{\$80}{(1+0.1)^t} + \frac{\$1,000}{(1+0.1)^{10}}$$

$$= \$80 \times T_4(10\%,10) + \$1,000 \times T_3(10\%,10)$$

$$= \$80 \ (6.145) + \$1,000 \ (0.386)$$

$$= \$491.60 + 386.00$$

$$= \$877.60$$

If the interest is paid semiannually, then

$$V = \sum_{t=1}^{n} \frac{I}{(1+r)^t} + \frac{M}{(1+r)^n} = I \times T_4(r,n) + M \times T_3(r,n)$$

EXAMPLE 24.2

Assume the same data as in Example 24.1, except the interest is paid semiannually.

$$V = \sum_{t=1}^{2n} \frac{I/2}{(1+2/r)^t} + \frac{M}{(1+r/2)^{2n}} = \frac{I}{2} \times T_4(r/2, 2n) + MT_3(r/2, 2n)$$

$$= \sum_{t=1}^{20} \frac{\$40}{(1+0.05)^t} + \frac{\$1,000}{(1+0.5)^{20}}$$

$$= \$40 \times T_4 \ (5\%, 20) + \$1,000 \times T_3(5\%, 20)$$

$$= \$40 \ (12.462) + \$1,000 \ (0.377)$$

= $498.48 + $377.00

= $875.48

HOW TO VALUE COMMON STOCK

The value of a common stock is the present value of all future cash inflows expected to be received by the investor. The cash inflows expected to be received are dividends and the future price at the time of the sale of the stock.

Single Holding Period

For an investor holding a common stock for only 1 year, the value of the stock would be the present value of both the expected cash dividend to be received in 1 year (D_1) and the expected market price per share of the stock at year-end (P_1). If r represents an investor's required rate of return, the value of common stock (P_0) would be:

$$P_0 = \frac{D_1}{(1+r)^1} + \frac{P_1}{(1+r)^1}$$

EXAMPLE 24.3

Assume an investor is considering the purchase of stock A at the beginning of the year. The dividend at year-end is expected to be $1.50, and the market price by the end of the year is expected to be $40. If the investor's required rate of return is 15%, the value of the stock would be:

$$P_0 = \frac{D_1}{(1+r)^1} + \frac{P_1}{(1+r)^1} = \frac{\$1.50}{(1+0.15)} + \frac{\$40}{(1+0.15)}$$

$$= \$1.50 \times T_3(15\%,1) + \$40 \times T_3(15\%,1)$$

$$= \$1.50(0.870) + \$40(0.870)$$

$$= \$1.31 + \$34.80 = \$36.11$$

Multiple Holding Period

Because common stock has no maturity date and is held for many years, a more general, multiperiod model is needed. The general common stock valuation model is defined as follows:

$$P_0 = \sum_{t=1}^{\infty} \frac{D_t}{(1+r)^t}$$

where

D_t = dividend in period t.

Two cases of growth in dividends are explained below. They are zero growth and constant growth.

Zero Growth Case

In the case of zero growth (i.e., $D_0 = D_1 = \ldots = D$), then the valuation model reduces to the formula:

$$P_0 = \frac{D}{r}$$

This is the case with a perpetuity. This model is most applicable to the valuation of preferred stocks, as was discussed earlier, or the common stocks of very mature companies such as large utilities. *Note:* The *capitalization of earnings method* (discussed in Chapter 23) is based on the zero growth assumption.

EXAMPLE 24.4

Assuming dividends (D) equals $2.50 and r equals 10%, then the value of the stock is:

$$P_0 = \frac{\$2.50}{0.1} = \$25$$

Constant Growth Case

In the case of constant growth, if we assume that dividends grow at a constant rate of g every year [i.e., $D_t = D_0(1+g)^t$], then the general model is simplified to:

$$P_0 = \frac{D_1}{r - g}$$

In words,

$$\text{Commons stock value} = \frac{\text{Dividend in year 1}}{\text{(Required rate of return)} - \text{(Growth rate)}}$$

This formula is known as the *Gordon's valuation model*. This model is most applicable to the valuation of the common stocks of very large or broadly diversified firms.

EXAMPLE 24.5

Consider a common stock that paid a $3 dividend per share at the end of the last year and is expected to pay a cash dividend every year at a growth rate of 10%. Assume the investor's required rate of return is 12%. The value of the stock would be:

$$D_1 = D_0(1 + g) = \$3(1 + 0.10) = \$3.30$$

$$P_0 = \frac{D_1}{(r - g)} = \frac{\$3.30}{0.12 - 0.10} = \$1.65$$

HOW TO FORECAST STOCK PRICE—A PRAGMATIC APPROACH

Many common stock analysts use the simple formula:

Forecasted at the end of year price =
Estimated EPS in year t × Estimated P/E ratio

where EPS = earnings per share and P/E = price earnings ratio or earnings multiple. Of course, for this method to be effective in forecasting the future value of a stock, earnings need to be correctly projected and the appropriate P/E multiple must be applied.

Forecasting EPS is not an easy task. Some accountants use a simple method of forecasting EPS. They use a sales forecast combined with an after-tax profit margin, as follows:

- Estimated after-tax earnings in year earnings t =
  Estimated sales in year t × After-tax profit margin expected in year margin t

- Estimated EPS in year *t* =
Estimated earnings in year earnings *t* / Number of common shares outstanding in year *t*

EXAMPLE 24.6

Assume that a company reported sales of $100 million, and its estimated sales will grow at a 6% annual rate, while the profit margin is about 8%. The company had 2 million shares outstanding. The company's P/E ratio was 15 times earnings and is expected to continue for the next year. Projected sales next year will equal $106 million ($100 million × 1.06).

Estimated after-tax earnings next year is:

$$\$106 \text{ million} \times 8\% = \$8.48 \text{ million}$$
$$\text{Estimated EPS next year} = \$8.48 \text{ million}/2 \text{ million} = \$4.24$$

Then, the company's stock should be trading at a price of $63.60 by the end of next year:

$$\text{Estimated share price next year} = \$4.24 \times 15 = \$63.60$$

Note: If you are looking for an advisory service's estimated EPS for the next year for a company in which you are interested, you can obtain it from publications such as *Value Line Investment Survey, First Call, Zacks Research, Nelson's*, and *IBES*. These firms constantly poll brokerages for their earnings estimates. From that survey, these companies publish a compilation that includes the high, low, and mean prediction for a company's upcoming quarterly and fiscal year results. Earnings expectations are available on many electronic quotation services such as *Bloomberg Business News*. The *Wall Street Journal* publishes a short list on notable surprises each day along with its daily listings of quarterly corporate results. Many brokerage houses have information from these two services available. On the Internet, Zack's web site at www.zacks.com is an excellent free resource.

WHAT ARE THE DETERMINANTS OF THE PRICE–EARNINGS RATIO?

The determination of the P/E multiple is very complex. Empirical evidence seems to suggest the following factors:

- Historical growth rate in earnings
- Forecasted earnings
- Average dividend payout ratio
- *Beta,* the company's systematic (uncontrollable) risk
- Instability of earnings
- Financial leverage
- Other factors such as competitive position, management ability
- Economic conditions

HOW TO READ BETA

Beta measures a security's volatility relative to an average security. Put another way, it is a measure of a security's return over time to that of the overall market. For example, if ABC's beta is 2.0, it means that if the stock market goes up 10%, ABC's common stock goes up 20%; if the market goes down 10%, ABC goes down 20%. *Note:* Generally, the higher the beta for a security, the greater the return expected (or demanded) by the investor.

Here is a guide for how to read betas:

Beta	What It Means
0	The security's return is independent of the market. An example is a risk-free security such as a T-bill.
0.5	The security is only half as responsive as the market.
1.0	The security has the same response or risk as the market (i.e., average risk). This is the beta value of the market portfolio such as Standard & Poor's 500.
2.0	The security is twice as responsive, or risky, as the market.

Note: Beta of a particular stock is useful in predicting how much the security will go up or down, provided that investors know which way the market will go. Beta helps to figure out risk and expected return.

Betas for stocks are widely available in many investment newsletters (e.g., *Value Line Investment Survey*) and online services such as *AOL* and *MSN Money Central* (http://moneycentral.msn.com/investor/home.asp). Table 24.1 presents examples of betas for selected stocks.

TABLE 24.1 Betas for Some Selected Coroporations

Company	Ticker Symbol	Beta
Microsoft	MSFT	1.49
Pfizer	PFE	0.89
Dow	DOW	0.90
Wal-Mart	WMT	1.20
McDonald's	MCD	0.93
Honda	HMC	0.87
Nokia	NOK	1.91
IBM	IBM	1.07

Source: AOL Personal Finance Channel and MSN Money Central Investor (http://moneycentral.msn.com/investor/home.asp), May 22, 2000.

WHAT DOES IT MEAN WHEN A FIRM'S STOCK SELLS ON A HIGH OR LOW P/E RATIO?

To answer this question, the *Gordon's growth model* can be helpful. If a company's dividends are expected to grow at a constant rate, then:

$$P_0 = \frac{D_1}{(r - g)}$$

where P_0 = the current price of stock, D_1 = the expected dividend next year, r = the return required by investors from similar investments, and g = the expected growth in dividends. In order to find the P/E ratio, dividing by expected EPS yields:

$$\frac{P_0}{\text{EPS}} = \frac{D_1}{\text{EPS}} \times \frac{1}{r - g}$$

Thus, a high P/E ratio may indicate that:

- Investors expect high dividend growth (g), *or*
- The stock has low risk and, therefore investors are content with a low prospective return (r), *or*
- The company is expected to achieve average growth while paying out a high proportion of earnings (D_1/EPS).

TABLE 24.2 P/E Ratios

Company	Industry	1998
Boeing	Aerospace	32
General Motors	Cars and trucks	21
Goodyear	Tire and rubber	13
Gap	Retailing	52
Intel	Semiconductor	37
Pfizer	Drugs and research	88

Source: *Corporate Scorecard*, by *Business Week*, McGraw-Hill, March 1999, pp. 75–91.

Table 24.2 shows price–earnings ratios of certain companies. Online computer investment databases such as www.marketguide.com contain such information.

CONCLUSION

In this chapter we have discussed the valuation of bonds, preferred stock, and common stock. Valuation is essentially a present value concept that involves estimating future cash flows and discounting them at a required rate of return. The value of a bond is essentially the present value of all future interest and principal payments. Stock price may be expressed as a function of the expected future dividends and a rate of return required by investors. The Gordon's valuation model reflects this process.

25 Forensic Accounting*

WHAT IS FORENSIC ACCOUNTING?

Forensic accounting is a science (i.e., a department of systemized knowledge) dealing with the application of accounting facts gathered through auditing methods and procedures to resolve legal problems. Forensic accounting is very different from traditional auditing. The main purpose of a traditional audit is to examine the financial statements of an organization and express an opinion on the fairness of the financial statements. In other words, auditors give an opinion whether the financial statements have been prepared in accordance with generally accepted accounting principles. Auditors employ limited procedures and use extensive testing and sampling techniques. Audits are performed by independent accountants and are not conducted with a view to present the evidence in a judicial forum. An audit is not an investigation; its main objective is not to uncover fraud.

Forensic accounting, on the other hand, is for investigation of an allegation with the assumption that the forensic accountant will have to present the evidence in a judicial forum. A forensic accountant often employs specialists in other areas as part of a team to gather evidence. In order to present the evidence in court, there must be absolute assurance; thus testing and sampling methods are usually not employed as part of the evidence-gathering procedures. The scope of the investigation is limited because it is determined by the client.

---

*This chapter is contributed by Frank Grippo, Dean, School of Business, William Paterson University.

Forensic accounting, therefore, is a specialty requiring the integration of investigative, accounting, and auditing skills. The forensic accountant looks at documents and financial and other data in a critical manner in order to draw conclusions and to calculate values, and to identify irregular patterns and/or suspicious transactions. A forensic accountant understands the fraud risk areas and has extensive fraud knowledge. A forensic accountant does not merely look at the numbers but rather, looks *behind* the numbers.

One can extend this definition to say that forensic accounting is a discipline consisting of two areas of specialization; namely, litigation support specialists and investigation or fraud accountants. Litigation support specialists concern themselves with business valuation, testimony as expert witnesses, future earnings' evaluation, and income and expense analysis. On the other hand, fraud accountants apply their skills to investigate areas of alleged criminal misconduct in order to support or dispel damages. These fields overlap—a forensic accountant may do litigation support work on one engagement and act as a fraud accountant on another. Both of these engagements could result in expert testimony by the forensic accountant. Thus, forensic accounting can be defined in a more generic way: It is merely a discipline where auditing, accounting, and investigative skills are used to assist in disputes involving financial issues and data, and where there is suspicion or allegation of fraud. The expertise of the forensic accountant may be used to support a plaintiff who is trying to establish a claim, or to support a defendant in order to minimize the impact of a claim against him or her. Usually such investigations involve litigation; sometimes, however, such disputes are settled by negotiation. In either case, persuasive and authoritative evidence resulting from the financial and investigative skills of the forensic accountant is imperative. Therefore, the forensic accountant must be a good businessperson and be aware of statutory law, common law, and the laws of evidence and procedure.

Usually the forensic accountant's findings are based on facts, not opinions. Facts can be investigated, and the forensic accountant can prepare a definitive report on these facts. Nevertheless, there are situations where the forensic accountant may rely on professional judgment and present findings using an opinion-type report. Needless to say, the reports based on facts usually do not present problems in court cases because they are supported by underlying documentation. Opinion reports, on the other hand, are subjective and require the forensic accountant to demonstrate competency and to provide adequate logic for the stated opinion.

Two points are often overlooked when one is involved in a case as a forensic accountant; namely, (1) the other side usually employs a forensic accountant as well; and (2) the credibility of a forensic accountant is extremely important. Thus the forensic accountant must have high professional standards and ethics.

WHY IS FORENSIC ACCOUNTING NECESSARY?

Business and criminal activities have become so complex that lawyers and criminal investigators often do not have the expertise necessary to discharge their responsibilities. This fact plus the marked increase in white-collar crime, marital and business disputes, and other claims have created the need for the new industry of forensic accounting. Although this specialty is not limited to fraud issues, nevertheless, the reality of forensic accounting is that most of the work does involve fraud investigations. In the case of fraud, the work of a forensic accounting team is crucial, as the survival of the business may rest on the outcome. Good businesspeople must realize that fraud is a permanent risk in any and all businesses. Thus company leaders must devise ways to prevent fraud rather than trying to manage the consequences of fraud. The instances of fraud have increased because of lack of government commitment, more sophisticated criminals, inefficiency of the judicial system, more complex technology, lack of adequate penalties and deterrents, and "old fashioned" greed and arrogance. Studies have shown that fraud will continue to increase. Currently, about 75% of fraud results from employees; other sources of fraud include customers, management, suppliers, and service providers. In addition, about 55% of fraud is discovered as a result of strong internal controls. Other methods of discovery include whistle blowers, customers, internal auditors, and by accident or formal investigation.

WHEN DOES ONE EMPLOY A FORENSIC ACCOUNTANT?

Clients retain forensic accountants when they are interested in either litigation support or investigations.

Litigation Support

This is a situation where the forensic accountant is asked to give an opinion either on known facts or facts yet uncovered. The forensic accountant is an integral part of the legal team, helping to substantiate allegations, analyze facts, dispute claims, and develop motives. The amount of involvement and the point at which the forensic accountant gets involved varies from case to case. Sometimes the forensic accountant is called upon from the beginning of the case; other times the forensic accountant is summoned before the case is scheduled to go to court and after out-of-court settlements have failed. Thus, in litigation support, the forensic accountant assists in obtaining documentation to support or dispel a claim, to review documentation to give an assessment of the case to the legal team, and/or to identify areas where loss occurred. Moreover, the forensic accountant may be asked to get involved during the discovery stage to help formulate questions and may be asked to review the opposing expert's witness report to give an evaluation of its strengths and weaknesses. During trial the forensic accountant may serve as an expert witness, help to provide questions for cross-examination, and assist with settlement discussions after the trial.

Investigations

Investigations most often involve fraud and are associated with criminal matters. Typically, an investigative accounting assignment would result from a client's suspicion that there is employee fraud. Other parties, such as regulatory agencies, police forces, and attorneys, may retain a forensic accountant to investigate securities fraud, kickbacks, insurance fraud, money-laundering schemes, and asset search and analysis.

WHERE IS A FORENSIC ACCOUNTANT USED?

A forensic accountant is used in a number of situations, including, but not limited to the following:

- *Business valuations:* A forensic accountant evaluates the current value of a business for various personal or legal matters.
- *Personal injury and fatal accident claims:* A forensic accountant may help to establish lost earnings (i.e., those earnings that the plaintiff would have accrued except for the actions of the defendant) by gathering and analyzing a variety of information and then issuing a report based on the outcome of the analyses.
- *Professional negligence:* A forensic accountant helps to determine if a breach of professional ethics or other standards of professional practice

has occurred. (e.g., failure to apply generally accepted auditing standards by a CPA when performing an audit). In addition, the forensic accountant may help to quantify the loss.

- *Insurance claims evaluations:* A forensic accountant may prepare financial analyses for an insurance company of claims, business income losses, expenses, and disability, liability or workmen's compensation insurance losses.
- *Arbitration:* A forensic accountant is sometimes retained to assist with alternative dispute resolution (ADR) by acting as a mediator to allow individuals and businesses to resolve disputes in a timely manner with a minimum of disruption.
- *Partnership and corporation disputes:* A forensic accountant may be asked to help settle disputes between partners or shareholders. Detailed analyses are often necessary of many records spanning a number of years. Most of these disputes relate to compensation and benefit issues.
- *Civil and criminal actions concerning fraud and financial irregularities:* These investigations are usually performed by the forensic accountant for police forces. A report is prepared to assist the prosecutor's office.
- *Fraud and white-collar crime investigations:* These types of investigations can be prepared on behalf of police forces as well or for private businesses. They usually result from such activities as purchasing/kickback schemes, computer fraud, labor fraud, and falsification of inventory. The investigation by the forensic accountant often involves fund tracing, asset identification, and recovery.

HOW DOES A FORENSIC ACCOUNTANT WORK?

Although each case is distinct and requires accounting and auditing procedures unique to the assignment, many forensic accounting assignments would include the following steps:

- *Meet with the client*: The forensic accountant should meet with the client to determine the scope of the engagement. In addition, it is advisable to obtain an engagement letter specifying the terms of the engagement.
- *Determine independence*: It is understood that a CPA should be independent when performing an audit or other attest services for clients. It is mandatory as well that the forensic accountant be independent, other-

wise the credibility of the forensic accountant will be questioned if the engagement results in a legal case.

- *Plan the engagement*: Proper, advance planning is essential to any type of engagement. The plan should be similar to an audit program, detailing objectives and procedures in a form that addresses the scope of the engagement so that some type of conclusion can be reached.
- *Gather evidence and perform analyses:* The forensic accountant should match the auditing, accounting, or investigative technique, employed with the type of evidence to be obtained. A specific technique may satisfy more than one objective. When the forensic accountant, for example, performs an audit technique for a particular account, evidence for other accounts may be discovered based on the double-entry system of accounting. Forensic accountants use a variety of techniques including inquiry, confirmation, physical examination, observation, inspection, reconciliation, tracing, vouching, reperformance, and analytical procedures.
- *Make a conclusion and prepare the report*: The forensic accountant should write the final report in a manner that clearly explains the nature of the assignment and the scope of the work. It should indicate the approach used for discovery of information, and detail findings and/or opinions.

A CASE IN FORENSIC ACCOUNTING

The following is an actual case involving the purchase of a business. The plaintiff alleges that the records shown to him were not accurate and that the lawyer who handled the closing for him was negligent.

MAGYAR, INC.
A Case Study in Fraud

"Since I was a little boy, I wanted to own a business. I never wanted to work for anyone else," Omar Saleem said to his wife, Sylvia.

Omar Saleem was 50 years old, came to the United States 30 years ago, and has worked for a large furniture manufacturer for 28 years. One day, he was reading the classified advertisements of the newspaper and noticed an office business for sale in the next town. He discussed the idea with his wife and she approved. So he contacted the seller and made an appointment.

Three days later Omar met with Rahman Magyar, the sole owner of Magyar, Inc. Rahman was an engaging individual, very smooth and personable. Omar was very impressed with Rahman's knowledge of the business and with his self-confidence. Rahman told Omar that he was selling the business because he was bored with it. He had built the company from nothing into a very successful business and now wanted to try something else. Omar believed everything that Rahman said. Rahman said he would be glad to open his books to Omar, but would require a good-faith, refundable deposit of $1,000. Omar agreed and made another appointment for the following week.

Omar met with Rahman and gave the $1,000 good-faith deposit. Rahman in turn showed Omar his equipment and inventory and explained more about the business. Specifically he told him that he averages about $120,000 per year in office supplies and equipment sales, and about $30,000 in services. The latter is a mail service where he prepares and mails packages for customers. Rahman produced a fee schedule and claimed that this end of the business has been very lucrative. After showing Omar the inventory, Rahman flashed some papers and tax returns in front of Omar to show him the growth since he opened the business in February 1994. Rahman said that the business has averaged about 20% growth each year. Omar looked at the papers, but actually didn't know what he was looking at. Furthermore, Rahman assured him that the paperwork was in order since his brother-in-law prepared them. He said his brother-in-law, Raj Kupar, was a CPA and that everything was in order. Rahman said that he would sell the business for $160,000, which is less than the normal selling price for this type of business. He said that the selling price is usually one times annual sales. He further said that "since you and I are from the same country, I will help you out. I prefer to sell to you over someone else."

He convinced Omar that he could easily make $75,000 from the business. Furthermore, he suggested that Omar move fast as there were a number of people interested in the business. Omar said that he would have to get an attorney. He promised to get back to Rahman in a week or so. Rahman even suggested an attorney.

Omar was quite excited and couldn't wait to get home to tell his wife. His wife was very supportive. Therefore, Omar asked his good friend, Stanley, if he knew an attorney. Stanley referred him to Neil Klavin, an attorney in town. On the following Monday, Omar called the attorney and made an appointment for Friday of that week. Before the meeting, Omar called Rahman and asked if he would accept $150,000 for the business. Rahman said that he would, but wanted cash and that he would not want to finance the business. Omar said that he had $110,000 in cash, but would require a loan of $40,000. Rahman surprisingly agreed to finance $40,000, but wanted 8% interest. They verbally agreed. Omar said that he was going to see an attorney on Friday to explain the deal. Rahman said "great."

On Friday, Omar went to the attorney, Neil Klavin, with his wife. Omar and the attorney discussed the business deal at length. Klavin said that he would be happy to represent Omar and would gladly review the contract drawn up by Rahman's attorney. Omar told the attorney that he had seen some documentation regarding income and expenses including the tax returns. Omar told Klavin that he would like him to review the documentation as well. The attorney said "fine." Omar left the office and then contacted Rahman. He gave Rahman his attorney's name and told him to have his lawyers draw up the paperwork. Omar's wife asked if he was moving a little too fast. Omar said that he had to move fast as it was a good deal and that Rahman had other interested buyers. He felt comfortable that his attorney would say it was a good deal after the attorney reviewed the numbers.

About two weeks later, Neil Klavin received the financial information from Rahman's attorney along with a contract of sale and promissory note for $40,000 at 8% interest. Neil reviewed the information and appeared to find everything in order. Although he did not understand the financials and tax returns that well, he did not suggest to Omar that anything was improper. Nor did he suggest soliciting the help of an expert. For example, he did not suggest contacting a CPA to review the books, financials and tax returns. The closing was scheduled for December 27, 1996. Rahman and Omar appeared at the closing with their wives. The contract and promissory note were signed. Omar was to start on the following Monday. Rahman agreed to stay around for a month to train both Omar and his wife. Since this was a family business (husband and wife), they only had the need for occasional casual labor. Rahman never had a payroll.

Omar showed up on January 2, 1997 eager to learn all about the business. He met Rahman, who turned over the keys to the store. Rahman was very gracious and patient as he explained things to Omar and his wife. This went on for the whole month as agreed upon at closing. During the month, Omar and his wife discussed the relative inactivity. They even mentioned this to Rahman, who replied that January is always slow because it is after the holidays. Rahman said "don't worry as December more than makes up for January." Omar and his wife didn't think too much about it.

Omar was now on his own. He and his wife worked diligently at the business each day. His wife prepared advertisements for the newspaper and ran a number of specials. They methodically kept track of daily revenues and expenses. It became apparent after seven months that the volume was nothing like Rahman had said. They both wondered what they were doing wrong. They were somewhat in denial and did not want to think that they may have been misled and/or tricked. They talked between themselves and decided to talk to an attorney, but not Neil Klavin. Instead they discussed the matter with one of their customers, an attorney named Ted Rich. Ted often went into the store to buy supplies and do special mailings of packages. He took a personal interest in both Omar and his wife, Sylvia. Therefore, he suggested that they make an appointment and discuss the matter further.

Omar and Sylvia talked more about the problem. Another two months went by without any appreciable increase in sales numbers. Finally they made an appointment with Ted Rich. Omar did most of the talking. He also brought copies of all the paperwork that he had including any financial information that he received from Rahman. He also included summaries of his revenues and expenses for the last nine months. They discussed alternatives. Ted asked a number of pertinent questions including whether Omar had an accountant, preferably a CPA, to review the financial information that he received from Rahman. Omar said that he didn't. He said that he gave all the information to his attorney to review. Omar made it clear to Ted that he depended on his attorney, Neil Klavin, for advice. Ted was not in the business of suing other attorneys; however, he was upset that Klavin was so sloppy with the closing. He knew that Omar and his wife were naïve. Nevertheless, that was no excuse for not following due diligence procedures. He believed that Klavin should have realized this and looked out for the welfare of his client. Not wanting to make an immediate decision, Ted told Omar that he would review the information and get back to them in a couple of weeks.

A few days later, Ted reviewed the file and decided that the best way to handle the case was to get an accountant to review the financial information including the tax returns for 1994, 1995, and 1996. Ted called Omar to ask for approval to retain an accountant. Omar agreed.

The next day Ted called George Spyros, a CPA and CFE (certified fraud examiner). George has a small forensic practice and had done work for Ted in the past. Ted and George met for about an hour the following day. George looked at the financial statements and tax returns. The first thing George did was check to see if Rahman's brother-in-law was indeed a CPA. He was not. The reason he did that first was because his cursory review of the tax returns revealed gross preparation errors. It only took George about eight hours to do a detailed review of the paperwork. George then prepared a report for Ted (Exhibit A).

Ted reviewed the report prepared by Spyros and Company. Based on the report and his discussions with George Spyros, he decided to take the case and pursue suing Neil Klavin. Over the next few months, Ted diligently worked on the case including obtaining interrogatories from a number of individuals including Omar and his wife, Rahman Magyar, and Neil Klavin.

Ted knew that the case was not solid. Therefore, he asked for the opinion of another attorney, Richard Darius of Darius and Spivack. He also asked for a second opinion from Edward Caruso. Both of these attorneys had experience suing other attorneys. Their opinions can be found in Exhibit B and Exhibit C, respectively.

Since the two attorneys had different opinions, Ted thought that it would be in the best interest of his client to try to settle out of court.

EXHIBIT A

SPYROS AND COMPANY
CERTIFIED PUBLIC ACCOUNTANTS
447 PEARL STREET
WOODBRIDGE, NEW JERSEY 07095

Mr. Theodore R. Rich
400 Pearl Street
Woodbridge, New Jersey 07095

Dear Mr. Rich,

In accordance with your request, we have reviewed the Federal income tax returns (Form 1120) of Magyar, Inc. for the eleven months ended December 31, 1994, and the years ended December 31, 1995 and 1996. The purpose of our review was to obtain reasonable assurance about whether the tax returns are free of material misstatement. Our review included examining the propriety of the amounts presented on the returns based on analytical procedures. Specifically, we have determined that:

(1) The company employed the accrual basis of accounting (see box checked on page 2 of the 1994 return). Since the balance sheets each year do not show any accounts receivable or accounts payable, one can logically conclude that all revenues and expenses were for cash.

(2) Based on the conclusion reached in (1) above, the cash balances reflected on the balance sheets on page 4 of the 1995 and 1996 tax returns are not reasonable. This fact can be supported by the following reconciliation:

Increase (decrease) in cash—	
Cash balance at inception	$ —
Issuance of stock in 1994	7,536
Loans in 1994	29,438
Equipment	(16,251)
Sales	101,792
Cost of sales	(118,326)
Expenses (excluding depreciation of $638)	(25,812)
Cash balance on December 31, 1994 should be	$ (21,623)
Cash balance on December 31, 1994 per tax return	$ 250

Comments:
It is unreasonable for cost of sales to be more than sales.
Cash is misstated by $21,873.

Recalculated cash balance on January 1, 1995	$ (21,623)
Additional issuance of stock in 1995	23,960
Payoff of loans	(29,438)
Sales	141,158
Cost of sales	(139,617)
Expenses (excluding depreciation of $638	(38,102)
Cash balance on December 31, 1995 should be	$ (63,662)
Cash balance on December 31, 1995 per tax return	$ 250

Comments:
It is unreasonable for cost of sales to be 99% of sales.
Cash is misstated cumulatively by $63,912.

Recalculated cash balance on January 1, 1996	$ (63,662)
Sales	157,572
Cost of sales	(145,710)
Expenses (excluding depreciation of $638)	(24,417)
Cash balance on December 31, 1996 should be	$(76,217)
Cash balance on December 31, 1996 per tax return	$295

Comments:
It is unreasonable for cost of sales to be 93% of sales.
Cash is misstated cumulatively by $76,512.

We also compared the tax returns to the internal financial statements prepared by Raj Kupar, who we understand is a CPA and brother-in-law of the prior owner of the business, Rahman Magyar. Please be advised that we could not find a relationship between the financial statements and the tax returns. The tax returns were materially different from the internal financial statements. Revenues on the internal financials were approximately $15,000 higher in 1994, $18,000 lower in 1995 and $30,000 higher in 1996. There appeared to be only a partial listing of expenses, such that 1994 showed a profit of $70,000, 1995 a profit of $65,000 and 1996 a profit of $74,000. The costs and expenses were substantially less than those shown on the tax returns. In addition, the tax returns reflected substantial losses each year. Finally, the internal financial statements were not prepared in accordance with generally accepted accounting principles.

You also asked us to check whether or not Mr. Kupar is a practicing CPA in New Jersey. We did check with the New Jersey State Board of Public Accountants. He is neither a licensed CPA nor licensed public accountant.

Thank you for the opportunity of serving you. If you have any questions about this report, please contact us directly.

Woodbridge, New Jersey
July 24, 1998

EXHIBIT B

DARIUS AND SPIVACK
One Main Street
Hackensack, NJ 07601

March 25, 1999

Theodore R. Rich, Esq.
100 Pearl Street
Woodbridge, New Jersey 07095

    Re: Saleem v. Klavin

Dear Mr. Rich:

This report relates to an action for legal malpractice brought by your clients, **Omar and Sylvia Saleem against Neil Klavin**, a member of the New Jersey Bar. It derives from your request for my opinion as to whether third party defendant Klavin breached any duty to his former clients, the third party plaintiffs herein, when he undertook to represent them in July, 1996, with respect to the purchase of a certain office supply and mail box business, known as Magyar, Inc., located at 189 Princeton Road, Woodbridge, New Jersey.

For purposes of this report, I have read, analyzed and relied upon multiple documents contained in all your litigation files, including the February 9, 1998 depositions of Omar Saleem, Sylvia Saleem and Rahman Magyar; the December 27, 1996 Contract of Sale between Magyar, Inc., and Omar and Sylvia Saleem; the January 4, 1997 addendum to closing statement; the January 2, 1997 Lease between Magyar, Inc. and Marjama Company; Rahman Magyar's answers to interrogatories; the December 27, 1996 note from Omar and Sylvia Saleem to Rahman Magyar; correspondence between attorneys D'Orio (for seller) and Klavin (for buyer) dated respectively October 14, 1996 and November 2, 1996 and December 3, 1996. Kindly note that the documents listed above do not include all the materials examined by me, such as all correspondence between and among the parties, all pleadings, all discovery, and the like. Most especially did I review and analyze the July 24, 1998 expert report of Spyros and Company, Certified Public Accountants, rendered on behalf of Omar and Sylvia Saleem.

STATEMENT OF FACTS

In early 1996, Omar Saleem, a native of Syria, but living and working in the United States since 1966, expressed interest in buying a small business. He read about a business for sale in the local newspaper. He answered the advertisement and soon met one Rahman Magyar, the owner of Magyar, Inc., a company engaged in the office supply and mail service business. Later, at a meeting held in Rahman Magyar's office, Omar verbally said that he was interested in purchasing the business. About a week later Saleem called Magyar. The two agreed on a price of $150,000 including a $40,000 promissory note to Magyar. During the course of the preliminary negotiations, Magyar had assured the Saleems that the business was a very simple operation which they would have no problem understanding and that he would agree to work a month in the business free of charge to train both Omar and his wife. For whatever reason, Magyar never offered the Saleems an opportunity to examine the books and records of the Company, or to have them examined by an outside accountant. However, he did show them some tax returns and financial statements prepared by his brother-in-law, whom he alleged was a CPA. After the closing, Magyar did provide on-the-job training, but it was hurried and did not afford the Saleems hardly any opportunity to understand the economics of the business.

The essential complaint of the Saleems is that their attorney Klavin failed to provide them with appropriate legal advice and counsel in connection with the actual purchase of the business. In this regard the Saleems contend that Klavin failed to incorporate certain conditions and contingencies in the December 27, 1997 contract which would have made the sale subject to a review of all books, records, income tax returns, and the like, by a Certified Public Accountant acting on behalf of the buyers. Thus, instead of advising the Saleems not to sign the contract and make any substantial deposit until the Saleems had all the books and records examined by their accountant; and having, alternatively, failed to incorporate such protective contingencies and conditions in the contract, Klavin put his clients on the horns of a dilemma faced, as they unfortunately were, with either losing their $1,000 deposit or purchasing the business in total ignorance of its monthly income and expenses.

CONCLUSIONS OF LAW

The matter of attorney negligence arising out of this matter, must, of course, be evaluated and judged in accordance with the standard of care applicable in legal malpractice actions. In this regard, it is settled that an attorney is obligated to exercise on behalf of his client the knowledge, skill and ability ordinarily possessed and exercised by members of the legal profession similarly situated, and to employ reasonable care and prudence in connection therewith. *McCullough v. Sullivan*, 102 N.J.L. 381, 384 (E. & A. 1926); *Sullivan v. Stoudt*, 120 N.J.L. 304, 308 (E. & A. 1938); *Taylor v. Shepard*, 136 NJ Super. 85, 90 (App. Div. 1982); *Saint Pius X House of Retreats v. Camden Diocese*, 88 N.J. 571, 588, (1982). Perhaps the most quoted statement of the rule of care applicable to attorney negligence suits is found in *Hodges v. Carter*, 239 N.C. 517, 80 S.E. 2nd 144 (1954):

> "Ordinarily when an attorney engages in the practice of the law and contracts to prosecute an action in behalf of his client, he impliedly represents that (1) he possesses the requisite degree of learning, skill and ability necessary to the practice of his profession and which others similarly situated ordinarily possess; (2) he will exercise his best judgment in the prosecution of the litigation entrusted to him; and (3) he will exercise into reasonable and ordinary care and diligence in the use of his skill and in the application of his knowledge to his client's cause." (Id. at 519, 80 S.E. 2nd at 145146).

What constitutes a reasonable degree of care is not to be considered in a vacuum. On the contrary, it must be the facts and circumstances of each specific case, and the type of service the attorney undertakes therein. With this in mind, I now proceed to examine the conduct of the subject defendant attorney in connection with his professional duties and conduct in the management of the above matter.

The record shows an egregious failure on the part of attorney Klavin to safeguard and protect the interests of his clients when he undertook to represent them in the purchase of Magyar, Inc. This conclusion is based upon the fact that defendant Klavin made no attempt to follow the standard and elementary procedures mandated for any attorney representing a buyer in the acquisition of a corporation. Thus, if Klavin had truly represented the interests of the Saleems, he would not only have examined all Magyar Inc.'s Federal and State tax returns, he would also, as a part of that investigation, have conducted a lien search in every place that Magyar conducted its business; would have obtained from Magyar an up-to-date financial statement in order to understand the economic aspects of the deal; would have obtained an independent audit of that financial statement; would have checked the terms, acceleration clauses and restrictions on any notes or mortgages or other indebtedness of the corporation; would have examined all insurance policies to discover what unknown liabilities existed; would have examined the viability and collectability of all accounts receivable; would have made a complete physical inventory of all corporate assets, together with a current market evaluation of same; would have examined the important contracts of Magyar and its customers, which constituted the life blood of that corporation; and would have performed other common sense duties, such as talking to the main customers of Magyar, all for the overall purpose of insuring that the interests of his clients, the Saleems, were fully protected and safeguarded.

It is my opinion that if Klavin had conducted this type of basic and common sense investigation, as he was bound to do in accordance with his duties as an attorney of this state, the Saleems would not have undertaken to purchase Magyar, and would thereby have escaped all the financial damage, loss of time, mental stress and anguish which they unfortunately suffered as a result of this purchase. Indeed, we now know that as a direct result of his negligence, Klavin caused his clients to lose at least $110,000 due to the misrepresentations made by the seller. In short, I find on the facts and the law that defendant Klavin, in his attorney–client relationship with the Saleems, fell below the standard of care and prudence exercised by ordinary members of the New Jersey Bar. Otherwise put, attorney Klavin, in his relationship with the Saleems, deviated substantially from the standard of care expected of New Jersey attorneys.

But it remains basic to the Saleems' cause of action for legal malpractice that the wrongful conduct or failures of attorney Klavin are a proximate cause of their injuries. In order to establish "causation," the burden is clearly upon the Saleems to prove that the negligence of Klavin was "more likely than not" a substantial factor in causing the unfavorable result. *Lecral Malpractice, Mallen & Levit*, at pg. 502; and also see *Lieberman v. Employers Ins. of Wassau*, 85 N.J. 325, 341 (1980); *Hoppe y. Ranzini*, 58 N.J. Super. 233, 238239 (App. Div. 1975), certif. den. 70 N.J. 144 (1976); *Lamb v. Barbour*, 188 N.J. Super. 6, 12 (App. Div. 1982); and as to the test of proximate cause see *State v. Jersey Central Power & Light Co.*, 69 N.J. 102, 100 (1976); *Ettin v. Ava Truck Leasing Inc.*, 153 N.J. 463, 483 (1969). And plaintiff is obliged to carry this burden of proof by the presentation of competent, credible evidence, which proves material facts; and not conjecture, surmise or suspicion. *Long v. Landy*, 35 N.J. 44, 54 (1961); *Modla v. United States*, 15 F. Supp. 198, 201, (D.N.J. 1957). Otherwise stated, third party plaintiffs herein must establish a chain of causation between their damages and the negligence or other wrongful conduct on the part of defendant Klavin. *Catto v. Schnepp*, 21 N.J. supra. 506, 511 (App. Div.) aff1d o.b. 62 N.J. 20 (1972).

Based upon the facts presented to me, and the applicable law, it is my view that the inexplicable failure of defendant Klavin to inspect or provide for the inspection of all Magyar, Inc. tax returns and corporate books and records, were the immediate factors that caused the Saleems to sustain heavy losses. It follows, therefore, that third party defendant Klavin is liable to the third party plaintiffs Saleems for legal malpractice and all causally related damages.

Very truly yours,

Richard M. Darius

EXHIBIT C

EDWARD J. CARUSO
Counselor at Law
300 Broad Street
Newark, New Jersey 07104

June 8, 1999

Theodore R. Rich, Esq.
100 Pearl Street
Woodbridge, New Jersey 07095

    Re: Saleem v. Klavin

Dear Mr. Rich:

Please be advised that this opinion relates to an action for legal malpractice brought by your clients, Omar and Sylvia Saleem against Neil Klavin, a member of the New Jersey Bar. It derives from your request for my opinion as to whether third party defendant Klavin breached any duty to his former clients, the third party plaintiffs herein, when he undertook to represent them in July, 1996, with respect to the purchase of a certain office supply and mail box business, known as Magyar, Inc., located at 189 Princeton Road, Woodbridge, New Jersey.

For purposes of this report, I have read, analyzed and relied upon the following documents contained in all your litigation files:

- February, 9, 1998 depositions of Omar Saleem, Sylvia Saleem and Rahman Magyar;
- December 27, 1996 Contract of Sale between Magyar, Inc., and Omar and Sylvia Saleem;
- January 4, 1997 addendum to closing statement;
- January 2, 1997 Lease between Magyar, Inc. and Marjama Company;
- Rahman Magyar answers to interrogatories;
- December 27, 1996 note from Omar and Sylvia to Rahman Magyar;
- correspondence between attorneys D'Orio (for seller) and Klavin (for buyer) dated respectively October 14, 1996 and November 2, 1996 and December 3, 1996;
- July 24, 1998 expert report prepared by the CPA firm of Spyros and Company; and
- March 25, 1999 expert opinion of Darius and Spivack.

Also please note that the documents listed above do not include all the materials examined by me, such as all correspondence between and among the parties, all pleadings, all discovery, and the like.

I have reviewed the documents referred to above in order to provide you with my opinion as to whether Neil Klavin deviated from the standard of care, which would be applicable in this transaction. Based on my review of all the documents set forth above, I am of the opinion that Mr. Klavin did not deviate from the standard of care for the reasons set forth below.

The transaction that is the subject of the litigation and this report involved the purchase of a business known as Magyar, Inc. The plaintiffs, Omar and Sylvia Saleem, executed a contract to purchase the aforesaid business from Magyar, Inc. In connection with the original negotiations relative to the business, the plaintiffs received a document showing projection of income and return on equity in connection with the business. This document was reviewed by the plaintiffs prior to the execution of the contract. The document was, in fact, executed by both of the plaintiffs, namely Omar and Sylvia Saleem.

After the parties agreed on all relevant terms for the transaction, the seller's attorney, Louis D'Orio, prepared a contract of sale. Ultimately, the contract was taken to Mr. Klavin by Omar Saleem. After reviewing the contract, Klavin prepared a review letter dated November 2, 1996. The review letter set forth a number of contingencies including, but not limited to, the following:

1. Review and approval of the existing lease . . .
2. A requirement that the buyer be permitted to review the books of the seller . . . and
3. Inclusion in the contract of a more detailed listing of scheduled assets

The response to Mr. Klavin's letter was Mr. D'Orio's letter dated December 3, 1996. In that letter Mr. D'Orio advised Mr. Klavin that a lease contingency was not necessary since the lease had already been reviewed and approved by Mr. Klavin's clients. Mr. Klavin did question his clients in connection with the aforesaid lease and ultimately was satisfied that his clients read, understood, and were willing to accept same.

The next item discussed in Mr. D'Orio's letter was Mr. Klavin's request that his clients be permitted access to the books and records of the selling corporation. Mr. D'Orio requested that the review period be limited to five days and that there be some ascertainable standard as to whether or not the review was "acceptable" or "unacceptable." In the last section of his letter, Mr. D'Orio provides Mr. Klavin with a more detailed schedule of assets.

It is obvious that the contents of Mr. D'Orio's letter were reviewed by Mr. Klavin and further reviewed by Mr. Klavin with his clients. I note that Mr. D'Orio requested that Mr. Klavin and/or his clients execute the letter so same could be incorporated as a part of the contract. I further note that Mr. Klavin, in fact, had his clients execute the letter after he reviewed same with him.

It is interesting that when Mr. Klavin forwarded the December 3, 1996 letter, which was executed by his clients, he included a cover letter in an effort to resolve the issue relative to a satisfactory review of the books and records. In that letter, Mr. Klavin indicates that his clients' review of the books would be acceptable provided the books and records indicate gross receipts in excess of $175,000. I believe it is unequivocally clear that Mr. Klavin was sensitive to his clients' needs to review the books and records and furthermore had a discussion with his clients in connection with same. Stated another way, Mr. Klavin had placed his clients in a position where they were able to have access to the books and records before performing the contract.

In addition, the other elements of the transaction, including lease review, etc., were all properly handled by Mr. Klavin. All of the critical issues in connection with the purchase of a business were considered and reviewed with the client and were also the subject of informed consent.

In the opinion letter of Darius and Spivak, Mr. Darius suggests that "Klavin failed to incorporate certain conditions and contingencies in the December 27, 1996 contract, which would have made the sale subject to a review of all books . . ." This obviously is inapposite to the existing fact pattern, since the letter of December 3, 1996 clearly incorporates that contingency. Mr. Darius goes on to indicate that Mr. Klavin should have advised the Saleems not to sign the contract and make a deposit until the Saleems had all the books and records examined by their accountant This simply flies in the face of the normal business practice in connection with the sale of a business. Having conducted numerous business closings over my 31 years of practice, it is my opinion that it would be extremely unusual to be involved in a transaction where a seller would let a buyer review books on any basis unless a substantial good faith deposit was made and a contract was executed by the parties.

Finally, Mr. Darius suggests that Mr. Klavin put his clients "on the horns of a dilemma," which resulted in their being faced with either losing a deposit or purchasing a business in total ignorance of the monthly income. This dilemma was not created by Klavin. Mr. Klavin clearly gave his clients the opportunity to have the books and records reviewed. He received representations from his clients that they were reviewed and understood. If Mr. Klavin's clients had, in fact, performed their due diligence and reviewed the books and were unsatisfied with the result of their review, the contract could have been voided provided the review occurred within the contractual period. It was only at the day of the closing that the plaintiffs first indicated that *they* had not an opportunity to review the books and records of the corporation.

At that point, Mr. Klavin properly advised his clients that in the event they refused to consummate the transaction, they faced a possible loss of their deposit, and possibly other damages for breach of contract, since they did not avail themselves of the accounting contingency within the time period set forth in the contract.

I note that Mr. Darius states in his report "that if Klavin had truly represented the interest of the Saleems, he would not only have examined all Magyar's Federal and State tax returns; he would also, as part of the investigation, have conducted a lien search . . ." It appears that Mr. Darius is suggesting that Mr. Klavin should fulfill the role of an accountant and examine the books and records of the corporation. This is simply not an accurate statement, nor an accurate reflection of the duty of a closing attorney. Insofar as the lien search is concerned, same was, in fact, conducted by Mr. Klavin who ordered what is the normal and customary business search in connection with the proposed closing.

Mr. Darius goes on to indicate in his letter various undertakings that should have been performed by Mr. Klavin. Many of the undertakings set forth in Mr. Darius' letter do not fall in the ambit of a lawyer's duty to his client. Many of the functions would be performed by an accountant or other professional and not within the scope of a duty owed by an attorney to his client.

In the case at bar, I believe it is clear from the deposition transcript and the correspondence referred to above, that Mr. Klavin adequately performed these duties.

Very truly yours,

Edward J. Caruso

Appendix

BUDGETING, FINANCIAL ANALYSIS, AND OPTIMIZATION SOFTWARE

There is a variety of computer software packages designed specifically for budgeting and financial modeling. Some are *stand-alone* packages, others are *templates*, and still others are spreadsheet *add-ins*.

1. Budget Express
Budget Express "understands" the structure of financial worksheets and concepts such as months, quarters, years, totals, and subtotals, speeding up budget and forecast preparation. The program creates column headers for months, automatically totals columns and rows, and calculates quarterly and yearly summaries. For sophisticated "what if" analyses, just specify your goal and Budget Express displays your current and target values as you make changes. (*add-in*)

2. ProPlans
It creates your financial plan automatically and accurately—and slices months from your annual planning and reporting process. Just enter your forecast data and assumptions into easy-to-follow, comprehensive data-entry screens, and ProPlans automatically creates the detailed financials you need to run your business for the next year—your income statement, balance sheet, cash flow statement, receipts and disbursements cash flow statements, and ratio reports. (*template*)

3. Profit Planner
It provide titles and amounts for revenues, cost of sales, expenses, assets, liabilities, and equity in a ready-to-use 1-2-3 template. Financial tables are automatically generated on screen.

    It presents results in 13 different table formats, including a pro forma earnings statement, balance sheet, and cash flow. Profit Planner even compares your earnings statement, balance sheet, and ratios against industry averages, so you're not working in a vacuum. (*template*)

4. Up Your Cash Flow
The program generates cash flow and profit and loss forecasts; detailed sales by product/product line and payroll by employee forecasts; monthly

balance sheets; bar graphs; ratio and break-even analyses and more. (*stand-alone*)

5. Cash Collector
It assists you in reviewing and aging receivables. You always know who owes what; nothing "falls through the cracks." What happens when collection action is required? Simply click through menu-driven screens to automatically generate letters and other professionally written collection documents (all included) that are proven to pull in the payments. (*stand-alone*)

6. Cash Flow Analysis
This software provides projections of inflow and cash outflow. You input data into eight categories: sales, cost of sales, general and administrative expense, long-term debt, other cash receipts, inventory build-up/reduction, capital expenditures (acquisition of long-term assets such as store furniture), and income tax. The program allows changes in assumptions and scenarios and provides a complete array of reports. (*stand-alone*)

7. Budget Maestro
Planet's Budget Maestro is probably the best answer to distributed budgeting, strategic planning, and financial control. Budget Maestro shortens your budgeting cycle and puts you in control of the process. Its information-driven environment guides you through budgeting, planning, modeling, forecasting, resource management, consolidation, analysis, and reporting.

CFOs and budget managers can plan, analyze, and manage in ways never before possible. Look at a user's screen and make changes directly without ever being there. Deliver budget models and deploy reconfigured software updates to many users at once. Manage budgetary information—even enterprise-wide information systems—with a single consistent interface. Planet's Budget Maestro is designed to put CFOs and financial managers in control of all aspects of managing budgets, creating financial models, and building and deploying financial plans. Budget Maestro allows business managers unparalleled flexibility in analyzing cash flow and business performance throughout the enterprise. Budget Maestro Enterprise Edition enables multiple independent budgets and plans to be consolidated into a unified enterprise model. (*stand-alone*)

8. Interactive Financial Planning System (IFPS/Plus)

Comshare's IFPS/Plus is a multipurpose, interactive financial modeling that supports and facilitates the building, solving, and asking of "what if" questions of financial models. It is a powerful modeling and analysis tool, designed to handle large complicated problems with lots of data. It is unsurpassed for large corporate-wide applications—especially those that get data directly from enterprise relational data base. Originally marketed by Execucom in the 1970s, IFPS is currently used by more than 600 businesses. The data and models created through IFPS/PLUS can be shared throughout the organization because the model logic is self documenting. The capabilities of the program include the ability to explain and perform spreadsheet-type editing, produce reports, and perform built-in business functions. Some of the capabilities of the system are forecasting, linear regression, and automatic extrapolation. The most current version of IFPS/PLUS is 5.1.1, which introduces Visual IFPS. This is a Microsoft Windows application that acts as the "client in the client–server application." The application runs on the PC and is connected to the IFPS/PLUS running on the server. In other words, IFPS/PLUS can access and take the data from the organization's main data base and send the results directly to the user. The user is not inundated with all of the data, but just presented with the results. This keeps the network from getting bogged down. Thus, the user has the power of the server on a PC and all the benefit of IFPS/PLUS. (Prospective users of IFPS/Plus are encouraged to contact Comshare, 3001 S. State St., P.O. Box 1588, Ann Arbor, Michigan 48106.) (*stand-alone*)

9. CFO Spreadsheet Applications

These ready-to-use spreadsheet templates offer easy ways to make many financial decisions. They are divided into four modules: cash management, tax strategies, capital budgeting, and advanced topics. (*template*)

10. SPREDGAR 2000

SPREDGAR 2000, an Excel add-in, rapidly calculates and graphs 30 standard financial ratios from the 10-K and 10-Q filings stored on the Securities and Exchange Commission's EDGAR data base. It also generates free cash flow analysis and plots ratios over time. You may download a full-featured evaluation copy from the web site at http://www.spredgar.com. SPREDGAR 2000 adds the power of stock portfolios, one-click access to EDGAR filings (by company name, stock ticker, or SIC code), tabular comparison of ratios, and over 9,000 company/ticker names. (*add-in*)

11. CapPLANS

It evaluates profitability based on Net Preset Value (NPV), Internal Rate of Return (IRR), and payout period. Choose among five depreciation methods, including Modified Accelerated Cost Recovery System (MACRS), run up to four sensitivity analyses, and project profitability over a 15-year horizon. In addition to a complete report of your analysis, CapPLANS generates a concise, 4-page executive summary—great for expediting approval. Add ready-made graphs to illustrate profitability clearly, at a glance. (*template*)

12. Project Evaluation Toolkit

It calculates the dollar value of your project based on six valuation methods, including discounted cash flow and effect on the corporate balance sheet. Assess intangibles such as influence on corporate strategy, investors, or labor relations. Use scenario planning to show the effects of changing start dates, sales forecasts, and other critical variables. (*template*)

13. What's Best!

If you have limited resources—for example, people, inventory, materials, time, or cash—then What's Best! can tell you how to allocate these resources in order to maximize or minimize a given objective, such as profit or cost. What's Best! uses a proven method—linear programming—to help you achieve your goals. This product can solve a variety of business problems that cut across every industry at every level of decision-making. (*stand-alone*)

14. Inventory Analyst

Inventory Analyst tells precisely how much inventory to order, and when to order it. Choose from four carefully explained ordering methods: economic order quantity (EOQ), fixed order quantity, fixed months requirements, and level load by work days. Inventory Analyst ensures that you'll always have enough stock to get you through your ordering period.

Just load up to 48 months' worth of inventory history, and Inventory Analyst makes the forecast based on one of three forecasting methods: time series, exponential smoothing, or moving averages. It explains which method is best for you. Inventory Analyst will adjust your forecast for seasonality, too. (*template*)

15. Palisade's DecisionTools Suite

Palisade's DecisionTools Suite is a DSS tool in the area of risk and decision analysis. It includes such programs as @RISK, @RISK for Project, TopRank, PrecisionTree, BestFit, and RISKview. These programs analyze risk, run Monte

Carlo simulations, perform sensitivity analyses, and fit data to distributions. (*stand-alone*)

- @RISK is a risk analysis and simulation add-in for Microsoft Excel and Lotus 1-2-3. It is the risk-analysis tool. Replace values in your spreadsheet with @RISK distributions to represent uncertainty, then simulate your model using powerful Monte Carlo simulation methods. @RISK recalculates your spreadsheet hundreds (or thousands) of times. The results: distributions of possible outcome values! Results are displayed graphically and through detailed statistical reports.
- @RISK for Project adds the same powerful Monte Carlo techniques to your Microsoft Project models allowing users to answer questions such as "What is the chance the project will be completed on schedule?"
- TopRank is a "what if" analysis add-in for either Microsoft Excel or Lotus 1-2-3 for Windows. Take any spreadsheet model, select the cells that hold your results, and TopRank automatically determines which spreadsheet values affect your results the most. TopRank then ranks the values in order of importance. Your results can be displayed in Tornado, Spider, and Sensitivity high-resolution graphs, allowing the user to easily understand the outcome at a glance. TopRank works easily and effectively with @RISK by identifying the critical cells users should concentrate on when running Monte Carlo simulations.
- PrecisionTree is a powerful, innovative decision-analysis tool. Enter decision trees and influence diagrams directly in your spreadsheet models. Detail all available decision options and identify the optimal decision. Your decision analysis factors in your attitudes toward risk and the uncertainty present in your model. Sensitivity analysis identifies the critical factors that affect the decision you'll make. It is a real plus for outlining all available options for a decision, or identifying and presenting the best course of action.
- BestFit takes data sets (up to 30,000 data points or pairs) and finds the distribution that best fits the data. BestFit accepts three types of data from text files: direct entry, cut and paste, or direct link to data within Excel or Lotus 1-2-3 spreadsheets. BestFit tests up to 26 distribution types using advanced optimization algorithms. Results are displayed graphically and through an expanded report which includes goodness-of-fit statistics. BestFit distributions can be used directly in @RISK for Excel, Lotus 1-2-3, and Microsoft Project models.

492   Appendix

- RISKview is the distribution viewing companion to @RISK, @RISK for Project, or BestFit. It is a powerful tool for viewing, assessing and creating probability distributions.

FORECASTING AND STATISTICAL SOFTWARE

There are numerous computer software programs that are used for forecasting purposes. They are broadly divided into two major categories: forecasting software and general purpose statistical software. A brief summary of some popular programs follows.

1. Forecast Pro

Forecast Pro, a *stand-alone* forecasting software, uses artificial intelligence. A built-in expert system examines your data, then guides you to state-of-the-art forecasting techniques (exponential smoothing, Box–Jenkins, dynamic regression, Croston's model, event models, and multiple-level models)—whichever method suits the data best. (Business Forecast Systems, Inc., 68 Leonard St., Belmont, MA 02178, 617-484-5050, 617-484-9219 [fax]; http://ourworld.compuserve.com/homepages/ForecastPro)

2. Easy Forecaster Plus I and II

Easy Forecaster Plus I and II are *stand-alone* forecasting softwares, developed by the Institute of Business Forecasting. Features include the following models: naïve, moving averages, exponential smoothing (single, double, and Holt's), linear trend line, and multiple regression. The program selects the optimal model automatically and prepares monthly or quarterly forecasts using seasonal indices. (Institute of Business Forecasting, P.O. Box 670159, Station C, Flushing, NY 11367-9086; 718-463-3914, 718-544-9086 [fax]; e-mail: IBF@ibf.org; http://www.ibf.org)

3. LifeCast Pro

LifeCast Pro is a *stand-alone* new product forecasting software. It quickly allows the integration of different marketing assumptions, prices, market research, competitive intelligence, historical similarities, and expert judgment—all within a graphically based product life-cycle framework. LifeCast Pro will help you "sell" your forecasts as believable, because it merges statistical diffusion theory with your own assumptions in a way easy to explain to management. Features include:

- Data availability options (high/medium/or none)
- Incorporation of price scenarios and elasticities
- Jackknife stability analysis
- Automatic search for best saturation
- Search area analysis and precision estimates
- Life-cycle analysis for mature products
- Statistical forecasting equations
- Easy to use

(LifeCast Pro, 6516 Wedgewood Way, Tucker, GA 30084; e-mail: huntertec @mindspring.com; http://www.mindspring.com/~jimstrick/hunter.htm)

4. Sales & Market Forecasting Toolkit

Sales & Market Forecasting Toolkit is a *spreadsheet template* that produces sales and market forecasts, even for new products with limited historical data. It includes: eight powerful methods for more accurate forecasts, as well as spreadsheet models, complete with graphing, ready-to-use with your numbers.

Sales & Market Forecasting Toolkit provides a variety of forecasting methods to help you generate accurate business forecasts—even in new or changing markets with limited historical data. They include:

- Customer poll
- Whole market penetration
- Chain method
- Strategic modeling
- Moving averages, exponential smoothing, and linear regressions

The customer poll method helps build a forecast from the ground up, by summing the individual components such as products, stores, or customers. Whole market penetration, market share, and the chain method are top-down forecasting methods used to predict sales for new products and markets lacking sales data. The strategic modeling method develops a forecast by projecting the impact of changes to pricing and advertising expenditures. Statistical forecasting methods include exponential smoothing, moving averages, and linear regression. You can use the built-in macros to enter data into your forecast automatically. For example, enter values for the first and last months of a 12-month forecast. The compounded growth-rate macro will automatically compute and enter values for the other 10 months. (Lotus Selects, P.O. Box 9172, Cambridge, MA 02139-9946; 800-635-6887; 617-693-3981)

5. Forecast! GFX*

Forecast! GFX* is a *stand-alone* forecasting system that can perform five types of time-series analyses: seasonal adjustment, linear and nonlinear trend analysis, moving-average analysis, exponential smoothing, and decomposition. Trend analysis supports linear, exponential, hyperbolic, S-curve, and polynomial trends. Hyperbolic trend models analyze data that indicate a decline toward a limit, such as the output of an oil well or the price of a particular model of personal computer. Forecast! GFX* can perform multiple-regression analysis with up to ten independent variables. (Intex Solutions, 35 Highland Circle, Needham, MA 01294; 617-449-6222; 617-444-2318 [fax])

6. ForeCalc

ForeCalc, a *spreadsheet add-in*, features nine forecasting techniques, including both automatic and manual modes, and eliminates the need to export or reenter data. In automatic mode, just highlight the historical data in your spreadsheet, such as sales, expenses, or net income; then ForeCalc tests several exponential-smoothing models and picks the one that best fits your data.

Forecast results can be transferred to your spreadsheet with upper and lower confidence limits. ForeCalc generates a line graph showing the original data, the forecasted values, and confidence limits.

ForeCalc can automatically choose the most accurate forecasting technique:

- Simple one-parameter smoothing
- Holt's two-parameter smoothing
- Winters's three-parameter smoothing
- Trendless seasonal models
- Dampened versions of Holt's and Winters's smoothing

ForeCalc's manual mode lets you select the type of trend and seasonality—yielding nine possible model combinations. You can vary the type of trend (constant, linear, or dampened), as well as the seasonality (nonseasonal, additive, or multiplicative). (Business Forecast Systems, Inc., 68 Leonard Street, Belmont, MA 02178; 617-484-5050; 617-484-9219 [fax])

7. StatPlan IV

StatPlan IV is a *stand-alone* program for those who understand how to apply statistics to business analyses. You can use it for market analysis, trend forecasting, and statistical modeling. StatPlan IV lets you analyze data by range, mean, median, standard deviation, skewdness, kurtosis, correlation analysis, one- or two-way analysis of variance (ANOVA), cross tabulations, and *t*-test. The forecasting methods include multiple regression, stepwise multiple regression, polynomial regression, bivariate curve fitting, autocorrelation analysis, trend and cycle analysis, and exponential smoothing. Data can be displayed in X–Y plots, histograms, time-series graphs, autocorrelation plots, actual vs. forecast plots, or frequency and percentile tables. (Lotus Selects, P.O. Box 9172, Cambridge, MA 02139-9946; 800-635-6887; 617-693-3981)

8. Geneva Statistical Forecasting

Geneva Statistical Forecasting, a *stand-alone*, can batch-process forecasts for thousands of data series, if the series are all measured in the same time units (days, weeks, months, and so on). The software automatically tries out as many as nine different forecasting methods, including six linear and nonlinear regressions and three exponential-smoothing techniques, before picking the one that best fits your historical data.

The program incorporates provisions that simplify and accelerate the process of reforecasting data items. Once you complete the initial forecast, you can save a data file that records the forecasting method assigned to each line item. When it is time to update the data, simply retrieve the file and reforecast, using the same methods as before. (Pizzano & Co., 800 W. Cummings Park, Woburn, MA 01801; 617-935-7122)

9. SmartForecasts

SmartForecasts, a *stand-alone* forecasting software, features the following:

- Automatically chooses the right statistical method
- Lets you manually adjust forecasts to reflect your business judgment
- Produces forecast results

SmartForecasts combines the benefits of statistical and judgmental forecasting, determining which statistical method will give you the most accurate forecast, and handling all the math.

Forecasts can be modified using the program's EYEBALL utility. You may need to adjust a sales forecast to reflect an anticipated increase in advertising or a decrease in price. SmartForecasts summarizes data with descriptive statistics, plots the distribution of data values with histograms, plots variables in a scattergram, and identifies leading indicators.

You can forecast using single- and double-exponential smoothing, and simple- and linear-moving averages. It even builds seasonality into your forecasts using Winters's exponential smoothing, or you can eliminate seasonality by using times-series decomposition and seasonal adjustment. In addition, SmartForecasts features simultaneous multiseries forecasting of up to 60 variables and 150 data points per variable, offers multivariate regression to let you relate business variables, and has an Undo command for mistakes. (Smart Software, Inc., 4 Hill Road, Belmont, MA 02178; 800-762-7899; 617- 489-2748 [fax])

10. Tomorrow

Tomorrow, a *stand-alone* forecasting software, uses an optimized combination of linear regression, single exponential smoothing, adaptive rate response single exponential smoothing, Brown's one-parameter double exponential smoothing, Holt's two-parameter exponential smoothing, Brown's one-parameter triple exponential smoothing, and Gardner's three-parameter damped trend. Some of the main features are:

- Eliminates the need to reformat your existing spreadsheets. Tomorrow recognizes and forecasts formula cells (e.g., containing totals and subtotals). It handles both horizontally and vertically oriented spreadsheets, and accepts historical data in up to 30 separate ranges.
- Allows you to specify seasonality manually, or to calculate seasonality automatically.
- Allows several forecasts of different time-series simultaneously (e.g., sales data from different regions).
- Recognizes and forecasts time-series headings (names of months, etc.).
- Makes forecast optionality become a normal part of your spreadsheet.
- Restores the original spreadsheet with the Undo command.
- Allows you to look at any part of the spreadsheet using the Browse feature (including the forecast) without leaving Tomorrow.
- Checks for and prevents accidental overlaying of nonempty or protected cells.

- Labels forecast cells, calculates MAPE, and, when seasonality is automatically determined, describes the seasonality via the optional annotation mode.
- Provides comprehensive context-sensitive online help.

(Isogon Corp., 330 Seventh Avenue, New York, NY 10001; 212-967-2424)

11. MicroTSP

MicroTSP is a *stand-alone* software that provides the tools most frequently used in practical econometric and forecasting work. It covers:

Descriptive statistics and a wide range of single equation estimation techniques, including ordinary least squares (multiple regression), two-stage least squares, nonlinear least squares, and probit and logit.

Forecasting tools include: exponential smoothing including single exponential, double exponential, and Winters's smoothing, and Box–Jenkins methodology. (Quantitative Micro Software, 4521 Campus Drive, Suite 336, Irvine, CA 92715; 714-856-3368)

12. Sibyl/Runner

Sibyl/Runner is an interactive, *stand-alone* forecasting system. Besides allowing usage of all major forecasting methods, the package permits analysis of the data, suggests available forecasting methods, compares results, and provides several accuracy measures in a way that makes it easy for the user to select an appropriate method and to forecast needed data under different economic and environmental conditions. (For details, see Makridakis, Hodgsdon, and Wheelwright, "An Interactive Forecasting System," *American Statistician*, November 1974.) (Applied Decision Systems, Lexington, MA 02173, 614-424-9820)

13. Forecast Plus

Forecast Plus, a *stand-alone* forecasting software, uses artificial intelligence. A built-in expert system examines your data. Then it guides you to thirteen forecasting methods including exponential smoothing, Box–Jenkins, or regression—whichever method suits the data best. The software features a simple-to-use menu system; high-resolution graphic capability; an ability to choose an appropriate forecasting technique, handle all phases of forecasting analysis, and save forecasted data; and optimization of smoothing constants. (StatPac, Inc., 3814 Lyndale Avenue South, Minneapolis, MN 55409; 612-822-8252)

Other Forecasting Software

There are many other forecasting software programs available, such as Autocast II and 4 Cast (both from Delphus, Inc., 103 Washington Street #348, Morristown, NJ 07960; 973-267-9269) and Trendsetter Expert Version (Concentric Data Systems, 110 Turnpike Road, Westborough, MA 01581; 800-325-9035).

General Purpose Statistical Software

There are numerous, widely used statistical software programs that can be utilized to build a forecasting model. Some of the more popular ones include:

- SPSS
- Minitab (Minitab, Inc., 3081 Enterprise Drive, State College, PA 16801-3008; 814-231-2682; http://www.minitab.com)
- MathSoft's S-Plus (MathSoft Inc., Seattle, WA; 800-569-0123, 206-283-8802; http://www.mathsoft.com/splus)
- SAS Application System
- Systat
- Statgraphics
- PC-90
- RATS
- BMD

An example of their features and functionality is Minitab statistical software *(Release 11 for Windows)* includes numerous forecasting tools, such as time-series methods (trend analysis, decomposition, moving average, single and double smoothing, Winters's Method, and ARIMA), and regression analysis.

Index

Abnormal earnings approach, 450–51
Accounting, forensic, 465–85
Accounting estimates, 101–3
Accounting rate of return (ARR), 43–44
Accounts receivable, 68–70, 159–66
   management of, 159–66
Accrual accounting earnings, 446
Acquisition of another business, 219–35
   determining price, 223–24
Acquisition terms, determining, 222–24
Adjusted net assets method, 443
Advertising, 97
After-tax earnings, 444
Altman's "Z-score", 89–90
"Amount of". *See* Future value of money
Annual payment, 23, 24, 25
Annuity
   future value of, 28–31
   perpetuities, 38
   value of, 24, 32–38
Appraisal
   business valuation and, 440–42
   of solvency, 81–82
Arbitration, using forensic accountant, 469
ARR. *See* Accounting rate of return
Asset
   business valuation based on, 440
   deferring items, 97
   financial, 180–88
   given in acquisition, 225
   profile, 74
   quality, analyzing, 67–75
      accounts receivable, 68–70
      asset profile, 74
      cash, 68
      deferred charges, 73–74
      fixed assets, 71–72
      intangible assets, 72–73
      inventory, 70–71
   real, 180, 188–92
      gold, 190
      precious metals, 189–90
      real estate, 188–89
      silver, 190
Auditor relations and reports, 103
Autocorrelation, 278–79
Average earnings, 1-5

Bank credit, types of, 207–8
Bank loan, 207–8
Bankruptcy, 89–93, 395–400
Barron's, 176
Barron's Confidence Index, 195–96
Before-tax earnings, 444
Beta, 107, 462, *463*
Blue chip stocks, 180–81
Bonds, 85, 89, 176, 182, 191–92, 211, 456–58
   conversion, 85
   how to value, 456–58
   indicators of performance, 176
   mutual funds, 191–92
   ratings, 89
Book value per share, 223
Break-even analysis, 3–11
   applications of, 5
   assumptions of, 5
   benefits of, 5
   cash break-even point, 10–11
   computing, 4–9
   CVP analysis, 3–5
   guidelines for, 6–8
   sales mix, 9–10
Budget
   optimal, 379–89
   shortcut approach to formulating, 323
Budgeted balance sheet, 319–22
Budgeted income statement, 319, *320*
Budgeting
   financial planning and, 306–23
   forecast cash inflow for, 331–44
Budget Maestro, 400, 415
Business
   appraisal, 436–37
   combination, 232–35
      pooling-of-interest method, 232–34
      purchase method, 234–35
   financing, 205–17
Business Conditions Digest, 176–77
Business failure
   minimizing, 92–93
   potential for, 89–93
   predicting, 90–92
Business risk, 179
Business segments, evaluating, 135–51

499

500 Index

Business valuation
  assets, 442
  customers and markets, 441
  employees and management, 442
  general approaches to, 439–40
    assets, 440
    earnings, 440
    market comparison, 439–40
  historical and projected financial performance, 442
  industry outlook, 441
  methods, 443–53
    abnormal earnings approach, 450–51
    adjusted net assets method, 443
    capitalization of earnings method, 444–46
    combination valuation method, 451
    control premiums and discounts, 452–53
    discounted cash flow method, 449–50
    dividend payment method, 446–47
    earnings surprises, 452
    excess earnings return on assets method, 447–48
    excess earnings return on sales method, 448–49
    gross revenue multiplier method, 443–44
    marketability discounts, 452
    price-earnings ratio method, 446
  opportunities, 436
  products and services, 441
  using forensic accountant, 468

Call
  definition of, 184
  puts and calls, 198
Capital, cost of, 213–17
Capital budgeting, 41–66
Capitalization of earnings method, 444–46, 459
Cash, 68
Cash break-even point, 10–11
Cash budget, 315–19, 331
Cash flows, 444
  acceleration of, 155–56
  budgeting, forecasting, 331–44
  from operations, 99–100
Cash management, 154–59
Cash outlay, delay of, 156–59

Cash payments, delaying, 157–59
Cash receipts, means of accelerating, 155–56
Certainty equivalent, 64–65
Certified Public Accountants (CPA)
  involvement with perspective financial statements, 325–29
  types of engagements performed by, 327–29
Charting, 198–203
  bar chart, *200*
  Dow Theory, 201–3
  line chart, *199*
  moving average, 199–200
  relative strength analysis, 200–201
  support and resistance levels, 201
Checks, processing delays, 155
Classical decomposition, 255
Coefficient of determination, 271, 274–75
Combination valuation method, 451
Commercial paper, 208–9
Commodity contracts, 186–87
Common stock
  about, 180–81
  exchange during merger, 220, 227–30
  forecasting, 460–61
  how to value, 458–60
Company's value, general analysis of, 440–42
  assets, 442
  customers and markets, 441
  employees and management, 442
  historical and projected financial performance, 442
  industry outlook, 441
  products and services, 441
"Compound value." *See* Future value of money
Computer technology, 350. *See also* Software
Conditional operators, 373
Confidence interval, 275
Conglomerate merger, 220
Consolidation, 219
Constant growth case, 459–60
Consumer surveys, *243*, 245
Contingent proposals, 53
Contribution margin, 3, 11, 14–22
  advantages and disadvantages of income statement, 14–15

Index   501

analysis, 14–22
  statement for divisional performance evaluation, *139*
Control premiums and discounts, 452–53
Conversion of preferred stock, 85
Convertible bonds, 212
Convertible securities, 182
Corporate planning models, 347–62
  attitudes and problems, 353–56
  current trends, 351–53
  history of, 350–51
  reasons for discontinued, *355*
  recommended, 355–59
  success factors in, *358*
  supporting data base, 359–61
  types of, 348, 350
  typical questions about, 348–49
  typical structure of an integrated planning model, *357*
Corporate valuations, 435–54
Corporations, surveys of, 351–52, *353*
Correlation coefficient, 271, 274–75
Cost center, 136–38
Cost of capital, 213–17
Cost-volume—profit (CVP) analysis, 3–5
CPA. *See* Certified Public Accounts
Consumer price index (CPI), 145
Credit system, attributes of a good, 160–66
Current accrual accounting, 446
"Current value." *See* Present value of money
Customers
  flow of, *298*
  monthly cash collections from, 308–10
  retention, gain, and loss of, *298*
Cutoff rate. *See* Required rate of return
CVP. *See* Cost-volume-profit analysis
Cyclical stocks, 181

DCF. *See* Discounted cash flow method
Debt
  long-term, 215–16
  short-term, 213–15
Decentralization, 136, 139
Decision (probability) trees, 65–66
Decision Support System (DSS), 359–61
Default risk, 179
Defensive stocks, 181

Deferred charges, 73–74
Delphi method, *243*, 245, *246*
Deseasonalizing the time series, 260
Direct labor budget, 311
Direct material budget, 311
Discounted cash flow method, 41, 57, 449–50
Discounted payback, 46
"Discounted value." *See* Present value of money
Discretionary costs, 97–99
Distributable cash flow, 445
Diversification, 60
Dividend payment method, 446–47
Dividends, 223
Divisional manager, measuring performance of, 135–36
Dow Jones Industrial Average, 175–76
Dow Theory, 201–3
DSS. *See* Decision Support System
Durbin-Watson statistic, 278–79, *280–83*, 287

Earnings, 95–97, 105–9, 222, 440, 452
  business valuation based on, 440
  measuring stability of, 105–8
  quality of, 95–97
  stability elements, 108–9
  surprises, 452
  types of measurements, 105–8
    average earnings, 105
    beta, 107–8
    coefficient of variation, 106
    instability index of earnings, 106–7
    one-time gains or losses to net income and/or sales, 106
    standard deviation, 106
Earnings before interest and taxes (EBIT), 444
Earnings per share (EPS), 220, 227–30, 460–61, 463
  forecasting, 460–61
  merger's impact on, 227–30
EBIT. *See* Earnings before interest and taxes
EIS. *See* Executive Information Systems
Electronic data bases, 177–78
Encore! Plus, 400, 414–15
Ending finished goods inventory budget, 313–14
EPS. *See* Earnings per share

Equity securities, 212–13, 216–17
Excess earnings return
  on assets method, 447–48
  on sales method, 448–49
Exchange ratio, in acquisitions, 227, 228, 229
Executive Information Systems (EIS), 359–61
Executive management games, 423–31
Executive opinions, *243*, 244
Exponential smoothing method, 251–55, *256–58*, 272–73
EXPRESS, 400, 412–14

Factory overhead budget, 313
Fair market value, 438
Federal Reserve Bulletin, 176
Finance company loan, 208
Financial analysis, 1–131
  analyzing financial position, 67–93
  break-even, operating leverage, and contribution margin, 3–22
  discounting and compounding analysis techniques, 23–39
  evaluating capital investment proposals, 41–66
  firm's financial structure, 105–20
  techniques for analyzing operating performance, 95–104
  variance analysis as a financial tool, 121–31
Financial assets, 180–88
  bonds, 182
  common stock, 180–81
  convertible securities, 182
  futures contracts, 186–88
  options, 183–85
  preferred stock, 181
  warrants, 182–83
Financial budget, 306, 307
Financial forecasting, 237–344
  forecasting cash inflows for budgeting, 331–44
  as management tools, 239–48
  methods for financial planning, 249–64
  regression and Markov methods, 265–301
  techniques, 303–29
Financial futures, 187–88
Financial modeling, 345–434
  corporate planning methods, 347–62

management games for executive training, 419–34
optimization techniques, 379–89
simulation, 363–77
  autocorrelation, 278–79
  behavioral equations, 371–72
  comprehensive, 375–77
  decision rules, 373–74
  definitional equations, 370–71
  developing, 367–69
  F-statistic, 277–78
  lagged model structure, 374
  multicollinearity, 278
  practicing, 365–66
  quantitative techniques used in, 366–67
  r-bar squared, 277
  recursive and simultaneous models, 372
  specification, 369–74
  t-statistic, 277, 278
  types of, 364
  variables of, 367–69
spreadsheet and financial modeling languages, 391–417
Financial planning, 205–6, 249–64
  forecasting methods for, 249–64
Financial position, analyzing, 67–93
Financial projection, 327
Financial section of the Statement of Cash Flows, 84–85
Financial structure of firm, analyzing, 105–31
Financing sources, short- and intermediate-term, 206–10
Financing
  avenues of, 77
  long-term, 211–13
  short-term versus long-term, 210
Fixed assets, 71–72
Fixed cost, 12
Forecast
  cash inflows for budgeting, 331–44
  control of, 285–87
  evaluation of, 279–87
  measuring accuracy of, 284–85
Forecasting, 239–64, 272–73, 358, 395–400, 460–61
  business failures, 395–400
  decomposition of time series and, 255, 258–63

equations, choosing the best, 287
features and assumptions, 246–47
financial, 237–344
  methods, 241–44, 249–64, 272–73
    commonly used, 272–73
    financial planning, 249–64
  steps in process, 247
  stock price, 460–61
  who uses, 239–41
Forensic accounting, 465–85
  case study, 470–85
  when to employ an accountant, 467–70
Fraud. *See* Forensic accounting
Free cash flow, 445
F-statistic, 277–78
Fundamental analysis, 192
Future value of money, 23–39

Goal programming (GP), 385–87, *388–89*
"Going concern" value, 438–39
Gold, 190
Gordon's growth model, 463
GP. *See* Goal programming
Gross profit, *144*
Gross revenue multiplier method, 443–44
Growth stocks, 181

Hedges, 185
Hedging approach of financing, 154
Holding company, 219, 231–32
Holding period return, 178, 192
Horizontal merger, 220
Hurdle rate. *See* Required rate of return

IFPS. *See* Interactive Financial Planning System
Income stocks, 181
Index of Bearish Sentiment, 198
Installment loans, 208
Insurance claims evaluations, using forensic accountant, 469
Intangible assets, 72–73
Interactive Financial Planning System (IFPS), 400–9
Interest rate, 23, 89, 179
  risk, 179
Intermediate-term loans, 208
Internal control, 103
Internal rate of return (IRR), 53–57
Inventory, 70–71

financing, 209–10
planning and control, 166–72
Investigations, forensic accountant and, 468
Investing Section of the Statement of Cash Flows, 83–84
Investment center, 144
Investment decisions, two basic types of, 41
Investors Intelligence's Index of Bearish Sentiment, 198
IRR. *See* Internal rate of return

Key indicators of market and stock performance, 193–98
  Barron's Confidence Index, 195–96
  market breadth, 194–95
  mutual fund position, 196
  old lot theory, 197–98
  puts and calls, 198
  short selling, 196–97
  trading volume, 193–94
Kiplinger Washington Letter, 177

Lagged model structure, 374
Leasing, 210
Liabilities, 75–77
  overstated, 77
  undervalued or unrecorded, 77
Limited partnership, 189
LINDO (Linear Interactive and Discrete optimization) program, 382, *383–85, 388–89*
Linear programming (LP), 379–82, 385
Lines of credit, 207–8
Liquidation value, 438
Liquidity analysis, 77–81
Liquidity risk, 179
Litigation support, forensic accountant and, 467–68
Lockbox arrangement, 155
"Long position", 186
Long-term debt, 215–16
Lost earnings, using forensic accountant, 468
LP. *See* Linear programming

MAD. *See* Mean absolute deviation
Management games for executive training, 419–34
Management honesty, 103

Management information system (MIS), 358–61
Manager performance, appraising, 135–36
Marketability discounts, 452
Market breadth, 194–95
Market comparison, business valuation based on, 439–40
Marketing effectiveness, 113
Market price of stock, 223
Market risk, 179
Markov model, 291–300, 332–35
Mean absolute deviation (MAD), 284–85, 287
Mean squared error (MSE), 253, 284–85, 287
Merchandise purchase budget, 311
Mergers, 219–35, 396, 435, 436
  acquisitions and, 435, 436
  advantages and disadvantages, 221–22
  appraisal of potential, 222
  impact on net income and market price per share, 227–30
Method of least squares, 265–67
Microsoft Excel, 268–69
MIS. See Management information system
Money, present and future value of, 23
Money market, 192
Mortgages, 211
Moving average, 199–200, 250–51, 272–73
MSE. See Mean squared error
Multicollinearity, 278
Multiple discriminant analysis (MDA), 396
Multiple holding period, 458–60
Mutual funds, 190–203
  buying pattern of, 196
  types of, 191–92

Naïve forecasting models, 249
NASDAQ (National Association of Security Dealers Automated Quotation), 176
NAV (net asset value), 192
Net income, 12
Net present value, 46–51, 57
Net working capital per share, 223
New York Stock Exchange Index, 176
Nondiscretionary projects, 56–57

Odd lot theory, 197–98
One-time gains or losses, 106

Operating budget, 306–7
Operating leverage, 3, 11–14
  measuring and examining effects of, 11–14
  ratios to calculate, 12
Operating section of the Statement of Cash Flows, 83
Operations, cash flow from, 99–100
Optimal budgets, 379–89
Options, 183–85
Overstated liabilities, 77

Partnership disputes, using forensic accountant, 469
Payback, 44–46
Penny stocks, 181
P/E ratio (price earnings ratio), 460-64
  determinants of, 461–62
  selling on a high or low, 463–64
Percent-of-sales method, 303–6
Perpetuities, 38
Personal computers
  corporate planning models and, 359–61
  obtaining business data on, 177–78
PERT. See Program Evaluation and Review Technique
Piggy-back product lines, 112
PIMS. See Profit Impact of Market Strategy
PMLS (Planning and modeling languages), 359
Pooling-of-interest method, 232–34
Portfolio investment
  accounting aspects, 173
  analysis information, 173–203
  considerations in selecting, 175
  indicators of risk, 174
  obtaining information, 175–78
Precious metals, 189–90
Preferred stock, 85, 181, 212–13
  conversion of, 85
Present value of money, 23–39
Price-earnings ratio (P/E ratio) method, 89, 446
Probability matrix approach. See Markov approach
Production budget, 310
Product line characteristics, 109–13
  causing instability, 112
  marketing effectiveness, 113
  measures, 109–11
  promoting stability, 111–12

Standard error of the regression coefficient, 275–76
Statement of cash flows, analyzing, 82–85
  financing section, 84–85
  investing section, 83
  operating section, 83
  schedule of noncash financing and investing activities, 85
Stock
  beta of, 107–8
  blue chip, 180–81
  common, 180–81
  conversion of preferred stock, 85
  cyclical, 181
  defensive, 181
  given in acquisition, 225
  growth, 181
  income, 181
  market price of, 223
  penny, 181
  preferred, 85, 181, 212–13
  speculative, 181
  types of, 180–81
Straddles, 185
Strategic business unit (SBU), 360–61
Subsidiary, definition of, 219
"Sum of." *See* Future value of money
Support level, 201
Survey of Current Business, 176
Systematic risk, 180

Taxable income, 100–101
Technical analysis, 192–203
Tender offer, 220
Theil U-statistic, 285
Time-adjusted rate of return. *See* Internal rate of return
Timing, 41
Trade credit, 207
Trading volume, 193–94
Transfer pricing, 140–44
Transition probabilities, 298–99
Trend analysis, 269–73
Trial and error method, 53–56
t-statistic, 275, 277, 278

Unsecured loan, 207
Unsystematic risk, 180
U-Statistic, 285

Valuation, 435–54
  general approaches to, 439–40
  of security, 455–64
  reasons for, 435
  steps in, 437–42
Value
  definitions of, 438, *439*
  determination of, 435
Value Line, 176
Vertical merger, 219

Warrants, 182–83, 213
Working capital, evaluating, 153–54

"Year zero value." *See* Present value of money

Zero growth case, 459
Zero-base budgeting (ZBB), 324–25
Z score, 395–400

Profit, changes in, operating leverage, 11–14
Profitability index, 51–53, 57
Profit center, 138–44
Profit Impact of Market Strategy (PIMS), 359
Program Evaluation and Review Technique (PERT), 244–45
Purchase method, 234–35
Purchasing power risk, 179–80
Put
   and calls, 198
   definition of, 184

Qualitative approach to forecasting, 244–46
Quality of earnings, 95–97

r-bar squared, 277
Real assets, 180, 188–92
   gold, 190
   precious metals, 189–90
   real estate, 188–89
   silver, 190
Real estate, 188–89
Real estate investment trust (REIT), 188–89
Receivable financing, 209
Recursive models, 372
Regression, multiple, 276–79, 288–91
   statistics to look for, 276–79
Regression analysis for sales and earnings projection, 265–73, 396
Regression approach, 335–41
Regression statistics, 271–79
REIT. *See* Real estate investment trust
Relative strength analysis, 200–201
Replacement value, 438
Required rate of return, 53
Residual income, 101, 149–51
   statement for divisional evaluation purposes, *150*
Resistance level, 201
Return, versus risk, 178–80
Return on investment (ROI), 144, 145, 146–49, 151
Revenue sources, 108–9
Revolving credit, 208
Risk. *See also* Beta
   about, 41, 60–66
   acquisition and, 230
   certainty equivalent, 64–65
   decision (probability) trees, 65–66
   potential merger and, 222
   risk-adjusted discount rate, 60–62
   semivariance, 65
   sensitivity analysis, 65
   simulation, 65
   standard deviation and coefficient of variation, 62–64, 179
   types of, 179–80
   versus return, 178–80
Risk-adjusted discount rate, 60–62
Risk-return trade off method, 41
ROI. *See* Return on investment

Sales budget, 307–8
Sales-force polling, *243*, 244
Sales mix, 9–10
SBU. *See* Strategic business unit
Scenario analysis, 230
Seasonal index, 259
Security valuation, 455–64
Selling and administrative expense budget, 315
"Selling climax", 193
Semivariance, 65
Sensitivity analysis, 65, 230
"Short position", 186
Short selling, 196–97
Short-term debt, cost of, 213–15
Silver, 190
SIMPLAN, 400, 409–12, *413*, *414*
Simulation, 65
Single holding period, 458
Smoothing techniques, 249
Software, 268–69, 324, 342–44, 391, 416–17, 487–99
   cash flow budgeting, 342–44
   modeling, factors to consider when evaluating, 416–17
   used by financial planners, 391
Solvency, appraisal of, 81–82
Speculative stocks, 181
Spreads, 185
Spreadsheet program, 391–417
   in financial modeling, 392–95
   forecasting business failures with Z scores, 395–400
SSPS for Windows, 288–91
Standard & Poor's Index, 176
Standard deviation and coefficient of variation, 62–64, 179